Classic Papers in Natural Resource Economics

Also by Chennat Gopalakrishnan

NATURAL RESOURCES AND ENERGY: Theory and Policy
THE EMERGING MARINE ECONOMY OF THE PACIFIC
THE ECONOMICS OF ENERGY IN AGRICULTURE

Classic Papers in Natural Resource Economics

Edited by

Chennat Gopalakrishnan
Professor
University of Hawaii at Manoa
Honolulu
Hawaii

First published in Great Britain 2000 by
MACMILLAN PRESS LTD
Houndmills, Basingstoke, Hampshire RG21 6XS and London
Companies and representatives throughout the world

A catalogue record for this book is available from the British Library.

ISBN 0–333–77763–8

First published in the United States of America 2000 by
ST. MARTIN'S PRESS, INC.,
Scholarly and Reference Division,
175 Fifth Avenue, New York, N.Y. 10010

ISBN 0–312–23014–1

Library of Congress Cataloging-in-Publication Data
Classic papers in natural resource economics / edited by Chennat Gopalakrishnan.
p.   cm.
Includes bibliographical references and index.
ISBN 0–312–23014–1 (cloth)
1. Natural resources.   2. Environmental policy.   3. Externalities (Economics)
I. Gopalakrishnan, Chennat

HC59 .C574   2000
333.7—dc21
                                            99–048233

Editorial matter and selection © Chennat Gopalakrishnan 2000
Chapter 1 © *The Economic Journal* 1960
Chapters 2, 3, 8, 12 and 13 © *American Economic Association* 1970, 1974, 1968, 1967, 1968
Chapter 4 © MIT Press, 1974
Chapter 5 © *Journal of Law and Economics* 1960
Chapters 6, 7 and 10 © Basil Blackwell Ltd 1962
Chapters 9 and 11 © University of Chicago Press 1954, 1931
Chapter 14 © Oxford University Press 1971

This book is printed on paper suitable for recycling and made from fully managed and sustained forest sources.

10   9   8   7   6   5   4   3   2   1
09   08   07   06   05   04   03   02   01   00

Printed and bound in Great Britain by Antony Rowe Ltd, Chippenham, Wiltshire

Contents

Preface

The role of natural resources in the context of sustainable economic development, both at the micro and macro levels, has in recent years begun to engage the serious attention of academics, policymakers, planners, and even laymen. This increased interest is largely the result of looming threats in the quantity and quality of natural resources and their potential human and environmental impacts. One of the consequences of this steadily rising concern is a resurgence of interest in natural resource economics as a major area of academic inquiry within the broad field of economics. This renewed interest has aroused the curiosity of a large number of individuals, both in academia and elsewhere, in the intellectual history of natural resource economics. The present volume is a modest effort to meet this growing fascination with the early beginnings of the field.

This book brings together in a single volume a choice selection of key classics in the field of natural resource economics. The 14 papers included in this book are grouped into five parts: the intertemporal problem; externalities and market failure; property rights, institutions and public choice; the economics of exhaustible resources; and the economics of renewable resources. The papers span many facets of the discipline and give the reader informed insights into the complex issues involved in resource production, pricing, consumption, and allocation. Written by distinguished resource economists, among them five Nobelists, the papers in this volume probe, analyze, and illuminate the central issues in the discipline.

This volume is primarily aimed at an academic audience. Specifically, it is intended as a supplementary textbook for graduate and/or advanced undergraduate courses in natural resource economics. Mindful of the time constraints under which professors and students operate, the book has limited the number of papers to fit a one-semester or even a one-quarter course. The papers present an appealing mix of conceptual, empirical, and quantitative analyses. A concise overview of each of the 14 papers is given in the editor's Introduction. Further Readings at the end of the book provide a list of 75 titles selected by the editor to help readers further explore topics discussed in this volume. This book could also be of use to researchers, policy analysts, and others with a good grounding in economic theory and some knowledge of quantitative methods.

Many people have contributed directly or indirectly to the preparation of this book. Although it is not possible to acknowledge everyone who has assisted, I am grateful to all. A few, however, deserve special mention. I owe a special debt of gratitude to my publisher, Macmillan, for accepting my book proposal. To Sunder Katwala, who commissioned this volume, Alison Howson, who was most helpful throughout the completion of this book, and to Linda Auld, for her meticulous copy-editing, I offer my sincere thanks. Special appreciation goes to my daughter Shalini who prepared the Author Index for this volume. I am grateful to Frank S. Scott, Jr. and Linda Cox, my colleagues here at the University of Hawaii, for their support of my work over the years. I am also beholden to Eric Im, also of the University of Hawaii, who helped me with the renumbering of the equations in Chapters 9, 13 and 14. To my former graduate students, Prahlad Kasturi, Hossein Khaleghi, and Parashar Malla, all good friends now, I extend my thanks for cheering me on all these years. My student assistants, Andrew Nishida and Cynthia Tavares, deserve special mention for their exemplary assistance with word processing and assorted other tasks involved in preparing the manuscript for the publisher. As always, I am deeply indebted to my wife Malini and my daughter Shalini, without whose understanding and support this book would not have materialized.

Chennat Gopalakrishnan

Acknowledgments

The editor and publishers acknowledge with thanks the authors and publishers listed below for granting permission to use copyright material.

The Economic Journal for article:
Martin S. Feldstein (1964), "The Social Time Preference Discount Rate in Cost Benefit Analysis," *Economic Journal*, 74: 360–79.

American Economic Association for articles:
Kenneth J. Arrow and Robert C. Lind (1970), "Uncertainty and the Evaluation of Public Investment Decisions," *American Economic Review*, 60: 364–78; Robert M. Solow (1974), "The Economics of Resources or the Resources of Economics," *American Economic Review*, 64: 1–15; William F. Baumol (1968), "On the Social Rate of Discount," *American Economic Review*, 57: 347–59; Harold Demsetz (1967), *American Economic Review*, 57: 347–59; Vernon L. Smith (1968), "Economics of Production from Natural Resources," *American Economic Review*, 58: 409–32.

Basil Blackwell, Ltd. for articles:
James M. Buchanan and W. C. Stubblebine (1962), "Externality," *Economica*, 29: 371–84; James M. Buchanan (1962), "Politics, Policy and the Pigovian Margins," *Economica*, 29: 17–28; Ralph Turvey (1963), "On Divergence Between Social Cost and Private Cost," *Economica*, 30: 309–13.

University of Chicago Press for articles:
Harold M. Hotelling (1931), "The Economics of Exhaustible Resources," *Journal of Political Economy*, 39: 137–75; H. Scott Gordon (1954), "The Economic Theory of a Common Property Resource: The Fishery," *Journal of Political Economy*, 62: 124–42.

Journal of Law & Economics for article:
Ronald H. Coase (1960), "The Problem of Social Cost," *Journal of Law & Economics*, 3: 1–44.

MIT Press Journals for article:
Kenneth J. Arrow and Anthony C. Fisher (1974), "Environmental Preser-

vation, Uncertainty and Irreversibility," *Quarterly Journal of Economics*, 88: 312–19.

Oxford University Press for article:
Paul A. Samuelson (1976), "Economics of Forestry in an Evolving Society," *Economic Inquiry*, 14: 466–92.

List of Contributors

Kenneth J. Arrow, Stanford University.

William F. Baumol, New York University.

James M. Buchanan, George Mason University.

Ronald H. Coase, Professor Emeritus, University of Chicago.

Harold Demsetz, University of California, Los Angeles.

Martin S. Feldstein, National Bureau of Economic Research.

Anthony C. Fisher, University of California, Berkeley.

H. Scott Gordon, Professor Emeritus, Indiana University.

Harold Hotelling (deceased), (formerly with) Stanford University.

Robert C. Lind, Cornell University.

Paul A. Samuelson, Massachusetts Institute of Technology.

Vernon L. Smith, University of Arizona.

Robert M. Solow, Massachusetts Institute of Technology.

William C. Stubblebine, Claremont McKenna College.

Ralph Turvey, (formerly with) International Labour Organization.

Classic Papers in Natural Resource Economics: An Overview

Chennat Gopalakrishnan

Natural resource economics has been the subject of serious academic inquiry for the past seven decades. Although it is difficult to trace its intellectual antecedents precisely, it is probably fair to say that it dates back to the early 1930s. The year 1931 has a special significance in the annals of natural resource economics; it was in that year that Harold Hotelling published his path-breaking paper on the economics of exhaustible resources in the *Journal of Political Economy* (Chapter 11 in this book), an event that has left a lasting imprint on the direction and development of the body of knowledge that is known today as the discipline of natural resource economics.

The last seven decades (1930–2000) have witnessed a remarkable growth in the field of natural resource economics. The 14 papers included in this book attempt to capture the essence of discourse in the field, although on a modest scale. The papers are grouped into five parts: the intertemporal problem; externalities and market failure; property rights, institutions and public choice; the economics of exhaustible resources; and the economics of renewable resources. Each part represents a major area in natural resource economics. The five parts are presented in a logical sequence, each one leading up to the next. The same applies to papers included within each part.

The papers examine the leading issues in the field of natural resource economics such as resource production, pricing, consumption, allocation and conservation, among others. Written by resource economists, the papers attempt to elucidate, analyze and illuminate the central concerns of the field. A brief overview of each of the 14 papers included in this volume follows.

1

Part I   The intertemporal problem

In the face of progressively increasing resource scarcity and steadily deteriorating environmental quality, intertemporal allocation of natural resources has taken on a new importance for natural resource economists. The focus of this concern is on ensuring the well-being of the future generations through optimal control conditions designed to produce intertemporal efficiency, on the one hand, and intergenerational equity, on the other. This is clearly a daunting task, given the difficulties and uncertainties inherent in planning for the future. The four papers included in this part address the many issues involved and in the process offer a number of original insights.

The concept of the social time preference function is introduced and its derivation explained by Martin Feldstein (1964) in Chapter 1. The author defines the social time preference (STP) and the social opportunity cost (SOC) and suggests that the SOC also includes time preference. The paper explains why the perfect market interest rate does not reflect social time preference. This is followed by the justification and derivation of the STP. Feldstein points out that the STP rate may fluctuate through time in response to changes in the level of consumption and growth rate, the rate of population growth and pure time preference rate. He recommends the use of a shadow price that reflects STP and the productivity of funds in private investment as bases for public investment decisions. The paper concludes that the STP function cannot be derived on the basis of current market rates, but must be administratively determined as a matter of public policy. This is an important contribution to the literature on investment in public projects.

William Baumol (1968) examines some of the major issues surrounding the concept of the social rate of discount in his paper. His analysis suggests that risk and corporate taxes play a far more important role in the choice of the social discount rate than was ascribed to them in earlier studies. The key role of risk is explained in terms of the relative risklessness of investments from the perspective of society as a whole. Baumol argues that it is not possible to determine precisely the social rate of discount, given the complexity of our institutional arrangements. One of Baumol's major conclusions is that "it made little sense for present generations to consciously forego current consumption to invest in projects designed to benefit future generations, since history suggested that future generations would surely be richer than present generations, anyway" (Randall, 1981, p. 8).

Kenneth Arrow and Robert Lind (1970) address the issue of incorporating risk and uncertainty in public investment decisions in a rigorous essay. The implications of risk and uncertainty in private and public investments are discussed and the appropriateness of discounting public investments and private investments in the same manner is examined. The authors argue that individual preferences are not of normative significance for government decisions and suggest that time and risk preferences relevant for government decisions should be developed as a matter of national policy. This conclusion is based on an analysis of such factors as market contingent claims and time risk preferences, public cost of and actual allocation of risk bearing. Arrow and Lind recommend that if all benefits and costs accrue privately, and different individuals receive the benefits and pay the costs, the correct procedure should be to discount the stream of expected benefits at a rate higher than the certainty rate and cost at a rate lower than the certainty rate. This paper makes a convincing case for considering risk and uncertainty in public investment decisions and offers some useful guidelines for this purpose.

Kenneth Arrow and Anthony Fisher (1974) examine the public policy implications of "uncertainty surrounding estimates of the environmental costs of some economic activities." Cases in point are environmental amenities such as wilderness areas and scenic waterways, *in situ* resources, whose development invariably results in irreversible alteration. An accurate determination of the comparative economics of preservation versus development of a pristine natural area is often rendered difficult because of the uncertainty involved in the estimates of environmental costs. The authors conclude that if the proposed development results in a decrease in net benefits, the rule of thumb should be, in general, to develop less of the area. The paper is an important early contribution to the literature on the economic valuation of natural amenities.

Part II   Externalities and market failure

The divergence between private costs and social costs and its multiple ramifications constitute the essence of externalities. The concept, in its simplest form, dates back to Adam Smith, followed by Alfred Marshall and A. C. Pigou. Since then, an extensive body of writings on externalities has developed. Externalities have been broadly classified into pecuniary, technological (or production), and political externalities. Other classifications include ownership-; depletable-; undepletable-;

Pareto-relevant-; marginal- and inframarginal-externalities. The discussion of externalities has gained a new urgency as significantly expanded economic activities by private and public parties are imposing ever higher damages on and disruptions in the environment. The damages in many instances are wide-ranging with near-term as well as long-term consequences, the latter with pronounced transnational and intergenerational impacts. The three papers in this section address the central issues pertaining to externalities.

Ronald Coase (1960) in his celebrated paper on "The Problem of Social Cost" proposed a framework for optimal resource allocation, in the presence of externalities, without market interventions or governmental regulation. The heart of the Coasian approach lies in voluntary negotiated agreements among the affected parties. Such agreements, Coase argues, would result in efficient resource allocation, so long as the property rights are well-defined, the costs of negotiation or transaction are negligible, the parties involved are few, and there is perfect competition. If all these assumptions hold true, the court can allocate the entitlement to the polluter or the victim without affecting the efficiency of resource allocation. Clearly, the theorem is of considerable potential importance since it offers major new insights into the regulation of pollution without governmental control or intervention. To be sure, many of Coase's assumptions are somewhat unrealistic and his analysis ignores the distributional consequences (income and wealth effects) of the bargaining solution and fails to address pollution control involving a public goods externality. Despite these limitations, Coase has made a significant contribution to the fields of economics and law by presenting "a framework for analyzing the assignment of property rights and liability in economic terms" (Posner, 1977, p. 16).

The definition of the term "externality" is fraught with difficulties. An overly broad definition, though conceptually appropriate, renders the concept operationally nonviable. Buchanan and Stubblebine (1962) in their paper address this problem by adopting a narrower, more conventional approach to externality. The authors present three general types of technological externalities: (1) marginal or infra-marginal; (2) Pareto-relevant or Pareto-irrelevant; and (3) potentially relevant and irrelevant. Their emphasis is on externalities in consumption. Although from an analytical perspective the distinctions proposed by the authors is useful, from the perspective of the policy maker and the victims of externality, it may not be very satisfying.

The divergence between social cost and private cost as the source of externality has been the subject of scrutiny by a number of economists.

In his paper, Ralph Turvey (1963) provides a synthesis and summary of the arguments presented in three major articles, among them Coase, and Buchanan and Stubblebine (Chapters 5 and 6). The main conclusions, as we have seen, are that a bargaining solution is preferable to state intervention when affected parties are able and willing to negotiate, and no single policy instrument such as a tax will eliminate the difference between social and private costs. In some instances, resource misallocation may result from the imposition of a tax or effluent charge alone. Turvey concludes that the benefits and costs of the proposed remedial measures have to be carefully weighed before any decisions are made. He also points out that the basis for government intervention is one of justice and not of economic efficiency.

Part III   Property rights, institutions and public choice

Property rights, institutions and public choice are key concepts in the discourse on the ownership, allocation and use of natural resources. A property right is a bundle of entitlements defining and stipulating the owner's rights, privileges and limitations for the use of resources. A well-defined property right should possess four characteristics: universality, exclusivity, transferability, and enforceability.

The absence of one or more of the four characteristics would render a property right attenuated and externality may result. Situations involving natural resources where ownership is ill-defined or unspecified have been variously described as common property-, non-exclusive-, or open access-resources. To be sure, these categories do not represent identical situations, but nonetheless share the characteristic of common ownership. The problems arising out of commonality of ownership, nonexclusivity, and open access are also examined in this part.

Institutions and public choice also play a pivotal role in the context of natural resource management. "Institutions," according to Commons (1924), "are the going concerns that order the relationships among individuals in society. Institutions include laws, constitutions (laws about making laws), traditions, moral and ethical structures, and customary and accepted ways of doing things ... Institutions of one kind or another direct, control, restrain or at best influence almost every activity and interpersonal relationship in a society." They may be explicit as in the case of laws, rules and regulations or may be implicit as with norms, views and principles of society. Theoretically, therefore, institutions reflect public preferences or public choice and should change in response to changes in public choices. Nevertheless, institutions could become instruments of political expediency.

The elements of an economic theory of property rights are presented and examined by Harold Demsetz (1967) in his pioneering paper. The paper first explains briefly the concept and role of property rights in social systems. The main allocative function of property rights is the provision of incentives to ensure a "greater internalization of externalities." Property rights emerge from the desires of the interacting parties to adjust to new benefit-cost possibilities. These adjustments have occurred historically through gradual institutional changes such as social mores and common law precedents. The author illustrates this thesis with examples of the evolution of property rights among Native Americans. Demsetz concludes his paper with a typology of property ownership: communal ownership, private ownership, and state ownership. Some principles underlying the evolution of property rights into specific forms of ownership and their impact on the internalization of externalities are set forth in this section.

H. Scott Gordon (1954) in his famous paper explores the economic theory of natural resource utilization in the context of the ocean fishery. He applies the economic theory of production to the fishing industry and explains the "overfishing problem" in terms of the economic organization of the industry. Gordon shows the optimum utilization of a particular fishing ground to be at the level of fishing effort where the marginal product equals the marginal cost. Net economic rent or economic yield is maximized at this level of exploitation. This approach represented a major departure from the then-prevailing theory predicated on maximum sustained physical yield. The author concludes that "common property natural resources are free goods for the individual and scarce goods for the society." Barring regulation, this would obviously lead to a dissipation of rent. Private or public regulation by a "unified directing power" is the solution to this dilemma. Gordon's analysis is sufficiently broad to warrant its application to natural resources owned in common and exploited under conditions of individualistic competition.

James Buchanan (1962) in a remarkable essay questions the validity of one of the basic assumptions of theoretical welfare economics (Sidgwick, Marshall and Pigou, among others) that externalities are either reduced or eliminated by the shift of an activity from market to political organization. It is argued in this paper that this proposition will be found tenable "only under certain highly restricted assumptions about human behavior in modern political systems." The dichotomy between marginal "social" product (cost) and marginal private product (cost) loses much of its value when we relax these restrictive assumptions. Buchanan concludes convincingly that major imperfections are apt to arise "from the political attempts at applying the economists' efficiency criteria." This is viewed as a major limitation of much of the work of welfare economists and economists in general. In this paper Buchanan thus advances the concept of what might be called "political externality" – a concept that has taken on a special relevance and significance in the current policy debates in the United States and elsewhere.

Part IV   The economics of exhaustible resources

A major aspect of the policy debates on natural resource allocation, management and use pertains to the nonrenewable or exhaustible nature of many natural resources such as oil, natural gas, minerals, and groundwater. This concern has found expression early on in the writings of economists as well as noneconomists. The central issue here has to do with the determination of the optimal rate of depletion of exhaustible resources, given the fact that their supply cannot be replenished or augmented in a meaningful time frame for planning purposes. Such a rate clearly has important implications both for the current generation as well as future generations (the issue of intergenerational equity).

The beginnings of the conservation movement in the United States can be attributed in large measure to a fear of impending resource shortages from the unwise and profligate use of natural resources. And conservation called for restrictions on the depletion of fixed deposits of nonrenewable resources. Thus began the search for an optimal rate of depletion which found its most powerful early expression in the seminal article by Harold Hotelling (1931). In this paper, the author stated that the price of an exhaustible resource must grow at a rate equal to the rate of interest, both along an efficient extraction path and in a competitive resource industry equilibrium. In essence, this meant that "the present value of a unit of homogeneous but finite stock of the mineral must be identical regardless of when it is extracted" (Hartwick and Olewiler, 1986, p. 59). This dictum has come to be known as the Hotelling Principle. Hotelling's formulation has had a profound impact on subsequent writings in the field. Solow describes it as the "fundamental principle of the economics of exhaustible resources" (Solow, 1974, Chapter 12 in this book).

Hotelling's classic-to-be received relatively little attention when it was published. However, the 1970s witnessed a surge of interest in his ideas, instigated in part by the two oil price shocks and the policy debates on population explosion and "limits to growth." The result was a series of academic papers scrutinizing the different aspects of Hotelling's formulation. An important contribution to this discourse is that of Robert Solow (1974). In his well-known paper, Solow discusses the economic theory of exhaustible resources as a partial equilibrium market theory with interest rate and demand as given. He examines the issue from the perspectives of efficiency and intergenerational equity. He starts out with the premise that Hotelling's rule, the fundamental principle of natural resource economics, is a necessary condition for efficiency and therefore for social optimality. It is argued that market price can fall or stay constant if extraction costs are falling and it has been found that low-cost resources will be exploited first and that backstop technology will provide a ceiling for the market price of the natural resource. Solow points out that technical progress and substitutability between exhaustible resources and reproducible capital and labor will greatly affect the gravity of the resource exhaustion problem. Solow has made a significant contribution to the conceptualization of the problem of exploitation of exhaustible resources. Although the assumption of constant population and zero technical progress is not in accord with reality, the Solow paper nonetheless paved the way for further analysis of the important idea of sustainable consumption.

Part V   The economics of renewable resources

The focus of this section is renewable resources. These differ from exhaustible resources in a fundamental way because they can regenerate in a time frame conducive to human exploitation. The loss in biomass due to harvest, for instance, is offset by natural growth under normal conditions. Thus, the threat of extinction or exhaustion of the resource base is less likely in the case of renewable resources.

The optimal depletion rate for a renewable resource differs from that for a nonrenewable one. The governing principle was for many years the maximum sustainable yield (MSY) used by biologists, foresters and other resource managers. This was based on the natural growth law which states that growth is a function simply of the size of the resource stock. Economists, however, have found this explanation somewhat simplistic. Age structure, competition and symbiosis with other species, and stochastic variations in the environment are other important factors that have a bearing on the optimal depletion rate. Renewable resources are also subject to externalities, e.g. fisheries and forestry, and internalization of externalities is an important consideration for the policymaker. These and other issues relevant to renewable resource ownership, allocation and management are investigated in the two papers included in this section.

The dichotomy between exhaustible resources and renewable resources is not always clear cut. There are a number of situations where it is difficult to make such a distinction; the resource in question may possess some of the attributes or characteristics of each category. The 1960s witnessed an increase in the understanding of the damage caused by the extinction of species and depletion of renewable resources consisting mainly of biological and/or genetic resources provided by nature. This situation calls for a new theory capable of explaining the interactions of resources and economic activities. Vernon Smith in his paper (1968) attempts to develop such a unified theory of production from natural resources. He uses a single model of an industry to "describe a dynamic process of recovery from such technologically diverse resources as fish, timber, petroleum, and minerals." Recovery from each of these resources is explained as a special case of a general model, based on whether the resource is replenishable, and/or whether production shows pronounced externalities.

Paul Samuelson explores optimal forest management in his 1976 classic. A survey and synthesis of the historical debate on the maximum sustainable yield (MSY) of forestry set the stage for a discussion of a modified theory of optimal forest management. Samuelson shows that it is economically inefficient to wait until the time of MSY for harvesting to begin. Previous studies in forestry economics, with the possible exception of Faustmann's 1849 paper, seriously failed to accommodate land rent, labor input, wage rate, output price, etc., all subject to change, in determining the optimal rotation period in forestry. The author in this paper presents a model with variables including time, interest rate, propensity to save, labor, wage, output price, land rent and the growth function of forest. The optimal rotation period in Samuelson's model is shorter than MSY, but longer than in the other theoretical models. A sophisticated model capturing some of the essential features of real world forestry is the contribution of this paper.

Note

Quotations that are not attributed, and therefore not cited in the References, are from the respective papers under discussion. The reader should be able to readily locate these.

References

Commons, John R., *Legal Foundations of Capitalism*, Madison: University of Wisconsin Press, 1924.

Faustmann, M., 1849, "On the Determination of the Value Which Forest Land and Immature Stands Possess for Forestry," In: M. Gane, ed. *Martin Faustmann and the Evolution of Discounted Cash Flow* (Oxford Paper 42), 1968.

Hartwick, John M. and Olewiler, Nancy D., *The Economics of Natural Resource Use*, New York: Harper & Row, 1986.

Posner, Richard A., *Economic Analysis of Law*, Boston and Toronto: Little, Brown and Company, 1977.

Randall, Allan, *Resource Economics*, New York: John Wiley and Sons, 1981.

Part I
The Intertemporal Problem

1

The Social Time Preference Discount Rate in Cost Benefit Analysis

Martin S. Feldstein

Choosing between alternative time-streams of social benefits and costs is one of the most difficult and most important problems in the evaluation of public investment projects. As an example of the numerous choices of this kind that arise in both the design and final selection stages, we need only recall the common problem of choosing between a technique of production that requires large capital investment but has low operating costs and one with the opposite profile of expenditure: nuclear versus conventional power, electric versus diesel railroads, etc.

Determining a project's admissibility requires comparing its annual net benefit time-stream with the time-stream of consumption that would have occurred if funds had not been used in the particular project. In selecting among admissible projects that are mutually exclusive for technical reasons (e.g., two different techniques for producing the same output) it is only in the rare (and trivial) case that one project dominates all others, i.e., has a greater net benefit in each year than that of every other project. In general, it is necessary to choose between time-streams with different durations and profiles. Except in cases of dominance, selecting among alternative projects requires assigning a single-value measure to each time-stream. This is the purpose of the "interest-rate" or discount-rate calculations in public investment decision-making.

The most useful measure of a project's desirability is the present value of the net addition to consumption created by the project.[1] In the framework of present value investment rules, the discount-rate calculation defines a functional relationship that makes outputs at different points in time commensurable with each other by assigning to them equivalent present-values. In traditional capital theory a *single* interest rate equates the marginal time preference of savers with the marginal productivity of capital in investment. Today most economists have begun to recognise that in a mixed economy with market imperfections and multiple interest rates no single discount rate can be taken as a measure of *both* time preference and the productivity of capital. Nevertheless, much cost-benefit writing has been a search for such a single discount rate with normative significance for public expenditure decisions.[2]

Two types of discount rates have been advocated: social time preference (STP) and social opportunity cost (SOC). A social time preference function assigns current values to future consumptions: it is a normative function reflecting society's evaluation of the relative desirability of consumption at different points in time. The STP function need not take the form of a constant discount rate; the relation of an STP function to an STP rate is discussed in Section III below. The social opportunity cost (SOC) is a measure of the value to society of the next best alternative use to which funds employed in the public project might otherwise have been put. In a perfectly competitive world the opportunity cost of these funds could be represented by the market interest rate; but in our economy no single interest rate or rate of return can fully measure the SOC of funds. The SOC depends on the source of the particular funds and *must also itself reflect the STP function*. It is best therefore to allow for the SOC of funds directly by placing a "shadow price" on the funds used in the project and to make all intertemporal comparisons with an STP rate or function.[3]

The search for a "perfect" formula to specify the social time preference rate is futile. An STP function must reflect public policy and social ethics, as well as judgment about future economic conditions. Nevertheless, there is much to be gained by understanding why a social time preference rate is necessary and by examining the factors that must be considered in formulating such a rate.

In this paper we show that the STP function cannot be derived on the basis of existing market rates, but must be administratively determined as a matter of public policy. We then examine the characteristics of the STP function, its relation to an STP rate and the movement of the STP rate through time.

I   Inapplicability of a "perfect" market interest rate to public policy

The ubiquitous imperfections of the capital market[4] should be adequate reason for rejecting the use of any market interest rate in a public policy decision. Why, then, encumber ourselves with an investigation into the reasons why even the interest rate of a "perfect" capital market would lack normative significance? First, some writers have argued that if a perfect market rate existed it would be appropriate for evaluating public investment projects.[5] Such an opinion would no doubt influence an economist's conception of an appropriate social time preference rate for use in the absence of perfect capital market conditions. Eckstein, for example, writes, "I shall endeavour to present that set (of value judgments) which, in my view, most closely adheres to the principle of consumer sovereignty."[6] This adherence to the "consumer sovereignty" which a "perfect" market rate would reflect may not accord with the characteristics of the social time preference rate we would otherwise accept. Second, considering the faults of a perfect market rate will demonstrate a number of defects inherent in the use of any market rate, or rate derived from market rates.

Pre-Keynesian theories considered the interest rate to be a price induced by the productivity of capital and required as payment for postponing consumption. Although the emphasis of economic theorists has shifted from this idea that the interest rate is an equilibrator of "real" savings and investment schedules to the loanable funds and liquidity preference theories which emphasize the "non-real" monetary nature of interest rate determination,[7] normative discussions of the role of the interest rate are still based on the old notion that the interest rate in a perfect capital market would equate the marginal productivity of capital and the marginal time preference of consumers to produce a Paretian social optimum. It is the application of this theory that we shall criticise.

Such an interest rate would acquire its usefulness for public decisions because it would also be the price that guided *private* investors to maximise their welfare over time. But even the interest rate of a perfect capital market is inadequate for this task. Unless all other assumptions of perfect competition are also fulfilled, this particular price will have no normative significance.[8] Further, individual savers must foresee their future incomes and wants, as well as the future prices of all goods. But the future income of each individual (or household) depends on the savings and investment decisions of society as a whole. The individual cannot possibly have the information he requires for rationally redistributing his income through time.[9] Similarly, although investors must know the marginal efficiency of capital in each private investment option, they may be unable to obtain such knowledge. The internal rate of return of a net revenue time-stream may be non-unique or even non-existent.[10] In addition, the revenue time-stream will depend on the investment decisions of other entrepreneurs: the individual investor, just as the individual saver, cannot have the information necessary for rational intertemporal decision-making.[11]

More importantly, even if a perfect market interest rate could guide private investors to maximise their welfare over time, it would not produce socially optimal investment decisions. A perfect market would equate *private* demand (investor's rate of return) and net supply (willingness to save) schedules; to produce socially optimal decisions, an interest rate would instead have to equate the social productivity of investment schedule with a politically determined saving supply schedule.

The private demand schedule for investment funds, even if it equalled the investor's internal rate of return, would not reflect the social productivity of capital. Investment enhances the productivity of labour and other factors of production, and, as a result, increases their income. This is a cost to the private investor, who calculates his rate of return net of payments to other factors. But to society as a whole, those increased factor incomes should be treated as a gain. The *social* rate of return on investment, i.e., the marginal output – capital ratio, may therefore be much greater than the private marginal efficiency of capital.[12] This difference is important not only for the micro-economic question of the optimal rate of national investment[13] but for the public micro-economic problems of benefit-cost analysis. Surprisingly, however, economists have universally ignored this distinction in benefit–cost discussions by taking the market rate of interest (or some other estimate of the marginal efficiency of private investment) as a measure of the social productivity of funds withdrawn from private investment.

In any case, for public investment decisions we may wish to reject the market-determined evaluation of future consumption in favour of a politically determined social time preference function. We may, in short, wish to replace the weights given to the opinions of individuals by the distribution of income and wealth with other weights, such as those given them in the ballot box. For this reason, Eckstein has argued for a discount rate lower than the market rate, reminding us that "Our notion of efficiency is relative to a distribution of income."[14] Further, the divergence of social time preference from market-expressed time preference need not reflect conflicting opinions of different people. An individual's own time preference may depend on whether he is acting alone or collectively. Sen[15] and Marglin[16] have suggested that individuals, in their public role as citizens, may be willing to save for future generations if others are also willing to do so. Public investment and consumption by future generations could therefore be treated as Samuelsonian "public goods" which are "psychically consumed by every member of the community."[17] Using the Samuelson formulation, Marglin provides a mathematical proof that "an individual's marginal time preference in collective saving *vs.* consumption decisions is not based on the same parameters . . . as his marginal time preference in unilateral decisions."[18]

II   Public preference versus the "public good"

In an unusual departure from the safety of their habitual domain to the unfamiliar territory of political theory, economists have argued about the proper political determination of the social time preference rate. As we have seen, the political process may be invoked because the market cannot express the "collective" demand for investment to benefit the future and because we may prefer the weights of some political process to those of the market-place. The first of these is a matter of facilitating action on which all might agree; the second is the familiar problem of allowing democratically determined redistribution to alter the outcome of the market process. But two other important questions remain: should the Government endeavour to provide for the future welfare of the current generation in a more rational way than they would themselves? What should the Government's attitude be towards future generations? In terms more familiar to the political theorist, they ask: should the Government act in the best interests of the public or should it do what the public wants? Is the Government's responsibility only to the current population or should it show a concern for the welfare of future generations greater than that which the current electorate would sanction?

Economists have long believed that individuals irrationally discount future *pleasures* merely because of their futurity.[19] Should not the Government correct this error, the argument continues, by substituting its own interpretation of the "public good" for the opinions of public preference expressed through the market or ballot-box? Thus, Pigou wrote that although "our telescopic faculty is defective, and . . . we therefore see future pleasures, as it were, on a diminished scale, . . . (this) does not imply that any economic dissatisfaction would be suffered if future pleasures were substituted at full value for present ones."[20] Although Marshall showed that we cannot be certain whether or to what extent individuals actually do discount future *pleasures* as such,[21] a controversey has developed between those such as Ramsey, Dobb and Sen,[22] who would disregard personal preferences and substitute a "more rational" government time preference, and others such as Eckstein, Bain, Tinbergen, and Marglin,[23] who would base the social time preference rate on public opinion.

An irrational preference for immediate pleasures need not be the reason that individuals introduce a pure time discount into their decisions; a quite rational fear of death is sufficient explanation for positive personal discount rates.[24] But if government is "the trustee for unborn generations as well as for its present citizens," as Pigou has said,[25] is not the mortality of individuals irrelevant for social time preference calculations? Some, like Pigou, Dobb, Holzman, and Sen,[26] are willing to impose on the public a responsibility for the welfare of future generations; others, like Eckstein, Bain and Marglin,[27] believe that the interests of future generations should be recognised only to the extent that the current public sanctions them through the democratic process.

Our own view would be to allow administrative determination of the STP with whatever weight to the welfare of future generations these democratic administrators would allow. An administrative decision by an accountable government satisfies our notion of the requirement of democracy; democratic theory does not require that each decision represent a consensus, but that government action as a whole be acceptable to the electorate.

III   The two-period STP function

Despite their general agreement that social decisions should not be made on the interest-rate rules appropriate for private investors, the critics of using market or opportunity cost discount rates are not agreed on the proper nature of social time preference discounting. We begin by examining the factors that should affect an administrative determination of an STP function between any two years; this is presented in terms of the indifference curve analysis developed by Irving Fisher. From this we shall see what a single STP rate implies and consider the *ex ante* determinacy of the rate. In the final section we discuss two aspects of the multi-period problem: factors affecting the change of the STP rate through time and the length of the time horizon of the STP function.

Fisher's indifference-curve analysis
Fisher's indifference curve analysis of private investment decision-making provides a useful framework for describing an STP function and

defining an STP rate.[28] For convenience, we first present the Fisher analysis in terms of an individual and then extend it to the problems of public investment.

The two axes in Figure 1.1 indicate the amounts the investor consumes in each of two successive years. If he begins with no expected consumption in year 2, we may represent his situation by a point such as D on the horizontal axis, indicating that he could consume D in year 1 and nothing in year 2. This would place him on indifference curve U_2. The line DK represents the borrowing-lending possibility line, equivalent to the budget line in consumer behaviour analysis. The slope of this line, say m, indicates the interest rate, i; $i = -(1 + m)$. The individual may redistribute his consumption between the two years by moving to any point on this line. At point K he consumes nothing in year 1 and OK in year 2; but this places him on a lower indifference curve than before, U_1. The individual whose only way of redistributing consumption between the years is by lending and borrowing (i.e., who has no direct investment opportunities) reaches his highest accessible indifference curve by moving to point W; here he lends amount DB, consumes OB in year 1 and OG in year 2, and is on indifference curve U_3.

Curve DL indicates the real (i.e., physical) investment opportunities open to the investor. The slope of the curve indicates that the rate of transformation of present goods into future goods[29] decreases as the

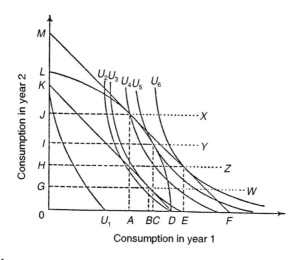

Figure 1.1

quantity of investment increases. If the investor follows the usual internal rate of return or present value rule he will invest the amount *DA*, bringing him to point *X*, where the marginal efficiency of capital is equal to the market interest rate. Here he will be on indifference curve U_4, consuming *OA* in year 1 and *OJ* in year 2. This is also the investment-consumption combination with maximum present value; the present value of the two-period consumption stream represented by point *X* is *OF*, the intercept of the interest rate line on the present year axis. It is obvious from the diagram that any other point on *DL* represents a lower present value.

Nevertheless, it is possible for the investor to reach higher indifference curves. If he invests *DC*, i.e., until the marginal efficiency of capital is equal to his marginal rate of substitution between consumption in years 1 and 2, he will be at point *Y*, on indifference curve U_5, consuming *OC* in period 1 and *OI* in period 2. This is still not the optimal strategy. The investor reaches his highest attainable indifference curve by following the internal rate of return rule (i.e., investing *DA*) and *then borrowing the amount AE* along the borrowing-lending line *MF*.[30] This brings him to point *Z* on indifference curve U_6, consuming *OE* in period 1 and *OH* in period 2.

Applications to public investment

Although this solution is necessarily determinate only for the two-period case, it is worthwhile examining some analogies between this analysis and the problem of public investment.

Curve *DL* represents the social productivity of investment for society as a whole, the possible transformations of present goods into future goods. This is the basis of the social opportunity cost of funds diverted from private investment to public expenditure.

For the community as a whole, it is impossible to redistribute consumption through time by merely monetary borrowing-lending transactions;[31] lines such as *KD* and *MF* are therefore irrelevant for the public investment decision. This inability to redistribute the time stream of social benefits of public investment by borrowing and lending has extremely important consequences for benefit-cost analysis which are ignored by those economists who would disregard social time preference and concentrate exclusively on social opportunity cost. Because society cannot redistribute the consumption of outputs of the public investment through time, any test or measure of the desirability of a public investment is inadequate if it does not take into account the social time preference function, i.e., the relative "weights" society places on consumption at different times in the future. Two net-benefit time streams *which differ in profile*, although they have the same unambiguous internal rate of return, are not necessarily equally desirable from society's point of view. A simple example will clarify this. Consider two possibilities of investing £100. One investment repays £200 after twelve years; the other repays £25,000 after a century. Both have internal rates of return of approximately 6%. A private investor might be indifferent between the two options because he could sell his investment whenever he wished; in effect, he could borrow against the future output of the project. But society as a whole cannot sell or borrow in this way; it must evaluate the alternative investments in terms of their specific time profiles.[32] If society's time preference discount rate[33] is more than 6% the £200 after twelve years is preferable to the £25,000 after a century; if society discounts consumption by less than 6% the £25,000 is preferable.

Characteristics of the two-period function

The indifference curves in the Fisher diagram represent two-period STP functions. The slope of such an indifference curve at any point indicates society's marginal rate of substitution of present for future goods, the STP rate between the two years. If the slope of the curve at a particular point is n we can express the STP rate, d, as: $d = -(1 + n)$. An STP *rate* is thus defined for each point in the consumption space in terms of the first derivative of an STP *function* at that point. This distinction between an STP function and an STP rate, although extremely important, is rarely recognised.[34]

Although Fisher's analytic technique provides a convenient framework for describing an STP function and defining an STP rate, it has never been used for this purpose. One reason may be the theoretical objections to extending Fisher's indifference curves from individuals to society.[35] Nevertheless, the social indifference curve is not unfamiliar in the literature of public expenditure; in this context, Samuelson has gone even further than we propose to go and has used both social and individual indifference curves simultaneously.[36] There are, however, problems peculiar to using intertemporal social utility curves; we return to these below in our discussion of the utility function.

It is important to clarify our measurement of consumption, i.e., the units of the axes. First, we assume that goods in each period have the prices that would prevail in a perfect market in which relative price changes occurred but the absolute price level remained constant. The reason for dealing in terms of a constant absolute price level requires no further discussion. If we are to be able to discount the specific outputs of a public project at the STP rate we must recognise that the relative utility of these goods (*vis à vis* other goods at the same time) may change reflecting changes in scarcity, taste, etc.[37] To do this, we must assign to them prices which indicate their relative social utility at the time of their consumption. Allowing directly for changes in relative utility permits us to ignore the arguments for applying different STP rates to different types of publicly produced goods. Second, we may choose between measuring total consumption or *per capita* consumption; the choice is only a matter of convenience, since, whichever we choose, we adjust our definition of the social utility-consumption map accordingly. In order to consider the growth of consumption and population separately, we shall use the *total* consumption as our unit of measure.

Exogenous consumption change

We noted above that society's location in the consumption space and the first derivative of the indifference curve at that point together determine the STP discount rate. The location in the consumption space reflects the exogenously determined consumption level in the first year and the rate of growth during the two years. A positive rate of growth of consumption is indicated by a point lying above a 45° ray through the origin. If the indifference curves have the "usual" properties of convexity higher growth rates imply higher STP rates.

To clarify this, we turn now to examine the factors which determine the shape of the social indifference curves: the social utility-consumption function, changes in population and the nature of the pure time discount, if any, that is imposed.

The social utility-consumption function

Precise definition of a utility-consumption function, capable of a normative evaluation of society's consumption through time, is obviously impossible. Even if we limited our aim to an ordinal function and ignored the distribution of consumption, we might still feel that changing population, tastes and levels of expectations presented insuperable problems of interpersonal and intertemporal comparison.[38] But impossibility is no excuse. Every intertemporal decision by government implies an underlying utility-consumption function; we turn therefore to examine the facets of this function which influence the social time preference rate.

Although we have stated our analysis in terms of total consumption, our basic belief is that the social consumption-utility function should reflect both total and *per capita* consumption. Previous writers have been far from unanimous on this subject. Ramsey safely evaded the problem by assuming that the population remained constant.[39] Tinbergen[40] and Chakravarty[41] do not mention population in discussing the social consumption-utility functions that they employ, but their growth equations clearly indicate that they are thinking in terms of total consumption rather than consumption *per capita*. Eckstein[42] explicitly introduces population growth and defines his social-welfare function strictly in terms of *per capita* consumption. Sen, while critical of Tinbergen's treatment, only commits himself to the comment that "Even if the size of the population is assumed to be independent of our decision, the choice (of techniques) will be affected by the fact that social utility depends, among other things, upon consumption *per capita*."[43] We would go further than Sen in seeking a middle position between Tinbergen and Eckstein. Although *per capita* consumption may be the underlying determinant of social welfare, we will say that social welfare increases if a nation that enjoys a high standard of living maintains the level of *per capita* consumption while the population increases. More explicitly, in terms of a general social utility-consumption function, $U = f\left(P, \dfrac{C}{P}\right)$, where U is social utility, C is total consumption and P is population, we shall say $\dfrac{\delta U}{\delta(C/P)} > 0$ and $\dfrac{\delta U}{\delta P} > 0$.[44] In terms of the Fisher indifference map, $\dfrac{\delta U}{\delta P} > 0$ and $\dfrac{\delta U}{\delta(C/P)} > 0$ are necessary conditions for movement outwards along a ray through the origin to lead to higher indifference levels.[45]

The shape of the Fisher indifference curves will reflect the second-order properties of the social utility-consumption function, i.e., our assumptions about diminishing marginal utility of consumption. Although economists have long accepted propositions that rest on diminishing marginal utility of consumption by an individual, there is no reason to assert that increasing *total* consumption would have diminishing marginal utility, even if *per capita* consumption were constant. Our notion of a social-welfare function is insufficiently well defined to make this assertion; the ethical propositions on which such a judgment would have to rest have never received adequate consideration.[46] A recognition of our uncertainty would yield a more acceptable interim solution. We would be safer if we assumed decreasing marginal utility of *per capita* consumption, $\left[\dfrac{\delta^2 U}{\delta(C/P)^2} < 0\right]$ but remained sceptical about the marginal utility of increasing total consumption due to increasing population $\left[\dfrac{\delta^2 U}{\delta P^2} \leq 0\right]$.[47]

The usual indifference curve convexity properties require that $\dfrac{\delta^2 U}{\delta C^2} < 0$; the stronger this inequality, the greater will be the convexity. Our second-order assumptions fulfil these conditions, except in the case where *per capita* consumption is constant and the population increase; here, unless $\dfrac{\delta^2 U}{\delta P^2} < 0$, the indifference curves would be straight lines. As we noted above, convex indifference curves imply that the STP rate is an increasing function of the rate of growth of consumption. If we assume that $\dfrac{\delta^2 U}{\delta P^2} = 0$, i.e., that there is no decreasing marginal utility of total consumption if *per capita* consumption remains constant, only the *per capita* consumption growth rate will influence the STP rate. If we allow that $\dfrac{\delta^2 U}{\delta P^2} < 0$ both total and *per capita* consumption growth rates are significant.[48]

Pure time discount

In terms of the Fisher indifference map, discounting future consumption merely because of its futurity, i.e., discounting future utility as such, means that all points (except those on the horizontal axis) lie on lower-value indifference curves; this further implies that if a pure time discount exists at all consumption levels and growth rates the indifference curves are steeper at all points. The economists who have included pure time discount in formal models have implicitly assumed that the extent of this pure time discount is the same for all consumption levels and growth rates,[49] i.e., that the slope of the indifference curves is everywhere made steeper to the same degree. But society's impatience for current consumption may well reflect the level of well-being and the rate of progress; the first may be subsumed in the utility-consumption function, but the effect of the growth rate can only be reflected in the pure time discount. More important, the pure time discount may be a function of calendar time: the Government may reject a pure time preference in the near future (say, twenty to fifty years), but may impose an increasing one after that date to reflect a decreasing concern of the current electorate with the welfare of future generations.

IV   The STP rate

A *single* STP rate is a measure of society's marginal rate of substitution of consumption in year $t + 1$ for consumption in year t; more formally, d_t, the STP rate applicable between years t and $t + 1$, may be defined: $1 - t\ d_t = \text{MRS}_{t+1-t} - 1$. The STP rate is thus determined by the consumption level and growth rate (society's location in the consumption space) and by the slope of the indifference curve at that point (which in turn reflects the social consumption-utility function, the rate of population growth and the pure time preference rate that is applied).

In an economy in which the total levels of both private and public investment were determined as a matter of national policy the location in the consumption space would be a point of tangency between the investment productivity curve and a social indifference curve. In Figure 1.2 this would occur at point X, where the social indifference curve U_2 is tangent to the investment productivity curve AB. Here the STP rate (as well as the marginal social productivity of investment) can be derived from the slope of line L_1, the tangent to the two curves at point X. But the Government may, for political as well as technical reasons, be unable to make private investment decisions conform to the STP discount rate; the marginal social productivity of private investment may therefore exceed the STP discount rate. In that case the Government can apply an STP rate (in combination with a measure of opportunity cost based on the marginal social productivity of private investment) only to its own investment decisions. Such a situation is represented in Figure 1.2 by point Y. For this location in the consumption space the STP rate is indicated by the slope of line L_2, the tangent to the indifference curve U_1 at point Y. Since private investment decisions have not been brought in line with social time preference, this is not a point of tangency with the investment productivity curve; funds transferred from private investment to the public sector will have an opportunity cost reflecting the marginal social productivity of private investment indicated by the slope of line L_3, the tangent to the investment productivity curve at point Y.[50]

Looking at the STP rate in terms of the Fisher indifference map, we see that there is no reason for it to remain constant through time. Changes in society's location in the consumption space, as well as changes in the shape of the indifference curves, can change the STP rate. We shall return to this below.

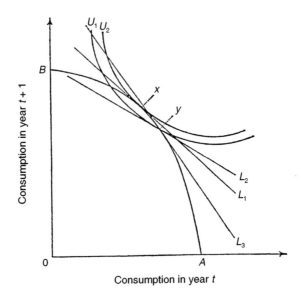

Figure 1.2

We are also better able to understand the meaning of a zero (or even negative) STP rate. In contrast to the assumptions of Dobb[51] and Tinbergen[52] that a positive discount rate is necessary to avoid investing the entire national income, we see that there is often a *zero* discount rate associated with at least one growth rate for the level of current consumption; for many points on the horizontal axis of the Fisher indifference map, there is a corresponding point vertically above it at which the slope of the social indifference curve is −1. Dobb and Tinbergen failed to see that the STP rate depends on the level of consumption and the rate of growth. If a nation reduces its consumption in order to invest more, the STP rate may rise. It is this, rather than the diminishing marginal productivity of investment, that precludes advice to invest the entire national income.[53] While we would expect that even in the absence of any pure time preference discount, the growth of *per capita* income would induce a positive STP rate, a zero or negative STP discount is not impossible.

A more serious question is whether the STP rate can be known in advance, and thus be available for use in the investment analyses or only emerges as a product of the investment decisions.[54] The STP rate appears at first both to determine and be determined by the Government's investment programme: the STP rate depends on society's

location in the consumption space; but, subject to the condition that
it must be on the investment-productivity curve, society's position in
the consumption space reflects the amount of investment and thus ultimately the STP rate.[55] It seems from this that the STP rate cannot be
known beforehand. An iterative method to solve for the optimum location on the investment productivity curve, and thus to yield simultaneously the amount of government investment, the marginal social
productivity of private investment, and the STP rate, would no doubt
be mathematically pleasing. It would, however, require that all projects
be considered simultaneously, that the precise shape of the investment
productivity curve be known and so forth. Extension of such a method
to more than two periods would be of even more dubious practicabil-
ity. In any case, its mathematical elegance would have little appeal to
the administrator who requires a method for evaluating individual projects. Is there any way in which we might be able to know the STP rate
in advance? Fortunately, although a precise *ex ante* estimate of the STP
rate is not possible, for practical purposes there would be no harm in
using such an advance estimate. The Government's range of total
amounts of investment between which the Government may choose,
i.e., the politically and economically feasible area in the consumption
space, is very limited. Although we have not been able to say anything
about the sensitivity of the STP rate to small changes in the consumption space location,[56] our uncertainty about the exact shape of the social
indifference curves leads us to the conclusion that as long as the area
of choice within which the Government may finally locate society is
narrowly prescribed, we are safe to estimate the STP rate in advance.
Our error in estimating the final location in the consumption space is
likely to be no greater than the error which would be associated with
an estimate of the STP rate after that location was known.

V The STP rate through time

The STP rate may vary through time if society's location in the consumption space changes or if the shapes or positions of the indifference
curves do not remain constant.[57] Both of these are likely. We begin with
the assumption that the social indifference map stays constant and
examine the effects of changing consumption levels and growth rates.
We then discuss the effects on the indifference map of changing the
pure time preference discount rate.

Changes in the absolute level of consumption, even if its rate of
growth remains constant, may alter the STP rate.[58] We have already seen

that the properties we ascribed to the social utility-consumption function imply that the social indifference curves have the convexity properties associated with the second-order condition $\frac{\delta^2 U}{\delta C^2} < 0$. The effect on the STP rate of a constant growth rate of *per capita* consumption will therefore depend on the function's third-order properties, i.e., on whether the marginal social utility of increasing consumption diminishes at a constant, accelerating or decelerating rate. In particular, the STP rate may increase through time as the level of consumption increases if the marginal utility of consumption diminishes at a sufficiently accelerating rate, i.e., if $\frac{\delta^3 U}{\delta C^3} > 0$.

In terms of a social indifference map that remains constant through time, society's time path in the consumption space would be a single ray through the origin with a slope equal to 1 plus the rate of growth of consumption. The STP rate would remain constant only if the first derivative of every social indifference curve at its point of intersection with the growth ray was the same. This occurs, for example, in Ramsey's constant elasticity of marginal utility function.[59]

A changing rate of growth of consumption will cause society to digress from a straight-line time path through the consumption space. Given the assumed convexity properties, an increased growth rate (i.e., a vertical displacement in the consumption space) will produce a higher STP rate.[60] Similarly, a decrease in the growth rate would, *ceteris paribus*, imply a lower STP rate.

The indifference curves may change shape through time in response to changes in the rate of population growth[61] and future changes in the social consumption-utility function. More importantly, the indifference curves will change through time in response to a change in the pure time discount rate. It is not unreasonable to suppose that a government that foregoes a pure time discount in early years will nevertheless wish to impose one for years that are further in the future. The common suggestion that a time horizon be imposed is an extreme example of this.[62] More appropriate, and perhaps a better reflection of the wishes of even the more intertemporally altruistic citizens, would be a pure time preference rate that increased through time. The result of this, *ceteris paribus*, would be that the curves of the Fisher indifference maps for later pairs of successive years would be more steeply sloped and, as a result, the STP rate would be higher. The process of slowly but continuously raising the pure time discount rate would seem to be the best compromise between those who would not have society look endlessly into the future and those who can see no moral justification for not doing so. It would have the further advantage of obviating the valuation of terminal capital, a problem that arises whenever a finite horizon is employed and which introduces peculiar results or arbitrary rules.[63]

Summary

(1) The interest rate even of a perfect capital market would be unsuitable for evaluating public investment projects.

(2) A social time preference (STP) rate, reflecting the Government's judgment of the relative social utility of consumption at different points in time, should be used.

(3) Fisher's indifference curve analysis shows the properties of the social time preference *function* (the indifference curves reflecting: the social consumption-utility function, the rate of population growth and the pure time preference discount rate) and its relationship with the social time preference *rate* (the first derivative of the social indifference curve at the point in the consumption space indicated by the consumption level and growth rate).

(4) A useful *ex ante* estimate of the STP rate can be made.

(5) The STP rate may vary through time in response to changes in the consumption level and growth rates, the rate of population growth and the pure time preference rate. It is not unreasonable to expect the STP rate to rise as a function of time.

(6) Public investment decisions must also reflect the social opportunity cost of the funds; this is best done by using a shadow price that reflects social time preference and the productivity of funds in private investment.

Notes

1 For a discussion of the superiority of the present value approach to the use of any measure of yield or internal rate of return, see: Hirshleifer *et al., op. cit.*, Chapters 6 and 7. The appropriate method of calculating the present value of the addition to consumption created by a project and of using this for public investment decision-making under a number of different conditions of capital rationing is developed in my "Net Social Benefit Calculation and the Public Investment Decision."

2 This has been particularly true in government discussions. But see also the works by Hirshleifer *et al.*, Kuhn, and McKean.

3 For a development of this idea and a method of combining STP and SOC, see my "Net Social Benefit Calculation and the Public Investment

Decision," especially Section I. Earlier work on this subject was done by Otto Eckstein (*Water Resource Development*; "A Survey of the Theory of Public Expenditure Criteria"), Peter Steiner (*op. cit.*) and Stephen Marglin ("Economic Factors Affecting System Design," "The Opportunity Costs of Public Investment").

4   In particular, institutional imperfections impeding access to credit, the divergence between lending and borrowing rates, the interference of risk and uncertainty and related problems that give rise to the simultaneous existence of multiple interest rates.

5   R. N. McKean suggests that in the absence of capital rationing "the market rate" should be used; *op. cit.*, pp. 76–81. Otto Eckstein develops his theory of intertemporal welfare economics because the absence of a "well-functioning capital market" prevents deriving these "social value judgments . . . directly from observable market behaviour" ("Investment Criteria for Economic Development and the Theory of Intertemporal Welfare Economics," p. 75). Although Maurice Dobb cites F. J. Atkinson as espousing the view that "the government should only invest . . . as much as it can raise by the sale of bonds to individuals" (quoted from M. Dobb, *An Essay on Economic Growth and Planning* (London: Routledge and Kegan Paul, 1960, p. 15), Atkinson himself is careful to explain that he attaches no normative significance to the proposition that a Socialist Government could allow the forces of a perfect capital market to determine the amount of investment by the public's willingness to absorb government bonds; he even comments, "It may be that it would be *better* for the state to decide the rate of accumulation . . . The validity of the norm of consumer's sovereignty is not discussed." ("Saving and Investment in a Socialist State," *Review of Economic Studies*, Vol. XV, 1948, p. 78).

6   O. Eckstein, "Investment Criteria for Economic Development and the Theory of Intertemporal Welfare Economics," pp. 75–6.

7   See the discussion by G. L. S. Shackle, "Recent Theories Concerning the Nature and Role of Interest," *Economic Journal*, Vol. LXXI (June 1961), pp. 209–54.

8   I. M. D. Little, *A Critique of Welfare Economics*, 2nd ed. (Oxford: Oxford University Press, 1957), p. 147. More generally, see R. G. Lipsey and K. Lancaster, "General Theory of the Second Best," *Review of Economic Studies*, Vol. XXIV (1956), pp. 11–12.

9   The necessary interdependence of rational savings decisions is developed by J. de V. Graaff, *Theoretical Welfare Economics* (Cambridge: Cambridge University Press, 1957), pp. 103–5, and by Maurice Dobb, *op. cit.*, pp. 17–18.

10   For a discussion of the ambiguity of the internal rate of return, see: J. Hirshleifer, "On the Theory of the Optimal Investment Decision," *Journal of Political Economy*, Vol. LXVI (August 1958), pp. 329–52; Pritchford and Hagger, "A Note on the Marginal Efficiency of Capital," *Economic Journal*, Vol. LXVII (1958), p. 597; and J. F. Wright, "Notes on the Marginal Efficiency of Capital," *Oxford Economic Papers*, Vol. XV (June 1963), p. 329.

11   Again see J. de V. Graaff, *op. cit.*, pp. 103–5.

12   This point was raised by A. K. Sen in discussing the optimal rate of national investment, "On Optimizing the Rate of Saving," *Economic Journal*, Vol. LXXI (September 1961), p. 487. J. Tinbergen, "The Optimum Rate of Saving,"

Economic Journal, Vol. LXVI (December 1956), pp. 603–4, made the mistake of treating the private marginal efficiency of capital as equal to the marginal output–capital ratio; his error was indicated by Branko Horvat, "The Optimum Rate of Saving: A Note," *Economic Journal,* Vol. LXVIII (March 1958), pp. 157–8. Mr John Flemming has pointed out to me that the private investors' demand schedule would not only be too low, but would show unequal bias for different industries and investments; although a perfect capital market would assure that the private marginal efficiency of investment was equal in all investments, there is no theoretical reason why the marginal output–capital ratio should be so.

13 The rule for determining the optimal rate of national investment should be: invest until the social rate of return on investment equals that rate of interest which reflects society's willingness to postpone consumption.

14 Otto Eckstein, *Water Resource Development: The Economics of Project Evaluation,* p. 100.

15 A. K. Sen, *op. cit.,* p. 488, discusses this as the "Isolation Paradox."

16 Stephen A. Marglin, "Economic Factors Affecting System Design," pp. 194–7.

17 Stephen A. Marglin, "The Social Rate of Discount and the Optimal Rate of Investment," p. 104. More generally, see P. A. Samuelson, "The Pure Theory of Public Expenditure," *Review of Economics and Statistics,* Vol. XXXVI (November 1957), pp. 387–9.

18 "The Social Rate of Discount and the Optimal Rate of Investment," p. 109.

19 Böhm-Bawerk remarked as early as 1888 that "to goods which are destined to meet the wants of the future, we ascribe a value which is really less than the true intensity of their future marginal utility." E. V. Böhm-Bawerk, *The Positive Theory of Capital* (1888), W. Smart translation (New York: G. E. Stechert and Company, 1891), p. 253. Marshall and Pigou called attention to this same phenomenon. A. Marshall, *Principles of Economics* (1920), 8th edition (London: Macmillan Company, 1959), pp. 100–2. A. C. Pigou, *Economics of Welfare* (1920), 4th edition (London: Macmillan Company, 1932), pp. 24–30.

20 *Op. cit.,* p. 25.

21 *Op. cit.,* pp. 101–2, especially the footnotes.

22 Discussing the optimal rate of national saving, F. P. Ramsey refers to pure time preference discounting as "a practice which is ethically indefensible and arises merely from weakness of the imagination." "A Mathematical Theory of Saving," *Economic Journal,* Vol. XXXVIII (December 1928), p. 543. Maurice Dobb's views are most recently expressed in *An Essay on Economic Growth and Planning,* Chapter 2. Sen rejects the "psychological discount" as irrational in *Choice of Techniques* (Oxford: Basil Blackwell, 1960), Chapter 8.

23 Otto Eckstein seeks to base his intertemporal comparisons on "the principle of consumer sovereignty," "Investment Criteria for Economic Development and the Theory of Intertemporal Welfare Economics," p. 75. Joe Bain states that the appropriate social discount rate "expressed the consensus of the electorate," "Criteria for Undertaking Water-Resource Developments," *American Economic Review,* Vol. L (May 1960), p. 315. Jan Tinbergen's optimum rate of saving reflects a "psychological discount rate," *op. cit.,* pp. 604–5. Stephen Marglin dismisses the opinions of Pigou and Dobb as

implying "an authoritarian rejection of individual preferences with which we are unwilling to associate ourselves" ("Economic Factors Affecting System Design," p. 197). Again, on a later occasion, he comments, "I, for one, do not accept the Pigovian formulation of social welfare . . . I want the government's social welfare function to reflect only the preferences of present individuals" ("The Social Rate of Discount and the Optimal Rate of Investment," p. 97).

24 This is developed by Otto Eckstein, "A Survey of the Theory of Public Expenditure Criteria," pp. 456–9; and A. K. Sen, *Choice of Techniques*, p. 83.

25 *Op. cit.*, p. 29.

26 A. C. Pigou, *op. cit.*, pp. 24–30; M. Dobb, *op. cit.*, p. 18. F. D. Holzman argues that true consumer sovereignty requires that the "wishes" of consumers of the future be represented in the decision; "Consumer Sovereignty and the Role of Economic Development," *Economia Internazionale*, Vol. XI (May 1958), pp. 193–207. Similarly, A. K. Sen says that a democratic solution to an intertemporal problem is impossible if the opinions of all who are concerned must be considered, "On Optimizing the Rate of Saving," p. 486.

27 See, note 23, p. 15. Marglin is not opposed to the government providing "education of today's citizens to the 'rightful claims' of future generations" ("The Social Rate of Discount and the Optimal Rate of Investment," (*op. cit.*, pp. 97–8).

28 Fisher's original presentation is in *The Theory of Interest* (New York: Macmillan Co., 1930). For a discussion and development of Fisher's approach, still with respect to private investment, see Jack Hirshleifer, "On the Theory of the Optimal Investment Decision."

29 This is the marginal efficiency of capital; since we are dealing with a two-period case, a unique internal rate of return may be calculated for each incremental pound of investment. In this case the present value and internal rate of return rules are also equivalent. For an amplification of the problem of a unique marginal efficiency of capital, see the discussions by Hirshleifer, *op. cit.*, and J. F. Wright, *op. cit.*

30 This line is parallel to *DK*, indicating that the interest rate is the same.

31 This is strictly true only for a closed economy; but for the large developed countries with which we are concerned, net international borrowing or lending would not be significant.

32 Thus, Tinbergen is misleading when he says, *à propos* the optimal rate of national saving and investment, "There need not be, in principle, any difference between the choice an individual makes and the choice made for a whole nation" (J. Tinbergen, "The Optimal Rate of Saving," p. 603). Similarly, we cannot agree with Kuhn's statement, "Time and interest problems arise in both public and private enterprise. By and large, the analytic treatment is identical." (Tillo E. Kuhn, *Public Enterprise Economics and Transport Problems*, p. 102.) The idea that private investment methods are directly applicable in the public sector is also found in R. N. McKean, *op. cit.*, and J. Hirshleifer *et al.*, *Water Supply: Economics, Technology and Policy.*

33 The meaning of society discounting future consumption will be explored below; for now we treat it merely as the discounting algorithm.

34 Two exceptions are: J. Hirshleifer, "Comment on Eckstein's Survey of the Theory of Public Expenditure Criteria," in James M. Buchanan (ed.), *op. cit.*,

pp. 495–50; S. Marglin, "The Social Rate of Discount and the Optimal Rate of Investment," footnote pp. 95–6. Neither of them, however, develops this point.

35 On the "impossibility" of constructing social indifference curves from individual indifference curves, see: P. A. Samuelson, "Social Indifference Curves," *Quarterly Journal of Economics*, Vol. LXX (February 1956), pp. 1–22; Kenneth Arrow, *Social Choice and Individual Values* (New York: Wiley, 1951).

36 Paul A. Samuelson, *op. cit.*, and also "Diagrammatic Exposition of a Theory of Public Expenditures," *Review of Economics and Statistics*, Vol. XXXVII (November 1955), pp. 350–6.

37 Marshall recognised that the utility (to an individual) of *specific* commodities might change with time, *op. cit.*, p. 101, especially the footnote. Later Hayek made this same point in his analysis of the relationship between the utility function and the interest rate; F. A. v. Hayek, "Utility Analysis and Interest," *Economic Journal*, Vol. XLVI (March 1936), p. 45.

38 Writers on social time preference have generally not been unaware of these problems. Some, such as Ramsey, assume that *ceteris* remain *paribus*. F. P. Ramsey, *op. cit.*, pp. 543–59. More appropriately, Sen recognises that while these problems may frustrate exact specification of a social utility-consumption function, they do not preclude all consideration of the subject. *Choice of Techniques*, p. 84. Still others, like Dobb, use these Duesenberry-cum-Veblen effects as reason for completely abandoning the subject of intertemporal comparison, *op. cit.*, pp. 19–22.

39 *Op. cit.*, p. 544.

40 *Op. cit.*

41 S. Chakravarty, "Optimal Savings with Finite Planning Horizon," *International Economic Review*, Vol. III (September 1962), pp. 338–55.

42 "Investment Criteria for Economic Development and the Theory of Intertemporal Welfare Economics," pp. 65–81.

43 *Choice of Techniques*, p. 85.

44 Note that $\frac{\delta U}{\delta P} > 0$ implies $\frac{\delta U}{\delta C} > 0$, i.e., social utility increasing when population increases with constant *per capita* consumption is equivalent to social utility increasing when total consumption increases. Throughout our discussion we ignore the cases of decreasing population and decreasing *per capita* consumption as practically unimportant.

45 If population remained constant, or if we redefined our measure of consumption in *per capita* terms, only $\frac{\delta U}{\delta(C/P)} > 0$ would be necessary.

46 Nevertheless, Tinbergen and Chakravarty both assume diminishing marginal utility of total consumption and define this relation without regard to population change; see notes 40 and 41. Eckstein goes further and implies that increasing total consumption has *zero* marginal utility when *per capita* consumption remains constant; "Investment Criteria for Economic Development and the Theory of Intertemporal Welfare Economics," pp. 65–81.

47 Such scepticism would also be appropriate for attempts to formulate particular functions with decreasing marginal utility of consumption, e.g.,

Ramsey's asymptotic Bliss or the Tinbergen–Eckstein constant-elasticity consumption-utility function.

48 This agrees with Eckstein's conclusion that higher growth rates of *per capita* consumption should imply higher STP discount rates: "Investment Criteria for Economic Development and the Theory of Intertemporal Welfare Economics" and "A Survey of the Theory of Public Expenditure Criteria." It also shows that this relationship need not rest on Eckstein's assumption that $\delta U/\delta P = 0$ (zero marginal utility of total consumption if *per capita* consumption is constant) but only requires that $\frac{\delta^2 U}{\delta P^2} = 0$ (*constant* marginal utility of total consumption if *per capita* consumption is constant). Further, we see that total as well as *per capita* consumption growth may influence the STP rate.

49 For example, Tinbergen and Eckstein. They also assume that it remains constant through time.

50 For a discussion of this problem and a method of calculating the opportunity cost "shadow price" of funds transferred from private investment, see M. S. Feldstein, "Net Social Benefit Calculation and the Public Investment Decision," especially Section I.

51 *Op. cit.*, pp. 27–8.

52 *Op. cit.*, pp. 604–5.

53 Horvat, replying to Tinbergen's argument about the need for a positive discount rate, stated that the law of diminishing returns would prevent investment of the total national income (*op. cit.*, p. 158). But if the STP rate remained zero this would be true only if the marginal social productivity diminished to zero.

54 In somewhat different frameworks, Dobb (*op. cit.*, p. 27) and Hirshleifer ("On the Theory of the Optimal Investment Decision," p. 329) argue that the investment criterion is itself a product of the analysis, and therefore cannot be available beforehand.

55 The STP rate determines the amount of public investment directly; private investment is affected by the taxation imposed to finance the programmes of public expenditure that are approved by calculations employing the STP rate.

56 Of course, for small enough movements along an indifference curve, the curve can be regarded as a straight line.

57 Julius Margolis has been the only writer to have suggested that the discount rate for evaluating public investment projects (not necessarily an STP rate) need not remain constant; he does not, however, develop the idea any further. "The Economic Evaluation of Water Resource Development," *American Economic Review*, Vol. LXIX (March 1959), p. 102. Marshall and Böhm-Bawerk have suggested that individuals' time preferences vary with time; see the discussion in R. Strotz, "Myopia and Inconsistency in Dynamic Utility Maximization," *Review of Economic Studies*, Vol. XXIII (1955–56), pp. 165–80.

58 This can, of course, happen if the rate of population growth changes. In our analysis this would imply a change in the social indifference map; we therefore ignore it at this point by assuming that the population

growth rate remains constant, and is less than the growth rate of total consumption.

59 *Op. cit.*

60 The only exception would be if $\dfrac{\delta^3 U}{\delta C^3} < 0$ to a great enough extent to counteract this.

61 A change in the rate of population growth would alter the growth rate of *per capita* consumption; the effects of this are discussed in the preceding paragraph.

62 A time horizon is used by Eckstein, *Water Resource Development*, Chapter 4; Peter Steiner, *op. cit.*, and has been recommended for official United States government use in: M. M. Hufschmidt, J. Krutilla, Julius Margolis and Stephen A. Marglin, *op. cit.*, p. 17 (Washington, DC: June 30, 1961, unpublished), p. 17.

63 Little thought has been given to the difficulties of introducing a finite planning horizon. Chakravarty's solution (*op. cit.*), although mathematically elegant, requires a number of strong assumptions about the national production function, can only be said to be optimal in the limit, and seems clearly beyond the realm of acceptance. A continually increasing pure time discount, while serving the same purpose, has none of these difficulties.

References

Eckstein, Otto, "Investment Criteria for Economic Development and the Theory of Intertemporal Welfare Economics," *Quarterly Journal of Economics*, Vol. LXXI (February 1957), pp. 56–85.

Eckstein, Otto, *Water Resource Development: The Economics of Project Evaluation* (Cambridge: Harvard University Press, 1958).

Eckstein, Otto, "A Survey of the Theory of Public Expenditure Criteria," in James M. Buchanan (ed.), *Public Finances: Needs, Sources and Utilization* (Princeton: Princeton University Press, 1961), pp. 439–95.

Feldstein, Martin S., "Net Social Benefit Calculation and the Public Investment Decision," *Oxford Economic Papers*, Vol. XVI (March 1964).

Hirshleifer, Jack, De Haven, J. C., and Milliman, J. W., *Water Supply: Economics, Technology and Policy* (Chicago: University of Chicago Press, 1960).

Hitch, Charles, J., and McKean, Roland N., *Economics of Defense in the Nuclear Age* (Cambridge: Harvard University Press, 1960).

Hufschmidt, Maynard M., Krutilla, John, Margolis, Julius, and Marglin, Stephen A., *Report of Panel of Consultants to the Bureau of the Budget on Standards and Criteria for Formulating and Evaluating Federal Water Resource Developments* (Washington, June 1961, unpublished).

Krutilla, John V., and Eckstein, Otto, *Multiple Purpose River Development* (Baltimore: Johns Hopkins Press, 1958).

Kuhn, Tillo E., *Public Enterprise Economics and Transport Problems* (Berkeley and Los Angeles: University of California Press, 1962).

Marglin, Stephen A., "Economic Factors Affecting System Design," in Maase, A., *et al., Design of Water Resource Systems* (Cambridge: Harvard University Press, 1962).

Marglin, Stephen A., "The Social Rate of Discount and the Optimal Rate of Investment," *Quarterly Journal of Economics*, Vol. LXXVII (February 1963), pp. 95–111.

Marglin, Stephen A., *Approaches to Dynamic Investment Planning* (Amsterdam: North-Holland Publishing Co., 1963).

Marglin, Stephen A., "The Opportunity Costs of Public Investment," *Quarterly Journal of Economics*, Vol. LXVII (May 1963), pp. 274–89.

McKean, Roland N., *Efficiency in Government through Systems Analysis, with Emphasis on Water Resource Development* (New York: John Wiley and Son, 1958).

Steiner, P. O., "Choosing Among Alternative Public Investments in the Water Resource Field," *American Economic Review*, Vol. XLIX (December 1959), pp. 893–916.

Turvey, R., "Present Value *Versus* Internal Rate of Return – An Essay in the Theory of the Third Best," *Economic Journal*, Vol. LXXIII (March 1963), pp. 93–8.

2
On the Social Rate of Discount

William J. Baumol

Few topics in our discipline rival the social rate of discount as a subject exhibiting simultaneously a very considerable degree of knowledge and a very substantial level of ignorance. Economists understand thoroughly just what this variable should measure: the opportunity cost of postponement of receipt of any benefit yielded by a public investment. They agree also on the components that should be considered in making up this figure: primarily the welfare foregone by not having these benefits available for immediate consumption or reinvestment and (perhaps) a premium corresponding to the risk incurred in undertaking government projects. Above all, economists are quite generally in accord on the view that a very serious misallocation of resources can result from the use of an incorrect estimate of the value of this variable in a cost-benefit calculation. Yet, while they agree that exernalities can play a significant role in the matter, there is some considerable question even about the direction of these effects. There is substantial obscurity and divergence of views in discussions of the implications of differences (if indeed there are any) in the degree of risk that is incurred when a given project is undertaken by a private firm on the one side and by government on the other. And as a result of these and other sources of shaky understanding of some basic principles, we are treated to what may with little exaggeration be described as a sorry spectacle – outstanding members of our profession providing in print estimates of the social discount rate ranging from $4\frac{1}{2}$ to 8 or 9 per cent. Some calculations by governmental agencies and others have even employed discount rates as low as three per cent (see March [10]) or have even discounted at a zero rate! (see Klarman [6]). Since the choice of investment projects can be so sensitive to the magnitude of this variable, little help is provided to the decision maker who is confronted by such a enormous range of estimates.

I do not presume in this paper to settle the major issues outstanding. But by going at the matter slowly and in terms of its elementary components I hope to introduce some illumination on these matters. It will be maintained however that there has been some misunderstanding of the relative magnitude of the components of the social discount rate.

I will conclude that both risk and corporate taxes play a more important role than is sometimes ascribed to them, though, curiously, risk derives its significance form the comparative risklessness of investments from the point of view of society, the very fact that has played a central part in the argument of those who oppose the inclusion of a risk premium in the discount rate for government projects.

Perhaps more important, I will show that, given our institutional arrangements, there is an unavoidable indeterminacy in the choice of that rate. The figure which is optimal from the point of view of the allocation of resources between the private and public sectors is necessarily higher than that which accords with the public's subjective time preference. As a result, neither the higher nor the lower figure that has been proposed can, by itself, satisfy the requirements for an optimal allocation of resources, and we find ourselves forced to hunt for a solution in the dark jungles of the second best.

Finally, I shall suggest that the intertemporal externalities that have been discussed in the literature are significant for the overall levels of the optimal private and public discount rates rather than for the *differential* between the two rates. That is, if, e.g., externalities were in fact to imply that society invests too little for the future, then this means that the private and social rates should both be lowered, not that public projects should be evaluated in terms of a rate that is low relative to the cost of capital to private industry. I shall, then, reexamine the externalities issue and review the nature of the misallocations which are likely to result if inappropriate policy decisions are made in response to them.

In covering our subject it will prove convenient to proceed by stages, first dealing with a world in which taxes are present but in which there is no uncertainty and the role of time preference and externalities are ignored. In subsequent sections these other influences will be reintroduced one at a time and so we will be able to see more clearly the consequences of each.

I   The basic model: the role of taxes

The basic premise on which the analysis will proceed is that the appropriate rate of discount for public projects is one which measures correctly the social opportunity cost. The decision to devote resources to investment in a public project means, given the overall level of employment in the economy, that these resource will become unavailable for use by the private sector. And this transfer should be undertaken whenever a potential project available to the government offers social benefits greater than the loss sustained by removing these resources from the private sector. The social rate of discount, then, must be chosen in such a way that it leads to a positive number for the evaluated net benefits of a public project if and only if its gross benefits exceed its opportunity costs in the private sector. I repeat this banality because it seems to me to be the criterion which is relevant for investigations of the discount rate, and because it forms the basis for all of the discussion that follows.

Let us begin with a very simple model that brings out some of the critical elements in the analysis. For these purposes I utilize the following assumptions in the discussion of the present section, many of which will be dropped later in the paper: (1) the overall level of employment of all resources by the economy is fixed so that any increase in the use of resources by the public sector unavoidably produces a concomitant decrease in their utilization by private enterprise; (2) there is no risk or uncertainty – the future returns of any investment project can be foreseen perfectly (we will return to the subject of risk in the next section); (3) all goods and services in the economy other than those provided by the government are supplied by corporations, an assumption which permits us to abstract from the difference in tax treatment of corporations and other types of firm; (4) corporations in this riskless world are financed entirely by equity; (5) corporate income is subject to a uniform tax rate of 50 per cent; (6) there is a unique rate of interest, r, at which the government borrows money.

Suppose now that the government considers undertaking a project whose construction requires the use of a set of input resources, R, for some given period of time. How does one calculate the opportunity cost of this use of resources? Since R is composed of inputs and since the corporations are the only alternative users of such items it follows that, in the first instance, R must all be obtained by taking it out of the hands of the corporations. The opportunity cost can then be calculated simply by determining the returns which could have been obtained if R had been left for corporate use during the period in question.

Our premises enable us to determine the equilibrium value of this magnitude, given the rate of interest on government securities. For in this riskless world investors will expect exactly the same rate of return on money invested either in the private or the public sectors. This means that the corporations must return r per cent to their stock-holders. But with a 50 per cent tax on corporate earnings it follows that corporate resources must provide a gross yield of $2r$. In other words, the resources, R, if left in the private sector would have produced a real rate of return evaluated by the market at $2r$. For this purpose it makes no difference whether or not product prices are affected by monopolistic elements or other influences causing them to depart from competitive levels.[1] The fact is simply that the transfer of our resources R has led to a reduction in outputs for which consumers would have been willing to pay enough to provide a rate of return $2r$ on corporate capital. Specifically, even if a monopoly charges prices above marginal cost, its sales will be cut sufficiently so that its outputs' prices still represent the money measure of the goods' marginal utilities to their consumers.[2] Hence, with the usual reservations about interpersonal comparisons and income distribution these amounts do still represent the opportunity costs of the outputs foregone.

The form of this argument can easily lead to one sort of misunder-standing. It would seem to suggest that all government projects must draw their resources from private investment and that none of them can be taken from private consumption. But nothing of this sort is implied or intended. It is obviously possible that the steel used in some governmental undertaking is all taken from consumers and so results in no reduction in the output of producers' goods. The consequent decrease in manufacture of automobiles, refrigerators and bird cages then represents the real cost of the government project. But this in no way conflicts with my way of regarding the matter which states only that this transfer of resources must take place *through the agency of the corporation*. The automobile factory will have fewer tons of steel to process, as will the producer of refrigerators and other steel product consumer's goods. And I am arguing only that the outlays of these firms on the steel which they would otherwise have used would hav brought them a rate of return of $2r$ *as a result of the consumers' marginal valuation of these commodities*.

In these simple circumstances that is all there is to the matter. But it is important to bring out clearly how this discussion differs from much of the standard literature. This it does in two respects; in method of approach and in its implications for policy. In method, the approach of this model avoids the technique associated with Krutilla and Eckstein [7, ch. 4], (see also Otto Eckstein [3, pp. 81–104]) the attempt to trace out the sources of the money funds "used to finance" the project. Their method is to ask whether the adoption of the project will lead to further taxes or will be financed by further borrowing and seeks to measure opportunity cost by estimating the real consequences for the taxpayers or lenders involved. Such a calculation can easily be questioned from the viewpoint of the literature of functional finance which tells us that, in the last analysis, the purpose of such fiscal measures is not to "pay for" governmental activity, but to offset inflationary pressures. Real resources can be transferred to the government without either increased taxation or added borrowing from the public, inflation being left the task of providing the necessary forced saving. And, looked at from this point of view it is by no means obvious that the tax equivalent of a D dollar government expenditure is exactly D dollars in taxes. The balanced budget multiplier literature suggests strongly that it takes more than D dollars in taxes and borrowing from the private sector to offset the impact of a D dollar public outlay. But whether or not one is prepared to go along with this functional finance criticism of the sources of funds approach to the estimation of opportunity cost one can surely argue that the method is unnecessarily complex. If it is true that, in real terms, what the government takes from the private sector is input resources, then to determine the relevant rate of discount one need not inquire beyond the rate of return currently being earned by users of such inputs. One can ignore in this calculation the subjective time preferences of consumers, the difference between the disutility of paying taxes and of lending and a host of other issues which clutter unnecessarily some of the public project discount rate calculations. That the government's use of resources does deprive consumers of some goods is true but beside the point because consumers implicitly but very definitely indicate how they feel about this foregone consumption through the rate of return they are currently providing to business firms. And the costs of taxation versus borrowing are considerations relevant to the choice of strategy of stabilization policy. They should not determine whether or not a specific project is undertaken.[3]

In addition, the proposed calculation has significant consequences for public policy, via its implication that, with a 5 per cent rate of interest on government bonds for the relevant time period, the correct rate of discount on government projects is not anything near 5 per cent but is on the order of 10 per cent per annum. This conclusion means that a number of longer-term government projects which are currently passing muster should be rejected. If this conclusion were accepted it might lead to very considerable changes in public investment programs – changes whose nature will be discussed later in this paper.[4]

II   Some modifications: the role of risk

So far the argument has deliberately abstracted from risk, a matter with which much of the discount rate discussion has concerned itself. A minor issue that arises from the presence of risk is that it leads corporations to finance themselves in part by means of debt rather than equity in the hope of attracting funds from investors who wish to limit their risk. Since in fact corporate income taxes apply neither to the interest payments on debt, nor to the earnings of firms which have avoided the corporate form of organization, one may conclude that our estimate of the opportunity cost of resources should be reduced somewhat below the figure of $2r$ arrived at in the preceding section. One should decrease the figure for the corporate sector perhaps proportionately to its use of debt financing and then the overall discount figure should presumably be reduced in proportion to the resources that would come from non-corporate enterprises.[5]

But this is not the main issue in the risk discussion, which has centered about the role of risk in private borrowing, where, in addition to tax payments, investments must produce a rate of return sufficiently high to compensate the investor for the risks he undertakes in providing the finances to the company. Thus, suppose a private corporation earns 16 per cent on investment, half of which goes into taxes and, that of the remaining 8 per cent we have reason to suppose 3 per cent is a risk premium. Should the social rate of discount be 10 per cent (the 5 per cent riskless rate of return plus the tax payment on that amount) or should it be 16 per cent?

The argument for exclusion of a risk premium from the discount rate on public investment has been provided by economists as eminent as Samuelson [12] and Arrow [1]. It proceeds somewhat as follows. The government undertakes a very large number of highly variegated projects. Thus, under the law of large numbers, the overall outcome becomes virtually certain. On insurance principles, each one should be evaluated in terms of its expected value with no distinction made between projects whose outcomes have different dispersions. In such a context a project offering two possible payoffs, $90 and $110 with equal probability, is neither better nor worse than another offering $50 or $150 since each has an expected value of $100.

It has been objected that one should take into account not only the total risk and the total expected yield of all government projects but also their *marginal* risk contribution and their *marginal* expected yield. It may appear at first glance that as a proportion of the government's total investment program both of these are apt to be insignificant for a single project, but that the ratio of the marginal risk to the marginal expected value contribution is not negligible. However, this view ignores some relevant considerations. If the outcomes of the various projects are independent, so that their covariance is zero (an assumption which is not obviously as valid a representation of the facts as is sometimes suggested – cf. Hirschleifer [5, pp. 268–75, esp. n. 6]), the distribution of the entire set of outcomes for all projects combined will tend to approach the normal distribution. Hence if the expected yield of a single representative project is y and its standard deviation is σ, for n projects the total expected yield will be yn while its standard deviation will be $\sqrt{n}\sigma$. A project's marginal contribution to expected yield will therefore be $dyn/dn = y$, while its contribution to standard deviation will be $\sigma/2\sqrt{n}$ which approaches zero with growing n. Thus if, for example, we consider as a rough measure of "safety level" (minimum anticipated earnings) a number k standard deviations below the mean, this figure for all government projects together will be $yn - \sqrt{n}k\sigma$ and a project's marginal contribution to safety level will be $y - k\sigma/2\sqrt{n}$ which for large values of n will be approximately equal to y, the project's expected yield.

But this still does not tell us about the opportunity cost. From the point of view of society (with the exception of one element that will be mentioned presently) a private project is equally riskless with a public one. Society benefits from the entire set of investment projects currently undertaken, whether they are public or private. The mere transfer of an investment's sponsorship from private hands to government does not *per se* affect its flow of benefits to society[6] nor does it mean that its risks are any more or less offsetable against the risks of other projects. That is to say, in line with the argument of the preceding paragraphs *all* investments should be evaluated at their expected earnings. Transfer into government hands may reduce the risk of an investment slightly in only one way. A private firm faces some danger of insolvency, in which case a project that has been undertaken may never be completed. Even here the distinction is not clear-cut; a change in administration with a new election can also cut off a public project before its invested resources can begin to bear fruit. But in any event, with increasing numbers of projects the marginal value of this sort of risk, too, will be negligible. Thus, from the social point of view the "law of large numbers" argument cuts both ways – it says that risk in either public or private projects is irrelevant for the returns society can expect.

But does this mean that the risk discount component in private cost of capital figures should be ignored in the social rate of discount calculation, as is often suggested in the literature? On the contrary, paradoxically, *the very absence of real risk means that the private risk discount should also enter the social discount rate*. Here private risk plays precisely the same role as the corporation tax. It induces firms to invest in such a way that the marginal investment yield is higher than it would otherwise be. And the transfer of resources from the private sector therefore imposes a correspondingly high opportunity cost. Take the example of our corporation earning a 16 per cent rate of return, which in the absence of a risk premium would be reduced to 10 per cent. The expected return on its investment is then in fact 16 per cent which, as we have seen, *is virtually certain from the viewpoint of society*. Then, clearly, the social opportunity cost of a transfer of resources from the corporate to the public sector is 16 and not 10 per cent, and that is all there is to be said on the subject. It is irrelevant to argue that this high return is produced by artificial distortions – taxes, risks which for society do not exist, etc. The fact that the source of this rate of return is "artificial" makes the resulting yield figure no less substantive. Society cannot come out ahead by taking resources that have been bringing in annual benefits amounting to 16 per cent of the resource values and transferring them to uses where they will yield only 5 per cent.

III Reassessment: total investment and its allocation between the public and private sectors

There are certain to be readers who find the preceding arguments to be offensive, and who will be led to this feeling by instincts that are perfectly reasonable. Surely, one may say, a 16 per cent discount rate means that far too little will be invested in the future. And in all this we have taken no account of the public's true preference and the relevant externalities. To some of these specific issues I will turn presently. But we should note first that this objection may well arise because we tend to overlook a distinction which has not often come across clearly in the literature. Involved in the choice of discount rate are several distinct issues:

(1) How much should be invested altogether?
(2) How should this investment activity be divided up between the private and public sectors?

(3) Given the level of investment of the public sector how much should be allocated to long-term projects – how much to short-term projects?

It must be emphasized that up to this point this paper has addressed itself exclusively to the second of these questions. It is perfectly consistent with what has been said for us to conclude in accord with the Pigovian point of view that our telescopic faculty is indeed defective. If so, the rate of interest on government securities should be lowered drastically. The value of r should perhaps be reduced by a cheap money policy to $2\frac{1}{2}$ per cent. *But this should serve to encourage longer-term investment by both the private and public sectors*, and, for example, in our riskless-world-with-corporate-tax model it does not in any way affect the conclusion that the rate of discount on public projects should be $2r$, a figure which would in these circumstances fall to 5 per cent.

Thus, nothing said so far argues for or against low rates of discount. It states merely that society will not benefit if it increases long-term investment in a wasteful and inefficient manner, by forcing the transfer of resources from employments with a high marginal yield to uses with a low marginal yield. For that is exactly what can be expected to result from the usual sort of figure of, say, 5 per cent for discount rates on pubic projects when the corporate rate of return is perhaps three times that high.

IV The role of consumers' subjective time preference

But so far our leading actor has only been lurking in the wings. Where in all this is the subjective time preference? Is this, too, equal to some multiple of the rate of interest on government bonds? A moment's thought indicates that it is not. Suppose all consumers were willing to purchase government bonds at r per cent and were not doing so merely in response to appeals to their patriotism. This means, surely, that they consider the proposition to be good business, i.e., their time discount rate must then be no higher than r per cent. In practice the motive in buying government bonds may often be somewhat mixed, and not all persons hold some of these instruments. But it seems safe to conclude that at least for some members of the public r per cent is the riskless rate of time preference.[7]

We are thus left with the following unpleasant pair of conclusions: as we saw in the preceding section, efficiency in resource allocation between the private and public sectors requires a social rate of discount equal to kr where k is some number considerably greater than unity, because otherwise one would end up drawing resources from uses providing a return of kr and putting them into uses providing a far lower yield. Yet the public's time preference calls for a discount rate of r per cent for otherwise one allocates to the future resources much smaller than the amount desired by society. This observation immediately suggests one explanation for the diversity of economists' views on our subject, a hypothesis which a study of the literature seems to confirm. Different writers seem to have focused on different optimality conditions – some on the requirement for efficiency in the allocation between public and private investments, and others on the requirements of the private subjective time preference rate, and each has concluded that the discount rate that satisfied the one corresponding optimality requirement was in fact optimal.

However, we see now that no optimal rate exists. The rate that satisfies the one requirement cannot possibly meet the conditions of the other. In part the difficulty is caused by the corporate income tax which, our discussion suggests, may well be a very serious cause of resource misallocation in our economy.[8]

But even if the corporation tax were eliminated it would not solve the problem because of the risk premium on private investments. Repeal of the corporate income tax might, in line with our numerical example, reduce the rate of return to corporate resources from perhaps 16 down to 8 per cent. But it would never get it down to the illustrative 5 per cent on government bonds because of the risk incurred by the individual who lends his money to a private firm, a risk which for society is negligible. Since the discount rate cannot simultaneously be 5 and 8 per cent, one of the optimality requirements must still be violated unless a negative tax (a subsidy) on corporate investment were substituted for the corporation income tax.[9]

In the absence of such a subsidy there remains an inescapable indeterminacy in the choice of discount rate on government projects. There is perhaps something to be said for a figure higher than that currently employed on the grounds discussed in the preceding section. But if the discount rate is raised it should surely be done by all government agencies simultaneously. For otherwise the change will only produce wastes in the interagency allocation of resources beyond those that already characterize the apportionment of inputs between the government and private enterprise.

V Investment as a public good: the externalities argument

Since the time when Pigou wrote on the subject there has been an increase in the sophistication of the argument against a market-deter-mined discount rate as the proper criterion for the quantity and durability of investment. But much of the literature seems to accept the view that a free market will make inadequate provision for the future and that therefore the social rate of discount should be lower than that which would produce market equilibrium.

Apparently the most widely accepted justification for this conclusion is one for which I must admit some degree of responsibility.[10] It maintains that the social yield of investment is characteristically higher than its private return so that on the usual logic of the externalities argument the market will not provide enough investment. Specifically, there are three reasons why this is apt to be the case:

(1) A project undertaken by an individual incurs a risk to him much greater than that which it imposes on society. Part of the source of this divergence has already been discussed – the insurance to society provided by the many projects simultaneously engaged in by the economy.

(2) But there is another and perhaps equally significant reason for the distinction. A project undertaken by a private individual may for financial or other reasons be taken from him before he receives all of its benefits; he may lose it by going bankrupt, or he may die without heirs. Yet in either of these cases the benefits accrue unimpaired to society. Inheritance taxes clearly cause a substantial divergence between private and public returns from long-term investment.

(3) Investment in the future is of the character of a public good. National pride leads many of us to want a promising future for our country. Or looked at the other way, many of us have an uneasy conscience at leaving to future generations a world despoiled and deprived of its productive capacity. But as with national defense, it is impossible to provide a brilliant future for the nation to one of today's citizens without simultaneously making it available to all.

These are all classic grounds for encouragement of additional supply and the direction of their force is clear. Yet when they were recently recapitulated, cogently argued and their implications explored by

Marglin, his conclusions were strongly disputed in two replies.[11] One of these dealt primarily with what, for present purposes, may be considered technicalities and so it need not concern us here, though it is certainly worth reading. However, the other note, that by Tullock, makes an important point which in my view goes far to offset the conclusions implied by the externalities argument.

Tullock points out that an increase in investment, aside from its allocative consequences, constitutes a redistribution of income from present to future generations. That being so, he reminds us, it is incumbent on us to ask ourselves whether we really want to undertake such a redistribution of income – as in any such redivision of the pie the answer depends heavily on who the recipients are to be, and on their economic circumstances. In particular, in our economy if past trends and current developments are any guide, a redistribution to provide more for the future may be described as a Robin Hood activity stood on its head – it takes from the poor to give to the rich. Average real per capita income a century hence is likely to be a sizeable multiple of its present value. Why should I give up part of my income to help support someone else with an income several times my own?[12]

Tullock puts the matter in a more attractive light by posing the alternative in a different way. Suppose we feel we can afford to give up some fixed amount for the benefit of others. We must then ask ourselves whether there are so few diseased, illiterate, underprivileged today, so few persons who excite our sympathy that we must look to the prospectively wealthy future for a source of worthy recipients of our bounty.

Let us then pull together the pieces of the argument and see where they lead. We have seen that there is a basic contradiction in the optimality requirements for the social rate of discount. The condition for efficiency in the allocation of resources between the private and public sectors requires a discount rate significantly higher than that called for by the public's time preferences. Only by the elimination of the corporate income tax and the substitution of a subsidy to private investment to offset the difference between public and private risks can the two requirements be reconciled. Since neither of these changes seems, to say the least, very likely to be instituted in the foreseeable future, some arbitrary choice will have to be made. It is my inclination at the moment to look with some favor at a figure toward the higher end of the range – at a discount rate closer to what may be considered the cost of capital to private firms. My grounds for this preference are hardly convincing even to me – they rest largely on the feeling that there is a very tangible loss in the transfer of resources from a high rate of return use to an employment in which their yield is very low. On the other hand I can attribute much less significance to a time preference rate which is constantly shifted about and made to adjust to the dictates of monetary policy.

My other major conclusion (which, unavoidably, is also largely a matter of opinion) would appear to be that in our economy, by and large, the future can be left to take care of itself. There is no need to lower artificially the social rate of discount in order to increase further the prospective wealth of future generations. The rate of interest should presumably then be set by the market and the needs of public policy – the requirements of stabilization, equilibrium in international trade, etc., and no attempt should be made to subsidize the future by artificial reductions in discount rates designed only for that purpose.

However, this does not mean that the future should in every respect be left to the mercy of the free market. There are important externalities and investments of the public goods variety which cry for special attention. Irreversibilities constitute a prime example. If we poison our soil so that never again will it be the same, if we destroy the Grand Canyon and turn it into a hydroelectric plant, we give up assets which like Goldsmith's bold peasantry, ". . . their country's pride, when once destroy'd can never be supplied." All the wealth and resources of future generations will not suffice to restore them. Investment in the preservation of such items then seems perfectly proper, but for this purpose the appropriate instrument would appear to be a set of selective subsidies rather than a low general discount rate that encourages indiscriminately all sorts of investment programs whether or not they are relevant.

Moreover, one can envision circumstances in which a more general program of encouragement to investment commends itself to us. In a country which is stagnating and where only a major restriction of current consumption can put life into its development program, one may well wish to make the sacrifice for tomorrow, for in such a case, without it the future generation will be as impoverished as the present.

There is a final consequence of the Tullock suggestion which should not be overlooked. The idea that we may want to redistribute income in favor of the poor of today's generation rather than the future poor is *not* an argument against government activity. On the contrary, it is perfectly consistent wit the rather persuasive Galbraithian view that the supply of public goods is far too small. We may want far more governmental activity than is currently being undertaken to remove today's slums, to combat today's air pollution, to help put down today's crime. But wanting *more* government projects is not tantamount to a desire for more *long-term* government projects. What our society's interests may well require is more but less durable government investments, and a low rate of discount on public projects is precisely the wrong way to go about their achievement.

Notes

1   However, externalities do make a difference. If a private firm obtains a private return on its investment but imposes external costs equivalent to 3 per cent, the net social yield will obviously be only 12 per cent. For precisely the same sort of reason, as will be observed later, we may well consider it desirable to subsidize further the production of public goods in order to increase their output beyond its current level.

  Note, incidentally, that the preceding argument does *not* necessarily imply that the individual firm can shift any or all of the burden of the corporate income tax. As with an increase in fixed costs under competitive equilibrium, the rise in taxes may raise the gross rate of return simply by driving some firms out of business even though no company can do anything about it.

2   Professor Abba Lerner, in a letter to me, has commented on this point, suggesting that the presence of monopoly in the private sector does make a difference. "It is true that a dollar spent on the monopolized article yields the same marginal utility as one spent on an item produced under perfect competition, but the marginal return on the monopolized investment derives from the *marginal revenue* received by the monopolist and this is less than the *price*, so that there is here an additional reason for not taking resources away from the monopolist whose marginal social product is greater than his marginal private product because of his monopolistic restriction."

  To put the argument another way, let p, mc, mr and I respectively represent price, marginal cost, marginal revenue and incremental investment, where the marginal cost includes no normal return, i.e., no "cost of capital." Then the monopolist will select an output at which his marginal rate of return on I is $2r$, i.e., at which $(mr - mc)/I = 2r$ so that

$$I = (mr - mc)/2r.$$

But, using price as the measure of marginal consumer benefits, the social rate of return will then be

$$(p - mc)/I = 2r(p - mc)/(mr - mc).$$

Since price is normally larger than the monopolist's marginal revenue, this social opportunity cost figure will then be greater than $2r$ and it may in fact be considerably greater. If, e.g., $p = \$2$, $mc = \$1.40$ and $mr = \$1.50$ the marginal social rate of return will then be $12r$ while if $mc = \$1.45$ this opportunity cost rate will rise to $22r$!

3　There is, however, a reasonable ground for objection to this last statement. If the decision to undertake a government project contributes to inflationary pressures the real cost or the cost of the counterinflationary measures should be deducted from the anticipated benefits of the project, and the reverse should hold in a period of unemployment where the calculation proposed in the text is incorrect in any event, since an increased use of resources by the government need require no corresponding reduction in their utilization by private industry.

4　Readers will recognize that this conclusion has much in common with the views of Hirshleifer, DeHaven and Milliman [4, pp. 139–50]. However, we come to this result not entirely for the same reasons, as will be noted presently. On the other hand my position on this particular point *is* similar to one taken by Machlup [9] and by Vickrey in some brief remarks [16].

5　That is, if e per cent of corporate financing is obtained from equity, and if c per cent of the government's input resources are derived from corporations, the social discount rate becomes

$$(1 - c)r + c[(1 - e)r + e(2r)] = r + cer$$

Thus if, say, 80 per cent of the nation's goods and services were produced by the corporate sector ($c = 0.8$) and 80 per cent of corporate finances were accounted for by equity, one might estimate the discount rate for public projects at $(1.64)r$.

Even this smaller ratio may overstate the proper differential between this allocative discount rate and the bond rate of interest. It is easy to show that if a company's earnings are growing at a rate g per annum then a 50 per cent tax rate will reduce the company's rate of return from P to P' where these are related by $P = 2P' - g$. Hence if $g = 0$ the company will indeed have to earn $2r$ to provide an investor a net reurn of r neglecting the considerations of the preceding paragraph. But if, say, $g = 0.03$ and P', the desired after tax rate, is 0.05, then P, the before tax rate, will be only $2P' - g = 0.07$ per cent. I am indebted to E. P. Howrey for this observation.

6　In a letter William Whipple Jr. of Rutgers University has pointed out to me that this conclusion is not quite correct as it stands. When the resources are in private hands, the risk involved in their use constitutes a disutility to the investor, a psychic cost which has no counterpart in public investment. Hence, the removal of resources from the private sector where they yield a rate of return S involves an opportunity cost lower than S by the amount of this psychic cost to investors. It may perhaps even be argued that this investor risk disutility is exactly equal to the risk premium on private investment so that for this reason the rate of discount on government projects should include no risk premium, contrary to what is argued in this section on the basis of the evaluation of the yield of the resources *by consumers*. In any event, it is clear that the opportunity cost of the transfer must be larger than one would have thought if one had believed the returns to the private project to be uncertain from the point of view of society and there must therefore be some distortion in a discount rate on government projects that does not take into account the low social risk of private projects.

7   Or, more accurately, r per cent *exceeds* their time preference rate by the expected rate of rise in the price level plus some risk premium corresponding to the lenders' risk of being repaid in depreciated money.

In any event, the r per cent rate to be used in this calculation is surely the market yield to maturity of some government bond with a suitably long period of time to maturity. This observation offers no support to the rather curious discount rate calculation procedure currently utilized (under presidential directive) by the Corps of Engineers in the evaluation of water resource projects. Their figure is obtained by averaging the coupon rates (!) on all government securities *"which upon original issue, had terms to maturity of 15 years or more."* Thus the June 30, 1965 discount rate of $3\frac{1}{8}$ per cent apparently included in its average bonds which had less than two years left to run and whose (nominal) coupon rate was $2\frac{1}{2}$ per cent.

8   Or as Professor Lerner, in a letter to me, prefers to put it, "for avoidance of bias between public and private investment the public investment should pay the same taxes." Some writers, e.g., Whipple, have argued that tax-induced differences in opportunity cost rate such as that between the corporate and noncorporate sectors are a matter of deliberate policy, suggesting, in effect, that corporate activity generates undesirable externalities which Congress, in its wisdom, has implicitly decided to discourage. My opinion is that this is an excessively charitable view of the logic of the legislation which is a compound of expediency and failure to consider its consequences with sufficient care. Surely it requires a heroic reinterpretation of history to take the selection of a source of tax funds that is likely to cause little damage to the career of a politician and elevate it into a decision of high social principle.

9   Hirshleifer [5, p. 270] recognizes the appropriateness of the risk compensating subsidy in these circumstances, and makes the very cogent remark that a larger subsidy would have to be paid to the small firm that incurs a substantial private risk than is given, say, to General Motors whose substantial number of investments offset one another's private risk to a considerable extent.

10   See Baumol [2], pp. 131–32. On the subsequent literature see Marglin [11] and Sen [13] [14]. The more recent of Sen's papers makes a very useful distinction between two related arguments on these matters: the "isolation paradox" whereby it pays no individual to save an optimal amount, whether or not everyone else does so, and the "assurance problem" in which the individual will save enough only if he is assured that others will also do so. Sen is right in pointing out that my argument seems to fall into the latter category. But that is a matter of careless phrasing on my part. On this I need not merely rely on distant memory which reminds me that I was well aware of the relevance of the prisoner's dilemma analogy when I wrote the passage in question. The discussion in Section 3 of my Chapter 11 makes the distinction between the two cases in some detail even if in a somewhat obscure manner.

11   See Lind [8] and Tullock [15].

12   Of course, if the capital market were perfect the discount rate would fully take into account the prospective rate of increase in real incomes. This is

why I find Sen's argument [14] convincing for the pure competitive model but not for decision making in practice. Under pure competition the differences in present and future wealth will be reflected fully in the market's discount rate so that the reluctance to invest described by the Marglin-Sen-Baumol argument will certainly make for a misallocation of resources. In practice, where capital markets are riddled with imperfections and subject to the tergiversations of government policy it is my judgment that the probable wealth of future generations is given inadequate weight in interest rate policy so that the Marglin-Sen-Baumol externalities may well prove benign in their effects.

References

1 K. J. Arrow, "Discounting and Public Investment Criteria," in A. V. Kneese and S. C. Smith, eds., *Water Research*, Baltimore 1966.
2 W. J. Baumol, *Welfare Economics and the Theory of the State*, 2nd ed. Cambridge Mass. 1965.
3 Otto Eckstein, *Water-Resource Development: The Economics of Project Evaluation*. Cambridge, Mass. 1961.
4 Jack Hirshleifer, J. C. DeHaven and J. J. Milliman, *Water Supply; Economics, Technology and Policy*. Chicago 1960.
5 Jack Hirshleifer, "Investment Decision Under Uncertainty: Applications of the State-Preference Approach," *Quart. Jour. Econ.*, May 1966, *80*, 252–77.
6 H. E. Klarman, "Syphilis Control Programs," in Robert Dorfman, ed., *Measuring Benefits of Government Investments*, Washington 1965.
7 J. V. Krutilla and Otto Eckstein, *Multiple Purpose River Development*. Baltimore 1958.
8 R. C. Lind, "Further Comment," *Quart. Jour. Econ.*, May 1964, *78*, 336–44.
9 Fritz Machlup, Discussion of a paper by Weisbrod, in Dorfman, editor [6].
10 M. S. March, Discussion of a paper by Weisbrod, in Dorfman, editor [6].
11 S. A. Marglin, "The Social Rate of Discount and the Optimal Rate of Investment," *Quart. Jour. Econ.*, Feb. 1963, *77*, 95–112.
12 P. A. Samuelson, "Principles of Efficiency: Discussion," *Am. Econ. Rev.*, Proc., May 1964, *54*, 93–96.
13 A. K. Sen, "On Optimizing the Rate of Saving," *Econ. Jour.*, Sept. 1961, *71*, 479–96.
14 ——, "Isolation, Assurance and the Social Rate of Discount," *Quart. Jour. Econ.*, Feb. 1967, *81*, 112–24.
15 Gordon Tullock, "The Social Rate of Discount and the Optimal Rate of Investment: Comment," *Quart. Jour. Econ.*, May 1964, *78*, 331–36.
16 William Vickrey, "Principles of Efficiency: Discussion," *Am. Econ. Rev.*, Proc., May 1964, *54*, 88–92.

3
Uncertainty and the Evaluation of Public Investment Decisions

Kenneth J. Arrow and Robert C. Lind

The implications of uncertainty for public investment decisions remain controversial. The essence of the controversy is as follows. It is widely accepted that individuals are not indifferent to uncertainty and will not, in general, value assets with uncertain returns at their expected values. Depending upon an individual's initial asset holdings and utility function, he will value an asset at more or less than its expected value. Therefore, in private capital markets, investors do not choose investments to maximize the present value of expected returns, but to maximize the present value of returns properly adjusted for risk. The issue is whether it is appropriate to discount public investments in the same way as private investments.

There are several positions on this issue. The first is that risk should be discounted in the same way for public investments as it is for private investments. It is argued that to treat risk differently in the public sector will result in overinvestment in this sector at the expense of private investments yielding higher returns. The leading proponent of this point of view is Jack Hirshleifer.[1] He argues that in perfect capital markets, investments are discounted with respect to both time and risk and that the discount rates obtaining in these markets should be used to evaluate public investment opportunities.

A second position is that the government can better cope with uncertainty than private investors and, therefore, government investments should not be evaluated by the same criterion used in private markets. More specifically, it is argued that the government should ignore uncertainty and behave as if indifferent to risk. The government should then evaluate investment opportunities according to their present value computed by discounting the expected value of net returns, using a rate of discount equal to the private rate appropriate for investments with certain returns. In support of this position it is argued that the government invests in a greater number of diverse projects and is able to pool risks to a much greater extent than private investors.[2] Another supporting line of argument is that many of the uncertainties which arise in private capital markets are related to what may be termed moral hazards. Individuals involved in a given transaction may hedge against the possibility of fraudulent behavior on the part of their associates. Many such risks are not present in the case of public investments and, therefore, it can be argued that it is not appropriate for the government to take these risks into account when choosing among public investments.

There is, in addition, a third position on the government's response to uncertainty. This position rejects the notion that individual preferences as revealed by market behavior are of normative significance for government investment decisions, and asserts that time and risk preferences relevant for government action should be established as a matter of national policy. In this case the correct rules for action would be those established by the appropriate authorities in accordance with their concept of national policy. The rate of discount and attitude toward risk would be specified by the appropriate authorities and the procedures for evaluation would incorporate these time and risk preferences. Two alternative lines of argument lead to this position. First, if one accepts the proposition that the state is more than a collection of individuals and has an existence and interests apart from those of its individual members, then it follows that government policy need not reflect individual preferences. A second position is that markets are so imperfect that the behavior observed in these markets yields no relevant information about the time and risk preferences of individuals. It follows that some policy as to time and risk preference must be established in accordance with other evidence of social objectives. One such procedure would be to set national objectives concerning the desired rate of growth and to infer from this the appropriate rate of discount.[3] If this rate were applied to the expected returns from all alternative investments, the government would in effect be behaving as if indifferent to risk.

The approach taken in this paper closely parallels the approach taken by Hirshleifer, although the results differ from his. By using the state-preference approach to market behavior under uncertainty, Hirshleifer demonstrates that investments will not, in general, be valued at the sum of the expected returns discounted at a rate appropriate for investments with certain returns.[4] He then demonstrates that using this discount rate for public investments may lead to non-optimal results, for two reasons. First, pooling itself may not be desirable.[5] If the government has the opportunity to undertake only investments which pay off in states where the payoff is highly valued, to combine such investments with ones that pay off in other states may reduce the value of the total investment package. Hirshleifer argues that where investments can be undertaken separately they should be evaluated separately, and that returns should be discounted at rates determined in the market. Second, even if pooling were possible and desirable, Hirshleifer argues correctly that the use of a rate of discount for the public sector which is lower than rates in the private sector can lead to the displacement of private investments by public investments yielding lower expected returns.[6]

For the case where government pooling is effective and desirable, he argues that rather than evaluate public investments differently from private ones, the government should subsidize the more productive private investments. From this it follows that to treat risk differently for public as opposed to private investments would only be justified if it were impossible to transfer the advantages of government pooling to private investors. Therefore, at most, the argument for treating public risks differently than private ones in evaluating investments is an argument for the "second best."[7]

The first section of this paper addresses the problem of uncertainty, using the state-preference approach to market behavior. It demonstrates that if the returns from any particular investment are independent of other components of national income, then the present value of this investment equals the sum of expected returns discounted by a rate appropriate for investments yielding certain returns. This result holds for both private and public investments. Therefore, by adding one plausible assumption to Hirshleifer's formulation, the conclusion can be drawn that the government should behave as an expected-value decision maker and use a discount rate appropriate for investments with certain returns. This conclusion needs to be appropriately modified when one considers the case where there is a corporate income tax.

While this result is of theoretical interest, as a policy recommendation it suffers from a defect common to the conclusions drawn by Hirshleifer. The model of the economy upon which these recommendations are based presupposes the existence of perfect markets for claims contingent on states of the world. Put differently, it is assumed that there are perfect insurance markets through which individuals may individually pool risks. Given such markets, the distribution of risks among individuals will be Pareto optimal. The difficulty is that many of these markets for insurance do not exist, so even if the markets which do exist are perfect, the resulting equilibrium will be sub-optimal. In addition, given the strong evidence that the existing capital markets are not perfect, it is unlikely that the pattern of investment will be Pareto optimal. At the margin, different individuals will have different rates of time and risk preference, depending on their opportunities to borrow or to invest, including their opportunities to insure.

There are two reasons why markets for many types of insurance do not exist. The first is the existence of certain moral hazards.[8] In particular, the fact that someone has insurance may alter his behavior so that the observed outcome is adverse to the insurer. The second is that such markets would require complicated and specialized contracts which are costly. It may be that the cost of insuring in some cases is so high that individuals choose to bear risks rather than pay the transaction costs associated with insurance.

Given the absence of some markets for insurance and the resulting sub-optimal allocation of risks, the question remains: how should the government treat uncertainty in evaluating public investment decisions? The approach taken in this paper is that individual preferences are relevant for public investment decisions, and government decisions should reflect individual valuations of costs and benefits. It is demonstrated in the second section of this paper that when the risks associated with a public investment are publicly borne, the total cost of risk-bearing is insignificant and, therefore, the government should ignore uncertainty in evaluating public investments. Similarly, the choice of the rate of discount should in this case be independent of considerations of risk. This result is obtained not because the government is able to pool investments but because the government distributes the risk associated with any investment among a large number of people. It is the risk-spreading aspect of government investment that is essential to this result.

There remains the problem that private investments may be displaced by public ones yielding a lower return if this rule is followed, although given the absence of insurance markets this will represent a Hicks-Kaldor improvement over the initial situation. Again the question must be asked whether the superior position of the government with respect to risk can be made to serve private investors. This leads to a discussion of the government's role as a supplier of insurance, and of Hirshleifer's recommendation that private investment be subsidized in some cases.

Finally, the results obtained above apply to risks actually borne by the government. Many of the risks associated with public investments are borne by private individuals, and in such cases it is appropriate to discount for risk as would these individuals. This problem is discussed in the final section of the paper. In addition, a method of evaluating public investment decisions is developed that calls for different rates of discount applied to different classes of benefits and costs.

I   Markets for contingent claims and time-risk preference[9]

For simplicity, consider an economy where there is one commodity and there are I individuals, S possible states of the world, and time is divided into Q periods of equal length. Further suppose that each individual acts on the basis of his subjective probability as to the states of nature; let π_{is} denote the subjective probability assigned to state s by individual i. Now suppose that each individual in the absence of trading owns claims for varying amounts of the one commodity at different points in time, given different states of the world. Let $\bar{x}_{isq}$ denote the initial claim to the commodity in period $q + 1$ if state s occurs which is owned by individual i. Suppose further that all trading in these claims takes place at the beginning of the first period, and claims are bought and sold on dated commodity units contingent on a state of the world. All claims can be constructed from basic claims which pay one commodity unit in period $q + 1$, given state s, and nothing in other states or at other times; there will be a corresponding price for this claim, $p_{sq}(s = 1, \ldots, S; q = 0, \ldots, Q - 1)$. After the trading, the individual will own claims x_{isq} which he will exercise when the time comes to provide for his consumption. Let $V_i(x_{i1,0}, \ldots, x_{i1,Q-1}, x_{i2,0}, \ldots, x_{iS,Q-1})$ be the utility of individual i if he receives claims x_{isq} $(s = 1, \ldots, S; q = 0, \ldots, Q - 1)$. The standard assumptions are made that V_i is strictly quasi-concave $(i = 1, \ldots, I)$.

Therefore each individual will attempt to maximize,

$$V_i(x_{i1,0}, \ldots, x_{i1,Q-1}, x_{i2,0}, \ldots, x_{iS,Q-1}) \tag{3.1}$$

subject to the constraint

$$\sum_{q=0}^{Q-1} \sum_{s=1}^{S} p_{sq} x_{isq} = \sum_{q=0}^{Q-1} \sum_{s=1}^{S} p_{sq} \bar{x}_{isq}$$

Using the von Neumann-Morgenstern theorem and an extension by Hirshleifer,[10] functions U_{is} $(s = 1, \ldots, S)$ can be found such that

$$V_i(x_{i1,0}, \ldots, x_{ix,Q-1}) = \sum_{s=1}^{S} \pi_{is} U_{is}(x_{is0}, x_{is1}, \ldots, x_{iS,Q-1}) \qquad (3.2)$$

In equation (3.2) an individual's utility, given any state of the world, is a function of his consumption at each point in time. The subscript s attached to the function U_{is} is in recognition of the fact that the value of a given stream of consumption may depend on the state of the world. The conditions for equilibrium require that

$$\pi_{is} = \frac{\partial U_{is}}{\partial x_{isq}} = \lambda_i p_{sq} \quad (i = 1, \ldots, I; s = 1, \ldots, S; q = 0, \ldots, Q-1) \qquad (3.3)$$

where λ_i is a Lagrangian multiplier.
From equation (3.3) it follows that

$$\frac{p_{sq}}{p_{rm}} = \frac{\pi_{is} \dfrac{\partial U_{is}}{\partial x_{isq}}}{\pi_{rm} \dfrac{\partial U_{ir}}{\partial x_{irm}}} \quad (i = 1, \ldots, I; r, s = 1, \ldots, S; m, q = 0, \ldots, Q-1) \qquad (3.4)$$

Insight can be gained by analyzing the meaning of the prices in such an economy. Since trading takes place at time zero, p_{sq} represents the present value of a claim to one commodity unit at time q, given state s. Clearly,

$$\sum_{s=1}^{S} p_{s0} = 1$$

since someone holding one commodity unit at time zero has a claim on one commodity unit, given any state of the world. It follows that p_{sq} is the present value of one commodity at time q, given state s, in terms of a certain claim on one commodity unit at time zero. Therefore, the implicit rate of discount to time zero on returns at time q, given state s, is defined by $p_{sq} = 1/1 + r_{sq}$.

Now suppose one considers a certain claim to one commodity unit at time q; clearly, its value is

$$p_q = \sum_{s=1}^{S} p_{sq}$$

and the rate of discount appropriate for a certain return at time q is defined by

$$\frac{1}{1+r_q} = \sum_{s=1}^{S}\frac{1}{1+r_{sq}} = \sum_{s=1}^{S}p_{sq} \tag{3.5}$$

Given these observations, we can now analyze the appropriate procedure for evaluating government investments where there are perfect markets for claims contingent on states of the world.[11] Consider an investment where the overall effect on market prices can be assumed to be negligible, and suppose the net return from this investment for a given time and state is h_{sq} ($s = 1, \ldots, S$; $q = 0, \ldots, Q - 1$). Then the investment should be undertaken if

$$\sum_{q=0}^{Q-1}\sum_{s=1}^{S}h_{sq}p_{sq} > 0, \tag{3.6}$$

and the sum on the left is an exact expression for the present value of the investment. Expressed differently, the investment should be adopted if

$$\sum_{q=0}^{Q-1}\sum_{s=1}^{S}\frac{h_{sq}}{1+r_{sq}} > 0 \tag{3.7}$$

The payoff in each time-state is discounted by the associated rate of discount. This is the essential result upon which Hirshleifer bases his policy conclusions.[12]

Now suppose that the net returns of the investment were (a) independent of the returns from previous investment, (b) independent of the individual utility functions, and (c) had an objective probability distribution, i.e., one agreed upon by everyone. More specifically, we assume that the set of all possible states of the world can be partitioned into a class of mutually exclusive and collectively exhaustive sets, E_t, indexed by the subscript t such that, for all s in any given E_t, all utility functions U_{is} are the same for any individual i ($i = 1, \ldots, I$), and such that all production conditions are the same. Put differently, for all s in E_t, U_{is} is the same for a given individual, but not necessarily for all individuals. At the same time there is another partition of the states of the world into sets, F_u, such that the return, h_{sq}, is the same for all s in F_u. Finally, we assume that the probability distribution of F_u is independent of E_t and is the same for all individuals.

Let E_{tu} be the set of all states of the world which lie in both E_t and F_u. For any given t and u, all states of the world in E_{tu} are indistinguishable for all purposes, so we may regard it as containing a single state.

Equations (3.3) and (3.5) and the intervening discussion still hold if we then replace s everywhere by tu. However, $U_{is} = U_{itu}$ actually depends only on the subscript, t, and can be written U_{it}. From the assumptions it is obvious and can be proved rigorously that the allocation x_{isq} also depends only on t, i.e., is the same for all states in E_t for any given t, so it may be written x_{itq}. Finally, let π_{it} be the probability of E_t according to individual i, and let π_u be the probability of F_u, assumed the same for all individuals. Then the assumption of statistical independence is written:

$$\pi_{itu} = \pi_{it}\pi_u \tag{3.8}$$

Then equation 3.3 can be written

$$\pi_{it}\pi_u \frac{\partial U_{it}}{\partial x_{itq}} = \lambda_i p_{tuq} \tag{3.9}$$

Since p_{tuq} and π_u are independent of i, so must be

$$\left(\pi_{it} \frac{\partial U_{it}}{\partial x_{itq}}\right)\Big/\lambda_i \,;$$

on the other hand, this expression is also independent of u and so can be written μ_{tq}. Therefore,

$$p_{tuq} = \mu_{tq}\pi_u \tag{3.10}$$

Since the new investment has the same return for all states s in F_u, the returns can be written h_{uq}. Then the left-hand side of equation (3.6) can, with the aid of equation (3.10), be written

$$\sum_{Q=0}^{Q-1}\sum_{s=1}^{S} h_{sq}p_{sq} = \sum_{q=0}^{Q-1}\sum_{t}\sum_{u} h_{uq}p_{tuq} = \sum_{q=0}^{Q-1}\left(\sum_{t}\mu_{tq}\right)\sum_{u}\pi_u h_{uq} \tag{3.11}$$

But from equation (3.10)

$$p_q = \sum_{s=1}^{S} p_{sq} = \sum_{t}\sum_{u} p_{tuq} = \left(\sum_{t}\mu_{tq}\right)\left(\sum_{u}\pi_u\right) = \sum_{t}\mu_{tq}, \tag{3.12}$$

since of course the sum of the probabilities of the F_u's must be 1. From equation (3.11),

$$\sum_{q=0}^{Q-1} \sum_{S=1}^{S} h_{sq} p_{sq} = \sum_{Q=0}^{Q-1} \frac{1}{1+r_q} \sum_u \pi_u h_{uq}$$ (3.13)

Equation (3.13) gives the rather startling result that the present value of any investment which meets the independence and objectivity conditions, equals the expected value of returns in each time period, discounted by the factor appropriate for a certain return at that time. This is true even though individuals may have had different probabilities for the events that governed the returns on earlier investments. It is also interesting to note that each individual will behave in this manner so that there will be no discrepancy between public and private procedures for choosing among investments.

The independence assumption applied to utility functions was required because the functions U_{is} are conditional on the states of the world. This assumption appears reasonable, and in the case where U_{is} is the same for all values of s, it is automatically satisfied. Then the independence condition is simply that the net returns from an investment be independent of the returns from previous investments.

The difficulty that arises if one bases policy conclusions on these results is that some markets do not exist, and individuals do not value assets at the expected value of returns discounted by a factor appropriate for certain returns. It is tempting to argue that while individuals do not behave as expected-value decision makers because of the nonexistence of certain markets for insurance, there is no reason why the government's behavior should not be consistent with the results derived above where the allocation of resources was Pareto optimal. There are two difficulties with this line of argument. First, if we are to measure benefits and costs in terms of individuals' willingness to pay, then we must treat risk in accordance with these individual valuations. Since individuals do not have the opportunities for insuring assumed in the state-preference model, they will not value uncertainty as they would if these markets did exist. Second, the theory of the second best demonstrates that if resources are not allocated in a Pareto optimal manner, the appropriate public policies may not be those consistent with Pareto efficiency in perfect markets. Therefore, some other approach must be found for ascertaining the appropriate government policy toward risk. In particular, such an approach must be valid, given the nonexistence of certain markets for insurance and imperfections in existing markets.

II The public cost of risk-bearing

The critical question is: what is the cost of uncertainty in terms of costs to individuals? If one adopts the position that costs and benefits should be computed on the basis of individual willingness to pay, consistency demands that the public costs of risk-bearing be computed in this way too. This is the approach taken here.

In the discussion that follows it is assumed that an individual's utility is dependent only upon his consumption and not upon the state of nature in which that consumption takes place. This assumption simplifies the presentation of the major theorem, but it is not essential. Again the expected utility theorem is assumed to hold. The presentation to follow analyzes the cost of risk-bearing by comparing the expected value of returns with the certainty equivalent of these returns. In this way the analysis of time and risk preference can be separated, so we need only consider one time period.

Suppose that the government were to undertake an investment with a certain outcome; then the benefits and costs are measured in terms of willingness to pay for his outcome. If, however, the outcome is uncertain, then the benefits and costs actually realized depend on which outcome in fact occurs. If an individual is risk averse, he will value the investment with the uncertain outcome at less than the expected value of its net return (benefit minus cost) to him. Therefore, in general the expected value of net benefits overstates willingness to pay by an amount equal to the cost of risk-bearing. It is clear that the social cost of risk-bearing will depend both upon which individuals receive the benefits and pay the costs and upon how large is each individual's share of these benefits and costs.

As a first step, suppose that the government were to undertake an investment and capture all benefits and pay all costs, i.e., the beneficiaries pay to the government an amount equal to the benefits received and the government pays all costs. Individuals who incur costs and those who receive benefits are therefore left indifferent to their pre-investment state. This assumption simply transfers all benefits and costs to the government, and the outcome of the investment will affect government disbursements and receipts. Given that the general taxpayer finances government expenditures, a public investment can be considered an investment in which each individual taxpayer has a very small share.

For precision, suppose that the government undertook an investment and that returns accrue to the government as previously described. In addition, suppose that in a given year the government were to have a balanced budget (or a planned deficit or surplus) and that taxes would be reduced by the amount of the net benefits if the returns are positive, and raised if returns are negative. Therefore, when the government undertakes an investment, each taxpayer has a small share of that investment with the returns being paid through changes in the level of taxes. By undertaking an investment the government adds to each individual's disposable income a random variable which is some fraction of the random variable representing the total net returns. The expected return to all taxpayers as a group equals expected net benefits.

Each taxpayer holds a small share of an asset with a random payoff, and the value of this asset to the individual is less than its expected return, assuming risk aversion. Stated differently, there is a cost of risk-bearing that must be subtracted from the expected return in order to compute the value of the investment to the individual taxpayer. Since each taxpayer will bear some of the cost of the risk associated with the investment, these costs must be summed over all taxpayers in order to arrive at the total cost of risk-bearing associated with a particular investment. These costs must be subtracted from the value of expected net benefits in order to obtain the correct measure for net benefits. The task is to assess these costs.

Suppose, as in the previous section, that there is one commodity, and that each individual's utility in a given year is a function of his income defined in terms of this commodity and is given by $U(Y)$. Further, suppose that U is bounded, continuous, strictly increasing, and differentiable. The assumptions that U is continuous and strictly increasing imply that U has a right and left derivative at every point and this is sufficient to prove the desired results; differentiability is assumed only to simplify presentation. Further suppose that U satisfies the conditions of the expected utility theorem.

Consider, for the moment, the case where all individuals are identical in that they have the same preferences, and their disposable incomes are identically distributed random variables represented by A. Suppose that the government were to undertake an investment with returns represented by B, which are statistically independent of A. Now divide the effect of this investment into two parts: a certain part equal to expected returns and a random part, with mean zero, which incorporates risk. Let $\bar{B} = E[B]$, and define the random variable X by $X = B - \bar{B}$. Clearly, X is independent of A and $E[X] = 0$. The effect of this investment is to add an amount $\bar{B}$ to government receipts along with a random component represented by X. The income of each taxpayer will be affected through taxes and it is the level of these taxes that determines the fraction of the investment he effectively holds.

Consider a specific taxpayer and denote his fraction of this investment by s, $0 \leq s \leq 1$. This individual's disposable income, given the public investment, is equal to $A + sB = A + s\bar{B} + sX$. The addition of sB to his disposable income is valued by the individual at its expected value less the cost of bearing the risk associated with the random component sX. If we suppose that each taxpayer has the same tax rate and that there are n taxpayers, then $s = 1/n$, and the value of the investment taken over all individuals is simply $\bar{B}$ minus n times the cost of risk-bearing associated with the random variable $(1/n)X$. The central result of this section of the paper is that this total of the costs of risk-bearing goes to zero as n becomes large. Therefore, for large values of n the value of a public investment almost equals the expected value of that investment.

To demonstrate this, we introduce the function

$$W(s) = E\left[U\left(A + s\bar{B} + sX\right)\right], \quad 0 \leq s \leq 1 \qquad (3.14)$$

In other words, given the random variables A and B representing his individual income before the investment and the income from the investment, respectively, his expected utility is a function of s which represents his share of B. From equation 3.14 and the assumption that U' exists, it follows that

$$W'(s) = E\left[U'\left(A + s\bar{B} + sX\right)\left(\bar{B} + X\right)\right] \qquad (3.15)$$

Since X is independent of A, it follows that $U'(A)$ and X are independent; therefore,

$$E[U'(A)X] = E[U'(A)]E[X] = 0$$

so that

$$W'(0) = E\left[U'(A)\left(\bar{B} + X\right)\right] = \bar{B}E[U'(A)] \qquad (3.16)$$

Equation (3.16) is equivalent to the statement

$$\lim_{s \to 0} \frac{E\left[U\left(A + s\bar{B} + sX\right) - U(A)\right]}{s} = \bar{B}E[U'(A)] \qquad (3.17)$$

Now let $s = 1/n$, so that equation (3.17) becomes

$$\lim_{n \to \infty} nE\left[U\left(A + \frac{\overline{B} + X}{n}\right) - U(A)\right] = \overline{B}E[U'(A)] \qquad (3.18)$$

If we assume that an individual whose preferences are represented by U is a risk-averter, then it is easily shown that there exists a unique number, $k(n) > 0$, for each value of n such that

$$E\left[U\left(A + \frac{\overline{B} + X}{n}\right)\right] = E\left[U\left(A + \frac{\overline{B}}{n} - k(n)\right)\right], \qquad (3.19)$$

or, in other words, an individual would be indifferent between paying an amount equal to $k(n)$ and accepting the risk represented by $(1/n)X$. Therefore, $k(n)$ can be said to be the cost of risk-bearing associated with the asset B. It can easily be demonstrated that $\lim_{n \to \infty} k(n) = 0$, i.e., the cost of holding the risky asset goes to zero as the amount of this asset held by the individual goes to zero. It should be noted that the assumption of risk aversion is not essential to the argument but simply one of convenience. If U represented the utility function of a risk preferrer, then all the above statements would hold except $k(n) < 0$, i.e., an individual would be indifferent between being paid $-k(n)$ and accepting the risk $(1/n)X$ (net of the benefit $(1/n)\overline{B}$).

We wish to prove not merely that the risk-premium of the representative individual, $k(n)$, vanishes, but more strongly that the total of the risk-premiums for all individuals, $nk(n)$, approaches zero as n becomes large.

From equations (3.18) and (3.19) it follows that

$$\lim_{n \to \infty} nE\left[U\left(A + \frac{\overline{B}}{n} - k(n)\right) - U(A)\right] = \overline{B}E[U'(A)] \qquad (3.20)$$

In addition, $\overline{B}/n - k(n) \to 0$, when $n \to \infty$. It follows from the definition of a derivative that

$$\lim_{n \to \infty} \frac{E\left[U\left(A + \frac{\overline{B}}{n} - k(n)\right) - U(A)\right]}{\frac{\overline{B}}{n} - k(n)} = E[U'(A)] > 0 \qquad (3.21)$$

Dividing equation (3.20) by (3.21) yields

$$\lim_{n \to \infty}\left[\overline{B} - nk(n)\right] = \overline{B} \qquad (3.22)$$

or

$$\lim_{n \to \infty} nk(n) = 0 \qquad (3.23)$$

The argument in equation (3.21) implies that $\overline{B}/n - k(n) \neq 0$. Suppose instead the equality held for infinitely many n. Substitution into the left-hand side of (3.20) shows that $\overline{B}$ must equal zero, so that $k(n) = 0$ for all such n, and hence $nk(n) = 0$ on that sequence, confirming equation (3.23).

Equation (3.23) states that the total of the costs of risk-bearing goes to zero as the population of taxpayers becomes large. At the same time the monetary value of the investment to each taxpayer, neglecting the cost of risk, is $(1/n)\overline{B}$, and the total, summed over all individuals, is $\overline{B}$, the expected value of net benefits. Therefore, if n is large, the expected value of net benefits closely approximates the correct measure of net benefits defined in terms of willingness to pay for an asset with an uncertain return.

In the preceding analysis, it was assumed that all taxpayers were identical in that they had the same utility function, their incomes were represented by identically distributed variables, and they were subject to the same tax rates. These assumptions greatly simplify the presentation; however, they are not essential to the argument. Different individuals may have different preferences, incomes, and tax rates; and the basic theorem still holds, provided that as n becomes larger the share of the public investment borne by any individual becomes arbitrarily smaller.

The question necessarily arises as to how large n must be to justify proceeding as if the cost of publicly-borne risk is negligible. This question can be given no precise answer; however, there are circumstances under which it appears likely that the cost of risk-bearing will be small. If the size of the share borne by each taxpayer is a negligible component of his income, the cost of risk-bearing associated with holding it will be small. It appears reasonable to assume, under these conditions, that the total cost of risk-bearing is also small. This situation will exist where the investment is small with respect to the total wealth of the taxpayers. In the case of a federally sponsored investment, n is not only large but the investment is generally a very small fraction of national income even though the investment itself may be large in some absolute sense.

The results derived here and in the previous section depend on returns from a given public investment being independent of other components of national income. The government undertakes a wide range of public investments and it appears reasonable to assume that their returns are independent. Clearly, there are some government investments which are interdependent; however, where investments are interrelated they should be evaluated as a package. Even after such groupings are established, there will be a large number of essentially independent projects. It is sometimes argued that the returns from public investments are highly correlated with other components of national income through the business cycle. However, if we assume that stabilization policies are successful, then this difficulty does not arise. It should be noted that in most benefit-cost studies it is assumed that full employment will be maintained so that market prices can be used to measure benefits and costs. Consistency requires that this assumption be retained when considering risk as well. Further, if there is some positive correlation between the returns of an investment and other components of national income, the question remains as to whether this correlation is so high as to invalidate the previous result.

The main result is more general than the specific application to public investments. It has been demonstrated that if an individual or group holds an asset which is statistically independent of other assets, and if there is one or more individuals who do not share ownership, then the existing situation is not Pareto-efficient. By selling some share of the asset to one of the individuals not originally possessing a share, the cost of risk-bearing can be reduced while the expected returns remain unchanged. The reduction in the cost of risk-bearing can then be redistributed to bring about a Pareto improvement. This result is similar to a result derived by Karl Borch. He proved that a condition for Pareto optimality in reinsurance markets requires that every individual hold a share of every independent risk.

When the government undertakes an investment it, in effect, spreads the risk among all taxpayers. Even if one were to accept that the initial distribution of risk was Pareto-efficient, the new distribution of risk will not be efficient as the government does not discriminate among the taxpayers according to their risk preferences. What has been shown is that in the limit the situation where the risk of the investment is spread over all taxpayers is such that there is only a small deviation from optimality with regard to the distribution of that particular risk. The overall distribution of risk may be sub-optimal because of market imperfections and the absence of certain insurance markets. The great advantage of the results of this section is that they are not dependent on the existence of perfect markets for contingent claims.

This leads to an example which runs counter to the policy conclusions generally offered by economists. Suppose that an individual in the private sector of the economy were to undertake a given investment and, calculated on the basis of expected returns, the investment had a rate of return of 10 per cent. Because of the absence of perfect insurance markets, the investor subtracted from the expected return in each period a risk premium and, on the basis of returns adjusted for risk, his rate of return is 5 per cent. Now suppose that the government could invest the same amount of money in an investment which, on the basis of expected returns, would yield 6 per cent. Since the risk would be spread over all taxpayers, the cost of risk-bearing would be negligible, and the true rate of return would be 6 per cent. Further, suppose that if the public investment were adopted it would displace the private investment. The question is: should the public investment be undertaken? On the basis of the previous analysis, the answer is yes. The private investor is indifferent between the investment with the expected return of 10 per cent, and certain rate of return of 5 per cent. When the public investment is undertaken, it is equivalent to an investment with a certain rate of return of 6 per cent. Therefore, by undertaking the public investment, the government could more than pay the opportunity cost to the private investor of 5 per cent associated with the diversion of funds from private investment.

The previous example illustrates Hirshleifer's point that the case for evaluating public investments differently from private ones is an argument for the second best. Clearly, if the advantages of the more efficient distribution of risk could be achieved in connection with the private investment alternative, this would be superior to the public investment. The question then arises as to how the government can provide insurance for private investors and thereby transfer the risks from the private sector to the public at large. The same difficulties arise as before, moral hazards and transaction costs. It may not be possible for the government to provide such insurance, and in such cases second-best solutions are in order. Note that if the government could undertake any investment, then this difficulty would not arise. Perhaps one of the strongest criticisms of a system of freely competitive markets is that the inherent difficulty in establishing certain markets for insurance brings about a sub-optimal allocation of resources. If we consider an investment, as does Hirshleifer, as an exchange of certain present income for uncertain future income, then the misallocation will take the form of under-investment.

Now consider Hirshleifer's recommendation that, in cases such as the one above, a direct subsidy be used to induce more private investment rather than increase public investment. Suppose that a particular private investment were such that the benefits would be a marginal increase in the future supply of an existing commodity, i.e., this investment would neither introduce a new commodity nor affect future prices. Therefore, benefits can be measured at each point in time by the market value of this output, and can be fully captured through the sale of the com-modity. Let $\bar{V}$ be the present value of expected net returns, and let V be the present value of net returns adjusted for risk where the certainty rate is used to discount both streams. Further, suppose there were a public investment, where the risks were publicly borne, for which the present value of expected net benefits was P. Since the risk is publicly borne, from the previous discussion it follows that P is the present value of net benefits adjusted for risk. Now suppose that $\bar{V} > P > V$. According-ing to Hirshleifer, we should undertake the private investment rather than the public one, and pay a subsidy if necessary to induce private entrepreneurs to undertake this investment. Clearly, if there is a choice between one investment or the other, given the existing distribution of risk, the public investment is superior. The implication is that if a risky investment in the private sector is displaced by a public investment with a lower expected return but with a higher return when appropriate adjustments are made for risks, this represents a Hicks-Kaldor improve-ment. This is simply a restatement of the previous point that the gov-ernment could more than pay the opportunity cost to the private entrepreneur.

Now consider the case for a direct subsidy to increase the level of private investment. One can only argue for direct subsidy of the private investment if $V < 0 < \bar{V}$. The minimum subsidy required is $|V|$. Suppose the taxpayers were to pay this subsidy, which is a transfer of income from the public at large to the private investor, in order to cover the loss from the investment. The net benefits, including the cost of risk-bearing, remain negative because while the subsidy has partially offset the cost of risk-bearing to the individual investor, it has not reduced this cost. Therefore, a direct public subsidy in this case results in a less efficient allocation of resources.

We can summarize as follows: it is implied by Hirshleifer that it is better to undertake an investment with a higher expected return than one with a lower expected return. (See 1965, p. 270.) This proposition is not in general valid, as the distribution of risk-bearing is critical. This statement is true, however, when the costs of risk-bearing associated with both investments are the same. What has been shown is that when risks are publicly borne, the costs of risk-bearing are negligible; therefore, a public investment with an expected return which is less than that of a given private investment may nevertheless be superior to the private alternative. Therefore, the fact that public investments with lower expected return may replace private investment is not necessarily cause for concern. Furthermore, a program of providing direct subsidies to encourage more private investment does not alter the cost of risk-bearing and, therefore, will encourage investments which are inefficient when the costs of risk are considered. The program which produces the desired result is one to insure private investments.

One might raise the question as to whether risk-spreading is not associated with large corporations so that the same result would apply, and it is easily seen that the same reasoning does apply. This can be made more precise by assuming there were n stockholders who were identical in the sense that their utility functions were identical, their incomes were represented by identically distributed random variables, and they had the same share in the company. When the corporation undertakes an investment with a return in a given year represented by B, each stockholder's income is represented by $A + (1/n)B$. This assumes, of course, that a change in earnings was reflected in dividends, and that there were no business taxes. Clearly, this is identical to the situation previously described, and if n is large, the total cost of risk-bearing to the stockholders will be negligible. If the income or wealth of the stockholders were large with respect to the size of the investment, this result would be likely to hold. Note that whether or not the investment is a large one, with respect to the assets of the firm, is not relevant. While an investment may constitute a major part of a firm's assets if each stockholder's share in the firm is a small component of his income, the cost of risk-bearing to him will be very small. It then follows that if managers were acting in the interest of the firm's shareholders, they would essentially ignore risks and choose investments with the highest expected returns.

There are two important reasons why large corporations may behave as risk averters. First, in order to control the firm, some shareholder may hold a large block of stock which is a significant component of his wealth. If this were true, then, from his point of view, the costs of risk-bearing would not be negligible, and the firm should behave as a risk averter. Note in this case that the previous result does not hold because the cost of risk-bearing to each stockholder is not small, even though the number of stockholders is very large. Investment behavior in this case is essentially the same as the case of a single investor.

The second case is when, even though from the stockholder's point of view, risk should be ignored, it may not be in the interest of the corporate managers to neglect risk. Their careers and income are intimately related to the firm's performance. From their point of view, variations in the outcome of some corporate action impose very real costs. In this case, given a degree of autonomy, the corporate managers, in considering prospective investments, may discount for risk when it is not in the interest of the stockholders to do so.

Suppose that this were the case and also suppose that the marginal rate of time preference for each individual in the economy was 5 per cent. From the point of view of the stockholders, risk can be ignored and any investment with an expected return which is greater than 5 per cent should be undertaken. However, suppose that corporate managers discount for risk so that only investments with expected rates of return that exceed 10 per cent are undertaken. From the point of view of the stockholders, the rate of return on these investments, taking risk into account, is over 10 per cent. Given a marginal rate of time preference of 5 per cent, it follows that from the point of view of the individual stockholder there is too little investment. Now suppose further that the government were considering an investment with an expected rate of return of 6 per cent. Since the cost of risk-bearing is negligible, this investment should be undertaken since the marginal rate of time preference is less than 6 per cent. However, in this case, if the financing were such that a private investment with a 10 per cent expected rate of return is displaced by the public investment, there is a loss because in both cases the risk is distributed so as to make the total cost of risk-bearing negligible. The public investment should be undertaken, but only at the expense of consumption.

III   The actual allocation of risk

In the idealized public investment considered in the last section, all benefits and costs accrued to the government and were distributed among the taxpayers. In this sense, all uncertainty was borne collectively. Suppose instead that some benefits and costs of sizeable magnitudes accrued directly to individuals so that these individuals incurred the attendant costs of risk-bearing. In this case it is appropriate to discount for the risk, as would these individuals. (Such a situation would arise in the case of a government irrigation project where the benefits accrued to farmers as increased income.) The changes in farm income would be uncertain and, therefore, should be valued at more or less than their expected value, depending on the states in which they occur. If these increases were independent of other components of farm income, and if we assume that the farmer's utility were only a function of his income and not the state in which he receives that income, then he would value the investment project at less than the expected increase in his income, provided he is risk averse. If, however, the irrigation project paid out in periods of drought so that total farm income was not only increased but also stabilized, then the farmers would value the project at more than the expected increase in their incomes.

In general, benefits and costs will accrue to the government and the uncertainties involved will be publicly borne; other benefits and costs will accrue to individuals and the attendant uncertainties will be borne privately. In the first case the cost of risk-bearing will be negligible; in the second case these costs may be significant. Therefore, in calculating the present value of returns from a public investment a distinction must be made between private and public benefits and costs. The present value of public benefits and costs should be evaluated by estimating the expected net benefits in each period and discounting them, using a discount factor appropriate for investments with certain returns. On the other hand, private benefits and costs must be discounted with respect to both time and risk in accordance with the preferences of the individuals to whom they accrue.

From the foregoing discussion it follows that different streams of benefits and costs should be treated in different ways with respect to uncertainty. One way to do this is to discount these streams of returns at different rates of discount ranging from the certainty rate for benefits and costs accruing to the government and using higher rates that reflect discounting for risk for returns accruing directly to individuals. Such a procedure raises some difficulties of identification, but this problem does not appear to be insurmountable. In general, costs are paid by the government, which receives some revenue, and the net stream should be discounted at a rate appropriate for certain returns. Benefits accruing directly to individuals should be discounted according to individual time and risk preferences. As a practical matter, Hirshleifer's suggestion of finding the marginal rate of return on assets with similar payoffs in the private sector, and using this as the rate of discount, appears reasonable for discounting those benefits and costs which accrue privately.

One problem arises with this latter procedure which has received little attention. In considering public investments, benefits and costs are aggregated and the discussion of uncertainty is carried out in terms of these aggregates. This obscures many of the uncertainties because benefits and costs do not in general accrue to the same individuals and the attendant uncertainties should not be netted out when considering the totals. To make this clear, consider an investment where the benefits and costs varied greatly, depending on the state of nature, but where the difference between total benefits and total costs was constant for every state. Further, suppose that the benefits and costs accrued to different groups. While the investment is certain from a social point of view, there is considerable risk from a private point of view. In the case of perfect markets for contingent claims, each individual will discount the stream of costs and benefits accruing to him at the appropriate rate for each time and state. However, suppose that such markets do not exist. Then risk-averse individuals will value the net benefits accruing to them at less than their expected value. Therefore, if net benefits accruing to this individual are positive, this requires discounting expected returns at a higher rate than that appropriate for certain returns. On the other hand, if net benefits to an individual are negative, this requires discounting expected returns at a rate lower than the certainty rate. Raising the rate of discount only reduces the present value of net benefits when they are positive. Therefore, the distinction must be made not only between benefits and costs which accrue to the public and those which accrue directly to individuals, but also between individuals whose net benefits are negative and those whose benefits are positive. If all benefits and costs accrued privately, and different individuals received the benefits and paid the costs, the appropriate procedure would be to discount the stream of expected benefits at a rate higher than the certainty rate, and costs at a rate lower than the certainty rate. This would hold even if the social totals were certain.

Fortunately, as a practical matter this may not be of great importance as most costs are borne publicly and, therefore, should be discounted using the certainty rate. Benefits often accrue to individuals, and where there are attendant uncertainties it is appropriate to discount the expected value of these benefits at higher rates, depending on the nature of the uncertainty and time-risk preferences of the individuals who receive these benefits. It is somewhat ironic that the practical implication of this analysis is that for the typical case where costs are borne publicly and benefits accrue privately, this procedure will qualify fewer projects than the procedure of using a higher rate to discount both benefits and costs.

Notes

1 J. Hirshleifer (1965, 1966) and Hirshleifer, J. C. De Haven, and J. W. Milliman (pp. 139–50).
2 For this point of view, see P. A. Samuelson and W. Vickrey.
3 For this point of view, see O. Eckstein and S. Marglin.
4 Hirshleifer (1965 pp. 523–34); (1966, pp. 268–75).
5 Hirshleifer (1966, pp. 270–75).
6 Hirshleifer (1966, pp. 270–75).
7 Hirshleifer (1966, p. 270).
8 For a discussion of this problem see M. V. Pauly and Arrow (1968).
9 For a basic statement of the state-preference approach, see Arrow (1964) and G. Debreu.
10 J. von Neumann and O. Morgenstern, and Hirshleifer (1965, pp. 534–36).
11 The following argument was sketched in Arrow (1966, pp. 28–30).
12 Hirshleifer (1965, pp. 523–34).

References

K. J. Arrow, "The Role of Securities in the Optimal Allocation of Risk-Bearing," *Rev. Econ. Stud.*, Apr. 1964, *31*, 91–96.
——, "Discounting and Public Investment Criteria," in A. V. Kneese and S. C. Smith, eds., *Water Research*. Baltimore 1966.
——, "The Economics of Moral Hazard: Further Comment," *Amer. Econ. Rev.*, June 1968, *58*, 537–38.
G. Debreu, *Theory of Value*. New York 1959.
O. Eckstein, "A Survey of the Theory of Public Expenditure," and "Reply," *Public Finances: Needs, Sources, and Utilization*, Nat. Bur. Econ. Res., Princeton 1961, 493–504.
J. Hirshleifer, "Investment Decision under Uncertainty: Choice-Theoretic Approaches," *Quart. J. Econ.*, Nov. 1965, *79*, 509–36.
——, "Investment Decision under Uncertainty: Applications of the State-Preference Approach," *Quart. J. Econ.*, May 1966, *80*, 252–77.
——, J. C. De Haven, and J. W. Milliman, *Water Supply: Economics, Technology, and Policy*; Chicago 1960.
S. Marglin, "The Social Rate of Discount and the Optimal Rate of Investment," *Quart. J. Econ.*, Feb. 1963, *77*, 95–111.
M. V. Pauly, "The Economics of Moral Hazard: Comment," *Amer. Econ. Rev.*, June 1968, *58*, 531–37.
P. A. Samuelson and W. Vickrey, "Discussion," *Amer. Econ. Rev. Proc.*, May 1964, *59*, 88–96.
J. von Neumann and O. Morgenstern, *Theory of Games and Economic Behavior*, 2nd ed., New York 1964.

4

Environmental Preservation, Uncertainty, and Irreversibility

Kenneth J. Arrow and Anthony C. Fisher

I

A number of recent contributions by economists have provided a clear insight into the causes of the varied forms of environmental deterioration, and have also suggested, implicitly or explicitly, policies for more efficient management of environmental as well as other resources.[1] Yet, as Allen Kneese has pointed out in a review of empirical studies of pollution damages, "a general shortcoming of [these studies] has been that they have treated a stochastic or probabilistic phenomenon as being deterministic."[2] The purpose of this paper is to explore the implications of uncertainty surrounding estimates of the environmental costs of some economic activities. It is shown in particular that the existence of uncertainty will, in certain important cases, lead to a reduction in net benefits from an activity with environmental costs. In such cases the implication for an efficient control policy will generally involve some restriction of the activity.

Any discussion of public policy in the face of uncertainty must come to grips with the problem of determining an appropriate attitude toward risk on the part of the policy maker. Thus in the essay quoted above, Kneese asks, "Is the concept of mathematical expectation applicable here or must we give attention to higher moments of the probability distribution . . . ?"[3] Although the question has not, to our knowledge, received consideration in just this form in the environmental literature, received theory does shed some light on the issue it poses.

Burton Weisbrod first suggested that where there is uncertainty in demand for a publicly provided good or service, there may be some benefit ("option value") to the individual in addition to the conventional price-compensating consumer surplus.[4] More recently Charles J.

Cicchetti and A. Myrick Freeman III have shown that, where there is uncertainty in either demand or supply, Weisbrod's option value will be positive for risk-averse individuals.[5] In the Cicchetti-Freeman analysis this extra benefit from the public good is in fact equivalent to a premium for risk bearing. Examples of such goods in the environmental sector (to which we will return) might be the preservation of certain valuable natural phenomena or the abatement of pollution.

At this point a very interesting corollary question arises. It is this: even assuming a nonneutral attitude toward risk, hence the need for some adjustment of expected benefits and costs *to the individual*, as demonstrated by Cicchetti and Freeman, does it necessarily follow that the social calculus should properly make the same adjustment? It does seem plausible, but a challenge to this point of view has been put forward in an analysis of the evaluation of benefits from more traditional public investments by Arrow and Lind.[6] They show that, as the net returns to an investment of given size are shared by an increasingly large number of individuals, the individual risk premium, and more importantly and perhaps unexpectedly, the aggregate of all such premiums go to zero. Only expected returns, then, should be taken into account in evaluating the investment.

This is the approach taken in the next section, in which the discussion focuses on a decision as to how far, if at all, to proceed with some form of commercial development of an unspoiled natural area that is also capable of yielding benefits in its preserved state. In particular, the question considered is, does the introduction of uncertainty as to the costs or benefits of a proposed development have any effect on an appropriately formulated investment criterion beyond the replacement of known values with their expectations? It turns out that, if the development involves some irreversible transformation of the environment, hence a loss in perpetuity of the benefits from preservation, and if information about the costs and benefits of both alternatives realized in one period results in a change in their expected values for the next, the answer is yes – net benefits from developing the area are reduced and, broadly speaking, less of the area should be developed.

II

In this section we are concerned primarily with the effect of uncertainty on the criteria for choice between two alternative uses of a natural environment – preservation and development. As an example of the type of problem to which the analysis might be applied, consider the choice, at each moment in time, between preserving (part of) a virgin redwood forest for wilderness recreation, on the one hand, or opening (part of) it up to clear-cut logging, on the other. Although this sort of transformation may be technically reversible, the length of time required for regeneration of the forest for purposes of wilderness recreation is so great that, given some positive rate of time preference, it might as well be irreversible.

A problem having just these characteristics has in fact been studied by Fisher, Krutilla, and Cicchetti.[7] Without going into the structure of the problem in more detail, their results, following results obtained by Arrow[8] and by Arrow and Kurz[9] in dynamic optimization theory, can be summarized as follows. First, it will in general be optimal to refrain from some development that is currently profitable if in the near future "undevelopment," which is impossible, would be indicated. Second, if net benefits from development are in fact decreasing over time relative to benefits from preservation, as shown in an empirical application to proposed further development of hydroelectric capacity along the Hells Canyon reach of the Snake River, it will be optimal to develop either immediately or not at all. It is then shown that even the most profitable of current development projects there can be expected at this time to yield a smaller return than the preservation-recreation alternative.

The notion of "irreversibility" underlying these results might be spelled out a bit more. Ordinarily, it would be technical. Thus the construction of a major dam or series of dams in the Hells Canyon clearly could not be undone in such a way as to make possible the enjoyment of the recreational and other services currently provided by the free-flowing stream through the deepest canyon on the North American continent.

Conceivably, construction of an alternative power source could preclude development of the hydroelectric potential there. This would, however, be an economic decision, and one that might in any case be reversed – although this would not be indicated by a continuation of present trends in benefits from wilderness preservation versus power development there, as assumed in the Fisher-Krutilla-Cicchetti study.

Of course, a technically irreversible development could be characterized as one that would be infinitely costly to reverse. More generally, the cost of reversal may take intermediate values that would vary with the alternative chosen. For the remainder of this section, however, it may be helpful to rely on the intuitive notion of a technically irreversible development, such as the placing of a dam.

As the Fisher-Krutilla-Cicchetti study adopts the risk-neutral approach in its specification of only expected costs and gains in the investment criterion with no adjustment, for example, for option value in preserving, the bias against development is due solely to the restriction on reversibility. By joining to this restriction the additional and plausible assumption that realizations in one period affect expectations in the next, as spelled out in the following simple model, we discover, consistent with the continuing assumption of risk neutrality, a "quasi-option value" having an effect in the same direction as risk aversion, namely, a reduction in net benefits from development.

Consider, now, the development of an area d over a two-period time horizon consisting of a first period followed by all future intervals compressed into a single second period. Though not particularly elegant, this formulation seems sufficient to capture the essential features of the process described above.

Let d = unity (a normalized unit of land)
         d_1 = the amount of land developed in the first period
         d_2 = the amount of land developed in the second period
         b_p = benefits from preservation of d in first period
         b_d = benefits from development of d in first period
         β_p = expected benefits, conditional on b_p and b_d, from
              preservation of d in second period
         β_d = expected benefits, conditional on b_p and b_d, from
              development of d in second period
         c_1 = investment costs in first period
         c_2 = investment costs in second period.

Several remarks can be made concerning the structure of this model.

(1) Though explicitly dynamic, it need not deal with time discounting in any meaningful way. Thus the second-period benefits and costs β_p, β_d, and c_2 can be viewed as present values, and the results are not affected.

(2) It is assumed that development entails investment costs but preservation does not. Costs of preservation could easily be introduced (where meaningful) but again, results would not be affected, and extra terms would clutter the model. The real difference between the alternatives is that one is assumed to be reversible, and the other not.

(3) Note that second-period expectations are conditional on first-period realizations. Some amount of development is planned at the start of the first period, but the plan can be revised (at least in the direction of additional development) at the start of the second period, based upon information that has accumulated concerning benefits in the first period.

(4) Note, finally, that all benefits are specified as coefficients, so that constant returns to any level of development or preservation are assumed. Later on, this assumption is relaxed.

Let us focus now on the decision at the start of the second period. If $\beta_d - \beta_p > c_2$, then $d_2 = 1 - d_1$. If $\beta_d - \beta_p < c_2$, then $d_2 = 0$. Define $z = \beta_d - \beta_p$, $w = b_d - b_p - c_1$, and event A as $z > c_2$. If A occurs, total benefits from the area are

$$b_p(1 - d_1) + b_d d_1 - c_1 d_1 + \beta_d - c_2(1 - d_1) = w d_1 + c_2 d_1 + b_p + \beta_d - c_2. \quad (4.1)$$

If A does not occur, then benefits are

$$b_p(1 - d_1) + b_d d_1 - c_1 d_1 + \beta_p(1 - d_1) + \beta_d d_1 = w d_1 + z d_1 + b_p + \beta_p. \quad (4.2)$$

The expected benefits from developing $d_1 > 0$ in the first period are

$$E[(w + \min(c_2, z))d_1 + b_p + \max(\beta_d - c_2, \beta_p)]. \quad (4.3)$$

Now suppose that $d_1 = 0$. If A occurs, total benefits from the area are $b_p + \beta_d - c_2$; if A does not occur, benefits are $b_p + \beta_p$; and expected benefits are $E[b_p + \max(\beta_d - c_2, \beta_p)]$. Then the difference (in expected benefits) between developing $d_1 > 0$ and $d_1 = 0$ is

$$E[(w + \min(c_2, z))d_1 + b_p + \max(\beta_d - c_2, \beta_p)] - E[b_p + \max(\beta_d - c_2, \beta_p)]$$
$$= E[(w + \min(c_2, z))d_1]. \quad (4.4)$$

We are interested in the sign of the expression $E[w + \min(c_2, z)]$. If it is positive, it will be optimal to develop in the first period.

Now suppose that the decision maker ignores uncertainty, i.e., he lets z and w be replaced by known numbers $E[z]$ and $E[w]$, so that the criterion is $E[w] + \min(c_2, E[z])$. Either $c_2 < E[z]$, or $c_2 > E[z]$. Consider the case in which $c_2 < E[z]$, so that the criterion is $E[w] + c_2$. Clearly,

$$\min(c_2, z) \leq c_2; \quad (4.5)$$

with

$$P[\min(c_2, z) < c_2] > 0, \tag{4.6}$$

where $P[\ ]$ represents the probability of occurrence of the expression in brackets. Thus

$$E[\min(c_2, z)] < c_2; \tag{4.7}$$

and

$$E[w + \min(c_2, z)] < E[w] + c_2.$$

The expected value of benefits under uncertainty is seen to be less than the value of benefits under certainty. There exists a range of values for z and w for which development should not, then, take place under uncertainty but should under certainty. An interpretation of this result might be that, if we are uncertain about the payoff to investment in development, we should err on the side of under-investment, rather than overinvestment, since development is irreversible. Given an ability to learn from experience, underinvestment can be remedied before the second period, whereas mistaken overinvestment cannot, the consequences persisting in effect for all time.

Similarly, for the case in which $c_2 > E[z]$,

$$\min(c_2, z) \leq z; \tag{4.8}$$

with

$$P[\min(c_2, z) < z] > 0. \tag{4.9}$$

Thus

$$E[\min(c_2, z)] < E[z]. \tag{4.10}$$

Note that the assumed rigidity of the benefit (and cost) coefficient requires that, if the criterion is positive, the entire area be developed. Our result then states that the entire area is less likely to be developed under uncertainty. It might be desirable to have a result of this type in more flexible form, in particular that less of a given area be developed under uncertainty – rather than less chance of the entire area's being developed.

Let (as yet) undeveloped area d be divided into n units, $\mu_1, \mu_2, \ldots, \mu_n$, each with fixed coefficients. Suppose, now, we consider development of d on a unit-by unit basis, proceeding exactly as above, but with the benefit and cost coefficients referring, respectively, to the first unit considered, then the second, etc. Under the plausible assumption of diminishing returns to both development and preservation, it is easily verified that, if it does not pay to develop the first unit considered, then it does not pay to develop any of the others. If, on the other hand, it pays to develop the first unit, then the second must be considered and so on. Corner solutions are possible as before, but so are interior solutions of part preserved and part developed.

In order to avoid confusion over the terms "constant returns" and "diminishing returns," we can define them more precisely. Let each of the n units μ_i, $i = 1, \ldots, n$ be further divided into m subunits μ_{ij}, $i = 1, \ldots, n$, $j = 1, \ldots, m$, each with fixed coefficients. Constant returns to, say, first-period development within any unit μ_i can be represented as

$$b_{di_1} = b_{di_2} = \ldots = b_{di_m},$$

with

$$b_{di_1} + b_{di_2} + \ldots + b_{di_m} = b_{di},$$

where b_{di_1} = benefits from development in the first period of unit μ_{i_1}, etc. Diminishing returns to development across units μ_i can be represented as $\dfrac{db_{di}}{di} < 0$. (Note that $\dfrac{db_{pi}}{di} > 0$, as benefits from preserving the marginal unit increase with the number of units already developed.) In this formulation the size and number of units μ_i are defined by the condition that returns are constant within each.

III

The foregoing analysis indicates that, even where it is not appropriate to postulate risk aversion in evaluating an activity, something of the "feel" of risk aversion is produced by a restriction on reversibility. If one takes the view that some means of spreading the risk associated with the uncertain environmental costs of the activity is likely to be feasible in most cases, then there are clear policy implications to this result, as it sharply distinguishes between reversible and irreversible changes in the environment.

One such implication, however, is *not* the overthrow of marginal analysis. Just because an action is irreversible does not mean that it should not be undertaken. Rather, the effect of irreversibility is to reduce the benefits, which are then balanced against costs in the usual way.

The analysis can be applied to problems of pollution control as well. Let b_d and β_d represent the benefits from an investment, and c_1 and c_2 the direct costs, as before. Then b_p and β_p can be taken to represent the benefits (reduced losses) from the cleaner or less toxic air, or water, that would be enjoyed were the investment not made.

Of course, the dynamic model is relevant only if the pollution is in some sense irreversible, as is the extinction of a form of life, or the destruction of a unique geomorphological phenomenon. This is an empirical matter. Clearly, much pollution is short-lived, sufficiently diffused or degraded by the assimilative medium to render it negligible in concentration and harmless in effect beyond some point in time. To this type of pollution the model does not apply.

On the other hand, there is evidence that some pollution does accumulate in the environment, perhaps sufficiently to be considered irreversible. Recent research has shed light on the toxicity and the persistence, indeed the increasing concentration, of the "hard" or nondegradable pesticides such as DDT, for example, and of industrial substances such as lead. A decision on a project involving discharge into the ambient environment of any of these or other potentially harmful and persistent substances should then take into account the continuing effect, as in the analysis of the preceding section. The same reasoning would apply to cumulative "macro" environmental effects, such as the increasing concentration of carbon dioxide in the global atmosphere, with its attendant climatic changes, as predicted by some ecologists.

The point about uncertainty, information, and irreversibility might be made still more generally, i.e., without reference to environmental effects. Essentially, the point is that the expected benefits of an irreversible decision should be adjusted to reflect the loss of options it entails.[10]

Notes

1. Also some not so recent, as in the classic work of Pigou. For a review of some more recent contributions, see E. J. Mishan, "The Postwar Literature on Externalities: An Interpretative Essay," *Journal of Economic Literature*, Vol. 9 (March 1971), 1–28.

2. A. V. Kneese, *Economics and the Quality of the Environment – Some Empirical Experiences*, Reprint Number 71 (Washington, DC: Resources for the Future, 1968), p. 172.
3. *Ibid.*, p. 172.
4. B. A. Weisbrod, "Collective-Consumption Services of Individual-Consumption Goods," *Quarterly Journal of Economics*, Vol. 78 (Aug. 1964), 471–77.
5. C. J. Cicchetti and A. M. Freeman III, "Option Demand and Consumer Surplus: Further Comment," *Quarterly Journal of Economics*, Vol. 85 (Aug. 1971), 528–39.
6. K. J. Arrow and R. C. Lind, "Uncertainty and the Evaluation of Public Investment Decisions," *American Economic Review*, Vol. 60 (June 1970), 364–78.
7. A. C. Fisher, J. V. Krutilla, and C. J. Cicchetti, "The Economics of Environmental Preservation: A Theoretical and Empirical Analysis," *American Economic Review*, Vol. 62 (Sept. 1972), 605–19.
8. K. J. Arrow, "Optimal Capital Policy and Irreversible Investment," in J. N. Wolfe, ed., *Value, Capital and Growth* (Chicago: Aldine Publishing Company, 1968), pp. 1–20.
9. K. J. Arrow and M. Kurz, "Optimal Growth with Irreversible Investment in a Ramsey Model," *Econometrica*, Vol. 38 (March 1970), 331–44.
10. For an earlier statement see A. G. Hart, "Risk, Uncertainty, and the Unprofitability of Compounding Probabilities," in *Studies in Mathematical Economics and Econometrics*, ed. by O. Lange, F. McIntyre, and T. O. Yntema (Chicago: University of Chicago Press, 1942).

Part II
Externalities and Market Failure

5
The Problem of Social Cost

Ronald H. Coase

I The problem to be examined[1]

This paper is concerned with those actions of business firms which have
harmful effects on others. The standard example is that of a factory the
smoke from which has harmful effects on those occupying neighbouring properties. The economic analysis of such a situation has usually
proceeded in terms of a divergence between the private and social
product of the factory, in which economists have largely followed the
treatment of Pigou in *The Economics of Welfare*. The conclusions to
which this kind of analysis seems to have led most economists is that
it would be desirable to make the owner of the factory liable for the
damage caused to those injured by the smoke, or alternatively, to place
a tax on the factory owner varying with the amount of smoke produced
and equivalent in money terms to the damage it would cause, or finally,
to exclude the factory from residential districts (and presumably from
other areas in which the emission of smoke would have harmful effects
on others). It is my contention that the suggested courses of action are
inappropriate, in that they lead to results which are not necessarily, or
even usually, desirable.

II The reciprocal nature of the problem

The traditional approach has tended to obscure the nature of the choice
that has to be made. The question is commonly thought of as one in
which A inflicts harm on B and what has to be decided is: how should
we restrain A? But this is wrong. We are dealing with a problem of a
reciprocal nature. To avoid the harm to B would inflict harm on A. The
real question that has to be decided is: should A be allowed to harm B

or should B be allowed to harm A? The problem is to avoid the more serious harm. I instanced in my previous article[2] the case of a confectioner the noise and vibrations from whose machinery disturbed a doctor in his work. To avoid harming the doctor would inflict harm on the confectioner. The problem posed by this case was essentially whether it was worth while, as a result of restricting the methods of production which could be used by the confectioner, to secure more doctoring at the cost of a reduced supply of confectionery products. Another example is afforded by the problem of straying cattle which destroy crops on neighbouring land. If it is inevitable that some cattle will stray, an increase in the supply of meat can only be obtained at the expense of a decrease in the supply of crops. The nature of the choice is clear: meat or crops. What answer should be given is, of course, not clear unless we know the value of what is obtained as well as the value of what is sacrificed to obtain it. To give another example, Professor George J. Stigler instances the contamination of a stream.[3] If we assume that the harmful effect of the pollution is that it kills the fish, the question to be decided is: is the value of the fish lost greater or less than the value of the product which the contamination of the stream makes possible. It goes almost without saying that this problem has to be looked at in total *and* at the margin.

III   The pricing system with liability for damage

I propose to start my analysis by examining a case in which most economists would presumably agree that the problem would be solved in a completely satisfactory manner: when the damaging business has to pay for all damage caused *and* the pricing system works smoothly (strictly this means that the operation of a pricing system is without cost).

A good example of the problem under discussion is afforded by the case of straying cattle which destroy crops growing on neighbouring land. Let us suppose that a farmer and a cattle-raiser are operating on neighbouring properties. Let us further suppose that, without any fencing between the properties, an increase in the size of the cattle-raiser's herd increases the total damage to the farmer's crops. What happens to the marginal damage as the size of the herd increases is another matter. This depends on whether the cattle tend to follow one another or to roam side by side, on whether they tend to be more or less restless as the size of the herd increases and on other similar factors. For my immediate purpose, it is immaterial what assumption is made about marginal damage as the size of the herd increases.

To simplify the argument, I propose to use an arithmetical example. I shall assume that the annual cost of fencing the farmer's property is $9 and that the price of the crop is $1 per ton. Also, I assume that the relation between the number of cattle in the herd and the annual crop loss is as follows:

Table 5.1

Number in herd (steers)	Annual crop loss (tons)	Crop loss per additional steer (tons)
1	1	1
2	3	2
3	6	3
4	10	4

Given that the cattle-raiser is liable for the damage caused, the additional annual cost imposed on the cattle-raiser if he increased his herd from, say, two to three steers is $3 and in deciding on the size of the herd, he will take this into account along with his other costs. That is, he will not increase the size of the herd unless the value of the additional meat produced (assuming that the cattle-raiser slaughters the cattle), is greater than the additional costs that this will entail, including the value of the additional crops destroyed. Of course, if, by the employment of dogs, herdsmen, aeroplanes, mobile radio and other means, the amount of damage can be reduced, these means will be adopted when their cost is less than the value of the crop which they prevent being lost. Given that the annual cost of fencing is $9, the cattle-raiser who wished to have a herd with four steers or more would pay for fencing to be erected and maintained, assuming that other means of attaining the same end would not do so more cheaply. When the fence is erected, the marginal cost due to the liability for damage becomes zero, except to the extent that an increase in the size of the herd necessitates a stronger and therefore more expensive fence because more steers are liable to lean against it at the same time. But, of course, it may be cheaper for the cattle-raiser not to fence and to pay for the damaged crops, as in my arithmetical example, with three or fewer steers.

It might be thought that the fact that the cattle-raiser would pay for all crops damaged would lead the farmer to increase his planting if a cattle-raiser came to occupy the neighbouring property. But this is not so. If the crop was previously sold in conditions of perfect competition, marginal cost was equal to price for the amount of planting undertaken and any expansion would have reduced the profits of the farmer. In the new situation, the existence of crop damage would mean that the farmer would sell less on the open market but his receipts for a given production would remain the same, since the cattle-raiser would pay the market price for any crop damaged. Of course, if cattle-raising commonly involved the destruction of crops, the coming into existence of a cattle-raising industry might raise the price of the crops involved and farmers would then extend their planting. But I wish to confine my attention to the individual farmer.

I have said that the occupation of a neighbouring property by a cattle-raiser would not cause the amount of production, or perhaps more exactly the amount of planting, by the farmer to increase. In fact, if the cattle-raising has any effect, it will be to decrease the amount of planting. The reason for this is that, for any given tract of land, if the value of the crop damaged is so great that the receipts from the sale of the undamaged crop are less than the total costs of cultivating that tract of land, it will be profitable for the farmer and the cattle-raiser to make a bargain whereby that tract of land is left uncultivated. This can be made clear by means of an arithmetical example. Assume initially that the value of the crop obtained from cultivating a given tract of land is $12 and that the cost incurred in cultivating this tract of land is $10, the net gain from cultivating the land being $2. I assume for purposes of simplicity that the farmer owns the land. Now assume that the cattle-raiser starts operations on the neighbouring property and that the value of the crops damaged is $1. In this case $11 is obtained by the farmer from sale on the market and $1 is obtained from the cattle-raiser for damage suffered and the net gain remains $2. Now suppose that the cattle-raiser finds it profitable to increase the size of his herd, even though the amount of damage rises to $3; which means that the value of the additional meat production is greater than the additional costs, including the additional $2 payment for damage. But the total payment for damage is now $3. The net gain to the farmer from cultivating the land is still $2. The cattle-raiser would be better off if the farmer would agree not to cultivate his land for any payment less than $3. The farmer would be agreeable to not cultivating the land for any payment greater than $2. There is clearly room for a mutually satisfactory bargain which would lead to the abandonment of cultivation.[4] But the same argument applies not only to the whole tract cultivated by the farmer but also to any subdivision of it. Suppose, for example, that the cattle have a well-defined route, say, to a brook or to a shady area. In these circumstances, the amount of damage to the crop along the route may well be great and if so, it could be that the farmer and the cattle-raiser would find it profitable to make a bargain whereby the farmer would agree not to cultivate this strip of land.

But this raises a further possibility. Suppose that there is such a well-defined route. Suppose further that the value of the crop that would be obtained by cultivating this strip of land is $10 but that the cost of cultivation is $11. In the absence of the cattle-raiser, the land would not be cultivated. However, given the presence of the cattle-raiser, it could well be that if the strip was cultivated, the whole crop would be destroyed by the cattle. In which case, the cattle-raiser would be forced to pay $10 to the farmer. It is true that the farmer would lose $1. But the cattle-raiser would lose $10. Clearly this is a situation which is not likely to last indefinitely since neither party would want this to happen. The aim of the farmer would be to induce the cattle-raiser to make a payment in return for an agreement to leave this land uncultivated. The farmer would not be able to obtain a payment greater than the cost of fencing off this piece of land nor so high as to lead the cattle-raiser to abandon the use of the neighbouring property. What payment would in fact be made would depend on the shrewdness of the farmer and the cattle-raiser as bargainers. But as the payment would not be so high as to cause the cattle-raiser to abandon this location and as it would not vary with the size of the herd, such an agreement would not affect the allocation of resources but would merely alter the distribution of income and wealth as between the cattle-raiser and the farmer.

I think it is clear that if the cattle-raiser is liable for damage caused and the pricing system works smoothly, the reduction in the value of production elsewhere will be taken into account in computing the additional cost involved in increasing the size of the herd. This cost will be weighed against the value of the additional meat production and, given perfect competition in the cattle industry, the allocation of resources in cattle-raising will be optimal. What needs to be emphasized is that the fall in the value of production elsewhere which would be taken into account in the costs of the cattle-raiser may well be less than the damage which the cattle would cause to the crops in the ordinary course of events. This is because it is possible, as a result of market transactions, to discontinue cultivation of the land. This is desirable in all cases in which the damage that the cattle would cause, and for which the cattle-raiser would be willing to pay, exceeds the amount which the farmer would pay for use of the land. In conditions of perfect competition, the amount which the farmer would pay for the use of the land is equal to the difference between the value of the total production when the factors are employed on this land and the value of the additional product yielded in their next best use (which would be what the farmer would have to pay for the factors). If damage exceeds the amount the farmer would pay for the use of the land, the value of the additional product of the factors employed elsewhere would exceed the value of the total product in this use after damage is taken into account. It follows that it would be desirable to abandon cultivation of the land and to release the factors employed for production elsewhere. A procedure which merely provided for payment for damage to the crop caused by the cattle but which did not allow for the possibility of cultivation being discontinued would result in too small an employment of factors of production in cattle-raising and too large an employment of factors in cultivation of the crop. But given the possibility of market transactions, a situation in which damage to crops exceeded the rent of the land would not endure. Whether the cattle-raiser pays the farmer to leave the land uncultivated or himself rents the land by paying the landowner an amount slightly greater than the farmer would pay (if the farmer was himself renting the land), the final result would be the same and would maximise the value of production. Even when the farmer is induced to plant crops which it would not be profitable to cultivate for sale on the market, this will be a purely short-term phenomenon and may be expected to lead to an agreement under which the planting will cease. The cattle-raiser will remain in that location and the marginal cost of meat production will be the same as before, thus having no long-run effect on the allocation of resources.

IV The pricing system with no liability for damage

I now turn to the case in which, although the pricing system is assumed to work smoothly (that is, costlessly), the damaging business is not liable for any of the damage which it causes. This business does not have to make a payment to those damaged by its actions. I propose to show that the allocation of resources will be the same in this case as it was when the damaging business was liable for damage caused. As I showed in the previous case that the allocation of resources was optimal, it will not be necessary to repeat this part of the argument.

I return to the case of the farmer and the cattle-raiser. The farmer would suffer increased damage to his crop as the size of the herd increased. Suppose that the size of the cattle-raiser's herd is three steers (and that this is the size of the herd that would be maintained if crop damage was not taken into account). Then the farmer would be willing to pay up to $3 if the cattle-raiser would reduce his herd to two steers, up to $5 if the herd were reduced to one steer and would pay up to $6 if cattle-raising was abandoned. The cattle-raiser would therefore receive $3 from the farmer if he kept two steers instead of three. This $3 foregone is therefore part of the cost incurred in keeping the third steer. Whether the $3 is a payment which the cattle-raiser has to make if he adds the third steer to his herd (which it would be if the cattle-raiser was liable to the farmer for damage caused to the crop) or whether it is a sum of money which he would have received if he did not keep a third steer (which it would be if the cattle-raiser was not liable to the farmer for damage caused to the crop) does not affect the final result. In both cases $3 is part of the cost of adding a third steer, to be included along with the other costs. If the increase in the value of production in cattle-raising through increasing the size of the herd from two to three is greater than the additional costs that have to be incurred (including the $3 damage to crops), the size of the herd will be increased. Otherwise, it will not. The size of the herd will be the same whether the cattle-raiser is liable for damage caused to the crop or not.

It may be argued that the assumed starting point – a herd of three steers – was arbitrary. And this is true. But the farmer would not wish to pay to avoid crop damage which the cattle-raiser would not be able to cause. For example, the maximum annual payment which the farmer could be induced to pay could not exceed $9, the annual cost of fencing. And the farmer would only be willing to pay this sum if it did not reduce his earnings to a level that would cause him to abandon cultivation of this particular tract of land. Furthermore, the farmer would only be willing to pay this amount if he believed that, in the absence of any payment by him, the size of the herd maintained by the cattle raiser would be four or more steers. Let us assume that this is the case. Then the farmer would be willing to pay up to $3 if the cattle raiser would reduce his herd to three steers, up to $6 if the herd were reduced to two steers, up to $8 if one steer only were kept and up to $9 if cattle-raising were abandoned. It will be noticed that the change in the starting point has not altered the amount which would accrue to the cattle-raiser if he reduced the size of his herd by any given amount. It is still true that the cattle-raiser could receive an additional $3 from the farmer if he agreed to reduce his herd from three steers to two and that the $3 represents the value of the crop that would be destroyed by adding the third steer to the herd. Although a different belief on the part of the farmer (whether justified or not) about the size of the herd that the cattle-raiser would maintain in the absence of payments from him may affect the total payment he can be induced to pay, it is not true that this different belief would have any effect on the size of the herd that the cattle-raiser will actually keep. This will be the same as it would be if the cattle-raiser had to pay for damage caused by his cattle, since a receipt foregone of a given amount is the equivalent of a payment of the same amount.

It might be thought that it would pay the cattle-raiser to increase his herd above the size that he would wish to maintain once a bargain had been made, in order to induce the farmer to make a larger total payment. And this may be true. It is similar in nature to the action of the farmer (when the cattle-raiser was liable for damage) in cultivating land on which, as a result of an agreement with the cattle-raiser, planting would subsequently be abandoned (including land which would not be cultivated at all in the absence of cattle-raising). But such manoeuvres are preliminaries to an agreement and do not affect the long-run equilibrium position, which is the same whether or not the cattle-raiser is held responsible for the crop damage brought about by his cattle.

It is necessary to know whether the damaging business is liable or not for damage caused since without the establishment of this initial delimitation of rights there can be no market transactions to transfer and recombine them. But the ultimate result (which maximises the value of production) is independent of the legal position if the pricing system is assumed to work without cost.

V   The problem illustrated anew

The harmful effects of the activities of a business can assume a wide variety of forms. An early English case concerned a building which, by obstructing currents of air, hindered the operation of a windmill.[5] A recent case in Florida concerned a building which cast a shadow on the cabana, swimming pool and sunbathing areas of a neighbouring hotel.[6] The problem of straying cattle and the damaging of crops which was the subject of detailed examination in the two preceding sections, although it may have appeared to be rather a special case, is in fact but one example of a problem which arises in many different guises. To clarify the nature of my argument and to demonstrate its general applicability, I propose to illustrate it anew by reference to four actual cases.

Let us first reconsider the case of *Sturges v. Bridgman*[7] which I used as an illustration of the general problem in my article on "The Federal

Communications Commission." In this case, a confectioner (in Wigmore Street) used two mortars and pestles in connection with his business (one had been in operation in the same position for more than 60 years and the other for more than 26 years). A doctor then came to occupy neighbouring premises (in Wimpole Street). The confectioner's machinery caused the doctor no harm until, eight years after he had first occupied the premises, he built a consulting room at the end of his garden right against the confectioner's kitchen. It was then found that the noise and vibration caused by the confectioner's machinery made it difficult for the doctor to use his new consulting room. "In particular . . . the noise prevented him from examining his patients by auscultation[8] for diseases of the chest. He also found it impossible to engage with effect in any occupation which required thought and attention." The doctor therefore brought a legal action to force the confectioner to stop using his machinery. The courts had little difficulty in granting the doctor the injunction he sought. "Individual cases of hardship may occur in the strict carrying out of the principle upon which we found our judgment, but the negation of the principle would lead even more to individual hardship, and would at the same time produce a prejudicial effect upon the development of land for residential purposes."

The court's decision established that the doctor had the right to prevent the confectioner from using his machinery. But, of course, it would have been possible to modify the arrangements envisaged in the legal ruling by means of a bargain between the parties. The doctor would have been willing to waive his right and allow the machinery to continue in operation if the confectioner would have paid him a sum of money which was greater than the loss of income which he would suffer from having to move to a more costly or less convenient location or from having to curtail his activities at this location or, as was suggested as a possibility, from having to build a separate wall which would deaden the noise and vibration. The confectioner would have been willing to do this if the amount he would have to pay the doctor was less than the fall in income he would suffer if he had to change his mode of operation at this location, abandon his operation or move his confectionery business to some other location. The solution of the problem depends essentially on whether the continued use of the machinery adds more to the confectioner's income than it subtracts from the doctor's.[9] But now consider the situation if the confectioner had won the case. The confectioner would then have had the right to continue operating his noise and vibration-generating machinery without having to pay anything to the doctor. The boot would have been on the other foot: the doctor would have had to pay the confectioner to induce him to stop using the machinery. If the doctor's income would have fallen more through continuance of the use of this machinery than it added to the income of the confectioner, there would clearly be room for a bargain whereby the doctor paid the confectioner to stop using the machinery. That is to say, the circumstances in which it would not pay the confectioner to continue to use the machinery and to compensate the doctor for the losses that this would bring (if the doctor had the right to prevent the confectioner's using his machinery) would be those in which it would be in the interest of the doctor to make a payment to the confectioner which would induce him to discontinue the use of the machinery (if the confectioner had the right to operate the machinery). The basic conditions are exactly the same in this case as they were in the example of the cattle which destroyed crops. With costless market transactions, the decision of the courts concerning liability for damage would be without effect on the allocation of resources. It was of course the view of the judges that they were affecting the working of the economic system – and in a desirable direction. Any other decision would have had "a prejudicial effect upon the development of land for residential purposes," an argument which was elaborated by examining the example of a forge operating on a barren moor, which was later developed for residential purposes. The judges' view that they were settling how the land was to be used would be true only in the case in which the costs of carrying out the necessary market transactions exceeded the gain which might be achieved by any rearrangement of rights. And it would be desirable to preserve the areas (Wimpole Street or the moor) for residential or professional use (by giving non-industrial users the right to stop the noise, vibration, smoke, etc., by injunction) only if the value of the additional residential facilities obtained was greater than the value of cakes or iron lost. But of this the judges seem to have been unaware.

Another example of the same problem is furnished by the case of *Cooke v. Forbes*. [10] One process in the weaving of cocoa-nut fibre matting was to immerse it in bleaching liquids after which it was hung out to dry. Fumes from a manufacturer of sulphate of ammonia had the effect of turning the matting from a bright to a dull and blackish colour. The reason for this was that the bleaching liquid contained chloride of tin, which, when affected by sulphuretted hydrogen, is turned to a darker colour. An injunction was sought to stop the manufacturer from emitting the fumes. The lawyers for the defendant argued that if the plaintiff "were not to use . . . a particular bleaching liquid, their fibre would not be affected; that their process is unusual, not according to the custom of the trade, and even damaging to their own fabrics." The judge commented: ". . . it appears to me quite plain that a person has a right to carry on upon his own property a manufacturing process in which he uses chloride of tin, or any sort of metallic dye, and that his neighbour is not at liberty to pour in gas which will interfere with his manufacture. If it can be traced to the neighbour, then, I apprehend, clearly he will have a right to come here and ask for relief." But in view of the fact that the damage was accidental and occasional, that careful precautions were taken and that there was no exceptional risk, an injunction was refused, leaving the plaintiff to bring an action for damages if he wished. What the subsequent developments were I do not know. But it is clear that the situation is essentially the same as that found in *Sturges v. Bridgman,* except that the cocoa-nut fibre matting manufacture could not secure an injunction but would have to seek damages from the sulphate of ammonia manufacturer. The economic analysis of the situation is exactly the same as with the cattle which destroyed crops. To avoid the damage, the sulphate of ammonia manufacturer could increase his precautions or move to another location. Either course would presumably increase his costs. Alternatively he could pay for the damage. This he would do if the payments for damage were less than the additional costs that would have to be incurred to avoid the damage. The payments for damage would then become part of the cost of production of sulphate of ammonia. Of course, if, as was suggested in the legal proceedings, the amount of damage could be eliminated by changing the bleaching agent (which would presumably increase the costs of the matting manufacturer) and if the additional cost was less than the damage that would otherwise occur, it should be possible for the two manufacturers to make a mutually satisfactory bargain whereby the new bleaching agent was used. Had the court decided against the matting manufacturer, as a consequence of which he would have had to suffer the damage without compensation, the allocation of resources would not have been affected. It would pay the matting manufacturer to change his bleaching agent if the additional cost involved was less than the reduction in damage. And since the matting manufacturer would be willing to pay the sulphate of ammonia manufacturer an amount up to his loss of income (the increase in costs or the damage suffered) if he would cease his activities, this loss of income would remain a cost of production for the manufacturer of sulphate of ammonia. This case is indeed analytically exactly the same as the cattle example.

Bryant v. Lefever[11] raised the problem of the smoke nuisance in a novel form. The plaintiff and the defendants were occupiers of adjoining houses, which were of about the same height.

> Before 1876 the plaintiff was able to light a fire in any room of his house without the chimneys smoking; the two houses had remained in the same condition some thirty or forty years. In 1876 the defendants took down their house, and began to rebuild it. They carried up a wall by the side of the plaintiff's chimneys much beyond its original height, and stacked timber on the roof of their house, and thereby caused the plaintiff's chimneys to smoke whenever he lighted fires.

The reason, of course, why the chimneys smoked was that the erection of the wall and the stacking of the timber prevented the free circulation of air. In a trial before a jury, the plaintiff was awarded damages of £40. The case then went to the Court of Appeals where the judgment was reversed. Bramwell, LJ, argued:

> . . . it is said and the jury have found, that the defendants have done that which caused a nuisance to the plaintiff's house. We think there is no evidence of this. No doubt there is a nuisance, but it is not of the defendant's causing. They have done nothing in causing the nuisance. Their house and their timber are harmless enough. It is the plaintiff who causes the nuisance by lighting a coal fire in a place the chimney of which is placed so near the defendants' wall, that the smoke does not escape, but comes into the house. Let the plaintiff cease to light his fire, let him move his chimney, let him carry it higher, and there would be no nuisance. Who then, causes it? It would be very clear that the plaintiff did, if he had built his house or chimney after the defendants had put up the timber on theirs, and it is really the same though he did so before the timber was there. But (what is in truth the same answer), if the defendants cause the nuisance, they have a right to do so. If the plaintiff has not the right to the passage of air, except subject to the defendants' right to build or put timber on their house, then his right is subject to their right, and though a nuisance follows from the exercise of their right, they are not liable.

And Cotton LJ, said:

> Here it is found that the erection of the defendants' wall has sensi-
> bly and materially interfered with the comfort of human existence
> in the plaintiff's house, and it is said this is a nuisance for which
> the defendants are liable. Ordinarily this is so, but the defendants
> have done so, not by sending on to the plaintiff's property any smoke
> or noxious vapour, but by interrupting the egress of smoke from
> the plaintiff's house in a way to which . . . the plaintiff has no legal
> right. The plaintiff creates the smoke, which interferes with his
> comfort. Unless he has . . . a right to get rid of this in a particular way
> which has been interfered with by the defendants, he cannot sue the
> defendants, because the smoke made by himself, for which he has
> not provided any effectual means of escape, causes him annoyance.
> It is as if a man tried to get rid of liquid filth arising on his own
> land by a drain into his neighbour's land. Until a right had been
> acquired by user, the neighbour might stop the drain without incur-
> ring liability by so doing. No doubt great inconvenience would be
> caused to the owner of the property on which the liquid filth arises.
> But the act of his neighbour would be a lawful act, and he would not
> be liable for the consequences attributable to the fact that the man
> had accumulated filth without providing any effectual means of
> getting rid of it.

I do not propose to show that any subsequent modification of the
situation, as a result of bargains between the parties (conditioned by the
cost of stacking the timber elsewhere, the cost of extending the chimney
higher, etc.), would have exactly the same result whatever decision the
courts had come to since this point has already been adequately dealt
with in the discussion of the cattle example and the two previous cases.
What I shall discuss is the argument of the judges in the Court of
Appeals that the smoke nuisance was not caused by the man who
erected the wall but by the man who lit the fires. The novelty of the
situation is that the smoke nuisance was suffered by the man who lit
the fires and not by some third person. The question is not a trivial one
since it lies at the heart of the problem under discussion. Who caused
the smoke nuisance? The answer seems fairly clear. The smoke nuisance
was caused both by the man who built the wall *and* by the man who
lit the fires. Given the fires, there would have been no smoke nuisance
without the wall; given the wall, there would have been no smoke nuisance without the fires. Eliminate the wall *or* the fires and the smoke

nuisance would disappear. On the marginal principle it is clear that *both* were responsible and *both* should be forced to include the loss of amenity due to the smoke as a cost in deciding whether to continue the activity which gives rise to the smoke. And given the possibility of market transactions, this is what would in fact happen. Although the wall-builder was not liable legally for the nuisance, as the man with the smoking chimneys would presumably be willing to pay a sum equal to the monetary worth to him of eliminating the smoke, this sum would therefore become for the wall-builder, a cost of continuing to have the high wall with the timber stacked on the roof.

The judges' contention that it was the man who lit the fires who alone caused the smoke nuisance is true only if we assume that the wall is the given factor. This is what the judges did by deciding that the man who erected the higher wall had a legal right to do so. The case would have been even more interesting if the smoke from the chimneys had injured the timber. Then it would have been the wall-builder who suffered the damage. The case would then have closely paralleled *Sturges v. Bridgman* and there can be little doubt that the man who lit the fires would have been liable for the ensuing damage to the timber, in spite of the fact that no damage had occurred until the high wall was built by the man who owned the timber.

Judges have to decide on legal liability but this should not confuse economists about the nature of the economic problem involved. In the case of the cattle and the crops, it is true that there would be no crop damage without the cattle. It is equally true that there would be no crop damage without the crops. The doctor's work would not have been disturbed if the confectioner had not worked his machinery; but the machinery would have disturbed no one if the doctor had not set up his consulting room in that particular place. The matting was blackened by the fumes from the sulphate of ammonia manufacturer; but no damage would have occurred if the matting manufacturer had not chosen to hang out his matting in a particular place and to use a particular bleaching agent. If we are to discuss the problem in terms of causation, both parties cause the damage. If we are to attain an optimum allocation of resources, it is therefore desirable that both parties should take the harmful effect (the nuisance) into account in deciding on their course of action. It is one of the beauties of a smoothly operating pricing system that, as has already been explained, the fall in the value of production due to the harmful effect would be a cost for both parties.

Bass v. Gregory[12] will serve as an excellent final illustration of the problem. The plaintiffs were the owners and tenant of a public house called the Jolly Anglers. The defendant was the owner of some cottages and a yard adjoining the Jolly Anglers. Under the public house was a cellar excavated in the rock. From the cellar, a hole or shaft had been cut into an old well situated in the defendant's yard. The well therefore became the ventilating shaft for the cellar. The cellar "had been used for a particular purpose in the process of brewing, which, without ventilation, could not be carried on." The cause of the action was that the defendant removed a grating from the mouth of the well, "so as to stop or prevent the free passage of air from [the] cellar upwards through the well. . . . " What caused the defendant to take this step is not clear from the report of the case. Perhaps "the air . . . impregnated by the brewing operations" which "passed up the well and out into the open air" was offensive to him. At any rate, he preferred to have the well in his yard stopped up. The court had first to determine whether the owners of the public house could have a legal right to a current of air. If they were to have such a right, this case would have to be distinguished from *Bryant v. Lefever* (already considered). This, however, presented no difficulty. In the case the current of air was confined to "a strictly defined channel." In the case of *Bryant v. Lefever*, what was involved was "the general current of air common to all mankind." The judge therefore held that the owners of the public house could have the right to a current of air whereas the owner of the private house in *Bryant v. Lefever* could not. An economist might be tempted to add "but the air moved all the same." However, all that had been decided at this stage of the argument was that there could be a legal right, not that the owners of the public house possessed it. But evidence showed that the shaft from the cellar to the well had existed for over 40 years and that the use of the well as a ventilating shaft must have been known to the owners of the yard since the air, when it emerged, smelt of the brewing operations. The judge therefore held that the public house had such a right by the "doctrine of lost grant." This doctrine states "that if a legal right is proved to have existed and been exercised for a number of years the law ought to presume that it had a legal origin."[13] So the owner of the cottages and yard had to unstop the well and endure the smell.

The reasoning employed by the courts in determining legal rights will often seem strange to an economist because many of the factors on which the decision turns are, to an economist, irrelevant. Because of this, situations which are, from an economic point of view, identical will be treated quite differently by the courts. The economic problem in all cases of harmful effects is how to maximise the value of production. In the case of *Bass v. Gregory* fresh air was drawn in through the well which facilitated the production of beer but foul air was expelled through the well which made life in the adjoining houses less pleasant. The economic problem was to decide which to choose: a lower cost of beer and worsened amenities in adjoining houses or a higher cost of beer and improved amenities. In deciding this question, the "doctrine of lost grant" is about as relevant as the colour of the judge's eyes. But it has to be remembered that the immediate question faced by the courts is *not* what shall be done by whom *but* who has the legal right to do what. It is always possible to modify by transactions on the market the initial legal delimitation of rights. And, of course, if such market transactions are costless, such a rearrangement of rights will always take place if it would lead to an increase in the value of production.

VI   The cost of market transactions taken into account

The argument has proceeded up to this point on the assumption (explicit in Sections III and IV and tacit in Section V) that there were no costs involved in carrying out market transactions. This is, of course, a very unrealistic assumption. In order to carry out a market transaction it is necessary to discover who it is that one wishes to deal with, to inform people that one wishes to deal and on what terms, to conduct negotiations leading up to a bargain, to draw up the contract, to undertake the inspection needed to make sure that the terms of the contract are being observed, and so on. These operations are often extremely costly, sufficiently costly at any rate to prevent many transactions that would be carried out in a world in which the pricing system worked without cost.

In earlier sections, when dealing with the problem of the rearrangement of legal rights through the market, it was argued that such a rearrangement would be made through the market whenever this would lead to an increase in the value of production. But this assumed costless market transactions. Once the cost of carrying out market transactions are taken into account it is clear that such a rearrangement of rights will only be undertaken when the increase in the value of production consequent upon the rearrangement is greater than the costs which would be involved in bringing it about. When it is less, the granting of an injunction (or the knowledge that it would be granted) or the liability to pay damages may result in an activity being discontinued (or may prevent its being started) which would be undertaken if market transactions were costless. In these conditions the initial delimitation of legal rights does have an effect on the efficiency with which the economic system operates. One arrangement of rights may bring about a greater value of production than any other. But unless this is the arrangement of rights established by the legal system, the costs of reaching the same result by altering and combining rights through the market may be so great that this optimal arrangement of rights, and the greater value of production which it would bring, may never be achieved. The part played by economic considerations in the process of delimiting legal rights will be discussed in the next section. In this section, I will take the initial delimitation of rights and the costs of carrying out market transactions as given.

It is clear that an alternative form of economic organisation which could achieve the same result at less cost than would be incurred by using the market would enable the value of production to be raised. As I explained many years ago, the firm represents such an alternative to organising production through market transactions.[14] Within the firm individual bargains between the various cooperating factors of production are eliminated and for a market transaction is substituted an administrative decision. The rearrangement of production then takes place without the need for bargains between the owners of the factors of production. A landowner who has control of a large tract of land may devote his land to various uses taking into account the effect that the interrelations of the various activities will have on the net return of the land, thus rendering unnecessary bargains between those undertaking the various activities. Owners of a large building or of several adjoining properties in a given area may act in much the same way. In effect, using our earlier terminology, the firm would acquire the legal rights of all the parties and the rearrangement of activities would not follow on a rearrangement of rights by contract, but as a result of an administrative decision as to how the rights should be used.

It does not, of course, follow that the administrative costs of organising a transaction through a firm are inevitably less than the costs of the market transactions which are superseded. But where contracts are peculiarly difficult to draw up and an attempt to describe what the parties have agreed to do or not to do (e.g. the amount and kind of a smell or noise that they may make or will not make) would necessitate a lengthy and highly involved document, and, where, as is probable, a long-term contract would be desirable;[15] it would be hardly surprising if the emergence of a firm or the extension of the activities of an existing firm was not the solution adopted on many occasions to deal with the problem of harmful effects. This solution would be adopted whenever the administrative costs of the firm were less than the costs of the market transactions that it supersedes and the gains which would result from the rearrangement of activities greater than the firm's costs of organising them. I do not need to examine in great detail the character of this solution since I have explained what is involved in my earlier article.

But the firm is not the only possible answer to this problem. The administrative costs of organising transactions within the firm may also be high, and particularly so when many diverse activities are brought within the control of a single organisation. In the standard case of a smoke nuisance, which may affect a vast number of people engaged in a wide variety of activities, the administrative costs might well be so high as to make any attempt to deal with the problem within the confines of a single firm impossible. An alternative solution is direct government regulation. Instead of instituting a legal system of rights which can be modified by transactions on the market, the government may impose regulations which state what people must or must not do and which have to be obeyed. Thus, the government (by statute or perhaps more likely through an administrative agency) may, to deal with the problem of smoke nuisance, decree that certain methods of production should or should not be used (e.g. that smoke preventing devices should be installed or that coal or oil should not be burned) or may confine certain types of business to certain districts (zoning regulations).

The government is, in a sense, a super-firm (but of a very special kind) since it is able to influence the use of factors of production by administrative decision. But the ordinary firm is subject to checks in its operations because of the competition of other firms, which might administer the same activities at lower cost and also because there is always the alternative of market transactions as against organisation within the firm if the administrative costs become too great. The government is able, if it wishes, to avoid the market altogether, which a firm can never do. The firm has to make market agreements with the owners of the factors of production that it uses. Just as the government can conscript or seize property, so it can decree that factors of production should only be used in such-and-such a way. Such authoritarian methods save a lot of trouble (for those doing the organising). Furthermore, the government has at its disposal the police and the other law enforcement agencies to make sure that its regulations are carried out.

It is clear that the government has powers which might enable it to get some things done at a lower cost than could a private organisation (or at any rate one without special governmental powers). But the governmental administrative machine is not itself costless. It can, in fact, on occasion be extremely costly. Furthermore, there is no reason to suppose that the restrictive and zoning regulations, made by a fallible administration subject to political pressures and operating without any competitive check, will necessarily always be those which increase the efficiency with which the economic system operates. Furthermore, such general regulations which must apply to a wide variety of cases will be enforced in some cases in which they are clearly inappropriate. From these considerations it follows that direct governmental regulation will not necessarily give better results than leaving the problem to be solved by the market or the firm. But equally there is no reason why, on occasion, such governmental administrative regulation should not lead to an improvement in economic efficiency. This would seem particularly likely when, as is normally the case with the smoke nuisance, a large number of people are involved and in which therefore the costs of handling the problem through the market or the firm may be high.

There is, of course, a further alternative, which is to do nothing about the problem at all. And given that the costs involved in solving the problem by regulations issued by the governmental administrative machine will often be heavy (particularly if the costs are interpreted to include all the consequences which follow from the government engaging in this kind of activity), it will no doubt be commonly the case that the gain which would come from regulating the actions which give rise to the harmful effects will be less than the costs involved in government regulation.

The discussion of the problem of harmful effects in this section (when the costs of market transactions are taken into account) is extremely inadequate. But at least it has made clear that the problem is one of choosing the appropriate social arrangement for dealing with the harmful effects. All solutions have costs and there is no reason to suppose that government regulation is called for simply because the problem is not well handled by the market or the firm. Satisfactory views on policy can only come from a patient study of how, in practice, the market, firms and governments handle the problem of harmful effects. Economists need to study the work of the broker in bringing parties together, the effectiveness of restrictive covenants, the problems of the large-scale real-estate development company, the operation of government zoning and other regulating activities. It is my belief that economists, and policy-makers generally, have tended to over-estimate the advantages which come from governmental regulation. But this belief, even if justified, does not do more than suggest that government regulation should be curtailed. It does not tell us where the boundary line should be drawn. This, it seems to me, has to come from a detailed investigation of the actual results of handling the problem in different ways. But it would be unfortunate if this investigation were undertaken with the aid of a faulty economic analysis. The aim of this article is to indicate what the economic approach to the problem should be.

VII   The legal delimitation of rights and the economic problem

The discussion in Section V not only served to illustrate the argument but also afforded a glimpse at the legal approach to the problem of harmful effects. The cases considered were all English but a similar selection of American cases could easily be made and the character of the reasoning would have been the same. Of course, if market transactions were costless, all that matters (questions of equity apart) is that the rights of the various parties should be well-defined and the results of legal actions easy to forecast. But as we have seen, the situation is quite different when market transactions are so costly as to make it difficult to change the arrangement of rights established by the law. In such cases, the courts directly influence economic activity. It would therefore seem desirable that the courts should understand the economic consequences of their decisions and should, in so far as this is possible without creating too much uncertainty about the legal position itself, take these consequences into account when making their decisions. Even when it is possible to change the legal delimitation of rights through market transactions, it is obviously desirable to reduce the need for such transactions and thus reduce the employment of resources in carrying them out.

A thorough examination of the presuppositions of the courts in trying such cases would be of great interest but I have not been able to attempt it. Nevertheless it is clear from a cursory study that the courts have often recognised the economic implications of their decisions and are aware (as many economists are not) of the reciprocal nature of the problem. Furthermore, from time to time, they take these economic implications into account, along with other factors, in arriving at their decisions. The American writers on this subject refer to the question in a more explicit fashion than do the British. Thus, to quote Prosser on Torts, a person may make use of his own property or . . . conduct his own affairs at the expense of some harm to his neighbors. He may operate a factory whose noise and smoke cause some discomfort to others, so long as he keeps within reasonable bounds. It is only when his conduct is unreasonable, *in the light of its utility and the harm which results* [italics added], that it becomes a nuisance. . . . As it was said in an ancient case in regard to candle-making in a town, "Le utility del chose excusera le noisomeness del stink."

The world must have factories, smelters, oil refineries, noisy machinery and blasting, even at the expense of some inconvenience to those in the vicinity and the plaintiff may be required to accept some not unreasonable discomfort for the general good.[16]

The standard British writers do not state as explicitly as this that a comparison between the utility and harm produced is an element in deciding whether a harmful effect should be considered a nuisance. But similar views, if less strongly expressed, are to be found.[17] The doctrine that the harmful effect must be substantial before the court will act is, no doubt, in part a reflection of the fact that there will almost always be some gain to offset the harm. And in the reports of individual cases, it is clear that the judges have had in mind what would be lost as well as what would be gained in deciding whether to grant an injunction or award damages. Thus, in refusing to prevent the destruction of a prospect by a new building, the judge stated:

I know no general rule of common law, which . . . says, that building so as to stop another's prospect is a nuisance. Was that the case, there could be no great towns; and I must grant injunctions to all the new buildings in this town. . . .[18]

In *Webb v Bird*[19] it was decided that it was not a nuisance to build a schoolhouse so near a windmill as to obstruct currents of air and hinder the working of the mill. An early case seems to have been decided in an opposite direction. Gale commented:

In old maps of London a row of windmills appears on the heights to the north of London. Probably in the time of King James it was thought an alarming circumstance, as affecting the supply of food to the city, that anyone should build so near them as to take the wind out from their sails.[20]

In one of the cases discussed in Section V, *Sturges v. Bridgman*, it seems clear that the judges were thinking of the economic consequences of alternative decisions. To the argument that if the principle that they seemed to be following

> were carried out to its logical consequences ,it would result in the most serious practical inconveniences, for a man might go – say into the midst of the tanneries of *Bermondsey*, or into any other locality devoted to any particular trade or manufacture of a noisy or unsavoury character, and by building a private residence upon a vacant piece of land put a stop to such trade or manufacture altogether,

the judges answered that

> whether anything is a nuisance or not is a question to be determined, not merely by an abstract consideration of the thing itself, but in reference to its circumstances; What would be a nuisance in *Belgrave Square* would not necessarily be so in *Bermondsey*; and where a locality is devoted to a particular trade or manufacture carried on by the traders or manufacturers in a particular and established manner not constituting a public nuisance, judges and juries would be justified in finding, and may be trusted to find, that the trade or manufacture so carried on in that locality is not a private or actionable wrong.[21]

That the character of the neighborhood is relevant in deciding whether something is, or is not, a nuisance, is definitely established.

> He who dislikes the noise of traffic must not set up his abode in the heart of a great city. He who loves peace and quiet must not live in a locality devoted to the business of making boilers or steamships.[22]

What has emerged has been described as "planning and zoning by the judiciary."[23] Of course there are sometimes considerable difficulties in applying the criteria.[24]

An interesting example of the problem is found in *Adams v. Ursell*[25] in which a fried fish shop in a predominantly working-class district was set up near houses of "a much better character." England without fish-and-chips is a contradiction in terms and the case was clearly one of high importance. The judge commented:

It was urged that an injunction would cause great hardship to the defendant and to the poor people who get food at his shop. The answer to that is that it does not follow that the defendant cannot carry on his business in another more suitable place somewhere in the neighbourhood. It by no means follows that because a fried fish shop is a nuisance in one place it is a nuisance in another.

In fact, the injunction which restrained Mr Ursell from running his shop did not even extend to the whole street. So he was presumably able to move to other premises near houses of "a much worse character," the inhabitants of which would no doubt consider the availability of fish-and-chips to outweigh the pervading odour and "fog or mist" so graphically described by the plaintiff. Had there been no other "more suitable place in the neighbourhood," the case would have been more difficult and the decision might have been different. What would "the poor people" have had for food? No English judge would have said: "Let them eat cake."

The courts do not always refer very clearly to the economic problem posed by the cases brought before them but it seems probable that in the interpretation of words and phrases like "reasonable" or "common or ordinary use" there is some recognition, perhaps largely unconscious and certainly not very explicit, of the economic aspects of the questions at issue. A good example of this would seem to be the judgment in the Court of Appeals in *Andreae v. Selfridge and Company Ltd.*[26] In this case, a hotel (in Wigmore Street) was situated on part of an island site. The remainder of the site was acquired by Selfridges which demolished the existing buildings in order to erect another in their place. The hotel suffered a loss of custom in consequence of the noise and dust caused by the demolition. The owner of the hotel brought an action against Selfridges for damages. In the lower court, the hotel was awarded £4,500 damages. The case was then taken on appeal.

The judge who had found for the hotel proprietor in the lower court said:

> I cannot regard what the defendants did on the site of the first operation as having been commonly done in the ordinary use and occupation of land or houses. It is neither usual nor common, in this country, for people to excavate a site to depth of 60 feet and then to erect upon that site a steel framework and fasten the steel frames together with rivets . . . Nor is it, I think, a common or ordinary use of land, in this country, to act as the defendants did when they were

dealing with the site of their second operation – namely, to demolish all the houses that they had to demolish, five or six of them I think, if not more, and to use for the purpose of demolishing them pneumatic hammers.

Sir Wilfred Greene, MR, speaking for the Court of Appeals, first noted

that when one is dealing with temporary operations, such as demolition and re-building, everybody has to put up with a certain amount of discomfort, because operations of that kind cannot be carried on at all without a certain amount of noise and a certain amount of dust. Therefore, the rule with regard to interference must be read subject to this qualification. . . .

He then referred to the previous judgment:

With great respect to the learned judge, I take the view that he has not approached this matter from the correct angle. It seems to me that it is not possible to say . . . that the type of demolition, excavation and construction in which the defendant company was engaged in the course of these operations was of such an abnormal and unusual nature as to prevent the qualification to which I have referred coming into operation. It seems to me that, when the rule speaks of the common or ordinary use of land, it does not mean that the methods of using land and building on it are in some way to be stabilised for ever. As time goes on new inventions or new methods enable land to be more profitably used, either by digging down into the earth or by mounting up into the skies. Whether, from other points of view, that is a matter which is desirable for humanity is neither here nor there; but it is part of the normal use of land, to make use upon your land, in the matter of construction, of what particular type and what particular depth of foundations and particular height of building may be reasonable, in the circumstances, and in view of the developments of the day. . . . Guests at hotels are very easily upset. People coming to this hotel, who were accustomed to a quiet outlook at the back, coming back and finding demolition and building going on, may very well have taken the view that the particular merit of this hotel no longer existed. That would be a misfortune for the plaintiff; but assuming that there was nothing wrong in the defendant company's works, assuming the defendant company was carrying on the demolition and its building, productive of noise though it might be, with all reasonable skill, and taking all reasonable precautions not to cause annoyance to its neighbors, then the planitiff might lose all her clients in the hotel because they have lost the amenities of an open and quiet place behind, but she would have no cause of complaint. . . . [But those] who say that their interference with the comfort of their neighbors is justified because their operations are normal and usual and conducted with proper care and skill are under a specific duty . . . to use that reasonable and proper care and skill. It is not a correct attitude to take to say: "We will go on and do what we like until somebody complains!' . . . Their duty is to take proper precautions and to see that the nuisance is reduced to a minimum. It is no answer for them to say: 'But this would mean that we should have to do the work more slowly than we would like to do it, or it would involve putting us to some extra expense.' All these questions are matters of common sense and degree, and quite clearly it would be unreasonable to expect people to conduct their work so slowly or so expensively, of the purpose of preventing a transient inconvenience, that the cost and trouble would be prohibitive. . . . In this case, the defendant company's attitude seems to have been to go on until somebody complained, and, further, that its desire to hurry its work and conduct it according to its own ideas and its own convenience was to prevail if there was a real conflict between it and the comfort of its neighbors. That . . . is not carrying out the obligation of using reasonable care and skill. . . . The effect comes to this . . . the plaintiff suffered an actionable nuisance; . . . she is entitled, not to a nominal sum, but to a substantial sum, based upon those principles . . . but in arriving at the sum . . . I have discounted any loss of custom . . . which might be due to the general loss of amenities owing to what was going on at the back. . . .

The upshot was that the damages awarded were reduced from £4,500 to £1,000.

The discussion in this section has, up to this point, been concerned with court decisions arising out of the common law relating to nuisance. Delimitation of rights in this area also comes about because of statutory enactments. Most economists would appear to assume that the aim of governmental action in this field is to extend the scope of the law of nuisance by designating as nuisances activities which would not be recognised as such by the common law. And there can be no doubt that some statues, for example, the Public Health Acts, have had this effect.

But not all Government enactments are of this kind. The effect of much of the legislation in this area is to protect businesses from the claims of those they have harmed by their actions. There is a long list of legalised nuisances.

The position has been summarised in *Halsbury's Laws of England* as follows:

> Where the legislature directs that a thing shall in all events be done or authorises certain works at a particular place for a specific purposes or grants powers with the intention that they shall be exercised, although leaving some discretion as to the mode of exercise, no action will lie at common law for nuisance or damage which is the inevitable result of carrying out the statutory powers so conferred. This is so whether the act causing the damage is authorised for public purposes or private profit. Acts done under powers granted by persons to whom Parliament has delegated authority to grant such powers, for example, under provisional orders of the Board of Trade, are regarded as having been done under statutory authority. In the absence of negligence it seems that a body exercising statutory powers will not be liable to an action merely because it might, by acting in a different way, have minimised an injury.

Instances are next given of freedom from liability for acts authorised:

> An action has been held not to be against a body exercising its statutory powers without negligence in respect of the flooding of land by water escaping from watercourses, from water pipes, from drains, or from a canal; the escape of fumes from sewers; the escape of sewage: the subsidence of a road over a sewer; vibration or noise caused by a railway; fires caused by authorised acts; the pollution of a stream where statutory requirements to use the best known method of purifying before discharging the effluent have been satisfied; interference with a telephone or telegraph system by an electric tramway; the insertion of poles for tramways in the subsoil; annoyance caused by things reasonably necessary for the excavation of authorised works; accidental damage caused by the placing of a grating in a roadway; the escape of tar acid; or interference with the access of a frontager by a street shelter or safety railings on the edge of a pavement.[27]

The legal position in the United States would seem to be essentially the same as in England, except that the power of the legislatures to authorise what would otherwise be nuisances under the common law, at least without giving compensation to the person harmed, is somewhat more limited, as it is subject to constitutional restrictions.[28] Nonetheless, the power is there and cases more or less identical with the English cases can be found. The question has arisen in an acute form in connection with airports and the operation of aeroplanes. The case of *Delta Air Corporation v. Kersey, Kersey v. City of Atlanta*[29] is a good example. Mr Kersey bought land and built a house on it. Some years later the City of Atlanta constructed an airport on land immediately adjoining that of Mr Kersey. It was explained that his property was "a quiet, peaceful and proper location for a home before the airport was built, but dust, noises and low flying of airplanes caused by the operation of the airport have rendered his property unsuitable as a home," a state of affairs which was described in the report of the case with a wealth of distressing detail. The judge first referred to an earlier case, *Thrasher v. City of Atlanta*[30] in which it was noted that the City of Atlanta had been expressly authorized to operate an airport.

By this franchise aviation was recognised as a lawful business and also as an enterprise affected with a public interest . . . all persons using [the airport] in the manner contemplated by law are within the protection and immunity of the franchise granted by the municipality. An airport is not a nuisance per se, although it might become such from the manner of its construction or operation.

Since aviation was a lawful business affected with a public interest and the construction of the airport was autorised by statute, the judge next referred to *Georgia Railroad and Banking Co. v. Maddox*[31] in which it was said:

Where a railroad terminal yard is located and its construction authorized, under statutory powers, if it be constructed and operated in a proper manner, it cannot be adjudged a nuisance. Accordingly, injuries and inconveniences to persons residing near such a yard, from noises of locomotives, rumbling of cars, vibrations produced thereby, and smoke, cinders, soot and the like, which result from the ordinary and necessary, therefore proper, use and operation of such a yard, are not nuisances, but are the necessary concomitants of the franchise granted.

In view of this, the judge decided that the noise and dust complained of by Mr Kersey "may be deemed to be incidental to the proper operation of an airport, and as such they cannot be said to constitute a nuisance." But the complaint against low flying was different:

> . . . can it be said that flights . . . at such a low height [25 to 50 feet above Mr. Kersey's house] as to be imminently dangerous to . . . life and health . . . are a necessary concomitant of an airport? We do not think this question can be answered in the affirmative. No reason appears why the city could not obtain lands of an area [sufficiently large] . . . as not to require such low flights . . . For the sake of public convenience adjoining-property owners must suffer such inconvenience from noise and dust as result from the usual and proper operation of an airport, but their private rights are entitled to preference in the eyes of the law where the inconvenience is not one demanded by a properly constructed and operated airport.

Of course this assumed that the City of Atlanta could prevent the low flying and continue to operate the airport. The judge therefore added:

> From all that appears, the conditions causing the low flying may be remedied; but if on the trial it should appear that it is indispensable to the public interest that the airport should continue to be operated in its present condition, it may be said that the petitioner should be denied injunctive relief.

In the course of another aviation case, *Smith v. New England Aircraft Co.*,[32] the court surveyed the law in the United States regarding the legalizing of nuisances and it is apparent that, in the broad, it is very similar to that found in England:

> It is the proper function of the legislative department of government in the exercise of the police power to consider the problems and risks that arise from the use of new inventions and endeavor to adjust private rights and harmonize conflicting interests by comprehensive statutes for the public welfare. . . . There are . . . analogies where the invasion of the airspace over underlying land by noise, smoke, vibration, dust and disagreeable odors, having been authorized by the legislative department of government and not being in effect a condemnation of the property although in some measure depreciating its market value, must be borne by the landowner without compensation or remedy. Legislative sanction makes that lawful which

otherwise might be a nuisance. Examples of this are damages to adjacent land arising from smoke, vibration and noise in the operation of a railroad . . . ; the noise of ringing factory bells . . . ; the abatement of nuisances . . . ; the erection of steam engines and furnaces . . . ; unpleasant odors connected with sewers, oil refining and storage of naphtha. . . .

Most economists seem to be unaware of all this. When they are prevented from sleeping at night by the roar of jet planes overhead (publicly authorised and perhaps publicly operated), are unable to think (or rest) in the day because of the noise and vibration from passing trains (publicly authorised and perhaps publicly operated), find it difficult to breathe because of the odour from a local sewage farm (publicly authorised and perhaps publicly operated) and are unable to escape because their driveways are blocked by a road obstruction (without any doubt, publicly devised), their nerves frayed and mental balance disturbed, they proceed to declaim about the disadvantages of private enterprise and the need for government regulation.

While most economists seem to be under a misapprehension concerning the character of the situation with which they are dealing, it is also the case that the activities which they would like to see stopped or curtailed may well be socially justified. It is all a question of weighing up the gains that would accrue from eliminating these harmful effects against the gains that accrue from allowing them to continue. Of course, it is likely that an extension of government economic activity will often lead to this protection against action for nuisance being pushed further than is desirable. For one thing, the government is likely to look with a benevolent eye on enterprises which it is itself promoting. For another, it is possible to describe the committing of a nuisance by public enterprise in a much more pleasant way than when the same thing is done by private enterprise. In the words of Lord Justice Sir Alfred Denning:

> . . . the significance of the social revolution of today is that, whereas in the past the balance was much too heavily in favor of the rights of property and freedom of contract, Parliament has repeatedly intervened so as to give the public good its proper place.[33]

There can be little doubt that the Welfare State is likely to bring an extension of that immunity from liability for damage, which economists have been in the habit of condemning (although they have tended to assume that this immunity was a sign of too little Government intervention in the economic system). For example, in Britain, the powers of local authorities are regarded as being either absolute or conditional. In the first category, the local authority has no discretion in exercising the power conferred on it. "The absolute power may be said to cover all the necessary consequences of its direct operation even if such consequences amount to nuisance." On the other hand, a conditional power may only be exercised in such a way that the consequences do not constitute a nuisance.

> It is the intention of the legislature which determines whether a power is absolute or conditional. . . . [As] there is the possibility that the social policy of the legislature may change from time to time, a power which in one era would be construed as being conditional, might in another era be interpreted as being absolute in order to further the policy of the Welfare State. This point is one which should be borne in mind when considering some of the older cases upon this aspect of the law of nuisance.[34]

It would seem desirable to summarise the burden of this long section. The problem which we face in dealing with actions which have harmful effects is not simply one of restraining those responsible for them. What has to be decided is whether the gain from preventing the harm is greater than the loss which would be suffered elsewhere as a result of stopping the action which produces the harm. In a world in which there are costs of rearranging the rights established by the legal system, the courts, in cases relating to nuisance, are, in effect, making a decision on the economic problem and determining how resources are to be employed. It was argued that the courts are conscious of this and that they often make, although not always in a very explicit fashion, a comparison between what would be gained and what lost by preventing actions which have harmful effects. But the delimitation of rights is also the result of statutory enactments. Here we also find evidence of an appreciation of the reciprocal nature of the problem. While statutory enactments add to the list of nuisances, action is also taken to legalise what would otherwise be nuisances under the common law. The kind of situation which economists are prone to consider as requiring corrective government action is, in fact, often the result of government action. Such action is not necessarily unwise. But there is a real danger that extensive government intervention in the economic system may lead to the protection of those responsible for harmful effects being carried too far.

VIII   Pigou's treatment in The Economics of Welfare

The fountainhead for the modern economic analysis of the problem discussed in this article is Pigou's *Economics of Welfare* and, in particular, that section of Part II which deals with divergences between social and private net products which come about because

> one person A, in the course of rendering some service, for which payment is made, to a second person B, incidentally also renders services or disservices to other persons (not producers of like services), of such a sort that payment cannot be exacted from the benefited parties or compensation enforced on behalf of the injured parties.[35]

Pigou tells us that his aim in Part II of *The Economics of Welfare* is

> to ascertain how far the free play of self-interest, acting under the existing legal system, tends to distribute the country's resources in the way most favorable to the production of a large national dividend, and how far it is feasible for State action to improve upon "natural" tendencies.[36]

To judge from the first part of this statement, Pigou's purpose is to discover whether any improvements could be made in the existing arrangements which determine the use of resources. Since Pigou's conclusion is that improvements could be made, one might have expected him to continue by saying that he proposed to set out the changes required to bring them about. Instead, Pigou adds a phrase which contrasts "natural" tendencies with State action, which seems in some sense to equate the present arrangements with "natural" tendencies and to imply that what is required to bring about these improvements is State action (if feasible). That this is more or less Pigou's position is evident from Chapter I of Part II.[37] Pigou starts by referring to "optimistic followers of the classical economists"[38] who have argued that the value of production would be maximised if the Government refrained from any interference in the economic system and the economic arrangements were those which came about "naturally." Pigou goes on to say that if self-interest does promote economic welfare, it is because human institutions have been devised to make it so. (This part of Pigou's argument, which he develops with the aid of a quotation from Cannan, seems to me to be essentially correct.) Pigou concludes:

But even in the most advanced States there are failures and imperfections.... there are many obstacles that prevent a community's resources from being distributed ... in the most efficient way. The study of these constitutes our present problem.... its purpose is essentially practical. It seeks to bring into clearer light some of the ways in which it now is, or eventually may become, feasible for governments to control the play of economic forces in such ways as to promote the economic welfare, and through that, the total welfare, of their citizens as a whole.[39]

Pigou's underlying thought would appear to be: some have argued that no State action is needed. But the system has performed as well as it has because of State action. Nonetheless, there are still imperfections. What additional State action is required?

If this is a correct summary of Pigou's position, its inadequacy can be demonstrated by examining the first example he gives of a divergence between private and social products.

It might happen ... that costs are thrown upon people not directly concerned, through, say, uncompensated damage done to surrounding woods by sparks from railway engines. All such effects must be included – some of them will be positive, others negative elements – in reckoning up the social net product of the marginal increment of any volume of resources turned into any use or place.[40]

The example used by Pigou refers to a real situation. In Britain, a railway does not normally have to compensate those who suffer damage by fire caused by sparks from an engine. Taken in conjunction with what he says in Chapter 9 of Part II, I take Pigou's policy recommendations to be, first, that there should be State action to correct this "natural" situation and, second, that the railways should be forced to compensate those whose woods are burnt. If this is a correct interpretation of Pigou's position, I would argue that the first recommendation is based on a misapprehension of the facts and that the second is not necessarily desirable.

Let us consider the legal position. Under the heading "Sparks from engines," we find the following in Halsbury's *Laws of England*:

If railway undertakers use steam engines on their railway without express statutory authority to do so, they are liable, irrespective of any negligence on their part, for fires caused by sparks from engines.

Railway undertakers are, however, generally given statutory authority to use steam engines on their railway; accordingly, if an engine
is constructed with the precautions which science suggests against
fire and is used without negligence, they are not responsible at
common law for any damage which may be done by sparks. . . . In
the construction of an engine the undertaker is bound to use all the
discoveries which science has put within its reach in order to avoid
doing harm, provided they are such as it is reasonable to require the
company to adopt, having proper regard to the likelihood of the
damage and to the cost and convenience of the remedy; but it is
not negligence on the part of an undertaker if it refuses to use an
apparatus the efficiency of which is open to bona fide doubt.

To this general rule, there is a statutory exception arising from the
Railway (Fires) Act, 1905, as amended in 1923. This concerns agricultural land or agricultural crops.

In such a case the fact that the engine was used under statutory
powers does not affect the liability of the company in an action for
the damage. . . . These provisions, however, only apply where the
claim for damage . . . does not exceed £200, [£100 in the 1905 Act]
and where written notice of the occurrence of the fire and the inten-
tion to claim has been sent to the company within seven days of the
occurrence of the damage and particulars of the damage in writing
showing the amount of the claim in money not exceeding £200 have
been sent to the company within twenty-one days.

Agricultural land does not include moorland or buildings and agricultural crops do not include those led away or stacked.[41] I have not made
a close study of the parliamentary history of this statutory exception,
but to judge from debates in the House of Commons in 1922 and 1923,
this exception was probably designed to help the smallholder.[42]

Let us return to Pigou's example of uncompensated damage to
surrounding woods caused by sparks from railway engines. This is presumably intended to show how it is possible "for State action to improve
on 'natural' tendencies." If we treat Pigou's example as referring to the
position before 1905, or as being an arbitrary example (in that he
might just as well have written "surrounding buildings" instead of "surrounding woods"), then it is clear that the reason why compensation
was not paid must have been that the railway had statutory authority
to run steam engines (which relieved it of liability for fires caused by

sparks). That this was the legal position was established in 1860, in a case, oddly enough, which concerned the burning of surrounding woods by a railway,[43] and the law on this point has not been changed (apart from the one exception) by a century of railway legislation, including nationalisation. If we treat Pigou's example of "uncompensated damage done to surrounding woods by sparks from railway engines" literally, and assume that it refers to the period after 1905, then it is clear that the reason why compensation was not paid must have been that the damage was more than £100 (in the first edition of *The Economics of Welfare*) or more than £200 (in later editions) or that the owner of the wood failed to notify the railway in writing within seven days of the fire or did not send particulars of the damage, in writing, within twenty-one days. In the real world, Pigou's example could only exist as a result of a deliberate choice of the legislature. It is not, of course, easy to imagine the construction of a railway in a state of nature. The nearest one can get to this is presumably a railway which uses steam engines "without express statutory authority." However, in this case the railway would be obliged to compensate those whose woods it burnt down. That is to say, compensation would be paid in the absence of government action. The only circumstances in which compensation would not be paid would be those in which there had been government action. It is strange that Pigou, who clearly thought it desirable that compensation should be paid, should have chosen this particular example to demonstrate how it is possible "for State action to improve on 'natural' tendencies."

Pigou seems to have had a faulty view of the facts of the situation. But it also seems likely that he was mistaken in his economic analysis. It is not necessarily desirable that the railway should be required to compensate those who suffer damage by fires caused by railway engines. I need not show here that, if the railway could make a bargain with everyone having property adjoining the railway line and there were no costs involved in making such bargains, it would not matter whether the railway was liable for damage caused by fires or not. This question has been treated at length in earlier sections. The problem is whether it would be desirable to make the railway liable in conditions in which it is too expensive for such bargains to be made. Pigou clearly thought it was desirable to force the railway to pay compensation and it is easy to see the kind of argument that would have led him to this conclusion. Suppose a railway is considering whether to run an additional train or to increase the speed of an existing train or to install spark-preventing devices on its engines. If the railway were not liable for fire damage, then, when making these decisions, it would not take into account as a cost the increase in damage resulting from the additional train or the faster train or the failure to install spark-preventing devices. This is the source of the divergence between private and social net products. It results in the railway performing acts which will lower the value of total production – and which it would not do if it were liable for the damage. This can be shown by means of an arithmetical example.

Consider a railway, which is *not* liable for damage by fires caused by sparks from its engines, which runs two trains per day on a certain line. Suppose that running one train per day would enable the railway to perform services worth $150 per annum and running two trains a day would enable the railway to perform services worth $250 per annum. Suppose further that the cost of running one train is $50 per annum and two trains $100 per annum. Assuming perfect competition, the cost equals the fall in the value of production elsewhere due to the employment of additional factors of production by the railway. Clearly the railway would find it profitable to run two trains per day. But suppose that running one train per day would destroy by fire crops worth (on an average over the year) $60 and two trains a day would result in the destruction of crops worth $120. In these circumstances running one train per day would raise the value of total production but the running of a second train would reduce the value of total production. The second train would enable additional railway services worth $100 per annum to be performed. But the fall in the value of production elsewhere would be $110 per annum; $50 as a result of the employment of additional factors of production and $60 as a result of the destruction of crops. Since it would be better if the second train were not run and since it would not run if the railway were liable for damage caused to crops, the conclusion that the railway should be made liable for the damage seems irresistible. Undoubtedly it is this kind of reasoning which underlies the Pigovian position.

The conclusion that it would be better if the second train did not run is correct. The conclusion that it is desirable that the railway should be made liable for the damage it causes is wrong. Let us change our assumption concerning the rule of liability. Suppose that the railway is liable for damage from fires caused by sparks from the engine. A farmer on lands adjoining the railway is then in the position that, if his crop is destroyed by fires caused by the railway, he will receive the market price from the railway; but if his crop is not damaged, he will receive the market price by sale. It therefore becomes a matter of indifference to him whether his crop is damaged by fire or not. The position is very different when the railway is *not* liable. Any crop destruction through railway-caused fires would then reduce the receipts of the farmer. He would therefore take out of cultivation any land for which the damage is likely to be greater than the net return of the land (for reasons explained at length in Section III). A change from a regime in which the railway is *not* liable for damage to one in which it *is* liable is likely therefore to lead to an increase in the amount of cultivation on lands adjoining the railway. It will also, of course, lead to an increase in the amount of crop destruction due to railway-caused fires.

Let us return to our arithmetical example. Assume that, with the changed rule of liability, there is a doubling in the amount of crop destruction due to railway-caused fires. With one train per day, crops worth $120 would be destroyed each year and two trains per day would lead to the destruction of crops worth $240. We saw previously that it would not be profitable to run the second train if the railway had to pay $60 per annum as compensation for damage. With damage at $120 per annum the loss from running the second train would be $60 greater. But now let us consider the first train. The value of the transport services furnished by the first train is $150. The cost of running the train is $50. The amount that the railway would have to pay out as compensation for damage is $120. It follows that it would not be profitable to run any trains. With the figures in our example we reach the following result: if the railway is not liable for fire-damage, two trains per day would be run; if the railway is liable for fire-damage, it would cease operations altogether. Does this mean that it is better that there should be no railway? This question can be resolved by considering what would happen to the value of total production if it were decided to exempt the railway from liability for fire-damage, thus bringing it into operation (with two trains per day).

The operation of the railway would enable transport services worth $250 to be performed. It would also mean the employment of factors of production which would reduce the value of production elsewhere by $100. Furthermore it would mean the destruction of crops worth $120. The coming of the railway will also have led to the abandonment of cultivation of some land. Since we know that, had this land been cultivated, the value of the crops destroyed by fire would have been $120, and since it is unlikely that the total crop on this land would have been destroyed, it seems reasonable to suppose that the value of the crop yield on this land would have been higher than this. Assume it would have been $160. But the abandonment of cultivation would have released factors of production for employment elsewhere. All we know is that the amount by which the value of production elsewhere will increase will be less than $160. Suppose that it is $150. Then the gain from operating the railway would be $250 (the value of the transport services) minus $100 (the cost of the factors of production) minus $120 (the value of crops destroyed by fire) minus $160 (the fall in the value of crop production due to the abandonment of cultivation) plus $150 (the value of production elsewhere of the released factors of production). Overall, operating the railway will increase the value of total production by $20. With these figures it is clear that it is better that the railway should not be liable for the damage it causes, thus enabling it to operate profitably. Of course, by altering the figures, it could be shown that there are other cases in which it would be desirable that the railway should be liable for the damage it causes. It is enough for my purpose to show that, from an economic point of view, a situation in which there is "uncompensated damage done to surrounding woods by sparks from railway engines" is not necessarily undesirable. Whether it is desirable or not depends on the particular circumstances.

How is it that the Pigovian analysis seems to give the wrong answer? The reason is that Pigou does not seem to have noticed that his analysis is dealing with an entirely different question. The analysis as such is correct. But it is quite illegitimate for Pigou to draw the particular conclusion he does. The question at issue is not whether it is desirable to run an additional train or a faster train or to install smoke-preventing devices; the question at issue is whether it is desirable to have a system in which the railway has to compensate those who suffer damage from the fires which it causes or one in which the railway does not have to compensate them. When an economist is comparing alternative social arrangements, the proper procedure is to compare the total social product yielded by these different arrangements. The comparison of private and social products is neither here nor there. A simple example will demonstrate this. Imagine a town in which there are traffic lights. A motorist approaches an intersection and stops because the light is red. There are no cars approaching the intersection on the other street. If the motorist ignored the red signal, no accident would occur and the total product would increase because the motorist would arrive earlier at his destination. Why does he not do this? The reason is that if he ignored the light he would be fined. The private product from crossing the street is less than the social product. Should we conclude from this that the total product would be greater if there were no fines for failing to obey traffic signals? The Pigovian analysis shows us that it is possible to conceive of better worlds than the one in which we live. But the problem is to devise practical arrangements which will correct defects in one part of the system without causing more serious harm in other parts.

I have examined in considerable detail one example of a divergence between private and social products and I do not propose to make any further examination of Pigou's analytical system. But the main discussion of the problem considered in this article is to be found in Part II, Chapter 9 of Pigou's book dealing with his second class of divergence and it is of interest to see how Pigou develops his argument. Pigou's own description of this second class of divergence was quoted at the beginning of this section. Pigou distinguishes between the case in which a person renders services for which he receives no payment and the case in which a person renders disservices and compensation is not given to the injured parties. Our main attention has, of course, centred on this second case. It is therefore rather astonishing to find, as was pointed out to me by Professor Francesco Forte, that the problem of the smoking chimney – the "stock instance"[44] or "classroom example"[45] of the second case – is used by Pigou as an example of the first case (services rendered without payment) and is never mentioned, at any rate explicitly, in connection with the second case.[46] Pigou points out that factory owners who devote resources to preventing their chimneys from smoking render services for which they receive no payment. The implication, in the light of Pigou's discussion later in the chapter, is that a factory owner with a smokey chimney should be given a bounty to induce him to install smoke-preventing devices. Most modern economists would suggest that the owner of the factory with the smokey chimney should be taxed. It seems a pity that economists (apart from Professor Forte) do not seem to have noticed this feature of Pigou's treatment since a realisation that the problem could be tackled in either of these two ways would probably have led to an explicit recognition of its reciprocal nature.

In discussing the second case (disservices without compensation to those damaged), Pigou says that they are rendered "when the owner of a site in a residential quarter of a city builds a factory there and so destroys a great part of the amenities of neighbouring sites; or, in a less degree, when he uses his site in such a way as to spoil the lighting of the house opposite; or when he invests resources in erecting buildings in a crowded centre, which by contracting the air-space and the playing room of the neighbourhood, tend to injure the health and efficiency of the families living there."[47] Pigou is, of course, quite right to describe such actions as "uncharged disservices." But he is wrong when he describes these actions as "anti-social."[48] They may or may not be. It is necessary to weigh the harm against the good that will result. Nothing could be more "anti-social" than to oppose any action which causes any harm to anyone.

The example with which Pigou opens his discussion of "uncharged disservices" is not, as I have indicated, the case of the smokey chimney but the case of the overrunning rabbits: ". . . incidental uncharged disservices are rendered to third parties when the game-preserving activities of one occupier involve the overrunning of a neighbouring occupier's land by rabbits. . . ." This example is of extraordinary interest, not so much because the economic analysis of the case is essentially any different from that of the other examples, but because of the peculiarities of the legal position and the light it throws on the part which economics can play in what is apparently the purely legal question of the delimitation of rights.

The problem of legal liability for the actions of rabbits is part of the general subject of liability for animals.[49] I will, although with reluctance, confine my discussion to rabbits. The early cases relating to rabbits concerned the relations between the lord of the manor and commoners, since, from the thirteenth century on, it became usual for the lord of the manor to stock the commons with conies (rabbits), both for the sake of the meat and the fur. But in 1597, in *Boulston's* case, an action was brought by one landowner against a neighbouring landowner, alleging that the defendant had made coney-burrows and that the conies had increased and had destroyed the plaintiff's corn. The action failed for the reason that

. . . so soon as the coneys come on his neighbor's land he may kill them, for they are ferae naturae, and he who makes the coney-burrows has no property in them, and he shall not be punished for the damage which the coneys do in which he has no property, and which the other may lawfully kill.[50]

As *Boulston's* case has been treated as binding – Bray, J., in 1919, said that he was not aware that *Boulston's* case has ever been overruled or questioned[51] – Pigou's rabbit example undoubtedly represented the legal position at the time *The Economics of Welfare* was written.[52] And in this case, it is not far from the truth to say that the state of affairs which Pigou describes came about because of an absence of Government action (at any rate in the form of statutory enactments) and was the result of "natural" tendencies.

Nonetheless, *Boulston's* case is something of a legal curiousity and Professor Williams makes no secret of his distaste for this decision:

> The conception of liability in nuisance as being based upon owner-ship is the result, apparently, of a confusion with the action of cattle-trespass, and runs counter both to principle and to the medieval authorities on the escape of water, smoke and filth. . . . The pre-requisite of any satisfactory treatment of the subject is the final abandonment of the pernicious doctrine in *Boulston's* case. . . . Once *Boulston's* case disappears, the way will be clear for a rational restate-ment of the whole subject, on lines that will harmonize with the principles prevailing in the rest of the law of nuisance.[53]

The judges in *Boulston's* case were, of course, aware that their view of the matter depended on distinguishing this case from one involving nuisance:

> This cause is not like to the cases put, on the other side, of erecting a lime-kiln, dye-house, or the like; for there the annoyance is by the act of the parties who make them; but it is not so here, for the conies of themselves went into the plaintiff's land, and he might take them when they came upon his land, and make profit of them.[54]

Professor Williams comments:

> Once more the atavistic idea is emerging that the animals are guilty and not the landowner. It is not, of course, a satisfactory principle to introduce into a modern law of nuisance. If A. erects a house or plants a tree so that the rain runs or drips from it on to B.'s land, this is A.'s act for which he is liable; but if A. introduces rabbits into his land so that they escape from it into B.'s, this is the act of the rabbits for which A. is not liable – such is the specious distinction resulting from *Boulston's* case.[55]

It has to be admitted that the decision in *Boulston's* case seems a little odd. A man may be liable for damage caused by smoke or unpleasant smells, without it being necessary to determine whether he owns the smoke or the smell. And the rule in *Boulston's* case has not always been followed in cases dealing with other animals. For example, in *Bland v. Yates*,[56] it was decided that an injunction could be granted to prevent someone from keeping an *unusual and excessive* collection of manure in which flies bred and which infested a neighbour's house. The question of who owned the flies was not raised. An economist would not wish to object because legal reasoning sometimes appears a little odd. But there is a sound economic reason for supporting Professor Williams' view that the problem of liability for animals (and particularly rabbits) should be brought within the ordinary law of nuisance. The reason is not that the man who harbours rabbits is solely responsible for the damage; the man whose crops are eaten is equally responsible. And given that the costs of market transactions make a rearrangement of rights impossible, unless we know the particular circumstances, we cannot say whether it is desirable or not to make the man who harbours rabbits responsible for the damage committed by the rabbits on neighbouring properties. The objection to the rule in *Boulston's* case is that, under it, the harbourer of rabbits can *never* be liable. It fixes the rule of liability at one pole: and this is as undesirable, from an economic point of view, as fixing the rule at the other pole and making the harbourer of rabbits always liable. But, as we saw in Section VII, the law of nuisance, as it is in fact handled by the courts, is flexible and allows for a comparison of the utility of an act with the harm it produces. As Professor Williams says: "The whole law of nuisance is an attempt to reconcile and compromise between conflicting interests. . . ."[57] To bring the problem of rabbits within the ordinary law of nuisance would not mean *inevitably* making the harbourer of rabbits liable for damage committed by the rabbits. This is not to say that the sole task of the courts in such cases is to make a comparison between the harm and the utility of an act. Nor is it to be expected that the courts will always decide correctly after making such a comparison. But unless the courts act very foolishly, the ordinary law of nuisance would seem likely to give economically more satisfactory results than adopting a rigid rule. Pigou's case of the overrunning rabbits affords an excellent example of how problems of law and economics are interrelated, even though the correct policy to follow would seem to be different from that envisioned by Pigou.

Pigou allows one exception to his conclusion that there is a divergence between private and social products in the rabbit example. He adds: ". . . unless . . . the two occupiers stand in the relation of landlord and tenant, so that compensation is given in an adjustment of the rent."[58] This qualification is rather surprising since Pigou's first class of divergence is largely concerned with the difficulties of drawing up satisfactory contracts between landlords and tenants. In fact, all the recent cases on the problem of rabbits cited by Professor Williams involved disputes between landlords and tenants concerning sporting rights.[59] Pigou seems to make a distinction between the case in which no contract is possible (the second class) and that in which the contract is unsatisfactory (the first class). Thus he says that the second class of divergences between private and social net product

> cannot, like divergences due to tenancy laws, be mitigated by a modification of the contractual relation between any two contracting parties, because the divergence arises out of a service or disservice rendered to persons other than the contracting parties.[60]

But the reason why some activities are not the subject of contracts is exactly the same as the reason why some contracts are commonly unsatisfactory – it would cost too much to put the matter right. Indeed, the two cases are really the same since the contracts are unsatisfactory because they do not cover certain activities. The exact bearing of the discussion of the first class of divergence on Pigou's main argument is difficult to discover. He shows that in some circumstances contractual relations between landlord and tenant may result in a divergence between private and social products.[61] But he also goes on to show that government-enforced compensation schemes and rent-controls will also produce divergences.[62] Furthermore, he shows that, when the government is in a similar position to a private landlord, e.g. when granting a franchise to a public utility, exactly the same difficulties arise as when private individuals are involved.[63] The discussion is interesting but I have been unable to discover what general conclusions about economic policy, if any, Pigou expects us to draw from it.

Indeed, Pigou's treatment of the problems considered in this article is extremely elusive and the discussion of his views raises almost insuperable difficulties of interpretation. Consequently it is impossible to be sure that one has understood what Pigou really meant. Nevertheless, it is difficult to resist the conclusion, extraordinary though this may be in an economist of Pigou's stature, that the main source of this obscurity is that Pigou had not thought his position through.

IX The Pigovian tradition

It is strange that a doctrine as faulty as that developed by Pigou should have been so influential, although part of its success has probably been due to the lack of clarity in the exposition. Not being clear, it was never clearly wrong. Curiously enough, this obscurity in the source has not prevented the emergence of a fairly well-defined oral tradition. What economists think they learn from Pigou, and what they tell their students, which I term the Pigovian tradition, is reasonably clear. I propose to show the inadequacy of this Pigovian tradition by demonstrating that both the analysis and the policy conclusions which it supports are incorrect.

I do not propose to justify my view as to the prevailing opinion by copious references to the literature. I do this partly because the treatment in the literature is usually so fragmentary, often involving little more than a reference to Pigou plus some explanatory comment, that detailed examination would be inappropriate. But the main reason for this lack of reference is that the doctrine, although based on Pigou, must have been largely the product of an oral tradition. Certainly economists with whom I have discussed these problems have shown a unanimity of opinion which is quite remarkable considering the meagre treatment accorded this subject in the literature. No doubt there are some economists who do not share the usual view but they must represent a small minority of the profession.

The approach to the problems under discussion is through an examination of the value of physical production. The private product is the value of the additional product resulting from a particular activity of a business. The social product equals the private product minus the fall in the value of production elsewhere for which no compensation is paid by the business. Thus, if 10 units of a factor (and no other factors) are used by a business to make a certain product with a value of $105; and the owner of this factor is not compensated for their use, which he is unable to prevent; and these 10 units of the factor would yield products in their best alternative use worth $100; then, the social product is $105 minus $100 or $5. If the business now pays for one unit of the factor and its price equals the value of its marginal product, then the social product rises to $15. If two units are paid for, the social product rises to $25 and so on until it reaches $105 when all units of the factor are paid for. It is not difficult to see why economists have so readily accepted this rather odd procedure. The analysis focuses on the individual business decision and since the use of certain resources is not allowed for in costs, receipts are reduced by the same amount. But, of course, this means that the value of the social product has no social significance whatsoever. It seems to me preferable to use the opportunity cost concept and to approach these problems by comparing the value of the product yielded by factors in alternative uses or by alternative arrangements. The main advantage of a pricing system is that it leads to the employment of factors in places where the value of the product yielded is greatest and does so at less cost than alternative systems (I leave aside that a pricing system also eases the problem of the redistribution of income). But if through some God-given natural harmony factors flowed to the places where the value of the product yielded was greatest without any use of the pricing system and consequently there was no compensation, I would find it a source of surprise rather than a cause for dismay.

The definition of the social product is queer but this does not mean that the conclusions for policy drawn from the analysis are necessarily wrong. However, there are bound to be dangers in an approach which diverts attention from the basic issues and there can be little doubt that it has been responsible for some of the errors in current doctrine. The belief that it is desirable that the business which causes harmful effects should be forced to compensate those who suffer damage (which was exhaustively discussed in Section VIII in connection with Pigou's railway sparks example) is undoubtedly the result of not comparing the total product obtainable with alternative social arrangements.

The same fault is to be found in proposals for solving the problem of harmful effects by the use of taxes or bounties. Pigou lays considerable stress on this solution although he is, as usual, lacking in detail and qualified in his support.[64] Modern economists tend to think exclusively in terms of taxes and in a very precise way. The tax should be equal to the damage done and should therefore vary with the amount of the harmful effect. As it is not proposed that the proceeds of the tax should be paid to those suffering the damage, this solution is not the same as that which would force a business to pay compensation to those damaged by its actions, although economists generally do not seem to have noticed this and tend to treat the two solutions as being identical.

Assume that a factory which emits smoke is set up in district previously free from smoke pollution, causing damage valued at $100 per annum. Assume that the taxation solution is adopted and that the factory owner is taxed $100 per annum as long as the factory emits the smoke. Assume further that a smoke-preventing device costing $90 per annum to run is available. In these circumstances, the smoke-preventing device would be installed. Damage of $100 would have been avoided at an expenditure of $90 and the factory-owner would be better off by $10 per annum. Yet the position achieved may not be optimal. Suppose that those who suffer the damage could avoid it by moving to other locations or by taking various precautions which would cost them, or be equivalent to a loss in income of, $40 per annum. Then there would be a gain in the value of production of $50 if the factory continued to emit its smoke and those now in the district moved elesewhere or made other adjustments to avoid the damage. If the factory owner is to be made to pay a tax equal to the damage caused, it would clearly be desirable to institute double tax system and to make residents of the district pay an amount equal to the additional cost incurred by the factory owner (or the consumers of his products) in order to avoid the damage. In these conditions, people would not stay in the district or would take other measures to prevent the damage from occurring, when the costs of doing so were less than the costs that would be incurred by the producer to reduce the damage (the producer's object, of course, being not so much to reduce the damage as to reduce the tax payments). A tax system which was confined to a tax on the producer for damage caused would tend to lead to unduly high costs being incurred for the prevention of damage. Of course this could be avoided if it were possible to base the tax, not on the damage caused, but on the fall in the value of production (in its widest sense) resulting from the emission of smoke. But to do so would require a detailed knowledge of individual preferences and I am unable to imagine how the data needed for such a taxation system could be assembled. Indeed, the proposal to solve the smoke-pollution and similar problems by the use of taxes bristles with difficulties: the problem of calculation, the difference between average and marginal damage, the interrelations between the damage suffered on different properties, etc. But it is unnecessary to examine these problems here. It is enough for my purpose to show that, even if the tax is exactly adjusted to equal the damage that would be done to neighboring properties as a result of the emission of each additional puff of smoke, the tax would not necessarily bring about optimal conditions. An increase in the number of people living or of business operating in the vicinity of the smoke-emitting factory will increase the amount of harm produced by a given emission of smoke. The tax that would be imposed would therefore increase with an increase in the number of those in the vicinity. This will tend to lead to a decrease in the value of production of the factors employed by the factory, either because a reduction in production due to the tax will result in factors being used elsewhere in ways which are less valuable, or because factors will be diverted to produce means for reducing the amount of smoke emitted. But people deciding to establish themselves in the vicinity of the factory will not take into account this fall in the value of production which results from their presence. This failure to take into account costs imposed on others is comparable to the action of a factory-owner in not taking into account the harm resulting from his emission of smoke. Without the tax, there may be too much smoke and too few people in the vicinity of the factory; but with the tax there may be too little smoke and too many people in the vicinity of the factory. There is no reason to suppose that one of these results is necessarily preferable.

I need not devote much space to discussing the similar error involved in the suggestion that smoke producing factories should, by means of zoning regulations, be removed from the districts in which the smoke causes harmful effects. When the change in the location of the factory results in a reduction in production, this obviously needs to be taken into account and weighed against the harm which would result from the factory remaining in that location. The aim of such regulation should not be to eliminate smoke pollution but rather to secure the optimum amount of smoke pollution, this being the amount which will maximise the value of production.

X   A change of approach

It is my belief that the failure of economists to reach correct conclusions about the treatment of harmful effects cannot be ascribed simply to a few slips in analysis. It stems from basic defects in the current approach to problems of welfare economics. What is needed is a change of approach.

Analysis in terms of divergencies between private and social products concentrates attention on particular deficiencies in the system and tends to nourish the belief that any measure which will remove the deficiency is necessarily desirable. It diverts attention from those other changes in the system which are inevitably associated with the corrective measure, changes which may well produce more harm than the original deficiency. In the preceding sections of this article, we have seen many examples of this. But it is not necessary to approach the problem in this way. Economists who study problems of the firm habitually use an opportunity cost approach and compare the receipts obtained from a given combination of factors with alternative business arrangements. It would seem desirable to use a similar approach when dealing with questions of economic policy and to compare the total product yielded by alternative social arrangements. In this article, the analysis has been confined, as is usual in this part of economics, to comparisons of the value of production, as measured by the market. But it is, of course, desirable that the choice between different social arrangements for the solution of economic problems should be carried out in broader terms than this and that the total effect of these arrangements in all spheres of life should be taken into account. As Frank H. Knight has so often emphasised, problems of welfare economics must ultimately dissolve into a study of aesthetics and morals.

A second feature of the usual treatment of the problems discussed in this article is that the analysis proceeds in terms of a comparison between a state of *laissez-faire* and some kind of ideal world. This approach inevitably leads to a looseness of thought since the nature of the alternatives being compared is never clear. In a state of *laissez-faire*, is there a monetary, a legal or a political system and if so, what are they? In an ideal world, would there be a monetary, a legal or a political system and if so, what would they be? The answers to all these questions are shrouded in mystery and every man is free to draw whatever conclusions he likes. Actually very little analysis is required to show that an ideal world is better than a state of *laissez-faire*, unless the definitions of a state of *laissez-faire* and an ideal world happen to be the same. But the whole discussion is largely irrelevant for questions of economic policy since whatever we may have in mind as our ideal world, it is clear that we have not yet discovered how to get to it from where we are. A better approach would seem to be to start our analysis with a situation approximating that which actually exists, to examine the effects of a proposed policy change and to attempt to decide whether the new situation would be, in total, better or worse than the original one. In this way, conclusions for policy would have some relevance to the actual situation.

A final reason for the failure to develop a theory adequate to handle the problem of harmful effects stems from a faulty concept of a factor of production. This is usually thought of as a physical entity which the businessman acquires and uses (an acre of land, a ton of fertiliser) instead of as a right to perform certain (physical) actions. We may speak of a person owning land and using it as a factor of production but what the land-owner in fact possesses is the right to carry out a circumscribed list of actions. The rights of a land-owner are not unlimited. It is not even always possible for him to remove the land to another place, for instance, by quarrying it. And although it may be possible for him to exclude some people from using "his" land, this may not be true of others. For example, some people may have the right to cross the land. Furthermore, it may or may not be possible to erect certain types of buildings or to grow certain crops or to use particular drainage systems on the land. This does not come about simply because of government regulation. It would be equally true under the common law. In fact it would be true under any system of law. A system in which the rights of individuals were unlimited would be one in which there were no rights to acquire.

If factors of production are thought of as rights, it becomes easier to understand that the right to do something which has a harmful effect (such as the creation of smoke, noise, smells, etc.) is also a factor of production. Just as we may use a piece of land in such a way as to prevent someone else from crossing it, or parking his car, or building his house upon it, so we may use it in such a way as to deny him a view or quiet or unpolluted air. The cost of exercising a right (of using a factor of production) is always the loss which is suffered elsewhere in consequence of the exercise of that right – the inability to cross land, to park a car, to build a house, to enjoy a view, to have peace and quiet or to breathe clean air.

It would clearly be desirable if the only actions performed were those in which what was gained was worth more than what was lost. But in choosing between social arrangements within the context of which individual decisions are made, we have to bear in mind that a change in the existing system which will lead to an improvement in some decisions may well lead to a worsening of others. Furthermore, we have to take into account the costs involved in operating the various social arrangements (whether it be the working of a market or of a government department), as well as the costs involved in moving to a new system. In devising and choosing between social arrangements we should have regard for the total effect. This, above all, is the change in approach which I am advocating.

Notes

1 This article, although concerned with a technical problem of economic analysis, arose out of the study of the Political Economy of Broadcasting which I am now conducting. The argument of the present article was implicit in a previous article dealing with the problem of allocating radio and television frequencies (The Federal Communications Commission, 2 J. Law & Econ. [1959]) but comments which I have received seemed to suggest that it would be desirable to deal with the question in a more explicit way and without reference to the original problem for the solution of which the analysis was developed.
2 Coase, The Federal Communications Commission, 2 J. Law & Econ. 26–27 (1959).

3 G. J. Stigler, *The Theory of Price* 105 (1952).
4 The argument in the text has proceeded on the assumption that the alternative to cultivation of the crop is abandonment of cultivation altogether. But this need not be so. There may be crops which are less liable to damage by cattle but which would not be as profitable as the crop grown in the absence of damage. Thus, if the cultivation of a new crop would yield return to the farmer of $1 instead of $2, and the size of the herd which would cause $3 damage with the old crop would cause $1 damage with the new crop, it would be profitable to the cattle-raiser to pay any sum less than $2 to induce the farmer to change his crop (since this would reduce damage liability from $3 to $1) and it would be profitable for the farmer to do so if the amount received was more than $1 (the reduction in his return caused by switching crops). In fact, there would be room for a mutually satisfactory bargain in all cases in which a change of crop would reduce the amount of damage by more than it reduces the value of the crop (excluding damage) – in all cases, that is, in which a change in the crop cultivated would lead to an increase in the value of production.
5 See Gale on Easements 237–39 (13th ed. M. Bowles 1959).
6 See Fontainebleu Hotel Corp. v. Forty-Five Twenty-Five, Inc., 114 So. 2d 357 (1959).
7 11 Ch. D. 852 (1879).
8 Auscultation is the act of listening by ear or stethoscope in order to judge by sound the condition of the body.
9 Note that what is taken into account is the change in income after allowing for alterations in methods of production, location, character of product, etc.
10 L. R. 5 Eq. 166 (1867–1868).
11 4 C.P.D. 172 (1878–1879).
12 25 Q.B.D. 481 (1890).
13 It may be asked why a lost grant could not also be presumed in the case of the confectioner who had operated one mortar for more than 60 years. The answer is that until the doctor built the consulting room at the end of his garden there was no nuisance. So the nuisance had not continued for many years. It is true that the confectioner in his affidavit referred to "an invalid lady who occupied the house upon one occasion, about 30 years before" who "requested him if possible to discontinue the use of the mortars before eight o'clock in the morning" and that there was some evidence that the garden wall had been subjected to vibration. But the court had little difficulty in disposing of this line of argument: "... this vibration, even if it existed at all, was so slight, and the complaint, if it can be called a complaint, of the invalid lady ... was of so trifling a character, that ... the Defendant's acts would not have given rise to any proceeding either at law or in equity" (11 Ch.D. 863). That is, the confectioner had not committed a nuisance until the doctor built his consulting room.
14 See Coase, "The Nature of the Firm", 4 *Economica*, New Series, 386 (1937). Reprinted in *Readings in Price Theory*, 331 (1952).
15 For reasons explained in my earlier article, see *Readings in Price Theory*, n. 14 at 337.
16 See W. L. Prosser, *The Law of Torts* 398–99, 412 (2d ed. 1955). The quotation about the ancient case concerning candle-making is taken from Sir James Fitzjames Stephen, A General View of the Criminal Law of England 106 (1890).

Sir James Stephen gives no reference. He perhaps had in mind *Rex. v. Ronkett*, included in Seavey, Keeton and Thurston, *Cases on Torts* 604 (1950). A similar view to that expressed by Prosser is to be found in F. V. Harper and F. James, *The Law of Torts* 67–74 (1956); Restatement, Torts §§826, 827 and 828.

17 See Winfield on Torts 541–48 (6th ed. T. E. Lewis 1954); Salmond on the Law of Torts 181–90 (12th ed. R. F. V. Heuston 1957); H. Street, The Law of Torts 221–29 (1959).

18 *Attorney General v. Doughty*, 2 Ves. Sen. 453, 28 Eng. Rep. 290 (Ch. 1752). Compare in this connection the statement of an American judge, quoted in Prosser, op. cit. supra n. 16 at 413 n. 54: "Without smoke, Pittsburgh would have remained a very pretty village," Musmanno, J., in Versailles Borough v. McKeesport Coal & Coke Co., 1935, 83 Pitts. Leg. J. 379, 385.

19 10 C.B. (N.S.) 268, 142 Eng. Rep. 445 (1861); 13 C.B. (N.S.) 841, 143 Eng. Rep. 332 (1863).

20 See Gale on Easements 238, n. 6 (13th ed. M. Bowles 1959).

21 11 Ch.D. 865 (1879).

22 Salmond on the Law of Torts 182 (12th ed. R.F.V. Heuston 1957).

23 C. M. Haar, *Land-Use Planning, A Casebook on the Use, Misuse, and Re-use of Urban Land* 95 (1959).

24 See, for example, *Rushmer v. Polsue and Alfieri, Ltd.* [1906] 1 Ch. 234, which deals with the case of a house in a quiet situation in a noisy district.

25 [1913] 1 Ch. 269.

26 [1938] 1 Ch. 1.

27 See 30 Halsbury, *Laws of England* 690–91 (3d ed. 1960), Article on Public Authorities and Public Officers.

28 See Prosser, op. cit. supra n. 16 at 421; Harper and James, op. cit. supra n. 16 at 86–87.

29 Supreme Court of Georgia. 193 Ga. 862, 20 S.E. 2d 245 (1942).

30 178 Ga. 514, 173 S.E. 817 (1934).

31 116 Ga. 64, 42 S.E. 315 (1902).

32 270 Mass. 511, 523, 170 N.E. 385, 390 (1930).

33 See Sir Alfred Denning, *Freedom Under the Law* 71 (1949).

34 M. B. Cairns, *The Law of Tort in Local Government* 28–32 (1954).

35 A. C. Pigou, *The Economics of Welfare* 183 (4th ed. 1932). My references will all be to the fourth edition but the argument and examples examined in this article remained substantially unchanged from the first edition in 1920 to the fourth in 1932. A large part (but not all) of this nalysis had appeared previously in *Wealth and Welfare* (1912).

36 *Id.* at xii.

37 *Id.* at 127–30.

38 In *Wealth and Welfare*, Pigou attributes the "optimism" to Adam Smith himself and not to his followers. He there refers to the "highly optimistic theory of Adam Smith that the national dividend, in given circumstances of demand and supply, tends 'naturally' to a maximum" (p. 104).

39 Pigou, op. cit. supra n. 35 at 129–30.

40 *Id.* at 134.

41 See 31 Halsbury, *Laws of England* 474–75 (3d ed. 1960), Article on Railways and Canals, from which this summary of the legal position, and all quotations, are taken.

42 See 152 H.C. Deb. 2622–63 (1922); 161 H.C. Deb. 2935–55 (1923).
43 *Vaughan v. Taff Vale Railway Co.*, 3 H. and N. 743 (Ex. 1858) and 5 H. and N. 679 (Ex. 1860).
44 Sir Dennis Robertson, I *Lectures on Economic Principles* 162 (1957).
45 E. J. Mishan, "The Meaning of Efficiency in Economics," 189 *The Bankers' Magazine* 482 (June 1960).
46 Pigou, op. cit. supra n. 35 at 184.
47 *Id.* at 185–86.
48 *Id.* at 186 n.1. For similar unqualified statements see Pigou's lecture "Some Aspects of the Housing Problem" in B. S. Rowntree and A. C. Pigou, "Lectures on Housing," in 18 *Manchester Univ. Lectures* (1914).
49 See G. L. Williams, Liability for Animals – An Account of the Development and Present Law of Tortious Liability for Animals, Distress Damage Feasant and the Duty to Fence, in Great Britain, Northern Ireland and the Common Law Dominions (1939). Part Four, "The Action of Nuisance, in Relation to Liability for Animals," 236–62, is especially relevant to our discussion. The problem of liability for rabbits is discussed in this part, 238–47. I do not know how far the common law in the United States regarding liability for animals has diverged from that in Britain. In some Western States of the United States, the English common law regarding the duty to fence has not been followed, in part because "the considerable amount of open, uncleared land made it a matter of public policy to allow cattle to run at large" (Williams, op. cit. supra 227). This affords a good example of how a different set of circumstances may make it economically desirable to change the legal rule regarding the delimitation of rights.
50 5 Coke (Vol. 3) 104 b. 77 Eng. Rep., 216, 217.
51 See *Stearn v. Prentice Bros. Ltd.*, (1919) 1 KB, 395, 397.
52 I have not looked into recent cases. The legal position has also been modified by statutory enactments.
53 Williams, op. cit. supra n. 49 at 242, 258.
54 Boulston v. Hardy, Cro. Eliz., 547, 548, 77 Eng. Rep. 216.
55 Williams, op. cit. supra n. 49 at 243.
56 58 Sol. J. 612 (1913–1914).
57 Williams, op. cit. supra n. 49 at 259.
58 Pigou, op. cit. supra n. 35 at 185.
59 Williams, op. cit. supra n. 49 at 244–47.
60 Pigou, op. cit. supra n. 35 at 192.
61 *Id.* 174–75.
62 *Id.* 177–83.
63 *Id.* 175–77.
64 *Id.* 192–4, 381 and *Public Finance* 94–100 (3d ed. 1947).

6
Externality

James M. Buchanan and William C. Stubblebine

Externality has been, and is, central to the neo-classical critique of market organisation. In its various forms – external economies and diseconomies, divergencies between marginal social and marginal private cost or product, spillover and neighbourhood effects, collective or public goods – externality dominates theoretical welfare economics, and, in one sense, the theory of economic policy generally. Despite this importance and emphasis, rigorous definitions of the concept itself are not readily available in the literature. As Scitovosky has noted, "definitions of external economies are few and unsatisfactory".[1] The following seems typical:

> External effects exist in consumption whenever the shape or position of a man's indifference curve depends on the consumption of other men.
> [External effects] are present whenever a firm's production function depends in some way on the amounts of the inputs or outputs of another firm.[2]

It seems clear that operational and usable definitions are required.

In this paper, we propose to clarify the notion of externality by defining it rigorously and precisely. When this is done, several important, and often overlooked, conceptual distinctions follow more or less automatically. Specifically, we shall distinguish marginal and infra-marginal externalities, potentially relevant and irrelevant externalities, and Pareto-relevant and Pareto-irrelevant externalities. These distinctions are formally developed in Section I. As we shall demonstrate, the term, "externality", as generally used by economists, corresponds only to our definition of Pareto-relevant externality. There follows, in Section II,

138

an illustration of the basic points described in terms of a simple descriptive example. In Section III, some of the implications of our approach are discussed.

It is useful to limit the scope of the analysis at the outset. Much of the discussion in the literature has been concerned with the distinction between *technological* and *pecuniary* external effects. We do not propose to enter this discussion since it is not relevant for our purposes. We note only that, if desired, the whole analysis can be taken to apply only to technological externalities. Secondly, we shall find no cause for discussing production and consumption externalities separately. Essentially the same analysis appiies in either case. In what follows, "firms" may be substituted for "individuals" and "production functions" for "utility functions" without modifying the central conclusions. For expositional simplicity only, we limit the explicit discussion to consumption externalities.

I

We define an external effect, *an externality*, to be present when,

$$u^A = u^A(X_1, X_2, \ldots, X_m, Y_1). \tag{6.1}$$

This states that the utility of an individual, A, is dependent upon the "activities", $(X_1, X_2, \ldots, X_m)$, that are exclusively under his own control or authority, but also upon another single activity, Y_1, which is, by definition, under the control of a second individual, B, who is presumed to be a member of the same social group. We define an *activity* here as any distinguishable human action that may be measured, such as eating bread, drinking milk, spewing smoke into the air, dumping litter on the highways, giving to the poor, etc. Note that A's utility may, and will in the normal case, depend on other activities of B in addition to Y_1, and also upon the activities of other parties. That is, A's utility function may, in more general terms, include such variables as $(Y_2, Y_3, \ldots, Y_m; Z_1, Z_2, \ldots, Z_m)$. For analytical simplicity, however, we shall confine our attention to the effects of one particular activity, Y_1, as it affects the utility of A.

We assume that A will behave so as to maximise utility in the ordinary way, subject to the externally determined values for Y_1, and that he will modify the values for the X's, as Y_1 changes, so as to maintain a state of "equilibrium".

A marginal externality exists when,

$$u^A_{Y_1} \neq 0. \qquad (6.2)$$

Here, small u's are employed to represent the "partial derivatives" of the utility function of the individual designated by the superscript with respect to the variables designated by the subscript. Hence, $u^A_{Y_1} = \partial u^A / \partial Y_1$, assuming that the variation in Y_1 is evaluated with respect to a set of "equilibrium" values for the X's, adjusted to the given value for Y_1.

An infra-marginal externality holds at those points where,

$$u^A_{Y_1} = 0, \qquad (6.3)$$

and equation (6.1) holds.

These classifications can be broken down into economies and diseconomies: a marginal external economy existing when,

$$u^A_{Y_1} > 0, \qquad (6.2A)$$

that is, a small change in the activity undertaken by B will change the utility of A in the same direction; a marginal external diseconomy existing when,

$$u^A_{Y_1} < 0. \qquad (6.2B)$$

An infra-marginal external economy exists when for any given set of values for $(X_1, X_2, \ldots, X_m)$, say, $(C_1, C_2, \ldots, C_m)$,

$$u^A_{Y_1} = 0, \text{ and } \int_0^{Y_1} u^A_{Y_1} d_{Y_1} > 0. \qquad (6.3A)$$

This condition states that, while incremental changes in the extent of B's activity, Y_1, have no effect on A's utility, the total effect of B's action has increased A's utility. An infra-marginal diseconomy exists when equation (6.1) holds, and, for any given set of values for $(X_1, X_2, \ldots, X_m)$, say, $(C_1, C_2, \ldots, C_m)$, then,

$$u^A_{Y_1} = 0, \text{ and } \int_0^{Y_1} u^A_{Y_1} d_{Y_1} < 0. \qquad (6.3B)$$

Thus, small changes in B's activity do not change A's level of satisfaction, but the total effect of B's undertaking the activity in question is harmful to A.

We are able to classify the effects of *B*'s action, or potential action, on *A*'s utility by evaluating the "partial derivative" of *A*'s utility function with respect to Y_1 over all possible values for Y_1. In order to introduce the further distinctions between *relevant* and *irrelevant* externalities, however, it is necessary to go beyond consideration of *A*'s utility function. Whether or not a relevant externality exists depends upon the extent to which the activity involving the externality is carried out by the person empowered to take action, to make decisions. Since we wish to consider a single externality in isolation, we shall assume that *B*'s utility function includes only variables (activities) that are within his control, including Y_1. Hence, *B*'s utility function takes the form,

$$u^B = u^B(Y_1, Y_2, \ldots, Y_m). \tag{6.4}$$

Necessary conditions for utility maximisation by *B* are,

$$u^B_{Y_1} / u^B_{Y_j} = f^B_{Y_1} / f^B_{Y_j}, \tag{6.5}$$

where Y_j is used to designate the activity of *B* in consuming or utilising some numeraire commodity or service which is, by hypothesis, available on equal terms to *A*. The right-hand term represents the marginal rate of substitution in "production" or "exchange" confronted by *B*, the party taking action on Y_1, his production function being defined as,

$$f^B = f^B(Y_1, Y_2, \ldots, Y_m), \tag{6.6}$$

where inputs are included as activities along with outputs. In other words, the right-hand term represents the marginal cost of the activity, Y_1, to *B*. The equilibrium values for the Y_i's will be designated as Y_i's.

An externality is defined as *potentially relevant* when the activity, to the extent that it is actually performed, generates *any* desire on the part of the externally benefited (damaged) party (*A*) to modify the behaviour of the party empowered to take action (*B*) through trade, persuasion, compromise, agreement, convention, collective action, etc. An externality which, to the extent that it is performed, exerts no such influence is defined as *irrelevant*. Note that, so long as equation (6.1) holds, an externality remains; utility functions remain interdependent.

A potentially relevant marginal externality exists when,

$$u^A_{Y_1}\big|_{Y_1=\bar{Y}_1} \neq 0. \tag{6.7}$$

This is a potentially relevant marginal external economy when equation (6.7) is greater than zero, a diseconomy when equation (6.7) is less than zero. In either case, A is motivated, by B's performance of the activity, to make some effort to modify this performance, to increase the resources devoted to the activity when equation (6.7) is positive, to decrease the quantity of resources devoted to the activity when equation (6.7) is negative.

Infra-marginal externalities are, by definition, irrelevant for small changes in the scope of B's activity, Y_1. However, when large or discrete changes are considered, A is motivated to change B's behaviour with respect to Y_1 in all cases *except* that for which,

$$u_{Y_1}^A\big|_{Y_1=\bar{Y}_1} = 0, \text{ and}$$
$$u^A(C_1, C_2, \ldots, C_m, \bar{Y}_1) \geq u^A(C_1, C_2, \ldots, C_m, Y_1), \text{ for all}$$
$$Y_1 \neq \bar{Y}_1. \tag{6.8}$$

When equation (6.8) holds, A has achieved an absolute maximum of utility with respect to changes over Y_1, given any set of values for the X's. In more prosaic terms, A is satiated with respect to Y_1.[3] In all other cases, where infra-marginal external economies or diseconomies exist, A will have some desire to modify B's performance; the externality is potentially relevant. Whether or not this motivation will lead A to seek an expansion or contraction in the extent of B's performance of the activity will depend on the location of the infra-marginal region relative to the absolute maximum for any given values of the X's.[4]

Pareto relevance and irrelevance may now be introduced. The existence of a simple desire to modify the behaviour of another, defined as potential relevance, need not imply the ability to implement this desire. An externality is defined to be Pareto-relevant when the extent of the activity may be modified in such a way that the externally affected party, A, can be made better off without the acting party, B, being made worse off. That is to say, "gains from trade" characterise the Pareto-relevant externality, trade that takes the form of some change in the activity of B as his part of the bargain.

A marginal externality is Pareto-relevant when[5]

$$(-)u_{Y_1}^A/u_{X_j}^A > \left[u_{Y_1}^B/u_{Y_j}^B - f_{Y_1}^B/f_{Y_j}^B\right]_{Y_1=\bar{Y}_1} \text{ and when } u_{Y_1}^A/u_{X_j}^A < 0, \text{ and}$$
$$u_{Y_1}^A/u_{X_j}^A > (-)\left[u_{Y_1}^B/u_{Y_j}^B - f_{Y_1}^B/f_{Y_j}^B\right]_{Y_1=\bar{Y}_1} \text{ when } u_{Y_1}^A/u_{X_j}^A > 0. \tag{6.9}$$

In equation (6.9), X_j and Y_j are used to designate, respectively, the activities of A and B in consuming or in utilising some numeraire commodity or service that, by hypothesis, is available on identical terms to each of them. As is indicated by the transposition of signs in equation (6.9), the conditions for Pareto relevance differ as between external diseconomies and economies. This is because the "direction" of change desired by A on the part of B is different in the two cases. In stating the conditions for Pareto relevance under ordinary two-person trade, this point is of no significance since trade in one good flows only in one direction. Hence, absolute values can be used.

The condition, equation (6.9), states that $A's$ marginal rate of substitution between the activity, Y_1, and the numeraire activity must be greater than the "net" marginal rate of substitution between the activity and the numeraire activity for B. Otherwise, "gains from trade" would not exist between A and B.

Note, however, that when B has achieved utility-maximising equilibrium,

$$u^B_{Y_1}/u^B_{Y_j} = f^B_{Y_1}/f^B_{Y_j}. \tag{6.10}$$

That is to say, the marginal rate of substitution in consumption or utilisation is equated to the marginal rate of substitution in production or exchange, i.e., to marginal cost. When equation (6.10) holds, the terms in the brackets in equation (6.9) mutually cancel. Thus, potentially relevant marginal externalities are also Pareto-relevant when B is in utility-maximising equilibrium. Some trade is possible.

Pareto equilibrium is defined to be present when,

$$(-)u^A_{Y_1}/u^A_{X_j} = \left[u^B_{Y_1}/u^B_{Y_j} - f^B_{Y_1}/f^B_{Y_j}\right], \text{ and when } u^A_{Y_1}/u^A_{X_j} < 0, \text{ and}$$
$$u^A_{Y_1}/u^A_{X_j} = (-)\left[u^B_{Y_1}/u^B_{Y_j} - f^B_{Y_1}/f^B_{Y_j}\right] \text{ when } u^A_{Y_1}/u^A_{X_j} > 0. \tag{6.11}$$

Condition equation (6.11) demonstrates that marginal externalities may continue to exist, even in Pareto equilibrium, as here defined. This point may be shown by reference to the special case in which the activity in question may be undertaken at zero costs. Here Pareto equilibrium is attained when the marginal rates of substitution in consumption or utilisation for the two persons are precisely offsetting, that is, where their interests are strictly opposed, and *not* where the left-hand term vanishes.

What vanishes in Pareto equilibrium are the Pareto-relevant

externalities. It seems clear that, normally, economists have been referring only to what we have here called Pareto-relevant externalities when they have, implicitly or explicitly, stated that external effects are not present when a postion on the Pareto optimality surface is attained.[6]

For completeness, we must also consider those potentially relevant infra-marginal externalities. Refer to the discussion of these as summarised in equation (6.8) above. The question is now to determine whether or not, A, the externally affected party, can reach some mutually satisfactory agreement with B, the acting party, that will involve some discrete (non-marginal) change in the scope of the activity, Y_1. If, over some range, any range, of the activity, which we shall designate by $\triangle Y_1$, the rate of substitution between Y_1 and X_j for A exceeds the "net" rate of substitution for B, the externality is Pareto-relevant. The associated changes in the utilisation of the numeraire commodity must be equal for the two parties. Thus, for external economies, we have

$$\frac{\triangle u^A}{\triangle Y_1}\bigg/\frac{\triangle u^A}{\triangle X_j} > (-)\left[\frac{\triangle u^B}{\triangle Y_1}\bigg/\frac{\triangle u^B}{\triangle Y_j} - \frac{\triangle f^B}{\triangle Y_1}\bigg/\frac{\triangle f^B}{\triangle Y_j}\right]_{Y_1=\bar{Y}_1}, \text{ and the} \qquad (6.12)$$

same with the sign in parenthesis transposed for external diseconomies. The difference to be noted between equation (6.12) and equation (6.9) is that, with infra-marginal externalities, potential relevance need not imply Pareto relevance. The bracketed terms in (equation 6.12) need not sum to zero when B is in his private utility-maximising equilibrium.

We have remained in a two-person world, with one person affected by the single activity of a second. However, the analysis can readily be modified to incorporate the effects of this activity on a multi-person group. That is to say, B's activity, Y_1, may be allowed to affect several parties simultaneously, several A's, so to speak. In each case, the activity can then be evaluated in terms of its effects on the utility of each person. Nothing in the construction need be changed. The only stage in the analysis requiring modification explicitly to take account of the possibilities of multi-person groups being externally affected is that which involves the condition for Pareto relevance and Pareto equilibrium.

For a multi-person group $(A_1, A_2, \ldots, A_n)$, any one or all of whom may be externally affected by the activity, Y_1, of the single person, B, the condition for Pareto relevance is,

$$(-)\sum_{i=1}^{n} u_{Y_1}^{A_i} \Big/ u_{X_j}^{A_i} > \left[u_{Y_1}^{B} \Big/ u_{Y_j}^{B} - f_{Y_1}^{B} \Big/ f_{Y_j}^{B} \right]_{Y_1 = \bar{Y}_1} \text{ when } u_{Y_1}^{A_i} \Big/ u_{X_j}^{A_i} < 0, \text{ and,}$$

$$\sum_{i=1}^{n} u_{Y_1}^{A_i} \Big/ u_{X_j}^{A_i} > (-) \left[u_{Y_1}^{B} \Big/ u_{Y_j}^{B} - f_{Y_1}^{B} \Big/ f_{Y_j}^{B} \right]_{Y_1 = \bar{Y}_1} \text{ when } u_{Y_1}^{A_i} \Big/ u_{X_j}^{A_i} > 0. \qquad (6.9A)$$

That is, the summed marginal rates of substitution over the members of the externally affected group exceed the offsetting "net" marginal evaluation of the activity by *B*. Again, in private equilibrium for *B*, marginal externalities are Pareto-relevant, provided that we neglect the important element involved in the costs of organising group decisions. In the real world, these costs of organising group decisions (together with uncertainty and ignorance) will prevent realisation of some "gains from trade" – just as they do in organised markets. This is as true for two-person groups as it is for larger groups. But this does not invalidate the point that potential "gains from trade" are available. The condition for Pareto equilibrium and for the infra-marginal case summarised in equation (6.11) and equation (6.12) for the two-person model can readily be modified to allow for the externally affected multi-person group.

II

The distinctions developed formally in Section I may be illustrated diagrammatically and discussed in terms of a simple descriptive example. Consider two persons, *A* and *B*, who own adjoining units of residential property. Within limits to be noted, each person values privacy, which may be measured quantitatively in terms of a single criterion, the height of a fence that can be constructed along the common boundary line. We shall assume that *B*'s desire for privacy holds over rather wide limits. His utility increases with the height of the fence up to a reasonably high level. Up to a certain minimum height, *A*'s utility also is increased as the fence is made higher. Once this minimum height is attained, however, *A*'s desire for privacy is assumed to be fully satiated. Thus, over a second range, *A*'s total utility does not change with a change in the height of the fence. However, beyond a certain limit, *A*'s view of a mountain behind *B*'s property is progressively obscured as the fence goes higher. Over this third range, therefore, *A*'s utility is reduced as the fence is constructed to higher levels. Finally, *A* will once again become wholly indifferent to marginal changes in the fence's height when his view is totally blocked out.

We specify that *B* possesses the sole authority, the only legal right, to construct the fence between the two properties.

The preference patterns for *A* and for *B* are shown in Figure 6.1, which is drawn in the form of an Edgeworth-like box diagram. Note, however, that the origin for *B* is shown at the upper left rather than the upper right corner of the diagram as in the more normal usage. This modification is necessary here because only the numeraire good, measured along the ordinate, is strictly divisible between *A* and *B*. Both must adjust to the same height of fence, that is, to the same level of the activity creating the externality.

As described above, the indifference contours for *A* take the general shape shown by the curves *aa, a'a'*, while those for *B* assume the shapes, *bb, b'b'*. Note that these contours reflect the relative evaluations, for *A* and *B*, between money and the activity, Y_1. Since the costs of undertaking the activity, for *B*, are not incorporated in the diagram, the "contract locus" that might be derived from tangency points will have little

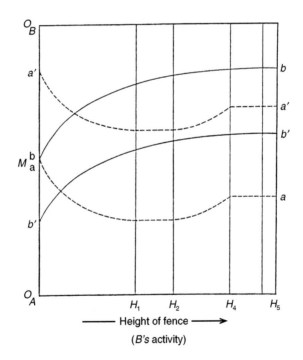

Figure 6.1

relevance except in the special case where the activity can be undertaken at zero costs.

Figure 6.2 depicts the marginal evaluation curves for *A* and *B*, as derived from the preference fields shown in Figure 6.1, along with some incorporation of costs. These curves are derived as follows: assume an initial distribution of "money" between *A* and *B*, say, that shown at *M* on Figure 6.1. The marginal evaluation of the activity for *A* is then derived by plotting the negatives (i.e., the mirror image) of the slopes of successive indifference curves attained by *A* as *B* is assumed to increase the height of the fence from zero. These values remain positive for a range, become zero over a second range, become negative for a third, and, finally, return to zero again.[7]

B's curves of marginal evaluation are measured downward from the upper horizontal axis or base line, for reasons that will become apparent. The derivation of *B*'s marginal evaluation curve is somewhat more complex than that for *A*. This is because *B*, who is the person authorised to undertake the action, in this case the building of the fence, must also bear the full costs. Thus, as *B* increases the scope of the activity, his real income, measured in terms of his remaining goods and services, is reduced. This change in the amount of remaining goods and services will, of course, affect his marginal evaluation of the activity in question.

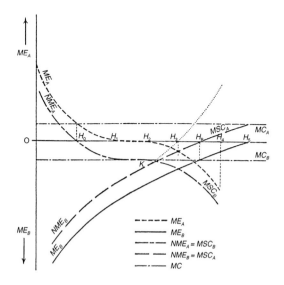

Figure 6.2

Thus, the marginal cost of building the fence will determine, to some degree, the marginal evaluation of the fence. This necessary interdependence between marginal evaluation and marginal cost complicates the use of simple diagrammatic models in finding or locating a solution. It need not, however, deter as from presenting the solution diagrammatically, if we postulate that the marginal evaluation curve, as drawn, is based on a single presumed cost relationship. This done, we may plot B's marginal evaluation of the activity from the negatives of the slopes of his indifference contours attained as he constructs the fence to higher and higher levels. B's marginal evaluation, shown in Figure 6.2, remains positive throughout the range to the point H_5, where it becomes zero.

The distinctions noted in Section I are easily related to the construction in Figure 6.2. To A, the party externally affected, B's potential activity in constructing the fence can be assessed independently of any prediction of B's actual behaviour. Thus, the activity of B would,

(1) exert marginal external economies which are potentially relevant over the range OH_1;
(2) exert infra-marginal external economies over the range H_1H_2, which are clearly irrelevant since no change in B's behaviour with respect to the extent of the activity would increase A's utility;
(3) exert marginal external diseconomies over the range H_2H_4 which are potentially relevant to A; and,
(4) exert infra-marginal external economies or diseconomies beyond H_4, the direction of the effect being dependent on the ratio between the total utility derived from privacy and the total reduction in utility derived from the obstructed view. In any case, the externality is potentially relevant.

To determine Pareto relevance, the extent of B's predicted performance must be determined. The necessary condition for B's attainment of "private" utility-maximising equilibrium is that marginal costs, which he must incur, be equal to his own marginal evaluation. For simplicity in Figure 6.2, we assume that marginal costs are constant, as shown by the curve, MC. Thus, B's position of equilibrium is shown at H_B, within the range of marginal external diseconomies for A. Here the externality imposed by B's behaviour is clearly Pareto-relevant: A can surely work out some means of compensating B in exchange for B's agreement to reduce the scope of the activity – in this example, to reduce the height of the fence between the two properties.

Diagrammatically, the position of Pareto equilibrium is shown at H_3 where the marginal evaluation of A is equal in absolute value, but negatively, to the "net" marginal evaluation of B, drawn as the curve NME_B. Only in this position are the conditions specified in equation (6.11), above, satisfied.[8]

III

Aside from the general classification of externalities that is developed, the approach here allows certain implications to be drawn, implications that have not, perhaps, been sufficiently recognised by some welfare economists.

The analysis makes it quite clear that externalities, external effects, may remain even in full Pareto equilibrium. That is to say, a position may be classified as Pareto-optimal or efficient despite the fact that, at the marginal, the activity of one individual externally affects the utility of another individual. Figure 6.2 demonstrates this point clearly. Pareto equilibrium is attained at H_3, yet B is imposing marginal external diseconomies on A.

This point has significant policy implications for it suggests that the observation of external effects, taken alone, cannot provide a basis for judgment concerning the desirability of some modification in an existing state of affairs. There is not a *prima facie* case for intervention in all cases where an externality is observed to exist.[9] The internal benefits from carrying out the activity, net of costs, may be greater than the external damage that is imposed on other parties.

In full Pareto equilibrium, of course, these internal benefits, measured in terms of some numeraire good, net of costs, must be just equal, at the margin, to the external damage that is imposed on other parties. This equilibrium will always be characterised by the strict opposition of interests of the two parties, one of which may be a multi-person group.

In the general case, we may say that, at full Pareto equilibrium, the presence of a marginal external diseconomy implies an offsetting marginal *internal* economy, whereas the presence of a marginal external economy implies an offsetting marginal *internal* diseconomy. In "private" equilibrium, as opposed to Pareto equilibrium, these net internal economies and diseconomies would, of course, be eliminated by the utility-maximising acting party. In Pareto equilibrium, these remain because the acting party is being compensated for "suffering" internal economies and diseconomies, that is, divergencies between "private" marginal costs and benefits, *measured in the absence of compensation.*

As a second point, it is useful to relate the whole analysis here to the more familiar Pigovian discussion concerning the divergence between marginal social cost (product) and marginal private cost (product). By saying that such a divergence exists, we are, in the terms of this paper, saying that a marginal externality exists. The Pigovian terminology tends to be misleading, however, in that it deals with the acting party to the exclusion of the externally affected party. It fails to take into account the fact that there are always two parties involved in a single externality relationship.[10] As we have suggested, a marginal externality is Pareto-relevant except in the position of Pareto equilibrium; gains from trade can arise. But there must be two parties to any trading arrangement. The externally affected party must compensate the acting party for modifying his behaviour. The Pigovian terminology, through its concentration on the decision-making of the acting party alone, tends to obscure the two-sidedness of the bargain that must be made.

To illustrate this point, assume that A, the externally affected party in our model, successfully secures, through the auspices of the "state", the levy of a marginal tax on B's performance of the activity, Y_1. Assume further that A is able to secure this change without cost to himself. The tax will increase the marginal cost of performing the activity for B, and, hence, will reduce the extent of the activity attained in B's "private" equilibrium. Let us now presume that this marginal tax is levied "correctly" on the basis of a Pigovian calculus; the rate of tax at the margin is made equal to the negative marginal evaluation of the activity to A. Under these modified conditions, the effective marginal cost, as confronted by B, may be shown by the curve designated as MSC_B in Figure 6.2. A new "private" equilibrium for B is shown at the quantity, H_3, the same level designated as Pareto equilibrium in our earlier discussion, if we neglect the disturbing interdependence between marginal evaluation and marginal costs. Attention solely to the decision calculus of B here would suggest, perhaps, that this position remains Pareto-optimal under these revised circumstances, and that it continues to qualify as a position of Pareto equilibrium. There is no divergence between marginal private cost and marginal social cost in the usual sense. However, the position, if attained in this manner, is clearly neither one of Pareto optimality, nor one that may be classified as Pareto equilibrium.

In this new "private" equilibrium for B,

$$u_{Y_1}^B \big/ u_{Y_j}^B = f_{Y_1}^B \big/ f_{Y_j}^B - u_{Y_1}^A \big/ u_{X_j}^A \,, \tag{6.13}$$

where u^A_{Y1}/u^A_{Xj} represents the marginal tax imposed on B as he performs the activity, Y_1. Recall the necessary condition for Pareto relevance defined in equation (6.9) above, which can now be modified to read,

$$(-)u^A_{Y_1}/u^A_{X_j} > \left[u^B_{Y_1}/u^B_{Y_j} - f^B_{Y_1}/f^B_{Y_j} + u^A_{Y_1}/u^A_{X_j}\right]_{Y_1=\bar{\bar{Y}}_1}, \text{ when } u^A_{Y_1}/u^A_{X_j} < 0,$$

$$\text{and } u^A_{Y_1}/u^A_{X_j} > (-)\left[u^B_{Y_1}/u^B_{Y_j} - f^B_{Y_1}/f^B_{Y_j} + u^A_{Y_1}/u^A_{X_j}\right]_{Y_1=\bar{\bar{Y}}_1}, \text{ when } u^A_{Y_1}/u^A_{X_j} > 0. \quad (6.9\text{B})$$

In equation (6.9B), $\tilde{Y}_1$ represents the "private" equilibrium value for Y_1, determined by B, after the ideal Pigovian tax is imposed. As before, the bracketed terms represent the "net" marginal evaluation of the activity for the acting party, B, and these sum to zero when equilibrium is reached. So long as the left-hand term in the inequality remains non-zero, a Pareto-relevant marginal externality remains, despite the fact that the full "Pigovian solution" is attained.

The apparent paradox here is not difficult to explain. Since, as postulated, A is not incurring any cost in securing the change in B's behaviour, and, since there remains, by hypothesis, a marginal diseconomy, further "trade" can be worked out between the two parties. Specifically, Pareto equilibrium is reached when,

$$(-)u^A_{Y_1}/u^A_{X_j} = \left[u^B_{Y_1}/u^B_{Y_j} - f^B_{Y_1}/f^B_{Y_j} + u^A_{Y_1}/u^A_{X_j}\right] \text{ when } u^A_{Y_1}/u^A_{X_j} < 0, \text{ and}$$

$$u^A_{Y_1}/u^A_{X_j} = (-)\left[u^B_{Y_1}/u^B_{Y_j} - f^B_{Y_1}/f^B_{Y_j} + u^A_{Y_1}/u^A_{X_j}\right] \text{ when } u^A_{Y_1}/u^A_{X_j} > 0. \quad (6.11\text{A})$$

Diagrammatically, this point may be made with reference to Figure 6.2. If a unilaterally imposed tax, corresponding to the marginal evaluation of A, is placed on B's performance of the activity, the new position of Pareto equilibrium may be shown by first subtracting the new marginal cost curve, drawn as MSC_B, from B's marginal evaluation curve. Where this new "net" marginal evaluation curve, shown as the dotted curve between points H_3 and K, cuts the marginal evaluation curve for A, a new position of Pareto equilibrium falling between H_2 and H_3 is located, neglecting the qualifying point discussed in note 8 in the Notes section.

The important implication to be drawn is that full Pareto equilibrium can never be attained via the imposition of unilaterally imposed taxes and subsidies until all marginal externalities are eliminated. If a tax-subsidy method, rather than "trade", is to be introduced, it should involve bi-lateral taxes (subsidies). Not only must B's behaviour be modified so as to insure that he will take the costs externally imposed on A into account, but A's behaviour must be modified so as to insure that he will take the costs "internally" imposed on B into account. In such a double tax-subsidy scheme, the necessary Pareto conditions would be readily satisfied.[11]

In summary, Pareto equilibrium in the case of marginal externalities cannot be attained so long as marginal externalities remain, until and unless those benefiting from changes are required to pay some "price" for securing the benefits.

A third point worthy of brief note is that our analysis allows the whole treatment of externalities to encompass the consideration of purely collective goods. As students of public finance theory will have recognised, the Pareto equilibrium solution discussed in this paper is similar, indeed is identical, with that which was presented by Paul Samuelson in his theory of public expenditures.[12] The summed marginal rates of substitution (marginal evaluation) must be equal to marginal costs. Note, however, that marginal costs may include the negative marginal evaluation of other parties, if viewed in one way. Note, also, that there is nothing in the analysis which suggests its limitations to purely collective goods or even to goods that are characterised by significant externalities in their use.

Our analysis also lends itself to the more explicit point developed in Coase's recent paper.[13] He argues that the same "solution" will tend to emerge out of any externality relationship, regardless of the structure of property rights, provided only that the market process works smoothly. Strictly speaking, Coase's analysis is applicable only to inter-firm externality relationships, and the identical solution emerges only because firms adjust to prices that are competitively determined. In our terms of reference, this identity of solution cannot apply because of the incomparability of utility functions. It remains true, however, that the basic characteristics of the Pareto equilibrium position remain unchanged regardless of the authority undertaking the action. This point can be readily demonstrated, again with reference to Figure 6.2. Let us assume that Figure 6.2 is now redrawn on the basis of a different legal relationship in which A now possesses full authority to construct the fence, whereas B can no longer take any action in this respect. A will, under these conditions, "privately" construct a fence only to the height H_0, where the activity clearly exerts a Pareto-relevant marginal external economy on B. Pareto equilibrium will be reached, as before, at H_3, determined, in this case, by the intersection of the "net" marginal evaluation curve for A (which is identical to the previously defined marginal social cost curve, *MSC*, when B is the acting party) and the marginal evaluation curve for B.[14] Note that, in this model, A will allow himself to suffer an internal marginal diseconomy, at equilibrium, provided that he is compensated by B, who continues, in Pareto equilibrium, to enjoy a marginal *external* economy.

Throughout this paper, we have deliberately chosen to introduce and to discuss only a single externality. Much of the confusion in the literature seems to have arisen because two or more externalities have been handled simultaneously. The standard example is that in which the output of one firm affects the production function of the second firm while, at the same time, the output of the second firm affects the production function of the first. Clearly, there are two externalities to be analysed in such cases. In many instances, these can be treated as separate and handled independently. In other situations, this step cannot be taken and additional tools become necessary.[15]

Notes

1 Tibor Scitovosky, "Two Concepts of External Economies", *Journal of Political Economy*, vol. LXII (1954), p. 143.
2 J. de V. Graaf, *Theoretical Welfare Economics*, Cambridge, 1957, p. 43 and p. 18.
3 Note that, $u^A_{y_1}|_{y_1=\bar{y}_1} = 0$, is a necessary, but not a sufficient, condition for irrelevance.
4 In this analysis of the relevance of externalities, we have assumed that B will act in such a manner as to maximise his own utility subject to the constraints within which he must operate. If, for any reason, B does not attain the equilibrium position defined in equation (6.5) above, the classification of his activity for A may, of course, be modified. A potentially relevant externality may become irrelevant and *vice versa*.
5 We are indebted to M. McManus of the University of Birmingham for pointing out to us an error in an earlier formulation of this and the following similar conditions.
6 This applies to the authors of this paper. For recent discussion of external effects when we have clearly intended only what we here designate as Pareto-relevant, see James M. Buchanan, "Politics, Policy, and the Pigovian Margins", *Economica*, vol. XXVIX (1962), pp. 17–28, and, also, James M. Buchanan and Gordon Tullock, *The Calculus of Consent*, Ann Arbor, 1962.
7 For an early use of marginal evaluation curves, see J. R. Hicks, "The Four Consumer's Surpluses", *Review of Economic Studies*, vol. XI (1943), pp. 31–41.
8 This diagrammatic analysis is necessarily oversimplified in the sense that the Pareto equilibrium position is represented as a unique point. Over the range between the "private" equilibrium for B and the point of Pareto equilibrium, the sort of bargains struck between A and B will affect the marginal evaluation curves of both individuals within this range. Thus, the more accurate

analysis would suggest a "contract locus" of equilibrium points. At Pareto equilibrium, however, the condition shown in the diagrammatic presentation holds, and the demonstration of this fact rather than the location of the solution is the aim of this diagrammatics.

9 Cf. Paul A. Samuelson, *Foundations of Economic Analysis*, Cambridge, Mass., 1948, p. 208, for a discussion of the views of various writers.

10 This criticism of the Pigovian analysis has been developed by R. H. Coase; see his "The Problem of Social Cost", *Journal of Law and Economics*, vol. III (1960), pp. 1–44.

11 Although developed in rather different terminology, this seems to be closely in accord with Coase's analysis. Cf. R. H. Coase, *loc. cit.*

12 Paul A. Samuelson, "The Pure Theory of Public Expenditure", *Review of Economics and Statistics*, vol. XXXVI (1954), pp. 386–9.

13 R. H. Coase, *loc. cit.*

14 The H_3 position, in this presumably redrawn figure, should not be precisely compared with the same position in the other model. We are using here the same diagram for two models, and, especially over wide ranges, the dependence of the marginal evaluation curves on income effects cannot be left out of account.

15 For a treatment of the dual externality problem that clearly shows the important difference between the separable and the non-separable cases, see Otto Davis and Andrew Whinston, "Externalities, Welfare, and the Theory of Games", *Journal of Political Economy*, vol. LXX (1962), pp. 241–62. As the title suggests, Davis and Whinston utilise the tools of game theory for the inseparable case.

7

On Divergences between Social Cost and Private Cost

Ralph Turvey

The notion that the resource-allocation effects of divergences between marginal social and private costs can be dealt with by imposing a tax or granting a subsidy equal to the difference now seems too simple a notion. Three recent articles have shown us this. First came Professor Coase's "The Problem of Social Cost", then Davis and Whinston's "Externalities, Welfare and the Theory of Games" appeared, and, finally, Buchanan and Stubblebine have published their paper "Externality".[1] These articles have an aggregate length of eighty pages and are by no means easy to read. The following attempt to synthesise and summarise the main ideas may therefore be useful. It is couched in terms of external diseconomies, i.e. an excess of social over private costs, and the reader is left to invert the analysis himself should he be interested in external economies.

The scope of the following argument can usefully be indicated by starting with a brief statement of its main conclusions. The first is that if the party imposing external diseconomies and the party suffering them are able and willing to negotiate to their mutual advantage, state intervention is unnecessary to secure optimum resource allocation. The second is that the imposition of a tax upon the party imposing external diseconomies can be a very complicated matter, even in principle, so that the *a priori* prescription of such a tax is unwise.

To develop these and other points, let us begin by calling A the person, firm or group (of persons or firms) which imposes a diseconomy, and B the person, firm or group which suffers it. How much B suffers will in many cases depend not only upon the *scale* of A's diseconomy-creating activity, but also upon the precise *nature* of A's activity and upon B's *reaction* to it. If A emits smoke, for example, B's loss will depend not only upon the quantity emitted but also upon the height of A's chimney and upon the cost to B of installing air-conditioning, indoor clothes-dryers or other means of reducing the effect of the smoke. Thus to ascertain the optimum resource allocation will frequently require an investigation of the nature and costs both of alternative activities open to A and of the devices by which B can reduce the impact of each activity. The optimum involves that kind and scale of A's activity and that adjustment to it by B which maximises the algebraic sum of A's gain and B's loss as against the situation where A pursues no diseconomy-creating activity. Note that the optimum will frequently involve B suffering a loss, both in total and at the margin.[2]

If A and B are firms, gain and loss can be measured in money terms as profit differences. (In considering a social optimum, allowance has of course to be made for market imperfections.) Now assuming that they both seek to maximise profits, that they know about the available alternatives and adjustments and that they are able and willing to negotiate, they will achieve the optimum without any government interference. They will internalize the externality by merger,[3] or they will make an agreement whereby B pays A to modify the nature or scale of its activity.[4] Alternatively,[5] if the law gives B rights against A, A will pay B to accept the optimal amount of loss imposed by A.

If A and B are people, their gain and loss must be measured as the amount of money they respectively would pay to indulge in and prevent A's activity. It could also be measured as the amount of money they respectively would require to refrain from and to endure A's activity, which will be different unless the marginal utility of income is constant. We shall assume that it is constant for both A and B, which is reasonable when the payments do not bulk large in relation to their incomes.[6] Under this assumption, it makes no difference whether B pays A or, if the law gives B rights against A, A compensates B.

Whether A and B are persons or firms, to levy a tax on A which is *not* received as damages or compensation by B may prevent optimal resource allocation from being achieved – still assuming that they can and do negotiate.[7] The reason is that the resource allocation which maximises A's *gain less B's loss* may differ from that which maximises A's *gain less A's tax less B's loss*.

The points made so far can usefully be presented diagrammatically (Figure 7.1). We assume that A has only two alternative activities, I and II, and that their scales and B's losses are all continuously variable. Let us temporarily disregard the dotted curve in the right-hand part of the diagram. The area under A's curves then gives the total gain to A. The area under B's curves gives the total loss to B after he has made the best

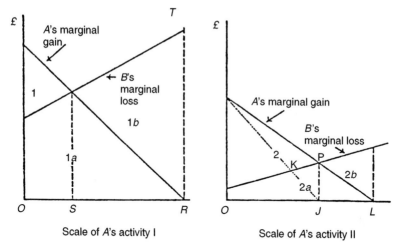

Figure 7.1

adjustment possible to *A*'s activity. This is thus the direct loss as reduced by adjustment, plus the cost of making that adjustment.

If *A* and *B* could not negotiate and if *A* were unhampered by restrictions of any sort, *A* would choose activity I at a scale of *OR*. A scale of *OS* would obviously give a larger social product, but the optimum is clearly activity II at scale *OJ*, since area 2 is greater than area 1. Now *B* will be prepared to pay up to $(1a + 1b - 2a)$ to secure this result, while *A* will be prepared to accept down to $(1 + 1a - 2 - 2a)$ to assure it. The difference is $(1b - 1 + 2)$, the maximum gain to be shared between them, and this is clearly positive.

If *A* is liable to compensate *B* for actual damages caused by either activity I or II, he will choose activity II at scale *OJ* (i.e. the optimum allocation), pay $2a$ to *B* and retain a net gain of 2. The result is the same as when there is no such liability, though the distribution of the gain is very different: *B* will pay *A* up to $(1a + 1b - 2a)$ to secure this result. Hence whether or not we should advocate the imposition of a liability on *A* for damages caused is a matter of fairness, not of resource allocation. Our judgment will presumably depend on such factors as who got there first, whether one of them is a non-conforming user (e.g. an establishment for the breeding of maggots on putrescible vegetable matter in a residential district), who is richer, and so on. Efficient resource allocation requires the imposition of a liability upon *A* only if we can show that inertia, obstinacy, etc. inhibit *A* and *B* from reaching a voluntary agreement.[8]

We can now make the point implicit in Buchanan-Stubblebine's argument, namely that there is a necessity for any impost levied on A to be paid to B when A and B are able to negotiate. Suppose that A is charged an amount equal to the loss he imposes on B; subtracting this from his marginal gain curve in the right-hand part of the diagram gives us the dotted line as his marginal net gain. If A moves to point J it will then pay B to induce him to move back to position K (which is sub-optimal) as it is this position which maximises the *joint* net gain to A and B together.

There is a final point to be made about the case where A and B can negotiate. This is that if the external diseconomies are reciprocal, so that each imposes a loss upon the other, the problem is still more complicated.[9]

We now turn to the case where A and B cannot negotiate, which in most cases will result from A and/or B being too large a group for the members to get together. Here there are certain benefits to be had from resource re-allocation which are not privately appropriable. Just as with collective goods,[10] therefore, there is thus a case for collective action to achieve optimum allocation. But all this means is that *if* the state can ascertain and enforce a move to the optimum position at a cost less than the gain to be had, and *if* it can do this in a way which does not have unfavourable effects upon income distribution, then it should take action.

These two "ifs" are very important. The second is obvious and requires no elaboration. The first, however, deserves a few words. In order to ascertain the optimum type and scale of A's activity, the authorities must estimate all of the curves in the diagrams. They must, in other words, list and evaluate all the alternatives open to A and examine their effects upon B and the adjustments B could make to reduce the loss suffered. When this is done, if it can be done, it is necessary to consider how to reach the optimum. Now, where the nature as well as the scale of A's activity is variable, it may be necessary to control both, and this may require two controls, not one. Suppose, for instance, that in the diagram, both activities are the emission of smoke: I from a low chimney and II from a tall chimney. To induce A to shift from emitting OR smoke from the low chimney to emitting OJ smoke from the tall chimney, it will not suffice to levy a tax of PJ per unit of smoke.[11] If this alone were done, A would continue to use a low chimney, emitting slightly less than OR smoke. It will also be necessary to regulate chimney heights. A tax would do the trick alone only if it were proportioned to losses imposed rather than to smoke emitted, and that would be very difficult.

These complications show that in many cases the cost of achieving optimum resource allocation may outweigh the gain. If this is the case, a second-best solution may be appropriate. Thus a prohibition of all smoke emission would be better than *OR* smoke from a low chimney (since 1 is less than 1*b*) and a requirement that all chimneys be tall would be better still (giving a net gain of 2 less 2*b*). Whether these requirements should be imposed on existing chimney-owners as well as on new ones then introduces further complications relating to the short run and the long run.

There is no need to carry the example any further. It is now abundantly clear that any general prescription of a tax to deal with external diseconomies is useless. Each case must be considered on its own and there is no *a priori* reason to suppose that the imposition of a tax is better than alternative measures or indeed, that any measures at all are desirable unless we assume that information and administration are both costless.[12]

To sum up, then: when negotiation is possible, the case for government intervention is one of justice not of economic efficiency; when it is not, the theorist should be silent and call in the applied economist.

Notes

1. *Journal of Law and Economics*, Vol. III, October, 1960, *Journal of Political Economy*, June, 1962, and *Economica*, November, 1962, respectively.
2. Buchanan-Stubblebine, pp. 380–1.
3. Davis-Whinston, pp. 244, 252, 256; Coase, pp. 16–17.
4. Coase, p. 6; Buchanan-Stubblebine agree, p. 383.
5. See previous references
6. Dr Mishan has examined the welfare criterion for the case where the only variable is the scale of *A*'s activity, but where neither *A* nor *B* has a constant marginal utility of income; Cf. his paper "Welfare Criteria for External Effects", *American Economic Review*, September, 1961.
7. Buchanan-Stubblebine, pp. 381–3.
8. Cf. the comparable argument on pp. 94–8 of my *The Economics of Real Property*, 1957, about the external economy to landlords of tenants' improvements.
9. Davis-Whinston devote several pages of game theory to this problem.
10. Buchanan-Stubblebine, p. 383.
11. Note how different *PJ* is from *RT*, the initial observable marginal external diseconomy.
12. Coase, pp. 18, 44.

References

Buchanan, J. M. and Stubblebine, W. C., "Externality", *Economica*, 29: 371–384.
Davis, O. and Whinston, A., "Externalities, Welfare, and the Theory of Games", *Journal of Political Economy*, Vol. LXX, 1962, pp. 24–62.
Coase, R. H., "The Problem of Social Cost", *Journal of Law and Economics*, Vol. III, 1960, pp. 1–44.

Part III

Property Rights, Institutions and Public Choice

8

Toward a Theory of
Property Rights

Harold Demsetz

When a transaction is concluded in the marketplace, two bundles of
property rights are exchanged. A bundle of rights often attaches to a
physical commodity or service, but it is the value of the rights that determines the value of what is exchanged. Questions addressed to the emergence and mix of the components of the bundle of rights are prior to
those commonly asked by economists. Economists usually take the
bundle of property rights as a datum and ask for an explanation of the
forces determining the price and the number of units of a good to which
these rights attach.

In this paper, I seek to fashion some of the elements of an economic
theory of property rights. The paper is organized into three parts. The
first part discusses briefly the concept and role of property rights in
social systems. The second part offers some guidance for investigating
the emergence of property rights. The third part sets forth some principles relevant to the coalescing of property rights into particular
bundles and to the determination of the ownership structure that will
be associated with these bundles.

The concept and role of property rights

In the world of Robinson Crusoe property rights play no role. Property
rights are an instrument of society and derive their significance from the
fact that they help a man form those expectations which he can reasonably hold in his dealings with others. These expectations find expression
in the laws, customs, and mores of a society. An owner of property rights
possesses the consent of fellowmen to allow him to act in particular ways.
An owner expects the community to prevent others from interfering

with his actions, provided that these actions are not prohibited in the specifications of his rights.

It is important to note that property rights convey the right to benefit or harm oneself or others. Harming a competitor by producing superior products may be permitted, while shooting him may not. A man may be permitted to benefit himself by shooting an intruder but be prohibited from selling below a price floor. It is clear, then, that property rights specify how persons may be benefited and harmed, and, therefore, who must pay whom to modify the actions taken by persons. The recognition of this leads easily to the close relationship between property rights and externalities.

Externality is an ambiguous concept. For the purposes of this paper, the concept includes external costs, external benefits, and pecuniary as well as nonpecuniary externalities. No harmful or beneficial effect is external to the world. Some person or persons always suffer or enjoy these effects. What converts a harmful or beneficial effect into an externality is that the cost of bringing the effect to bear on the decisions of one or more of the interacting persons is too high to make it worthwhile, and this is what the term shall mean here. "Internalizing" such effects refers to a process, usually a change in property rights, that enables these effects to bear (in greater degree) on all interacting persons.

A primary function of property rights is that of guiding incentives to achieve a greater internalization of externalities. Every cost and benefit associated with social interdependencies is a potential externality. One condition is necessary to make costs and benefits externalities. The cost of a transaction in the rights between the parties (internalization) must exceed the gains from internalization. In general, transacting cost can be large relative to gains because of "natural" difficulties in trading or they can be large because of legal reasons. In a lawful society the prohibition of voluntary negotiations makes the cost of transacting infinite. Some costs and benefits are not taken into account by users of resources whenever externalities exist, but allowing transactions increases the degree to which internalization takes place. For example, it might be thought that a firm which uses slave labor will not recognize all the costs of its activities, since it can have its slave labor by paying subsistence wages only. This will not be true if negotiations are permitted, for the slaves can offer to the firm a payment for their freedom based on the expected return to them of being free men. The cost of slavery can thus be internalized in the calculations of the firm. The transition from serf to free man in feudal Europe is an example of this process.

Perhaps one of the most significant cases of externalities is the extensive use of the military draft. The taxpayer benefits by not paying the full cost of staffing the armed services. The costs which the taxpayer escapes are the additional sums that would be needed to acquire men voluntarily for the services or those sums that would be offered as payment by draftees to taxpayers in order to be exempted. With either voluntary recruitment, the "buy-him-in" system, or with a "let-him-buy-his-way-out" system, the full cost of recruitment would be brought to bear on taxpayers. It has always seemed incredible to me that so many economists can recognize an externality when they see smoke but not when they see the draft. The familiar smoke example is one in which negotiation costs may be too high (because of the large number of interacting parties) to make it worthwhile to internalize all the effects of smoke. The draft is an externality caused by forbidding negotiation.

The role of property rights in the internalization of externalities can be made clear within the context of the above examples. A law which establishes the right of a person to his freedom would necessitate a payment on the part of a firm or of the taxpayer sufficient to cover the cost of using that person's labor if his services are to be obtained. The costs of labor thus become internalized in the firm's or taxpayer's decisions. Alternatively, a law which gives the firm or the taxpayer clear title to slave labor would necessitate that the slaveowners take into account the sums that slaves are willing to pay for their freedom. These costs thus become internalized in decisions although wealth is distributed differently in the two cases. All that is needed for internalization in either case is ownership which includes the right of sale. It is the prohibition of a property right adjustment, the prohibition of the establishment of an ownership title that can thenceforth be exchanged, that precludes the internalization of external costs and benefits.

There are two striking implications of this process that are true in a world of zero transaction costs. The output mix that results when the exchange of property rights is allowed is efficient and the mix is independent of who is assigned ownership (except that different wealth distributions may result in different demands).[1] For example, the efficient mix of civilians and military will result from transferable ownership no matter whether taxpayers must hire military volunteers or whether draftees must pay taxpayers to be excused from service. For taxpayers will hire only those military (under the "buy-him-in" property right system) who would not pay to be exempted (under the "let-him-buy-his-way-out" system). The highest bidder under the "let-him-buy-his-way-out" property right system would be precisely the last to volunteer under a "buy-him-in" system.[2]

We will refer back to some of these points later. But for now, enough groundwork has been laid to facilitate the discussion of the next two parts of this paper.

The emergence of property rights

If the main allocative function of property rights is the internalization of beneficial and harmful effects, then the emergence of property rights can be understood best by their association with the emergence of new or different beneficial and harmful effects.

Changes in knowledge result in changes in production functions, market values, and aspirations. New techniques, new ways of doing the same things, and doing new things – all invoke harmful and beneficial effects to which society has not been accustomed. It is my thesis in this part of the paper that the emergence of new property rights takes place in response to the desires of the interacting persons for adjustment to new benefit-cost possibilities.

The thesis can be restated in a slightly different fashion: property rights develop to internalize externalities when the gains of internalization become larger than the cost of internalization. Increased internalization, in the main, results from changes in economic values, changes which stem from the development of new technology and the opening of new markets, changes to which old property rights are poorly attuned. A proper interpretation of this assertion requires that account be taken of a community's preferences for private ownership. Some communities will have less well-developed private ownership systems and more highly developed state ownership systems. But, given a community's tastes in this regard, the emergence of new private or state-owned property rights will be in response to changes in technology and relative prices.

I do not mean to assert or to deny that the adjustments in property rights which take place need be the result of a conscious endeavor to cope with new externality problems. These adjustments have arisen in Western societies largely as a result of gradual changes in social mores and in common law precedents. At each step of this adjustment process, it is unlikely that externalities *per se* were consciously related to the issue being resolved. These legal and moral experiments may be hit-and-miss procedures to some extent but in a society that weights the achievement of efficiency heavily, their viability in the long run will depend on how well they modify behavior to accommodate to the externalities associated with important changes in technology or market values.

A rigorous test of this assertion will require extensive and detailed empirical work. A broad range of examples can be cited that are consistent with it: the development of air rights, renters' rights, rules for liability in automobile accidents, etc. In this part of the discussion, I shall present one group of such examples in some detail. They deal with the development of private property rights in land among American Indians. These examples are broad ranging and come fairly close to what can be called convincing evidence in the field of anthropology.

The question of private ownership of land among aboriginals has held a fascination for anthropologists. It has been one of the intellectual battlegrounds in the attempt to assess the "true nature" of man unconstrained by the "artificalities" of civilization. In the process of carrying on this debate, information has been uncovered that bears directly on the thesis with which we are now concerned. What appears to be accepted as a classic treatment and a high point of this debate is Eleanor Leacock's memoir on *The Montagnes "Hunting Territory" and the Fur Trade.*[3] Leacock's research followed that of Frank G. Speck[4] who had discovered that the Indians of the Labrador Peninsula had a long-established tradition of property in land. This finding was at odds with what was known about the Indians of the American Southwest and it prompted Leacock's study of the Montagnes who inhabited large regions around Quebec.

Leacock clearly established the fact that a close relationship existed, both historically and geographically, between the development of private rights in land and the development of the commercial fur trade. The factual basis of this correlation has gone unchallenged. However, to my knowledge, no theory relating privacy of land to the fur trade has yet been articulated. The factual material uncovered by Speck and Leacock fits the thesis of this paper well, and in doing so, it reveals clearly the role played by property right adjustments in taking account of what economists have often cited as an example of an externality – the overhunting of game.

Because of the lack of control over hunting by others, it is in no person's interest to invest in increasing or maintaing the stock of game. Overly intensive hunting takes place. Thus a successful hunt is viewed as imposing external costs on subsequent hunters – costs that are not taken into account fully in the determination of the extent of hunting and of animal husbandry.

Before the fur trade became established, hunting was carried on primarily for purposes of food and the relatively few furs that were required for the hunter's family. The externality was clearly present. Hunting could be practiced freely and was carried on without assessing its impact on other hunters. But these external effects were of such small significance that it did not pay for anyone to take them into account. There did not exist anything resembling private ownership in land. And in the *Jesuit Relations*, particularly Le Jeune's record of the winter he spent with the Montagnes in 1633–34 and in the brief account given by Father Druilletes in 1647–48, Leacock finds no evidence of private land holdings. Both accounts indicate a socioeconomic organization in which private rights to land are not well developed.

We may safely surmise that the advent of the fur trade had two immediate consequences. First, the value of furs to the Indians was increased considerably. Second, and as a result, the scale of hunting activity rose sharply. Both consequences must have increased considerably the importance of the externalities associated with free hunting. The property right system began to change, and it changed specifically in the direction required to take account of the economic effects made important by the fur trade. The geographical or distributional evidence collected by Leacock indicates an unmistakable correlation between early centers of fur trade and the oldest and most complete development of the private hunting territory.

> By the beginning of the eighteenth century, we begin to have clear evidence that territorial hunting and trapping arrangements by individual families were developing in the area around Quebec. . . . The earliest references to such arrangements in this region indicates a purely temporary allotment of hunting territories. They [Algonkians and Iroquois] divide themselves into several bands in order to hunt more efficiently. It was their custom . . . to appropriate pieces of land about two leagues square for each group to hunt exclusively. Ownership of beaver houses, however, had already become established, and when discovered, they were marked. A starving Indian could kill and eat another's beaver if he left the fur and the tail.[5]

The next step toward the hunting territory was probably a seasonal allotment system. An anonymous account written in 1723 states that the "principle of the Indians is to mark off the hunting ground selected by them by blazing the trees with their crests so that they may never encroach on each other. . . . By the middle of the century these allotted territories were relatively stabilized."[6]

The principle that associates property right changes with the emergence of new and reevaluation of old harmful and beneficial effects suggests in this instance that the fur trade made it economic to encourage the husbanding of fur-bearing animals. Husbanding requires the ability to prevent poaching and this, in turn, suggests that socioeconomic changes in property in hunting land will take place. The chain of reasoning is consistent with the evidence cited above. Is it inconsistent with the absence of similar rights in property among the southwestern Indians?

Two factors suggest that the thesis is consistent with the absence of similar rights among the Indians of the southwestern plains. The first of these is that there were no plains animals of commercial importance comparable to the fur-bearing animals of the forest, at least not until cattle arrived with Europeans. The second factor is that animals of the plains are primarily grazing species whose habit is to wander over wide tracts of land. The value of establishing boundaries to private hunting territories is thus reduced by the relatively high cost of preventing the animals from moving to adjacent parcels. Hence both the value and cost of establishing private hunting lands in the Southwest are such that we would expect little development along these lines. The externality was just not worth taking into account.

The lands of the Labrador Peninsula shelter forest animals whose habits are considerably different from those of the plains. Forest animals confine their territories to relatively small areas, so that the cost of internalizing the effects of husbanding these animals is considerably reduced. This reduced cost, together with the higher commercial value of fur-bearing forest animals, made it productive to establish private hunting lands. Frank G. Speck finds that family proprietorship among the Indians of the Peninsula included retaliation against trespass. Animal resources were husbanded. Sometimes conservation practices were carried on extensively. Family hunting territories were divided into quarters. Each year the family hunted in a different quarter in rotation, leaving a tract in the center as a sort of bank, not to be hunted over unless forced to do so by a shortage in the regular tract.

To conclude our excursion into the phenomenon of private rights in land among the American Indians, we note one further piece of corroborating evidence. Among the Indians of the Northwest, highly developed private family rights to hunting lands had also emerged – rights which went so far as to include inheritance. Here again we find that forest animals predominate and that the West Coast was frequently visited by sailing schooners whose primary purpose was trading in furs.[7]

The coalescence and ownership of property rights

I have argued that property rights arise when it becomes economic for those affected by externalities to internalize benefits and costs. But I have not yet examined the forces which will govern the particular form of right ownership. Several idealized forms of ownership must be distinguished at the outset. These are communal ownership, private ownership, and state ownership.

By communal ownership, I shall mean a right which can be exercised by all members of the community. Frequently the rights to till and to hunt the land have been communally owned. The right to walk a city sidewalk is communally owned. Communal ownership means that the community denies to the state or to individual citizens the right to interfere with any person's exercise of communally-owned rights. Private ownership implies that the community recognizes the right of the owner to exclude others from exercising the owner's private rights. State ownership implies that the state may exclude anyone from the use of a right as long as the state follows accepted political procedures for determining who may not use state-owned property. I shall not examine in detail the alternative of state ownership. The object of the analysis which follows is to discern some broad principles governing the development of property rights in communities oriented to private property.

It will be best to begin by considering a particularly useful example that focuses our attention on the problem of land ownership. Suppose that land is communally owned. Every person has the right to hunt, till, or mine the land. This form of ownership fails to concentrate the cost associated with any person's exercise of his communal right on that person. If a person seeks to maximize the value of his communal rights, he will tend to overhunt and overwork the land because some of the costs of his doing so are borne by others. The stock of game and the richness of the soil will be diminished too quickly. It is conceivable that those who own these rights, i.e., every member of the community, can agree to curtail the rate at which they work the lands if negotiating and policing costs are zero. Each can agree to abridge his rights. It is obvious that the costs of reaching such an agreement will not be zero. What is not obvious is just how large these costs may be.

Negotiating costs will be large because it is difficult for many persons to reach a mutually satisfactory agreement, especially when each hold-out has the right to work the land as fast as he pleases. But, even if an agreement among all can be reached, we must yet take account of the costs of policing the agreement, and these may be large, also. After such an agreement is reached, no one will privately own the right to work the land; all can work the land but at an agreed upon shorter workweek. Negotiating costs are increased even further because it is not possible under this system to bring the full expected benefits and expected costs of future generations to bear on current users.

If a single person owns land, he will attempt to maximize its present value by taking into account alternative future time streams of benefits and costs and selecting that one which he believes will maximize the present value of his privately-owned land rights. We all know that this means that he will attempt to take into account the supply and demand conditions that he thinks will exist after his death. It is very difficult to see how the existing communal owners can reach an agreement that takes account of these costs.

In effect, an owner of a private right to use land acts as a broker whose wealth depends on how well he takes into account the competing claims of the present and the future. But with communal rights there is no broker, and the claims of the present generation will be given an uneconomically large weight in determining the intensity with which the land is worked. Future generations might desire to pay present generations enough to change the present intensity of land usage. But they have no living agent to place their claims on the market. Under a communal property system, should a living person pay others to reduce the rate at which they work the land, he would not gain anything of value for his efforts. Communal property means that future generations must speak for themselves. No one has yet estimated the costs of carrying on such a conversation.

The land ownership example confronts us immediately with a great disadvantage of communal property. The effects of a person's activities on his neighbors and on subsequent generations will not be taken into account fully. Communal property results in great externalities. The full costs of the activities of an owner of a communal property right are not borne directly by him, nor can they be called to his attention easily by the willingness of others to pay him an appropriate sum. Communal property rules out a "pay-to-use-the-property" system and high negotiation and policing costs make ineffective a "pay-him-not-to-use-the-property" system.

The state, the courts, or the leaders of the community could attempt to internalize the external costs resulting from communal property by allowing private parcels owned by small groups of person with similar interests. The logical groups in terms of similar interests, are, of course, the family and the individual. Continuing with our use of the land ownership example, let us initially distribute private titles to land randomly among existing individuals and, further, let the extent of land included in each title be randomly determined.

The resulting private ownership of land will internalize many of the external costs associated with communal ownership, for now an owner, by virtue of his power to exclude others, can generally count on realizing the rewards associated with husbanding the game and increasing the fertility of his land. This concentration of benefits and costs on owners creates incentives to utilize resources more efficiently.

But we have yet to contend with externalities. Under the communal property system the maximization of the value of communal property rights will take place without regard to many costs, because the owner of a communal right cannot exclude others from enjoying the fruits of his efforts and because negotiation costs are too high for all to agree jointly on optimal behavior. The development of private rights permits the owner to economize on the use of those resources from which he has the right to exclude others. Much internalization is accomplished in this way. But the owner of private rights to one parcel does not himself own the rights to the parcel of another private sector. Since he cannot exclude others from their private rights to land, he has no direct incentive (in the absence of negotiations) to economize in the use of his land in a way that takes into account the effects he produces on the land rights of others. If he constructs a dam on his land, he has no direct incentive to take into account the lower water levels produced on his neighbor's land.

This is exactly the same kind of externality that we encountered with communal property rights, but it is present to a lesser degree. Whereas no one had an incentive to store water on any land under the communal system, private owners now can take into account directly those benefits and costs to their land that accompany water storage. But the effects on the land of others will not be taken into account directly.

The partial concentration of benefits and costs that accompany private ownership is only part of the advantage this system offers. The other part, and perhaps the most important, has escaped our notice. The cost of negotiating over the remaining externalities will be reduced greatly. Communal property rights allow anyone to use the land. Under this system it becomes necessary for all to reach an agreement on land use. But the externalities that accompany private ownership of property do not affect all owners, and, generally speaking, it will be necessary for only a few to reach an agreement that takes these effects into account. The cost of negotiating an internalization of these effects is thereby reduced considerably. The point is important enough to elucidate.

Suppose an owner of a communal land right, in the process of plowing a parcel of land, observes a second communal owner constructing a dam on adjacent land. The farmer prefers to have the stream as it is, and so he asks the engineer to stop his construction. The engineer says, "Pay me to stop." The farmer replies, "I will be happy to pay you, but what can you guarantee in return?" The engineer answers, "I can guarantee you that I will not continue constructing the dam, but I cannot guarantee that another engineer will not take up the task because this is communal property; I have no right to exclude him." What would be a simple negotiation between two persons under a private property arrangement turns out to be a rather complex negotiation between the farmer and everyone else. This is the basic explanation, I believe, for the preponderance of single rather than multiple owners of property. Indeed, an increase in the number of owners is an increase in the communality of property and leads, generally, to an increase in the cost of internalizing.

The reduction in negotiating cost that accompanies the private right to exclude others allows most externalities to be internalized at rather low cost. Those that are not are associated with activities that generate external effects impinging upon many people. The soot from smoke affects many homeowners, none of whom is willing to pay enough to the factory to get its owner to reduce smoke output. All homeowners together might be willing to pay enough, but the cost of their getting together may be enough to discourage effective market bargaining. The negotiating problem is compounded even more if the smoke comes not from a single smoke stack but from an industrial district. In such cases, it may be too costly to internalize effects through the market-place.

Returning to our land ownership paradigm, we recall that land was distributed in randomly sized parcels to randomly selected owners. These owners now negotiate among themselves to internalize any remaining externalities. Two market options are open to the negotiators. The first is simply to try to reach a contractual agreement among owners that directly deals with the external effects at issue. The second option is for some owners to buy out others, thus changing the parcel size owned. Which option is selected will depend on which is cheaper. We have here a standard economic problem of optimal scale. If there exist constant returns to scale in the ownership of different sized parcels, it will be largely a matter of indifference between outright purchase and contractual agreement if only a single, easy-to-police, contractual agreement will internalize the externality. But, if there are several externalities, so that several such contracts will need to be negotiated, or if the contractual agreements should be difficult to police, then outright purchase will be the preferred course of action.

The greater the diseconomies of scale to land ownership the more will contractual arrangement be used by the interacting neighbors to settle these differences. Negotiating and policing costs will be compared to costs that depend on the scale of ownership, and parcels of land will tend to be owned in sizes which minimize the sum of these costs.[8]

The interplay of scale economies, negotiating cost, externalities, and the modification of property rights can be seen in the most notable "exception" to the assertion that ownership tends to be an individual affair: the publicly-held corporation. I assume that significant economies of scale in the operation of large corporations is a fact and, also, that large requirements for equity capital can be satisfied more cheaply by acquiring the capital from many purchasers of equity shares. While economies of scale in operating these enterprises exist, economies of scale in the provision of capital do not. Hence, it becomes desirable for many "owners" to form a joint-stock company.

But if all owners participate in each decision that needs to be made by such a company, the scale economies of operating the company will be overcome quickly by high negotiating cost. Hence a delegation of authority for most decisions takes place and, for most of these, a small management group becomes the *de facto* owners. Effective ownership, i.e., effective control of property, is thus legally concentrated in management's hands. This is the first legal modification, and it takes place in recognition of the high negotiating costs that would otherwise obtain.

The structure of ownership, however, creates some externality difficulties under the law of partnership. If the corporation should fail, partnership law commits each shareholder to meet the debts of the corporation up to the limits of his financial ability. Thus, managerial *de facto* ownership can have considerable external effects on shareholders. Should property rights remain unmodified, this externality would make it exceedingly difficult for entrepreneurs to acquire equity capital from wealthy individuals. (Although these individuals have recourse to reimbursements from other shareholders, litigation costs will be high.) A second legal modification, limited liability, has taken place to reduce the effect of this externality. *De facto* management ownership and limited liability combine to minimize the overall cost of operating large enterprises. Shareholders are essentially lenders of equity capital and not owners, although they do participate in such infrequent decisions as those involving mergers. What shareholders really own are their shares and not the corporation. Ownership in the sense of control again becomes a largely individual affair. The shareholders own their shares, and the president of the corporation and possibly a few other top executives control the corporation.

To further ease the impact of management decisions on shareholders, that is, to minimize the impact of externalities under this ownership form, a further legal modification of rights is required. Unlike partnership law, a shareholder may sell his interest without first obtaining the permission of fellow shareholders or without dissolving the corporation. It thus becomes easy for him to get out if his preferences and those of the management are no longer in harmony. This "escape hatch" is extremely important and has given rise to the organized trading of securities. The increase in harmony between managers and shareholders brought about by exchange and by competing managerial groups helps to minimize the external effects associated with the corporate ownership structure. Finally, limited liability considerably reduces the cost of exchanging shares by making it unnecessary for a purchaser of shares to examine in great detail the liabilities of the corporation and the assets of other shareholders; these liabilities can adversely affect a purchaser only up to the extent of the price per share.

The dual tendencies for ownership to rest with individuals and for the extent of an individual's ownership to accord with the minimization of all costs is clear in the land ownership paradigm. The applicability of this paradigm has been extended to the corporation. But it may not be clear yet how widely applicable this paradigm is. Consider the problems of copyright and patents. If a new idea is freely appropriable by all, if there exist communal rights to new ideas, incentives for developing such ideas will be lacking. The benefits derivable from these ideas will not be concentrated on their originators. If we extend some degree of private rights to the originators, these ideas will come forth at a more rapid pace. But the existence of the private rights does not mean that their effects on the property of others will be directly taken into account. A new idea makes an old one obsolete and another old one more valuable. These effects will not be directly taken into account, but they can be called to the attention of the originator of the new idea through market negotiations. All problems of externalities are closely analogous to those which arise in the land ownership example. The relevant variables are identical.

What I have suggested in this paper is an approach to problems in property rights. But it is more than that. It is also a different way of viewing traditional problems. An elaboration of this approach will, I hope, illuminate a great number of social-economic problems.

Notes

1 These implications are derived by R. H. Coase, "The Problem of Social Cost," *J. of Law and Econ.*, Oct., 1960, pp. 1–44.
2 If the demand for civilian life is unaffected by wealth redistribution, the assertion made is correct as it stands. However, when a change is made from a "buy-him-in" system to a "let-him-buy-his-way-out" system, the resulting redistribution of wealth away from draftees may significantly affect their demand for civilian life; the validity of the assertion then requires a compensating wealth change. A compensating wealth change will not be required in the ordinary case of profit maximizing firms. Consider the farmer-rancher example mentioned by Coase. Society may give the farmer the right to grow corn unmolested by cattle or it may give the rancher the right to allow his cattle to stray. Contrary to the Coase example, let us suppose that if the farmer is given the right, he just breaks even; i.e., with the right to be compensated for corn damage, the farmer's land is marginal. If the right is transferred to the rancher, the farmer, not enjoying any economic rent, will not have the wherewithal to pay the rancher to reduce the number of head of cattle raised. In this case, however, it will be profitable for the rancher to buy the farm, thus merging cattle raising with farming. His self-interest will then lead him to take account of the effect of cattle on corn.
3 Eleanor Leacock, *American Anthropologist* (American Anthropological Asso.), Vol. 56, No. 5, Part 2, Memoir No. 78.
4 Cf., Frank G. Speck, "The Basis of American Indian Ownership of Land," *Old Penn Weekly Rev.* (Univ. of Pennsylvania), Jan. 16, 1915, pp. 491–95.
5 Eleanor Leacock, *op. cit.*, p. 15.
6 Eleanor Leacock, *op. cit.*, p. 15.
7 The thesis is consistent with the development of other types of private rights. Among wandering primitive peoples the cost of policing property is relatively low for highly portable objects. The owning family can protect such objects while carrying on its daily activities. If these objects are also very useful, property rights should appear frequently, so as to internalize the benefits and costs of their use. It is generally true among most primitive communities that weapons and household utensils, such as pottery, are regarded as private property. Both types of articles are portable and both require an investment of time to produce. Among agriculturally-oriented peoples, because of the relative fixity of their location, portability has a smaller role to play in the determination of property. The distinction is most clearly seen by comparing property in land among the most primitive of these societies, where crop rotation and simple fertilization techniques are unknown, or where land fertility is extremely poor, with property in land among primitive peoples who are more knowledgeable in these matters or who possess very superior land. Once

a crop is grown by the more primitive agricultural societies, it is necessary for them to abandon the land for several years to restore productivity. Property rights in land among such people would require policing cost for several years during which no sizable output is obtained. Since to provide for sustenance these people must move to new land, a property right to be of value to them must be associated with a portable object. Among these people it is common to find property rights to the crops, which, after harvest, are portable, but not to the land. The more advanced agriculturally based primitive societies are able to remain with particular land for longer periods, and here we generally observe property rights to the land as well as to the crops.

8 Compare this with the similar rationale given by R. H. Coase to explain the firm in "The Nature of the Firm," *Economica*, New Series, 1937, pp. 386–405.

9
The Economic Theory of a Common-Property Resource: The Fishery

H. Scott Gordon

I Introduction

The chief aim of this paper is to examine the economic theory of natural resource utilization as it pertains to the fishing industry. It will appear, I hope, that most of the problems associated with the words "conservation" or "depletion" or "overexploitation" in the fishery are, in reality, manifestations of the fact that the natural resources of the sea yield no economic rent. Fishery resources are unusual in the fact of their common-property nature; but they are not unique, and similar problems are encountered in other cases of common-property resource industries, such as petroleum production, hunting and trapping, etc. Although the theory presented in the following pages is worked out in terms of the fishing industry, it is, I believe, applicable generally to all cases where natural resources are owned in common and exploited under conditions of individualistic competition.

II Biological factors and theories

The great bulk of the research that has been done on the primary production phase of the fishing industry has so far been in the field of biology. Owing to the lack of theoretical economic research,[1] biologists have been forced to extend the scope of their own thought into the economic sphere and in some cases have penetrated quite deeply, despite the lack of the analytical tools of economic theory.[2] Many others, who have paid no specific attention to the economic aspects of the problem have nevertheless recognized that the ultimate question is not the ecology of life in the sea as such, but man's use of these resources for his own (economic) purposes. Dr Martin D. Burkenroad, for example, began a recent article on fishery management with a section on "Fishery Management as Political Economy," saying that "the management of fisheries is intended for the benefit of man, not fish; therefore effect of management upon fishstocks cannot be regarded as beneficial *per se*."[3] The great Russian marine biology theorist, T. I. Baranoff, referred to his work as "bionomics" or "bio-economics," although he made little explicit reference to economic factors.[4] In the same way, A. G. Huntsman, reporting in 1944 on the work of the Fisheries Research Board of Canada, defined the problem of fisheries depletion in economic terms: "Where the take in proportion to the effort fails to yield a satisfactory living to the fisherman";[5] and a later paper by the same author contains, as an incidental statement, the essence of the economic optimum solution without, apparently, any recognition of its significance.[6] Upon the occasion of its fiftieth anniversary in 1952, the International Council for the Exploration of the Sea published a *Rapport Jubilaire*, consisting of a series of papers summarizing progress in various fields of fisheries research. The paper by Michael Graham on "Overfishing and Optimum Fishing," by its emphatic recognition of the economic criterion, would lead one to think that the economic aspects of the question had been extensively examined during the last half-century. But such is not the case. Virtually no specific research into the economics of fishery resource utilization has been undertaken. The present state of knowledge is that a great deal is known about the biology of the various commercial species but little about the economic characteristics of the fishing industry.

The most vivid thread that runs through the biological literature is the effort to determine the effect of fishing on the stock of fish in the sea. This discussion has had a very distinct practical orientation, being part of the effort to design regulatory policies of a "conservation" nature. To the layman the problem appears to be dominated by a few facts of overriding importance. The first of these is the prodigious reproductive potential of most fish species. The adult female cod, for example, lays millions of eggs at each spawn. The egg that hatches and ultimately reaches maturity is the great exception rather than the rule. The various herrings (Clupeidae) are the most plentiful of the commercial species, accounting for close to half the world's total catch, as well as providing food for many other sea species. Yet herring are among the smallest spawners, laying a mere hundred thousand eggs a season, which, themselves, are eaten in large quantity by other species. Even in inclosed waters the survival and reproductive powers of fish appear to be very great. In 1939 the Fisheries Research Board of Canada deliberately tried to kill all the fish in one small lake by poisoning the water. Two years later more than ninety thousand fish were found in the lake, including only about six hundred old enough to have escaped from poisoning.

The picture one gets of life in the sea is one of constant predation of one species on another, each species living on a narrow margin of food supply. It reminds the economist of the Malthusian law of population; for, unlike man, the fish has no power to alter the conditions of his environment and consequently cannot progress. In fact, Malthus and his law are frequently mentioned in the biological literature. One's first reaction is to declare that environmental factors are so much more important than commercial fishing that man has no effect on the population of the sea at all. One of the continuing investigations made by fisheries biologists is the determination of the age distribution of catches. This is possible because fish continue to grow in size with age, and seasonal changes are reflected in certain hard parts of their bodies in much the same manner as one finds growth-rings in a tree. The study of these age distributions shows that commercial catches are heavily affected by good and bad brood years. A good brood year, one favourable to the hatching of eggs and the survival of fry, has its effect on future catches, and one can discern the dominating importance of that brood year in the commercial catches of succeeding years.[7] Large broods, however, do not appear to depend on large numbers of adult spawners, and this lends support to the belief that the fish population is entirely unaffected by the activity of man.

There is, however, important evidence to the contrary. World Wars I and II, during which fishing was sharply curtailed in European waters, were followed by indications of a significant growth in fish populations. Fish-marking experiments, of which there have been a great number, indicate that fishing is a major cause of fish mortality in developed fisheries. The introduction of restrictive laws has often been followed by an increase in fish populations, although the evidence on this point is capable of other interpretations which will be noted later.

General opinion among fisheries biologists appears to have had something of a cyclical pattern. During the latter part of the last century, the Scottish fisheries biologist, W. C. MacIntosh,[8] and the great Darwinian, T. H. Huxley, argued strongly against all restrictive measures on the basis of the inexhaustible nature of the fishery resources of the sea. As Huxley put it in 1883: "The cod fishery, the herring fishery, the pilchard fishery, the mackerel fishery, and probably all the great sea fisheries, are inexhaustible: that is to say that nothing we do seriously affects the number of fish. And any attempt to regulate these fisheries seems consequently, from the nature of the case, to be useless."[9] As a matter of fact, there was at this time relatively little restriction of fishing in European waters. Following the Royal Commission of 1866, England had repealed a host of restrictive laws. The development of steam-powered trawling in the 1880s, which enormously increased man's predatory capacity, and the marked improvement of the trawl method in 1923 turned the pendulum, and throughout the interwar years discussion centered on the problem of "overfishing" and "depletion." This was accompanied by a considerable growth of restrictive regulations.[10] Only recently has the pendulum begun to reverse again, and there has lately been expressed in biological quarters a high degree of skepticism concerning the efficacy of restrictive measures, and the Huxleyian faith in the inexhaustibility of the sea has once again begun to find advocates. In 1951 Dr Harden F. Taylor summarized the overall position of world fisheries in the following words:

> Such statistics of world fisheries as are available suggest that while particular species have fluctuated in abundance, the *yield of the sea fisheries as a whole or of any considerable region has not only been sustained, but has generally increased with increasing human populations,* and there is as yet no sign that they will not continue to do so. No single species so far as we know has ever become extinct, and no regional fishery in the world has ever been exhausted.[11]

In formulating governmental policy, biologists appear to have had a hard struggle (not always successful) to avoid oversimplification of the problem. One of the crudest arguments to have had some support is known as the "propagation theory," associated with the name of the English biologist, E. W. L. Holt.[12] Holt advanced the proposition that legal size limits should be established at a level that would permit every individual of the species in question to spawn at least once. This suggestion was effectively demolished by the age-distribution studies whose results have been noted above. Moreover, some fisheries, such as the "sardine" fishery of the Canadian Atlantic Coast, are specifically for *immature* fish. The history of this particular fishery shows no evidence whatever that the landings have been in any degree reduced by the practice of taking very large quantities of fish of prespawning age year after year.

The state of uncertainty in biological quarters around the turn of the century is perhaps indicated by the fact that Holt's propagation theory was advanced concurrently with its diametric opposite: "the thinning theory" of the Danish biologist, C. G. J. Petersen.[13] The latter argued that the fish may be too plentiful for the available food and that thinning out the young by fishing would enable the remainder to grow more rapidly. Petersen supported his theory with the results of transplanting experiments which showed that the fish transplanted to a new habitat frequently grew much more rapidly than before. But this is equivalent to arguing that the reason why rabbits multiplied so rapidly when introduced to Australia is because there were no rabbits already there with which they had to compete for food. Such an explanation would neglect all the other elements of importance in a natural ecology. In point of fact, in so far as food alone is concerned, thinning a cod population, say by half, would not double the food supply of the remaining individuals; for there are other species, perhaps not commercially valuable, that use the same food as the cod.

Dr Burkenroad's comment, quoted earlier, that the purpose of practical policy is the benefit of man, not fish, was not gratuitous, for the argument has at times been advanced that commercial fishing should crop the resource in such a way as to leave the stocks of fish in the sea completely unchanged. Baranoff was largely responsible for destroying this approach, showing most elegantly that a commercial fishery cannot fail to diminish the fish stock. His general conclusion is worth quoting, for it states clearly not only his own position but the error of earlier thinking:

> As we see, a picture is obtained which diverges radically from the hypothesis which has been favoured almost down to the present time, namely that the natural reserve of fish is an inviolable capital, of which the fishing industry must use only the interest, not touching the capital at all. Our theory says, on the contrary, that a fishery and a natural reserve of fish are incompatible, and that the exploitable stock of fish is a changeable quantity, which depends on the intensity of the fishery. The more fish we take from a body of water, the smaller is the basic stock remaining in it; and the less fish we take, the greater is the basic stock, approximating to the natural stock when the fishery approaches zero. Such is the nature of the matter.[14]

The general conception of a fisheries ecology would appear to make such a conclusion inevitable. If a species were in ecological equilibrium before the commencement of commercial fishing, man's intrusion would have the same effect as any other predator; and that can only mean that the species population would reach a new equilibrium at a lower level of abundance, the divergence of the new equilibrium from the old depending on the degree of man's predatory effort and effectiveness.

The term "fisheries management" has been much in vogue in recent years, being taken to express a more subtle approach to the fisheries problem than the older terms "depletion" and "conservation." Briefly, it focuses attention on the quantity of fish caught, taking as the human objective of commercial fishing the derivation of the largest sustainable catch. This approach is often hailed in the biological literature as the "new theory" or the "modern formulation" of the fisheries problem.[15] Its limitations, however, are very serious, and, indeed, the new approach comes very little closer to treating the fisheries problem as one of human utilization of natural resources than did the older, more primitive, theories. Focusing attention on the maximization of the catch neglects entirely the inputs of other factors of production which are used up in fishing and must be accounted for as costs. There are many references to such ultimate economic considerations in the biological literature but no analytical integration of the economic factors. In fact, the very conception of a *net economic yield* has scarcely made any appearance at all. On the whole, biologists tend to treat the fisherman as an exogenous element in their analytical model, and the behavior of fishermen is not made into an integrated element of a general and systematic "bionomic" theory. In the case of the fishing industry the large numbers of fishermen permit valid behavioristic generalization of their activities along the lines of the standard economic theory of production. The following section attempts to apply that theory to the fishing industry and to demonstrate that the "overfishing problem" has its roots in the economic organization of the industry.

III Economic theory of the fishery

In the analysis which follows, the theory of optimum utilization of fishery resources and the reasons for its frustration in practice are developed for a typical demersal fish. Demersal, or bottomdwelling fishes, such as cod, haddock, and similar species and the various flatfishes, are relatively nonmigratory in character. They live and feed on shallow continental shelves where the continual mixing of cold water maintains the availability of those nutrient salts which form the fundamental basis of marine-food chains. The various feeding grounds are separated by deep-water channels which constitute barriers to the movement of these species; and in some cases the fish of different banks can be differentiated morphologically, having varying numbers of vertebrae or some such distinguishing characteristic. The significance of this fact is that each fishing ground can be treated as unique, in the same sense as can a piece of land, possessing, at the very least, one characteristic not shared by any other piece: that is, location.

(Other species, such as herring, mackerel, and similar pelagic or surface dwellers, migrate over very large distances, and it is necessary to treat the resource of an entire geographic region as one. The conclusions arrived at below are applicable to such fisheries, but the method of analysis employed is not formally applicable. The same is true of species that migrate to and from fresh water and the lake fishes proper.)

We can define the optimum degree of utilization of any particular fishing ground as that which maximizes the net economic yield, the difference between total cost, on the one hand, and total receipts (or total value production), on the other.[16] Total cost and total production can each be expressed as a function of the degree of fishing intensity or, as the biologists put it, "fishing effort," so that a simple maximization solution is possible. Total cost will be a linear function of fishing effort, if we assume no fishinginduced effects on factor prices, which is reasonable for any particular regional fishery.

The production function – the relationship between fishing effort and total value produced – requires some special attention. If we were to follow the usual presentation of economic theory, we should argue that this function would be positive but, after a point, would rise at a diminishing rate because of the law of diminishing returns. This would not mean that the fish population has been reduced, for the law refers only to the *proportions* of factors to one another, and a fixed fish population, together with an increasing intensity of effort, would be assumed to show the typical sigmoid pattern of yield. However, in what follows it will be assumed that the law of diminishing returns in this pure sense is inoperative in the fishing industry. (The reasons will be advanced at a later point in this paper.) We shall assume that, as fishing effort expands, the catch of fish increases at a diminishing rate but that it does so because of the effect of catch upon the fish population.[17] So far as the argument of the next few pages is concerned, all that is formally necessary is to assume that, as fishing intensity increases, catch will grow at a diminishing rate. Whether this reflects the pure law of diminishing returns or the reduction of population by fishing, or both, is of no particular importance. The point at issue will, however, take on more significance in Section IV and will be examined there.

Our analysis can be simplified if we retain the ordinary production function instead of converting it to cost curves, as is usually done in the theory of the firm. Let us further assume that the functional relationship between average production (production-per-unit-of-fishing-effort) and the quantity of fishing effort is uniformly linear. This does not distort the results unduly, and it permits the analysis to be presented more simply and in graphic terms that are already quite familiar.

In Figure 9.1 the optimum intensity of utilization of a particular fishing ground is shown. The curves *AP* and *MP* represent, respectively, the average productivity and marginal productivity of fishing effort. The relationship between them is the same as that between average revenue and marginal revenue in imperfect competition theory, and *MP* bisects any horizontal between the ordinate and *AP*. Since the costs of fishing supplies, etc., are assumed to be unaffected by the amount of fishing effort, marginal cost and average cost are identical and constant, as shown by the curve *MC, AC*.[18] These costs are assumed to include an opportunity income for the fishermen, the income that could be earned in other comparable employments. Then *Ox* is the optimum intensity of effort on this fishing ground, and the resource will, at this level of exploitation, provide the maximum net economic yield indicated by the shaded area *apqc*. The maximum sustained physical yield that the biologists speak of will be attained when marginal productivity of fishing effort is zero, at *Oz* of fishing intensity in the chart shown. Thus, as one might expect, the optimum economic fishing intensity is less than that which would produce the maximum sustained physical yield.

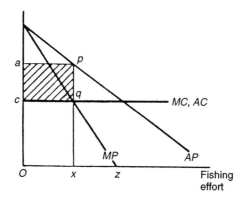

Figure 9.1

The area *apqc* in Figure 9.1 can be regarded as the rent yielded by the fishery resource. Under the given conditions, *Ox* is the best rate of exploitation for the fishing ground in question, and the rent reflects the productivity of that ground, not any artificial market limitation. The rent here corresponds to the extra productivity yielded in agriculture by soils of better quality or location than those on the margin of cultivation, which may produce an opportunity income but no more. In short, Figure 9.1 shows the determination of the intensive margin of utilization on an intramarginal fishing ground.

We now come to the point that is of greatest theoretical importance in understanding the primary production phase of the fishing industry and in distinguishing it from agriculture. In the sea fisheries the natural resource is not private property; hence the rent it may yield is not capable of being appropriated by anyone. The individual fisherman has no legal title to a section of ocean bottom. Each fisherman is more or less free to fish wherever he pleases. The result is a pattern of competition among fishermen which culminates in the dissipation of the rent of the intramarginal grounds. This can be most clearly seen through an analysis of the relationship between the intensive margin and the extensive margin of resource exploitation in fisheries.

In Figure 9.2, two fishing grounds of different fertility (or location) are shown. Any given amount of fishing effort devoted to ground *2* will yield a smaller total (and therefore average) product than if devoted to *1*. The maximization problem is now a question of the allocation of fishing effort between grounds *1* and *2*. The optimum is, of course,

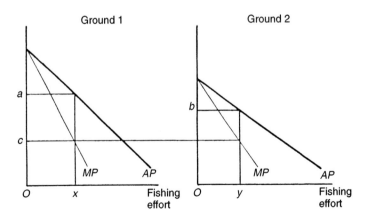

Figure 9.2

where the marginal productivities are equal on both grounds. In Figure 9.2, fishing effort of Ox on *1* and Oy on *2* would maximize the total net yield of $Ox + Oy$ effort if marginal cost were equal to Oc. But if under such circumstances the individual fishermen are free to fish on whichever ground they please, it is clear that this is not an equilibrium allocation of fishing effort in the sense of connoting stability. A fisherman starting from port and deciding whether to go to ground *1* or *2* does not care for *marginal* productivity but for *average* productivity, for it is the latter that indicates where the greater total yield may be obtained. If fishing effort were allocated in the optimum fashion, as shown in Figure 9.2, with Ox on *1*, and Oy on *2*, this would be a disequilibrium situation. Each fisherman could expect to get an average catch of Oa on *1* but only Ob on *2*. Therefore, fishermen would shift from *2* to *1*. Stable equilibrium would not be reached until the average productivity of both grounds was equal. If we now imagine a continuous gradation of fishing grounds, the extensive margin would be on that ground which yielded nothing more than outlaid costs plus opportunity income – in short, the one on which average productivity and average cost were equal. But, since average cost is the same for all grounds and the average productivity of all grounds is also brought to equality by the free and competitive nature of fishing, this means that the intramarginal grounds also yield no rent. It is entirely possible that some grounds would be exploited at a level of *negative* marginal productivity. What happens is that the rent which the intramarginal grounds are capable of yielding is dissipated through misallocation of fishing effort.

This is why fishermen are not wealthy, despite the fact that the fishery resources of the sea are the richest and most indestructible available to man. By and large, the only fisherman who becomes rich is one who makes a lucky catch or one who participates in a fishery that is put under a form of social control that turns the open resource into property rights.

Up to this point, the remuneration of fishermen has been accounted for as an opportunity-cost income comparable to earnings attainable in other industries. In point of fact, fishermen typically earn less than most others, even in much less hazardous occupations or in those requiring less skill. There is no effective reason why the competition among fishermen described above must stop at the point where opportunity incomes are yielded. It may be and is in many cases carried much further. Two factors prevent an equilibration of fishermen's incomes with those of other members of society. The first is the great immobility of fishermen. Living often in isolated communities, with little knowledge of conditions or opportunities elsewhere; educationally and often romantically tied to the sea; and lacking the savings necessary to provide a "stake," the fisherman is one of the least mobile of occupational groups. But, second, there is in the spirit of every fisherman the hope of the "lucky catch." As those who know fishermen well have often testified, they are gamblers and incurably optimistic. As a consequence, they will work for less than the going wage.[19]

The theory advanced above is substantiated by important developments in the fishing industry. For example, practically all control measures have, in the past, been designed by biologists, with sole attention paid to the production side of the problem and none to the cost side. The result has been a wide-open door for the frustration of the purposes of such measures. The Pacific halibut fishery, for example, is often hailed as a great achievement in modern fisheries management. Under international agreement between the United States and Canada, a fixed-catch limit was established during the early thirties. Since then, catch-per-unit-effort indexes, as usually interpreted, show a significant rise in the fish population. W. F. Thompson, the pioneer of the Pacific halibut management program, noted that "it has often been said that the halibut regulation presents the only definite case of sustained improvement of an overfished deep-sea fishery. This, I believe, is true and the fact should lend special importance to the principles which have been deliberately used to obtain this improvement."[20] Actually, careful study of the statistics indicates that the estimated recovery of halibut stocks could not have been due principally to the control measures, for the average catch was, in fact, greater during the recovery years than during the years of decline. The total amount of fish taken was only a small fraction of the estimated population reduction for the years prior to regulation.[21] Natural factors seem to be mainly responsible for the observed change in population, and the institution of control regulations almost a coincidence. Such coincidences are not uncommon in the history of fisheries policy, but they may be easily explained. If a long-term cyclical fluctuation is taking place in a commercially valuable species, controls will likely be instituted when fishing yields have fallen very low and the clamor of fishermen is great; but it is then, of course, that stocks are about due to recover in any case. The "success" of conservation measures may be due fully as much to the sociological foundations of public policy as to the policy's effect on the fish. Indeed, Burkenroad argues that biological statistics in general may be called into question on these grounds. Governments sponsor biological research when the catches are disappointing. If there are long-term cyclical fluc-tuations in fish populations, as some think, it is hardly to be wondered why biologists frequently discover that the sea is being depleted, only to change their collective opinion a decade or so later.

Quite aside from the *biological* argument on the Pacific halibut case, there is no clear-cut evidence that halibut fishermen were made rela-tively more prosperous by the control measures. Whether or not the recovery of the halibut stocks was due to natural factors or to the catch limit, the potential net yield this could have meant has been dissipated through a rise in fishing costs. Since the method of control was to halt fishing when the limit had been reached, this created a great incentive on the part of each fisherman to get the fish before his competitors. During the last twenty years, fishermen have invested in more, larger, and faster boats in a competitive race for fish. In 1933 the fishing season was more than six months long. In 1952 it took just twenty-six days to catch the legal limit in the area from Willapa Harbor to Cape Spencer, and sixty days in the Alaska region. What has been happening is a rise in the average cost of fishing effort, allowing no gap between average production and average cost to appear, and hence no rent.[22]

Essentially the same phenomenon is observable in the Canadian Atlantic Coast lobster-conservation program. The method of control here is by seasonal closure. The result has been a steady growth in the number of lobster traps set by each fisherman. Virtually all available lob-sters are now caught each year within the season, but at much greater cost in gear and supplies. At a fairly conservative estimate, the same quantity of lobsters could be caught with half the present number of traps. In a few places the fishermen have banded together into a local monopoly, preventing entry and controlling their own operations. By this means, the amount of fishing gear has been greatly reduced and incomes considerably improved.

That the plight of fishermen and the inefficiency of fisheries produc-tion stems from the common-property nature of the resources of the sea is further corroborated by the fact that one finds similar patterns of exploitation and similar problems in other cases of open resources. Perhaps the most obvious is hunting and trapping. Unlike fishes, the biotic potential of land animals is low enough for the species to be destroyed. Uncontrolled hunting means that animals will be killed for any short-range human reason, great or small: for food or simply for fun. Thus the buffalo of the western plains was destroyed to satisfy the most trivial desires of the white man, against which the long-term food needs of the aboriginal population counted as nothing. Even in the most civilized communities, conservation authorities have discovered that a bag-limit *per man* is necessary if complete destruction is to be avoided.

The results of anthropological investigation of modes of land tenure among primitive peoples render some further support to this thesis. In accordance with an evolutionary concept of cultural comparison, the older anthropological study was prone to regard resource tenure in common, with unrestricted exploitation, as a "lower" stage of development comparative with private and group property rights. However, more complete annals of primitive cultures reveal common tenure to be quite rare, even in hunting and gathering societies. Property rights in some form predominate by far, and, most important, their existence may be easily explained in terms of the necessity for orderly exploitation and conservation of the resource. Environmental conditions make necessary some vehicle which will prevent the resources of the community at large from being destroyed by excessive exploitation. Private or group land tenure accomplishes this end in an easily understandable fashion.[23] Significantly, land tenure is found to be "common" only in those cases where the hunting resource is migratory over such large areas that it cannot be regarded as husbandable by the society. In cases of group tenure where the numbers of the group are large, there is still the necessity of co-ordinating the practices of exploitation, in agricultural, as well as in hunting or gathering, economies. Thus, for example, Malinowski reported that among the Trobriand Islanders one of the fundamental principles of land tenure is the co-ordination of the productive activities of the gardeners by the person possessing magical leadership in the group.[24] Speaking generally, we may say that stable primitive cultures appear to have discovered the dangers of common-property tenure and to have developed measures to protect their resources. Or, if a more Darwinian explanation be preferred, we may say that only those primitive cultures have survived which succeeded in developing such institutions.

Another case, from a very different industry, is that of petroleum production. Although the individual petroleum producer may acquire undisputed lease or ownership of the particular plot of land upon which his well is drilled, he shares, in most cases, a common pool of oil with other drillers. There is, consequently, set up the same kind of competitive race as is found in the fishing industry, with attending overexpansion of productive facilities and gross wastage of the resource. In the United States, efforts to regulate a chaotic situation in oil production began as early as 1915. Production practices, number of wells, and even output quotas were set by governmental authority; but it was not until the federal "Hot Oil" Act of 1935 and the development of interstate agreements that the final loophole (bootlegging) was closed through regulation of interstate commerce in oil.

Perhaps the most interesting similar case is the use of common pasture in the medieval manorial economy. Where the ownership of animals was private but the resource on which they fed was common (and limited), it was necessary to regulate the use of common pasture in order to prevent each man from competing and conflicting with his neighbors in an effort to utilize more of the pasture for his own animals. Thus the manor developed its elaborate rules regulating the use of the common pasture, or "stinting" the common: limitations on the number of animals, hours of pasturing, etc., designed to prevent the abuses of excessive individualistic competition.[25]

There appears, then, to be some truth in the conservative dictum that everybody's property is nobody's property. Wealth that is free for all is valued by none because he who is foolhardy enough to wait for its proper time of use will only find that it has been taken by another. The blade of grass that the manorial cowherd leaves behind is valueless to him, for tomorrow it may be eaten by another's animal; the oil left under the earth is valueless to the driller, for another may legally take it; the fish in the sea are valueless to the fisherman, because there is no assurance that they will be there for him tomorrow if they are left behind today. A factor of production that is valued at nothing in the business calculations of its users will yield nothing in income. Common-property natural resources are free goods for the individual and scarce goods for society. Under unregulated private exploitation, they can yield no rent; that can be accomplished only by methods which make them private property or public (government) property, in either case subject to a unified directing power.

IV The bionomic equilibrium of the fishing industry

The work of biological theory in the fishing industry is, basically, an effort to delineate the ecological system in which a particular fish population is found. In the main, the species that have been extensively studied are those which are subject to commercial exploitation. This is due not only to the fact that funds are forthcoming for such research but also because the activity of commercial fishing vessels provides the largest body of data upon which the biologist may work. Despite this, however, the ecosystem of the fisheries biologist is typically one that excludes man.

Or, rather, man is regarded as an exogenous factor, having influence on the biological ecosystem through his removal of fish from the sea, but the activities of man are themselves not regarded as behaviorized or determined by the other elements of a system of mutual interdependence. The large number of independent fishermen who exploit fish populations of commercial importance makes it possible to treat man as a behavior element in a larger, "bionomic," ecology, if we can find the rules which relate his behavior to the other elements of the system. Similarly, in their treatment of the principles of fisheries management, biologists have overlooked essential elements of the problem by setting maximum physical landings as the objective of management, thereby neglecting the economic factor of input cost.

An analysis of the bionomic equilibrium of the fishing industry may, then, be approached in terms of two problems. The first is to explain the nature of the equilibrium of the industry as it occurs in the state of uncontrolled or unmanaged exploitation of a common-property resource. The second is to indicate the nature of a socially optimum manner of exploitation, which is, presumably, what governmental management policy aims to achieve or promote. These two problems will be discussed in the remaining pages.

In the preceding section it was shown that the equilibrium condition of uncontrolled exploitation is such that the net yield (total value landings *minus* total cost) is zero. The "bionomic ecosystem" of the fishing industry, as we might call it, can then be expressed in terms of four variables and four equations. Let P represent the population of the particular fish species on the particular fishing bank in question; L the total quantity taken or "landed" by man, measured in value terms; E the intensity of fishing or the quantity of "fishing effort" expended; and C the total cost of making such effort. The system, then, is as follows:

$$P = P(L), \tag{9.1}$$

$$L = L(P, E), \tag{9.2}$$

$$C = C(E), \tag{9.3}$$

$$C = L. \tag{9.4}$$

Equation (9.4) is the equilibrium condition of an uncontrolled fishery.

The functional relations stated in equations (9.1), (9.2), and (9.3) may be graphically presented as shown in Figure 9.3. Segment *1* shows the fish population as a simple negative function of landings. In segment *2* a map of landings functions is drawn. Thus, for example, if population were P_8, effort of Oe would produce Ol of fish. For each given level of population, a larger fishing effort will result in larger landings. Each population contour is, then, a production function for a given population level. The linearity of these contours indicates that the law of diminishing returns is not operative, nor are any landings-induced price effects assumed to affect the value landings graphed on the vertical axis. These assumptions are made in order to produce the simplest determinate solution; yet each is reasonable in itself. The assumption of a fixed product price is reasonable, since our analysis deals with one fishing ground, not the fishery as a whole. The cost function represented in equation (9.3) and graphed in segment *3* of Figure 9.3 is not really necessary to the determination, but its inclusion makes the matter somewhat clearer. Fixed prices of input factors – "fishing effort" – is assumed, which is reasonable again on the assumption that a small part of the total fishery is being analyzed.

Starting with the first segment, we see that a postulated catch of Ol connotes an equilibrium population in the biological ecosystem of Op. Suppose this population to be represented by the contour P_3 of segment *2*. Then, given P_3, Oe is the effort required to catch the postulated landings Ol. This quantity of effort involves a total cost of Oc, as shown in segment *3* of the graph. In full bionomic equilibrium, $C = L$, and if the particular values Oc and Ol shown are not equal, other quantities of all four variables, L, P, E, and C, are required, involving movements of these variables through the functional system shown. The operative movement is, of course, in fishing effort, E. It is the equilibrating variable in the system.

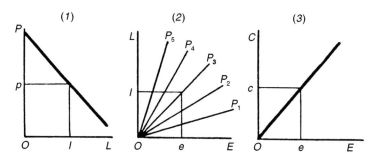

Figure 9.3

The equilibrium equality of landings (L) and cost (C), however, must be a position of stability, and $L = C$ is a necessary, though not in itself sufficient, condition for stability in the ecosystem. This is shown by Figure 9.4. If effort-cost and effort-landings functions were both linear, no stable equilibrium could be found. If the case were represented by C and L_1, the fishery would contract to zero; if by C and L_2, it would undergo an infinite expansion. Stable equilibrium requires that either the cost or the landings function be nonlinear. This condition is fulfilled by the assumption that population is reduced by fishing (equation (9.1) above). The equilibrium is therefore as shown in Figure 9.5. Now *Oe* represents a fully stable equilibrium intensity of fishing.

The analysis of the conditions of stable equilibrium raises some points of general theoretical interest. In the foregoing we have assumed that

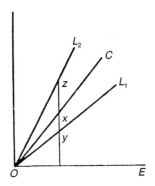

Figure 9.4

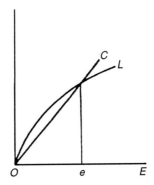

Figure 9.5

stability results from the effect of fishing on the fish population. In the standard analysis of economic theory, we should have employed the law of diminishing returns to produce a landings function of the necessary shape. Market factors might also have been so employed; a larger supply of fish, forthcoming from greater fishing effort, would reduce unit price and thereby produce a landings function with the necessary negative second derivative Similarly, greater fishing intensity might raise the unit costs of factors, producing a cost function with a positive second derivative. Any one of these three – population effects, law of diminishing returns, or market effects – is alone sufficient to produce stable equilibrium in the ecosystem.

As to the law of diminishing returns, it has not been accepted *per se* by fisheries biologists. It is, in fact, a principle that becomes quite slippery when one applies it to the case of fisheries. Indicative of this is the fact that Alfred Marshall, in whose *Principles* one can find extremely little formal error, misinterprets the application of the law of diminishing returns to the fishing industry, arguing, in effect, that the law exerts its influence through the reducing effect of fishing on the fish population.[26] There have been some interesting expressions of the law or, rather, its essential varying-proportions-of-factors aspect, in the biological literature. H. M. Kyle, a German biologist, included it in 1928 among a number of reasons why catch-per-unit-of-fishing-effort indexes are not adequate measures of population change.[27] Interestingly enough, his various criticisms of the indexes were generally accepted, with the significant exception of this one point. More recently, A. G. Huntsman warned his colleagues in fisheries biology that "[there] may be a decrease in the take-per-unit-of-effort without any decrease in the total take or in the fish population. . . . This may mean that there has been an increase in fishermen rather than a decrease in fish."[28] While these statements run in terms of average rather than marginal yield, their underlying reasoning clearly appears to be that of the law of diminishing returns. The point has had little influence in biological circles, however, and when, two years ago, I advanced it, as Kyle and Huntsman had done, in criticism of the standard biological method of estimating population change, it received pretty short shrift.

In point of fact, the law of diminishing returns is much more difficult to sustain in the case of fisheries than in agriculture or industry. The "proof" one finds in standard theory is not empirical, although the results of empirical experiments in agriculture are frequently adduced as subsidiary corroboration. The main weight of the law, however, rests on a *reductio ad absurdum*. One can easily demonstrate that, were it not for the law of diminishing returns, all the world's food could be grown on one acre of land. Reality is markedly different, and it is because the law serves to render this reality intelligible to the logical mind, or, as we might say, "explains" it, that it occupies such a firm place in the body of economic theory. In fisheries, however, the pattern of reality can easily be explained on other grounds. In the case at least of developed demersal fisheries, it cannot be denied that the fish population is reduced by fishing, and this relationship serves perfectly well to explain why an infinitely expansible production is not possible from a fixed fishing area. The other basis on which the law of diminishing returns is usually advanced in economic theory is the prima facie plausibility of the principle as such; but here, again, it is hard to grasp any similar reasoning in fisheries. In the typical agricultural illustration, for example, we may argue that the fourth harrowing or the fourth weeding, say, has a lower marginal productivity than the third. Such an assertion brings ready acceptance because it concerns a process with a zero productive limit. It is apparent that, ultimately, the land would be completely broken up or the weeds completely eliminated if harrowing or weeding were done in ever larger amounts. The law of diminishing returns signifies simply that such a zero limit is *gradually approached*, all of which appears to be quite acceptable on prima facie grounds. There is nothing comparable to this in fisheries at all, for there is no "cultivation" in the same sense of the term, except, of course, in such cases as oyster culture or pond rearing of fish, which are much more akin to farming than to typical sea fisheries.

In the biological literature the point has, I think, been well thought through, though the discussion does not revolve around the "law of diminishing returns" by that name. It is related rather to the fisheries biologist's problem of the interpretation of catch-per-unit-of-fishing-effort statistics. The essence of the law is usually eliminated by the assumption that there is no "competition" among units of fishing gear – that is, that the ratio of gear to fishing area and/or fish population is small. In some cases, corrections have been made by the use of the compound-interest formula where some competition among gear units is considered to exist.[29] Such corrections, however, appear to be based on the idea of an increasing catch-population ratio rather than an increasing effort-population ratio. The latter would be as the law of diminishing returns would have it; the idea lying behind the former is that the total population in existence represents the maximum that can be caught, and, since this maximum would be gradually approached, the ratio of catch to population has some bearing on the efficiency of fishing gear. It is, then, just an aspect of the population-reduction effect. Similarly, it has been pointed out that, since fish are recruited into the catchable stock in a seasonal fashion, one can expect the catch-per-unit-effort to fall as the fishing season progresses, at least in those fisheries where a substantial proportion of the stock is taken annually. Seasonal averaging is therefore necessary in using the catch-effort statistics as population indexes from year to year. This again is a population-reduction effect, not the law of diminishing returns. In general, there seems to be no reason for departing from the approach of the fisheries biologist on this point. The law of diminishing returns is not necessary to explain the conditions of stable equilibrium in a static model of the fishery, nor is there any prima facie ground for its acceptance.

Let us now consider the exploitation of a fishing ground under unified control, in which case the equilibrium condition is the maximization of net financial yield, $L - C$.

The map of population contours graphed in segment *2* of Figure 9.3 may be superimposed upon the total-landings and total-cost functions graphed in Figure 9.5. The result is as shown in Figure 9.6. In the system of interrelationships we have to consider, population changes affect,

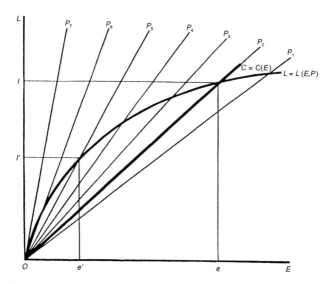

Figure 9.6

and are in turn affected by, the amount of fish landed. The map of population contours does not include this roundabout effect that a population change has upon itself. The curve labeled L, however, is a landings function which accounts for the fact that larger landings reduce the population, and this is why it is shown to have a steadily diminishing slope. We may regard the landings function as moving progressively to lower population contours P_7, P_6, P_5, etc., as total landings increase in magnitude. As a consequence, while each population contour represents many hypothetical combinations of E, L, and P, only one such combination on each is actually compatible in this system of interrelationships. This combination is the point on any contour where that contour is met by the landings function L. Thus the curve labeled L may be regarded as tracing out a series of combinations of E, L, and P which are compatible with one another in the system.

The total-cost function may be drawn as shown, with total cost, C, measured in terms of landings, which the vertical axis represents.[30] This is a linear function of effort as shown. The optimum intensity of fishing effort is that which maximizes $L - C$. This is the monopoly solution; but, since we are considering only a single fishing ground, no price effects are introduced, and the social optimum coincides with maximum monopoly revenue. In this case we are maximizing the yield of a natural resource, not a privileged position, as in standard monopoly theory. The rent here is a social surplus yielded by the resource, not in any part due to artificial scarcity, as is monopoly profit or rent.

If the optimum fishing intensity is that which maximizes $L - C$, this is seen to be the position where the slope of the landings function equals the slope of the cost function in Figure 9.6. Thus the optimum fishing intensity is Oe' of fishing effort. This will yield Ol' of landings, and the species population will be in continuing stable equilibrium at a level indicated by P_5.

The equilibrium resulting from uncontrolled competitive fishing, where the rent is dissipated, can also be seen in Figure 9.6. This, being where $C = L$, is at Oe of effort and Ol of landings, and at a stable population level of P_2. As can be clearly seen, the uncontrolled equilibrium means a higher expenditure of effort, higher fish landings, and a lower continuing fish population than the optimum equilibrium.

Algebraically, the bionomic ecosystem may be set out in terms of the optimum solution as follows. The species population in equilibrium is a linear function of the amount of fish taken from the sea:

$$P = a - bL. \qquad (9.5)$$

In this function, *a* may be described as the "natural population" of the species – the equilibrium level it would attain if not commercially fished. All natural factors, such as water temperatures, food supplies, natural predators, etc., which affect the population are, for the purposes of the system analyzed, locked up in *a*. The magnitude of *a* is the vertical intercept of the population function graphed in segment *1* of Figure 9.3. The slope of this function is *b*, which may be described as the "depletion coefficient," since it indicates the effect of catch on population. The landings function is such that no landings are forthcoming with either zero effort or zero population; therefore,

$$L = cEP. \qquad (9.6)$$

The parameter *c* in this equation is the technical coefficient of production or, as we may call it simply, the "production coefficient." Total cost is a function of the amount of fishing effort.

$$C = qE.$$

The optimum condition is that the total net receipts must be maximized, that is,

$$L - C \text{ to be maximized.}$$

Since *q* has been assumed constant and equal to unity (i.e., effort is counted in "dollars-worth" units), we may write *L* – *E* to be maximized. Let this be represented by *R*:

$$R = L - E, \qquad (9.7)$$

$$\frac{dR}{dE} = 0. \qquad (9.8)$$

The four numbered equations constitute the system when in optimality equilibrium. In order to find this optimum, the landings junction equation (9.6) may be rewritten, with the aid of equation (9.5), as:

$$L = cE(a - bL).$$

From this we have at once

$$L \, (1 + cEb) = cEa,$$

$$L = \frac{caE}{1 + cbE}.$$

To find the optimum intensity of effort, we have, from equation (9.3):

$$\frac{dR}{dE} = \frac{dL}{dE} - \frac{dE}{dE}$$

$$= \frac{(1 + cbE)(ca) - caE(cb)}{(1 + cbE)^2} - 1,$$

$$= \frac{ca}{(1 + cbE)^2} - 1;$$

for a maximum, this must be set equal to zero; hence,

$$ca = (1 + cbE)^2,$$

$$1 + cbE = \pm\sqrt{ca},$$

$$E = \frac{-1 \pm \sqrt{ca}}{cb}.$$

For positive E,

$$E = \frac{\sqrt{ca} - 1}{cb}.$$

This result indicates that the effect on optimum effort of a change in the production coefficient is uncertain, a rise in c calling for a rise in E in some cases and a fall in E in others, depending on the magnitude of the change in c. The effects of changes in the natural population and depletion coefficient are, however, clear, a rise (fall) in a calling for a rise (fall) in E, while a rise (fall) in b means a fall (rise) in E.

Notes

1 The single exception that I know is G. M. Gerhardsen, "Production Economics in Fisheries," *Revista de economia* (Lisbon), March, 1952.
2 Especially remarkable efforts in this sense are Robert A. Nesbit, "Fishery Management" US Fish and Wildlife Service, "Special Scientific Reports," No. 18 [Chicago, 1943]) (mimeographed), and Harden F. Taylor, *Survey of Marine Fisheries of North Carolina* (Chapel Hill, 1951); also R. J. H. Beverton, "Some Observations on the Principles of Fishery Regulation," *Journal du conseil*

permanent international pour l'exploration de la mer (Copenhagen), Vol. XIX, No. 1 (May, 1953); and M. D. Burkenroad, "Some Principles of Marine Fishery Biology," *Publications of the Institute of Marine Science* (University of Texas), Vol. II, No. 1 (September, 1951).

3 "Theory and Practice of Marine Fishery Management," *Journal du conseil permanent international pour l'exploration de la mer*, Vol. XVIII, No. 3 (January, 1953).

4 Two of Baranoff's most important papers – "On the Question of the Biological Basis of Fisheries" (1918) and "On the Question of the Dynamics of the Fishing Industry" (1925) – have been translated by W. E. Ricker, now of the Fisheries Research Board of Canada (Nanaimo, B. C.), and issued in mimeographed form.

5 "Fishery Depletion," *Science*, XCIX (1944), 534.

6 "The highest take is not necessarily the best. The take should be increased only as long as the extra cost is offset by the added revenue from sales" (A. G. Huntsman, "Research on Use and Increase of Fish Stocks," *Proceedings of the United Nations Scientific Conference on the Conservation and Utilization of Resources* [Lake Success, 1949]).

7 One example of a very general phenomenon: 1904 was such a successful brood year for Norwegian herrings that the 1904 year class continued to outweigh all others in importance in the catch from 1907 through to 1919. The 1904 class was some thirty times as numerous as other year classes during the period (Johan Hjort, "Fluctuations in the Great Fisheries of Northern Europe," *Rapports et Procèsverbaux, Conseil permanent international pour l'exploration de la mer*, Vol. XX [1914]; see also E. S. Russell, *The Overfishing Problem* [Cambridge, 1942], p. 57).

8 See his *Resources of the Sea* published in 1899.

9 Quoted in M. Graham, *The Fish Gate* (London, 1943). p. 111; see also T. H. Huxley, "The Herring," *Nature* (London), 1881.

10 See H. Scott Gordon, "The Trawler Question in the United Kingdom and Canada," *Dalhousie Review*, summer, 1951.

11 Taylor, *op. cit.*, p. 314 (Dr. Taylor's italics).

12 See E. W. L. Holt, "An Examination of the Grimsby Trawl Fishery," *Journal of the Marine Biological Association* (Plymouth), 1895.

13 See C. G. J. Petersen, "What Is Overfishing?" *Journal of the Marine Biological Association* (Plymouth), 1900–1903.

14 T. I. Baranoff, "On the Question of the Dynamics of the Fishing Industry," p. 5 (mimeographed).

15 See, e.g., R. E. Foerster, "Prospects for Managing Our Fisheries," *Bulletin of the Bingham Oceanographic Collection* (New Haven), May, 1948; E. S. Russell, "Some Theoretical Considerations on the Overfishing Problem," *Journal du conseil permanent international pour l'exploration de la mer*, 1931, and *The Overfishing Problem*, Lecture IV.

16 Expressed in these terms, this appears to be the monopoly maximum, but it coincides with the social optimum under the conditions employed in the analysis, as will be indicated below.

17 Throughout this paper the conception of fish population that is employed is one of *weight* rather than *numbers*. A good deal of the biological theory has been an effort to combine growth factors and numbers factors into

weight sums. The following analysis will neglect the fact that, for some species, fish of different sizes bring different unit prices.

18 Throughout this analysis, fixed costs are neglected. The general conclusions reached would not be appreciably altered, I think, by their inclusion, though the presentation would be greatly complicated. Moreover, in the fishing industry the most substantial portion of fixed cost – wharves, harbors, etc. – is borne by government and does not enter into the cost calculations of the operators.

19 "The gambling instinct of the men makes many of them work for less remuneration than they would accept as a weekly wage, because there is always the possibility of a good catch and a financial windfall" (Graham, *op. cit.*, p. 86).

20 W. F. Thompson, "Condition of Stocks of Halibut in the Pacific," *Journal du conseil permanent international pour l'exploration de la mer*, Vol. XVIII, No. 2 (August, 1952).

21 See M. D. Burkenroad, "Fluctuations in Abundance of Pacific Halibut," *Bulletin of the Bingham Oceanographic Collection*, May, 1948.

22 The economic significance of the reduction in season length which followed upon the catch limitation imposed in the Pacific halibut fishery has not been fully appreciated. For example, Michael Graham said in summary of the program in 1943: "The result has been that it now takes only five months to catch the quantity of halibut that formerly needed nine. This, *of course*, has meant profit, where there was none before" (*op. cit.*, p. 156; my italics). Yet, even when biologists have grasped the economic import of the halibut program and its results, they appear reluctant to declare against it. For example, W. E. Ricker: "This method of regulation does not necessarily make for more profitable fishing and certainly puts no effective brake on waste of effort, since an unlimited number of boats is free to join the fleet and compete during the short period that fishing is open. However, the stock is protected, and yield approximates to a maximum if quotas are wisely set; as biologists, perhaps we are not required to think any further. Some claim that any mixing into the economics of the matter might prejudice the desirable biological consequences of regulation by quotas" ("Production and Utilization of Fish Population," in a Symposium on Dynamics of Production in Aquatic Populations, Ecological Society of America, *Ecological Monographs*, XVI [October, 1946], 385). What such "desirable biological consequences" might be, is hard to conceive. Since the regulatory policies are made by man, surely it is necessary they be evaluated in terms of human, not piscatorial, objectives.

23 See Frank G. Speck, "Land Ownership among Hunting Peoples in Primitive America and the World's Marginal Areas," *Proceedings of the 22nd International Congress of Americanists* (Rome, 1926), II, 323–32.

24 B. Malinowski, *Coral Gardens and Their Magic*. Vol. I, chaps. xi and xii. Malinowski sees this as further evidence of the importance of magic in the culture rather than as a means of co-ordinating productive activity; but his discussion of the practice makes it clear that the latter is, to use Malinowski's own concept, the "function" of the institution of magical leadership, at least in this connection.

25 See P. Vinogradoff, *The Growth of the Manor* [London, 1905], chap. iv; E. Lipson, *The Economic History of England* [London, 1949], I, 72.

26 See H. Scott Gordon, "On a Misinterpretation of the Law of Diminishing Returns in Alfred Marshall's *Principles,*" *Canadian Journal of Economics and Political Science,* February, 1952.

27 "Die Statistik der Seefischerei Nordeuropas," *Handbuch der Seefischerei Nordeuropas* (Stuttgart, 1928).

28 A. G. Huntsman, "Fishing and Assessing Populations," *Bulletin of the Bingham Oceanographic Collection* (New Haven), May, 1948.

29 See, e.g., W. F. Thompson and F. H. Bell, *Biological Statistics of the Pacific Halibut Fishery, No. 2: Effect of Changes in Intensity upon Total Yield and Yield per Unit of Gear: Report of the International Fisheries Commission* (Seattle, 1934).

30 More correctly, perhaps, C and L are both measured in money terms.

10
Politics, Policy, and the Pigovian Margins[1]

James M. Buchanan

Since Sidgwick and Marshall, and notably since Pigou's *The Economics of Welfare*, economists have accepted the presence or absence of external effects in production and consumption as a primary criterion of market efficiency. When private decisions exert effects that are external to the decision-maker, "ideal" output is not obtained through the competitive organisation of economic activity even if the remaining conditions necessary for efficiency are satisfied. The market "fails" to the extent that there exist divergencies between marginal private products and marginal social products and/or between marginal private costs and marginal social costs. This basic Pigovian theorem has been theoretically refined and elaborated in numerous works, but its conceptual validity has rarely been challenged.[2] The purpose of this paper is to bring into question a fundamental implication of this aspect of theoretical welfare economics, namely, the implication that externalities are either reduced or eliminated by the shift of an activity from market to political organisation. I shall try to show that this implication will stand up to critical scrutiny only under certain highly restricted assumptions about human behaviour in modern political systems. When these restrictive assumptions are modified, the concept of divergence between marginal "social" product (cost) and marginal private product (cost) loses most of its usefulness.[3]

"Imperfection" and "failure" are descriptive nouns that tell something about the operation of the organism, the activity, or the organisation that is under discussion. These words, and others like them, are meaningful only if the alternative states of "perfection" and "success" are either specifically described or are assumed to be tacitly recognised by participants in the discussion. In the analysis of market organisation, the "perfectly-working" order has been quite carefully defined. The necessary conditions for Paretian optimality are now a part of the professional economist's stock-in-trade, and these conditions are known to be satisfied only when all of the relevant costs and benefits resulting from an action are incorporated into the calculus of the decision-maker that selects the action. By contrast with this state of perfection, almost all ordinary or real-world markets are "imperfect", in greater or lesser degree. Most private decisions exert external effects. So far, so good. If this were the end of it, however, there would be little point in all of the effort. Economists must imply or suggest that the imperfectly-working organisation is, in fact, "perfectible": that is, they must do so if they are to justify their own professional existence. The analysis of an existing social order must, almost by the nature of science itself, imply that some "improvement" in results can be produced by changes that can be imposed on the variables subject to social control.

Such improvements in the organisation of economic activity have almost without exception, involved the placing of restrictions on the private behaviour of individuals through the implementation of some *political* action. The various proposals that have been advanced by economists are sufficiently familiar to make a listing at this point unnecessary. They run the gamut from the relatively straightforward tax-subsidy schemes of Marshall to the more sophisticated and highly intricate proposals for multi-part pricing, counter-speculation, collective simulation of ideal market processes, and many other intriguing methods designed to promote and to insure the attainment of economic efficiency. Indeed, economists tend to be so enmeshed with efficiency notions that it seems extremely difficult for them to resist the ever-present temptation to propose yet more complex gimmicks and gadgets for producing greater "efficiency". In almost every case, and often quite unconsciously, the suggested improvement is assumed to be within the realm of the genuinely attainable. And, if some sceptic dare raise a question on this point, the economist is likely to respond to the effect that his task is not that of the politician, that he does not appropriately concern himself with the political feasibility or workability of his proposals. But if political obstacles to realisation are not in fact, discussed, the implication is clear that the proposals which are advanced are attainable as a result of some conceivable politically-imposed modifications in the institutional framework within which decisions are made. It seems fully appropriate to charge welfare economists, generally, with an implicit acceptance of this implication of their analyses. If this were not the case, it is difficult to see why, for example, William J. Baumol should have attempted to construct a theory of the state, of collective action, on the basis of the externality argument,[4] why K. W. Kapp should have entitled his work, *The Social Costs of Private Enterprise*,[5] and why Francis Bator should have called his recent summary analysis, "The Anatomy of Market Failure".[6]

I shall not be concerned here with the analysis of market imperfection or failure, as such. The primary criticism of theoretical welfare economics (and economists) that is advanced in this note is that its failure to include analyses of similar imperfections in realistic and attainable alternative solutions causes the analysis itself to take on implications for institutional change that are, at best, highly misleading. To argue that an existing order is "imperfect" in comparison with an alternative order of affairs that turns out, upon careful inspection, to be unattainable may not be different from arguing that the existing order is "perfect".[7] The existence of demonstrated imperfection in terms of an unattainable state of affairs should imply nothing at all about the possibility of actual improvement to an existing state. To take this step considerably more is required than the preliminary analysis of "ideal output". This is not to suggest, of course, that the preliminary analysis is not essential and important.

In what follows I shall try to show that, with consistent assumptions about human behaviour in both market and political institutions, any attempt to replace or to modify an existing market situation, admitted to be characterised by serious externalities, will produce solutions that embody externalities which are different, but precisely analogous, to those previously existing. Indeed, the Pigovian analysis lends itself readily to the analysis of political imperfection.

I

In order to analyse political processes in a manner that is even remotely similar to the methods of economic theory, great simplification and abstraction are required. To the political scientist, accustomed as he is to working with more "realistic" models of human behaviour, the simplified models with which the economist must analyse political institutions can only seem to be grossly inadequate caricatures of the operation of complex organisational structures. This rather sharp methodological gap between the two social sciences incorporated in "political economy" provides an important reason why the political scientist has not filled, and could hardly be expected to fill, the analytical void left open by the incompleteness of welfare economics.

I shall assume the existence of a community composed of separate individuals in which all collective decisions are reached by a voting rule of simple majority with universal suffrage. More complex, and realistic, models introducing representation, political parties, leadership, etc., could be employed but without significantly altering the conclusions reached. Almost any political order described by the term, "democratic", in the modern Western usage of this term may, for present purposes, be simplified into this extreme model of "pure" democracy. Characteristics of the political structure may modify the majority equivalent in the simple model. That is to say, a model of two-thirds or three-fourths majority may be more appropriate to the analysis of some political structures under certain conditions than the simple majority model. However, this quantitative variation in the voting rule equivalent does not affect the conclusions of this paper. Each particular rule, save that of unanimity, leads to conclusions that are identical to those reached in the simple majority model. The magnitude of the distortions produced is, of course, affected by the voting rule. The analysis here is concerned solely with indicating the direction of these effects, not with their magnitude. A distinction among the various "majority equivalents" is not, therefore, necessary.

In the first model, the orthodox assumptions of positive economics will be retained in so far as these concern individual motivation and action. Private individuals are assumed to be sufficiently informed and rational to conduct the required calculus and to reach decisions on the basis of a comparison of private costs and benefits at the relevant margins. No considerations of the "public" or the "social" interest are assumed to enter into this individual calculus within the relationship in question except in so far as this should coincide with individual interest. In determining his voting behaviour on each issue confronted by the group, the individual is assumed, quite simply, to act in that manner which he considers to advance his own interest. The model embodies, therefore, a rather straightforward extension of the behavioural assumptions of orthodox economic theory, as a predictive, explanatory theory, to political choice-making.

If no institutional restrictions are placed on this majority-rule model of the collective choice process, the characteristics of the "solution" should be intuitively clear. The minimum-size effective or dominating coalition of individuals, as determined by the voting rule, will be able to secure net gains at the expense of the other members of the political group. These gains, secured through the political process, will tend to be shared symmetrically (equally) among all members of the dominant coalition. In the simple majority-rule model, this involves, in the limit, fifty plus per cent. of the total membership in the dominating coalition and fifty minus per cent. of the total membership in the losing or minority coalition. That such a solution will, in fact, tend to emerge under the conditions of the model seems hardly subject to question. It is helpful, however, to note that such a solution, and only such, satisfies fully the Von Neumann-Morgenstern requirements for solutions to n-person games which, of course, all political "games" must be.[8]

It is useful to apply the familiar Pigovian calculus to this model of political behaviour. To the individual member of the effective majority, the political process provides a means through which he may secure private gain at the expense of other citizens. In determining the margins to which political activity shall be extended, the individual member of the dominant coalition will include in his calculus a share of the net benefits from public activity that will be larger than the offsetting individualised share or proportion of the net costs of the activity. In the calculus of the individuals effectively making the final collective decision, marginal private benefits will tend to exceed marginal social benefits and/or marginal private costs will tend to fall short of marginal social costs. The distortions produced are, therefore, precisely analogous, in opposing directions, to those present in the market solution characterised by the familiar Pigovian divergencies. In essence, the value of a political vote in this model lies in its potential power to impose external costs on other members of the group. Externalities must be present in any solution reached by the voting process under all less-than-unanimity rules. If the possible "perfectibility" of market organisation is to be determined under these conditions, it is clearly necessary to compare two separate imperfections, in each of which significant divergencies of the Pigovian sort may exist at the individualised margins of decision-making. Since there will be nothing in the collective choice process that will tend to produce the "ideal" solution, as determined by the welfare economist, the presence or absence of a Pigovian marginal divergency in the market solution, even of sufficient seriousness to warrant concern, provides in itself no implication for the desirability of institutional change.[9]

II

This conclusion holds so long as consistency in individual behaviour patterns over market and voting processes is retained, independently of the specific motivation that may be assumed to direct this behaviour.

The oversimplified model of Part I may be criticised on the grounds that individuals do not act in the way postulated: that is, they do not follow their own interests when they participate in the formation of social decisions for the community. Several responses might be advanced to such criticism, but it is not the purpose of this note to defend the validity, methodologically or otherwise, of the self-interest assumption about behaviour. The relevant response to the charge of unrealism at this point is surely the frank admission that, of course, individuals do not always act as the model of Part I postulates. A model is a construction that isolates one element of behaviour and, upon this, the analyst may erect conceptually refutable hypotheses. The model of majority rule in the simple pure democracy is not different in this respect from the competitive model of economic theory. Both models isolate that part of human behaviour that does reflect the rational pursuit of private gain by individuals in particular institutional relationships and both models fail to the extent that individuals do not, in fact, behave in this fashion in the relationships under consideration.[10]

Any number of models of individual behaviour can be constructed. The only real limitation lies, ultimately, in the testing of the predictions made. It will not be necessary, however, to develop any large number of additional and complex models to illustrate the central point of this note. One additional extremely simple model will suffice for this purpose. In this second model, I shall drop the assumption that individuals, in both their market and in their political behaviour, act in pursuit of their own narrowly defined self-interest. Instead, I now postulate that individuals act in the other extreme: I assume that each individual, in all aspects of his behaviour, tries to identify himself with the community of which he is a member and to act in accordance with his own view of the overall "public" or "social" interest. Each member of the group tries to act in the genuine interest of the whole group as this is determined for him through the application of some appropriately-chosen Kantian-like rule of action.

The results are again almost intuitively clear. Since each member of the group acts on the basis of identifying his own interest with that of the larger group, no deliberate exploitation of minority by majority can take place through the political process regardless of the voting rule that is applied. Differences that may arise, and which must be resolved by voting, stem solely from differences in individual conceptions of what the group interest on particular issues is. The Pigovian-type marginal divergencies between private and social costs or benefits disappear from the individual calculus in this model of behaviour. It is in application to market, rather than to political, behaviour that this model seems somewhat unorthodox. Under the assumptions of the model, the individual in his market behaviour will also try to identify himself with the group as a whole and to act in accordance with what he considers to be the "public" interest. If his chimney pours out smoke that soils his neighbours' laundry, he will assess these costs as if they were his own in reaching a decision concerning the possible introduction of a smoke-abatement device. The familiar analysis of welfare economics simply does not apply. Each individual decision-maker does, in fact, attempt to balance off "social" benefits against "social" costs at the margin. While, as in the collective sector, differences may arise among members of the group concerning the proper definition of social benefits and social costs, these differences cannot be interpreted in the standard way. The Pigovian divergence between marginal private product and marginal social product disappears in both the market and the political organisation of activity in this universal benevolence model. The policy conclusions are, however, identical with those reached from the use of the extreme self-interest model. If chimneys smoke, or if the majority is observed to impose discriminatory taxes on the minority, these facts carry with them no implications for institutional changes. In this case, they must represent the decision-makers' estimates of genuine community interest. Neither "real" nor "apparent" externalities can, in themselves, provide grounds for suggesting organisational changes.

III

From the analysis of these two extreme and contrasting models of human behaviour, the inference is clear that so long as individuals are assumed to be similarly motivated under market and under political institutions there can be no direct implications drawn about the organisational structure of an activity on the basis of a Pigovian-like analysis of observed externalities. The orthodox implication of Pigovian welfare economics follows only on the assumption that individuals respond to *different* motives when they participate in market and in political activity. The only behavioural model appropriate to the Pigovian analysis is that which has been called "the bifurcated man". Man must be assumed to shift his psychological and moral gears when he moves from the realm of organised market activity to that of organised political activity and *vice-versa*. Only if there can be demonstrated to be something in the nature of market organisation, as such, that brings out the selfish motives in man, and something in the political organisation, as such, which, in turn, suppresses these motives and brings out the more "noble" ones, can there be assumed to exist any "bridge" between the orthodox externality analysis and practical policy, even apart from problems of specific policy prescription.

The characteristics of the organisational structure within which choices must be made may affect the nature of the value system upon which individual action is based. It seems probable that the individual in his voting behaviour, will tend to choose among alternatives on the basis of a somewhat broader and more inclusive value scale than that which will direct his behaviour in the making of market choices. One reason for this is that, in political behaviour, the individual is made fully conscious of the fact that he is choosing *for* the whole group, that his individual action will exert external effects on other members of the group, that he is acting "socially". In his market behaviour, on the other hand, the external effects of individual choice are sensed only indirectly by the chooser.[11] But this recognition that the individual value scale may be, to some extent, modified by the institutional structure within which choice is exercised is quite different from accepting the idea that the motivation for individual action is wholly transformed as between two separate structures. While it may be acknowledged as "realistic" to assume that the model of individual choice based on self-interest motivation, the "economic" model, is somewhat more applicable to an analysis of markets than of voting processes, this is far removed from accepting the applicability of the universal benevolence model for the latter. At most, the influence of the different organisational structures, as such, on motivation would seem to be conceptually represented by a reasonably narrow distance on some motivational spectrum. If, at the elementary stages of analysis, a choice must be made between that conception of behaviour that assumes this possible institutionally-generated difference to be absent or negligible (models that I have called consistent) and the conception that assumes wholly different behavioural patterns solely due to the institutional structure, the first alternative seems obviously to be preferred. Yet, as I have shown, it is the second, and clearly extreme, conception of human behaviour that is implicit in much of the discussion of Pigovian welfare economics.

This assumption of behavioural dichotomy, as opposed to behavioural consistency, is most openly expressed in the early literature on socialism, especially that of the Christian and Fabian varieties. The criticism of the market order of affairs was often made by referring to the pursuit of private gain, and the case for socialism was based on the replacement of this pursuit of private gain by that of public good. Although this rather naive conception has perhaps lost some of its appeal since World War II, it continues to be implied in much of the popular discussion. While this is not in itself surprising, it does seem notable that the analytical structure based on this conception of human behaviour should have remained largely unchallenged in the scientific literature.[12]

IV

Up to this point the discussion has been concerned with the most general case in which no limitations are placed on the activities that may be organised through the political process. Can the implications of the Pigovian welfare analytics be rescued by restricting the movement of the political-institutional variables? If collective action can take place only within prescribed limits, which can be assumed to be fixed by constitutional rules, a model may be constructed in which the policy implications of the Pigovian-type of analysis do not run into immediate conflict with reasonable assumptions concerning human motivation. To accomplish this result, however, the range of possible political action must be restricted to such an extent as to make the analysis practically worthless.

Let it be assumed that constitutional rules dictate that all human activity shall be organised privately and voluntarily except that which involves the provision of genuinely collective goods and services. These are defined as those goods and services which, when a unit is made available to one individual member of the group, an equal amount, one unit, is also made available to each other member of the group. These goods and services are completely indivisible. Let it be further assumed that the constitution states that the provision of such goods and services, if politically organised, shall be financed by taxes that are levied on the "marginal benefit principle". That is to say, each individual shall be required to contribute a "tax-price" that is exactly proportional to his own marginal rate of substitution between the collective good and money (all other goods). This marginal tax will be different for different individuals in the group because, although the good is genuinely collective, the relative marginal utility of it will vary from individual to individual.

If the provision of such a good or service should be organised privately rather than collectively, and if individuals are assumed to be motivated by self-interest considerations, the market solution will be characterised by the presence of significant externalities. The individual, acting privately, will take into account only that share of total marginal benefit or product that he expects to enjoy. By comparison, he will take into account the full amount of the marginal costs which, by hypothesis, he must bear individually. In other words, he cannot exclude other members of the group from the enjoyment of the benefits provided by the good: but there is no way that he may include these other members of the group in the payment of the costs. This market organisation produces, therefore, the familiar result; the private calculus of individuals embodies the Pigovian divergence at the margins of decision. Compared to a Pareto-optimal situation, relatively too few resources will be devoted to the provision of the common good or service.

Under this situation, a shift in organisation from the private or market sector to the collective sector will, under the conditions specified, tend to eliminate the Pigovian divergence, even if the self-interest motivation of individual action is retained. If the individual, in making a political or voting choice concerning the possible marginal extension of the provision of the collective good or service, is required to include in his calculus a share of the total marginal cost of the extension that is proportional to his individualised share of the total marginal benefits provided by the extension, a "solution" will tend to be produced by political choice that will meet all of the necessary conditions for Pareto optimality. If the total marginal costs of extending the activity fall short of the total marginal benefits, individuals will not be in equilibrium and they will, accordingly, vote to extend the activity. At the "solution", all of the necessary conditions are satisfied, and total incremental benefits equal total marginal costs. No externalities exist.[13]

The reason for this result is not difficult to understand. By imposing the restriction that the individual voter must pay for the marginal unit of the collective good or service in proportion to the marginal benefit enjoyed, it is insured that the individual's private calculus becomes a miniature reflection of the aggregate or "social" calculus that would be made by an omniscient, benevolent despot acting in the interests of all persons in the community. The individual voter cannot, because of the restrictions on the model, impose external costs on others in the group through the political process. In his/her private voting decision he/she will recognise that additional units of the collective good will yield benefits to others than him/herself. But he/she will, under the self-interest assumption, not be influenced by these spillover benefits at all. There are, however, also spillover marginal costs that the provision of the additional units of the collective good will impose on the individual's fellows, and the neglected external benefits will tend to offset these neglected external costs.

This highly restricted model has several interesting features. First of all, note that the sharp difference in result as between the market and the political solution emerges only if the self-interest assumption about human motivation is consistently adopted and applied. If, by contrast, the universal benevolence assumption is introduced, the market organisation and the political organisation will tend to produce similar results, as in the earlier analyses. Secondly, if the self-interest assumption is adopted, the political result in the restricted model here will tend to be identical under *any* voting rule. Any rule will, under the constitutional restrictions imposed, tend to produce a solution that satisfies all of the necessary conditions for Pareto optimality. The single individual acting as a dictator, the simple majority, and the rule of unanimity: each of these will tend to produce the same results. These separate rules for making political decisions only become important because they reflect differences in the ability of some members of the group to impose costs on other members, an ability that is specifically eliminated by the constitutional restrictions postulated.

It is not, of course, surprising to find that the Pigovian analysis has relevant policy implications only for the provision of genuinely collective (perfectly indivisible) goods and services. Indeed, the statement that externalities exist in any private market solution is one means of stating that genuinely collective elements characterise the activity under consideration. This restricted model indicates clearly, however, that the good must be wholly collective if the implications of the Pigovian analysis are to apply. If an activity is only quasi-collective, that is to say, if it contains elements that are privately divisible as well as collective elements, the political solution must also involve externalities. The restricted model analysed here is perhaps even more useful in pointing up the extremely limited tax scheme that is required for the analysis to apply at all. Even for those goods and services that are wholly collective in nature, the provision of them through the political process will produce Pigovian-like externalities at the margin unless taxes are collected on the basis of marginal benefits. In the real world, very few, if any, goods and services are wholly collective. And even if these few could be isolated, they would not be financed by taxes levied on this principle of incremental benefits enjoyed. Such a principle is not only politically unimaginable in modern democracy: it is also conceptually impossible. Its application would require that the taxing authorities be able to determine, in advance, all individual preference functions. It must be concluded, therefore, that the restricted institutional model in which the implications of the standard externality analysis might apply is nothing but a conceptual toy. In the real world, political results must embody externalities to the extent that individuals follow self-interest in their capacities as collective decision makers: individuals are able, by political means, to impose costs on other individuals.

V

In Part III it was demonstrated that the generalised implications of the Pigovian analysis could be supported only on the adoption of a highly questionable conception of human motivation. In Part IV it was demonstrated that these implications would be drawn from a consistent motivational model only if this model should be so highly restricted as to make the analysis of little practical value. It is much easier, however, to explain the reasons for economists neglecting to examine these aspects of their analysis than it is to justify their neglect. As Knut Wicksell suggested many years ago, most economists are content with assuming the presence of a benevolent despot. In so far as their analysis points toward policy at all, as it must, the improvements in efficiency advanced are assumed to be attainable within the realm of the politically possible. The almost universal neglect of the imperfections that might arise from the political attempts at applying the economists' efficiency criteria represents a serious deficiency in the work of welfare economists and economists generally. To shy away from considerations of the politically feasible has been deemed an admirable trait, but to refuse to examine the politically possible is incomplete scholarship.

Notes

1 Although independently developed, this note draws upon and extends certain ideas that have been developed in a larger work undertaken in collaboration with Gordon Tullock. See, *The Calculus of Consent* 1962. I should acknowledge Tullock's indirect as well as his direct influence on the general ideas presented in this paper.
2 The work of my colleague, Ronald Coase, should be mentioned as a notable exception. Coase's criticism of the Pigovian analysis concerns the implications of externality for resource allocation. For a preliminary statement of Coase's position see his "The Federal Communications Commission", *Journal of Law and Economics*, vol. II (1959), especially pp. 26–7. A more complete

statement appears in "The Problem of Social Cost", *Journal of Law and Economics*, vol. III (1960).

3   It should be noted that I shall not be concerned with the conceptual ability of welfare economists to make specific policy prescriptions, a problem that has been central to much of the modern discussion. It is now widely acknowledged that welfare economics, as such, can provide few guides to positive policy-making in a specific sense. But the analysis continues to be employed for the purposes of demonstrating the existence of market failure. If, as J. de V. Graaff suggests, *"laissez-faire* welfare theory" was "largely concerned with demonstrating the optimal properties of free competition and the unfettered price system", it is surely equally accurate to suggest that modern welfare theory has been largely concerned with demonstrating that these conclusions are invalid: that is, that competitive markets do not satisfy the necessary conditions for optimality. Graaff's own work is, perhaps, the most elegant example. See his *Theoretical Welfare Economics*, 1957. (Citation from page 170.)

4   William J. Baumol, *Welfare Economics and the Theory of the State*, 1952.

5   K. W. Kapp, *The Social Costs of Private Enterprise*, 1950.

6   Francis Bator, "The Anatomy of Market Failure", *Quarterly Journal of Economics*, vol. LXXII (1958), pp. 351–79.

7   Professor Frank Knight's statement that "to call a situation hopeless is equivalent to calling it ideal" may be reversed. To call a situation ideal is merely another means of calling it hopeless: that is, not perfectible.

8   J. Von Neumann and O. Morgenstern, *Theory of Games and Economic Behavior*, third ed., 1953, p. 264.

9   I am not suggesting that deliberate exploitation of minority by majority need be the only purpose of collective activity, even in this polar model. The point is rather that, independently of the motivation for collective activity, majority-rule institutions of decision-making create opportunities within which Pigovian-like externalities may arise. There will, of course, arise situations in which the self-interest of the individual dictates the collectivisation of an activity in order that the application of general rules to *all* members of the group can be effected. It is precisely in such cases that, conceptually, unanimity may replace majority rule as the decision device, and the propositions of modern welfare economics become fully appropriate. But so long as majority rule prevails, the "political externalities" are present, whether these be purposeful or ancillary to collective action designed to accomplish other ends.

10 Care must be taken to distinguish between the self-interest assumption, as the basis for a "logic of choice" and the self-interest assumption as the basis of a predictive, explanatory theory of human action. In the first sense, all action of individuals must be based on self-interest, and it becomes meaningless to discuss alternative models of behaviour. The pure logic of individual choice is not without value, but it should be emphasised that the argument of this paper employs the second version of the self-interest assumption. If conceptually refutable hypotheses are to be developed, the behaviour of choice-making individuals must be externally observable in terms of measurable criteria of choice. In the market relationship, this degree of operational validity is often introduced by stating that the minimal

requirement is that individuals, when confronted with choice, choose "more" rather than "less". But "more" or "less" take on full operational meaning only when they become measurable in something other than subjective utility of the choosers. The "measuring rod of money" must be allowed to enter before the generalised logic of choice can produce even so much as the first law of demand.

11   For a further discussion on these points see my "Individual Choice in Voting and the Market", *Journal of Political Economy*, vol. LXII (1954), pp. 334–43.

12   The behavioural inconsistency here has been, of course, indirectly recognised by many writers. However, the only explicit reference to the private-cost social-cost analysis, to my knowledge, is contained in the paper by William H. Meckling and Armen A. Alchian, "Incentives in the United States", *American Economic Review*, vol. L (1960), pp. 55–61, and, even here, the reference is only a passing one.

13   This solution is that which has been rigorously defined by Paul A. Samuelson. See his "The Pure Theory of Public Expenditure", *Review of Economics and Statistics*, vol. XXXVI (1954), pp. 386–9; "Diagrammatic Exposition of a Theory of Public Expenditure", *Review of Economics and Statistics*, vol. XXXVII (1955), pp. 350–56.

Part IV

The Economics of Exhaustible Resources

11
The Economics of Exhaustible Resources

Harold Hotelling

I The peculiar problems of mineral wealth

Contemplation of the world's disappearing supplies of minerals, forests, and other exhaustible assets has led to demands for regulation of their exploitation. The feeling that these products are now too cheap for the good of future generations, that they are being selfishly exploited at too rapid a rate, and that in consequence of their excessive cheapness they are being produced and consumed wastefully has given rise to the conservation movement. The method ordinarily proposed to stop the wholesale devastation of irreplaceable natural resources, or of natural resources replaceable only with difficulty and long delay, is to forbid production at certain times and in certain regions or to hamper production by insisting that obsolete and inefficient methods be continued. The prohibitions against oil and mineral development and cutting timber on certain government lands have this justification, as have also closed seasons for fish and game and statutes forbidding certain highly efficient means of catching fish. Taxation would be a more economic method than publicly ordained inefficiency in the case of purely commercial activities such as mining and fishing for profit, if not also for sport fishing. However, the opposition of those who are making the profits, with the apathy of everyone else, is usually sufficient to prevent the diversion into the public treasury of any considerable part of the proceeds of the exploitation of natural resources.

In contrast to the conservationist belief that a too rapid exploitation of natural resources is taking place, we have the retarding influence of monopolies and combinations, whose growth in industries directly concerned with the exploitation of irreplaceable resources has been striking. If "combinations in restraint of trade" extort high prices from consumers and restrict production, can it be said that their products are too cheap and are being sold too rapidly?

It may seem that the exploitation of an exhaustible natural resource can never be too slow for the public good. For every proposed rate of production there will doubtless be some to point to the ultimate exhaustion which that rate will entail, and to urge more delay. But if it is agreed that the total supply is not to be reserved for our remote descendants and that there is an optimum rate of present production, then the tendency of monopoly and partial monopoly is to keep production below the optimum rate and to exact excessive prices from consumers. The conservation movement, in so far as it aims at absolute prohibitions rather than taxation or regulation in the interest of efficiency, may be accused of playing into the hands of those who are interested in maintaining high prices for the sake of their own pockets rather than of posterity. On the other hand, certain technical conditions most pronounced in the oil industry lead to great wastes of material and to expensive competitive drilling, losses which may be reduced by systems of control which involve delay in production. The government of the United States under the present administration has withdrawn oil lands from entry in order to conserve this asset, and has also taken steps toward prosecuting a group of California oil companies for conspiring to maintain unduly high prices, thus restricting production. Though these moves may at first sight appear contradictory in intent, they are really aimed at two distinct evils, a Scylla and Charybdis between which public policy must be steered.

In addition to these public questions, the economics of exhaustible assets presents a whole forest of intriguing problems. The static-equilibrium type of economic theory which is now so well developed is plainly inadequate for an industry in which the indefinite maintenance of a steady rate of production is a physical impossibility, and which is therefore bound to decline. How much of the proceeds of a mine should be reckoned as income, and how much as return of capital? What is the value of a mine when its contents are supposedly fully known, and what is the effect of uncertainty of estimate? If a mine-owner produces too rapidly, he will depress the price, perhaps to zero. If he produces too slowly, his profits, though larger, may be postponed farther into the future than the rate of interest warrants. Where is his golden mean? And how does this most profitable rate of production vary as exhaustion approaches? Is it more profitable to complete the extraction within a finite time, to extend it indefinitely in such a way that the amount remaining in the mine approaches zero as a limit, or to exploit so slowly that mining operations will not only continue at a diminishing rate forever but leave an amount in the ground which does not approach zero? Suppose the mine is publicly owned. How should exploitation take place for the greatest general good, and how does a course having such an objective compare with that of the profit-seeking entrepreneur? What of the plight of laborers and of subsidiary industries when a mine is exhausted? How can the state, by regulation or taxation, induce the mine-owner to adopt a schedule of production more in harmony with the public good? What about import duties on coal and oil? And for these dynamical systems what becomes of the classic theories of monopoly, duopoly, and free competition?

Problems of exhaustible assets are peculiarly liable to become entangled with the infinite. Not only is there infinite time to consider, but also the possibility that for a necessity the price might increase without limit as the supply vanishes. If we are not to have property of infinite value, we must, in choosing empirical forms for cost and demand curves, take precautions to avoid assumptions, perfectly natural in static problems, which lead to such conditions.

While a complete study of the subject would include semi-replaceable assets such as forests and stocks of fish, ranging gradually downward to such short-time operations as crop carryovers, this paper will be confined in scope to absolutely irreplaceable assets. The forests of a continent occupied by a new population may, for purposes of a first approximation at least, be regarded as composed of two parts, of which one will be replaced after cutting and the other will be consumed without replacement. The first part obeys the laws of static theory; the second, those of the economics of exhaustible assets. Wild life which may replenish itself if not too rapidly exploited presents questions of a different type.

Problems of exhaustible assets cannot avoid the calculus of variations, including even the most recent researches in this branch of mathematics. However, elementary methods will be sufficient to bring out, in the next few pages, some of the principles of mine economics, with the help of various simplifying assumptions. These will later be generalized in considering a series of cases taking on gradually some of the complexities of the actual situation. We shall assume always that the owner of an exhaustible supply wishes to make the present value of all his future profits a maximum. The force of interest will be denoted by γ, so that $e^{-\gamma t}$ is the present value of a unit of profit to be obtained after time t, interest rates being assumed to remain unchanged in the meantime. The case of variable interest rates gives rise to fairly obvious modifications.[1]

II   Free competition

Since it is a matter of indifference to the owner of a mine whether he receives for a unit of his product a price p_0 now or a price $p_0 e^{\gamma t}$ after time t, it is not unreasonable to expect that the price p will be a function of the time of the form $p = p_0 e^{\gamma t}$. This will not apply to monopoly, where the form of the demand function is bound to affect the rate of production, but is characteristic of completely free competition. The various units of the mineral are then to be thought of as being at any time all equally valuable, excepting for varying costs of placing them upon the market. They will be removed and used in order of accessibility, the most cheaply available first. If interest rates or degrees of impatience vary among the mine-owners, this fact will also affect the order of extraction. Here p is to be interpreted as the net price received after paying the cost of extraction and placing upon the market – a convention to which we shall adhere throughout.

The formula

$$p = p_0 e^{\gamma t} \tag{11.1}$$

fixes the relative prices at different times under free competition. The absolute level, or the value p_0 of the price when $t = 0$, will depend upon demand and upon the total supply of the substance. Denoting the latter by a, and putting

$$q = f(p, t)$$

for the quantity taken at time t if the price is p, we have the equation,

$$\int_0^T q \, dt = \int_0^T f(p_0 e^{\gamma t}, t) dt = a, \tag{11.2}$$

the upper limit T being the time of final exhaustion. Since q will then be zero, we shall have the equation

$$f(p_0 e^{\gamma t}, T) = 0 \tag{11.3}$$

to determine T.

The nature of these solutions will depend upon the function $f(p, t)$, which gives q. In accordance with the usual assumptions, we shall assume that it is a diminishing function of p, and depends upon the time, if at all, in so simple a fashion that the equations all have unique solutions.

Suppose, for example, that the demand function is given by

$$q = 5 - p, \quad (0 \le p \le 5)$$
$$q = 0 \text{ for } p \ge 5,$$

independently of the time.

As q diminishes and approaches zero, p increases toward the value 5, which represents the highest price anyone will pay. Thus at time T,

$$p_0 e^{\gamma T} = 5.$$

The relation (equation (11.2)) between the unknowns p_0 and T becomes in this case

$$a = \int_0^T (5 - p_0 e^{\gamma t}) dt = 5T - p_0 \left(e^{\gamma T} - 1\right) / \gamma.$$

Eliminating p_0, we have

$$a/5 = T + \left(e^{-\gamma T} - 1\right)/\gamma,$$

that is,

$$e^{-\gamma T} = 1 + \gamma(a/5 - T).$$

Now, if we plot as functions of T

$$y_1 = e^{-\gamma T}$$

and

$$y_2 = 1 + \gamma(a/5 - T),$$

we have a diminishing exponential curve whose slope where it crosses the y-axis is $-\gamma$, and a straight line with the same slope. The line crosses the y-axis at a higher point than the curve, since, when $T = 0$, $y_1 < y_2$. Hence there is one and only one positive value of T for which $y_1 = y_2$. This value of T gives the time of complete exhaustion. Clearly it is finite.

If the demand curve is fixed, the question whether the time until exhaustion will be finite or infinite turns upon whether a finite or infinite value of p will be required to make q vanish. For the demand function $q = e^{-bp}$, where b is a constant, the exploitation will continue forever, though of course at a gradually diminishing rate. If $q = \alpha - \beta p$, all will be exhausted in a finite time. In general, the higher the price anticipated when the rate of production becomes extremely small, compared with the price for a more rapid production, the more protracted will be the period of operation.

III   Maximum social value and state interference

As in the static case, there is under free competition in the absence of complicating factors a certain tendency toward maximizing what might be called the "total utility" but is better called the "social value of the resource." For a unit of time this quantity may be defined as

$$u(q) = \int_0^q p(q)dq, \tag{11.4}$$

where the integrand is a diminishing function and the upper limit is the quantity actually placed upon the market and consumed. If future enjoyment be discounted with force of interest γ, the present value is

$$V = \int_0^T u[q(t)]e^{-\gamma t}dt.$$

Since $\int_0^T q\,dt$ is fixed, the production schedule $q(t)$ which makes V a maximum must be such that a unit increment in q will increase the integrand as much at one time as at another. That is,

$$\frac{d}{dq}u[q(t)]e^{-\gamma t},$$

which by (equation (11.4)) equals $pe^{-\gamma t}$, is to be a constant. Calling this constant p_0, we have

$$p = p_0 e^{\gamma t},$$

the result (equation (11.1)) obtained in considering free competition. That this gives a genuine maximum appears from the fact that the second derivative is essentially negative, owing to the downward slope of the demand curve.

This conclusion does not, of course, supply any more justification for laissez faire with the exploitation of natural resources than with other pursuits. It shows that the true basis of the conservation movement is not in any tendency inherent in competition under these ideal conditions. However, there are in extractive industries discrepancies from our assumed conditions leading to particularly wasteful forms of exploitation which might well be regulated in the public interest. We have tacitly assumed all the conditions fully known. Great wastes arise from the suddenness and unexpectedness of mineral discoveries, leading to wild rushes, immensely wasteful socially, to get hold of valuable property.

Of this character is the drilling of "offset wells" along each side of a property line over a newly discovered oil pool. Each owner must drill and get the precious oil quickly, for otherwise his neighbors will get it all. Consequently great forests of tall derricks rise overnight at a cost of $50,000 or more each; whereas a much smaller number and a slower exploitation would be more economic. Incidentally, great volumes of natural gas and oil are lost because the suddenness of development makes adequate storage impossible.[2]

The unexpectedness of mineral discoveries provides another reason than wastefulness for governmental control and for special taxation. Great profits of a thoroughly adventitious character arise in connection with mineral discoveries, and it is not good public policy to allow such profits to remain in private hands. Of course the prospector may be said to have earned his reward by effort and risk; but can this be said of the landowner who discovers the value of his subsoil purely by observing the results of his neighbors' mining and drilling?

The market rate of interest γ must be used by an entrepreneur in his calculations, but should it be used in determinations of social value and optimum public policy? The use of $\int_0^T p\,dq$ as a measure of social value in a unit of time, whereas the smaller quantity pq would be the greatest possible profit to an owner for the same extraction of material, suggests that a similar integral be used in connection with the various rates of time-preference. There is, however, an important difference between the two cases in that the rate of interest is set by a great variety of forces, chiefly independent of the particular commodity and industry in question, and is not greatly affected by variations in the output of the mine or oil well in question. It is likely, therefore, that in deciding questions of public policy relative to exhaustible resources, no large errors will be made by using the market rate of interest. Of course, changes in this rate are to be anticipated, especially in considering the remote future. If we look ahead to a distant time when all the resources of the earth will be near exhaustion, and the human race reduced to complete poverty, we may expect very high interest rates indeed. But the exhaustion of one or a few types of resources will not bring about this condition.

The discounting of future values of u may be challenged on the ground that future pleasures are ethically equivalent to present pleasure of the same intensity. The reply to this is that capital is productive, that future pleasures are uncertain in a degree increasing with their remoteness in time, and that V and u are concrete quantities, not symbols for pleasure. They measure the social value of the mine in the sense concerned with the total production of goods, but not properly its utility or the happiness to which it leads, since this depends upon the distribution of wealth, and is greater if the products of the mine benefit chiefly the poor than if they become articles of luxury. A platinum mine is of greater general utility when platinum is used for electrical and chemical purposes than when it is pre-empted by the jewelry trade. However, we must leave questions of distribution of wealth to be dealt with otherwise, perhaps by graded income and inheritance taxes, and consider the effects of various schedules of operation upon the total value of goods produced. It is for this reason that we are concerned with V.

The general question of how much of its income a people should save has been beautifully treated by F. P. Ramsey.[3]

Money metals, of course, occasion very special cause for public concern. Not only does gold production tend to unstabilize prices; but if the uses in the arts can be neglected, the costs of discovery, extraction, and transportation from the mine are, from the social standpoint, wasted.

Still a different reason for caution in deducing a laissez faire policy from the theoretical maximizing of V under "free" competition is that the actual conditions, even when competition exists, are likely to be far removed from the ideal state we have been postulating. A large producing company can very commonly affect the price by varying its rate of marketing. There is then something of the monopoly element, with a tendency toward undue retardation of production and elevation of price. This will be considered further in our last section. The monopoly problem of course extends also to non-extractive industries; but in dealing with exhaustible resources there are some features of special interest, which will now be examined.

IV   Monopoly

The usual theory of monopoly prices deals with the maximum point of the curve

$$y = pq,$$

y being plotted as a function either of p or of q, each of these variables being a diminishing function of the other (Figure 11.1). We now consider the problem of choosing q as a function of t, subject to the condition

$$\int_0^\infty q\,dt = a, \tag{11.5}$$

so as to maximize the present value,

$$J = \int_0^\infty qp(q)e^{-\gamma t}\,dt, \tag{11.6}$$

of the profits of the owner of a mine. We do not restrict q to be a continuous function of t, though p will be considered a continuous function of q with a continuous first derivative which is nowhere positive. The upper limit of the integrals may be taken as ∞ even if the exploitation is to take place only for a finite time T, for then $q = 0$ when $t > T$.

This may or may not be considered a problem in the calculus of variations; some definitions of that subject would exclude our problem because no derivative is involved under the integral signs, though the methods of the science may be applied to it. However, the problem may be treated fairly simply by observing that

$$qp(q)e^{-\gamma t} - \lambda q, \tag{11.7}$$

where λ is a Lagrange multiplier, is to be a maximum for every value of t. We must therefore have

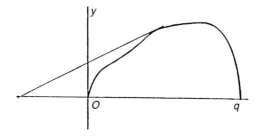

Figure 11.1 $y = pq$. The tangent turns counterclockwise. The value of the mine is proportional to the distance to O from the intersection of the tangent with the q-axis.

$$e^{-\gamma t}\frac{d}{dq}(pq) - \lambda = 0, \tag{11.8}$$

and also

$$e^{-\gamma t}\frac{d^2}{dq^2}(pq) < 0. \tag{11.9}$$

Evidently (equation (11.8)) may also be written

$$y' = \frac{d}{dq}(pq) = p + q\frac{dp}{dq} = \lambda e^{\gamma t}, \tag{11.10}$$

the contrast with the competitive conditions of the last section appearing in the term $q\,dp/dq$.

The constant λ is determined by solving (equation (11.8)) or (equation (11.10)) for q as a function of λ and t and substituting in (equation (11.5)). Upon integrating from 0 to T an equation will then be obtained for λ in terms of T and of the amount a initially in the mine, which is here assumed to be known. The additional equation required to determine T is obtained by putting $q = 0$ for $t = T$.

In general, if p takes on a finite value K as q approaches zero, $q\,dp/dq$ also remaining finite, (11.8) or (11.10) can be written

$$\frac{d(pq)}{dq} = Ke^{\gamma(t-T)},$$

Suppose, for example, that the demand function is

$$p = (1 - e^{-Kq})/q,$$
$$= K - K^2 q/2! + K^3 q^2/3! - \ldots,$$

where K is a positive constant. For every positive value of q this expression is positive and has a negative derivative. As q approaches zero, p approaches K. We have

$$y = pq = 1 - e^{-Kq},$$
$$y' = Ke^{-Kq} = \lambda e^{\gamma t}$$

whence

$$q = (\log K/\lambda - \gamma t)/K,$$

this expression holding when t is less than T, the time of ultimate exhaustion. When $t = T$, q is of course zero. We have, therefore, putting $q = 0$ for $t = T$,

$$\log K/\lambda = \gamma T;$$

and from (equation (11.5))

$$a = \int_0^T (\log K/\lambda - \gamma t)\, dt/K = \gamma \int_0^T (T - t)\, dt/K = \gamma T^2/2K$$

so that

$$T = \sqrt{2Ka/\gamma},$$
$$\log K/\lambda = \sqrt{2K\gamma a},$$

giving finally,

$$q = \gamma(\sqrt{2Ka/\gamma} - t)/K.$$

V Graphical study: discontinuous solutions

The interpretation of (equation (11.10)) in terms of Figure 11.1 is that the rate of production is the abscissa of the point of tangency of a tangent line which rotates counterclockwise. The slope of this line is proportional to a sum increasing at compound interest.

Other graphical representations of the exhaustion of natural resources are possible. Drawing a curve giving $y' = d(pq)/dq$ as a function of q (Figure 11.2), we have for the most profitable rate of extraction the length of a horizontal line RS which rises like compound interest.

The waviness with which these curves have been drawn suggests that the solution obtained in this way is not unambiguous. Such waviness will arise if the demand function is, for example

$$p = b - (q - 1)^3, \tag{11.11}$$

the derivative of which,

$$-3(q - 1)^2,$$

is never positive. Here b is a constant, taken as 1 for Figure 11.2. For this demand function

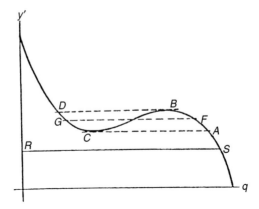

Figure 11.2   RS rises with increasing speed. Its length is the rate of production and diminishes.

$$y' = b - (4q - 1)(q - 1)^2.$$

When the rising line *RS* reaches the position *AC*, the point *S* whose abscissa represents the rate of production might apparently continue along the curve to *B* and then jump to *D*; or it might jump from *A* to *C* and then move on through *D*; or it might leave the arc *AB* at a point between *A* and *B*. At first sight there would seem to be another possibility, namely, to jump from *A* to *C*, to move up the curve to *B*, and then to leap to *D*. But this would mean increasing production for a period. This is never so profitable as to run through the same set of values of *q* in reverse order, for the total profit would be the same but would be received on the average more quickly if the most rapid production takes place at the beginning of the period. Hence we may regard *q* as always diminishing, though in this case with a discontinuity.

The values of *q* between which the leap is made in this case will be determined in Section X; it will be shown that the maximum profit will be reached if the monopolist moves horizontally from a certain point *F* on *AB* to a point *G* on *CD*.

VI   Value of a mine monopoly

To find the present value

$$J_{t_1}^{t_2} = \int_{t_1}^{t_2} pqe^{-\gamma t}\, dt$$

of the profits which are to be realized in any interval t_1 to t_2 during which the maximizing value of q is a continuous function of t, we integrate by parts:

$$J_{t_1}^{t_2} = -\frac{pqe^{-\gamma t}}{\gamma}\bigg]_{t_1}^{t_2} + \frac{1}{\gamma}\int_{t_1}^{t_2}\frac{d(pq)}{dq}\frac{dq}{dt}e^{-\gamma t}\,dt.$$

When we put

$$y = pq \tag{11.12}$$

and apply (equation (11.10)), the last integral takes a simple form admitting direct integration. This gives, after applying (equation (11.10)) also to eliminate $e^{-\gamma t}$ from the first term,

$$J_{t_1}^{t_2} = \frac{\lambda}{\gamma}\left(q - \frac{y}{y'}\right)\bigg]_{t_1}^{t_2}. \tag{11.13}$$

Now upon differentiating (equation (11.12)), we find

$$qy' = y + q^2\frac{dp}{dq}.$$

Hence (equation (11.13)) can be written

$$J_{t_1}^{t_2} = \frac{\lambda}{\gamma}\frac{q^2}{y'}\frac{dp}{dq}\bigg]_{t_1}^{t_2}. \tag{11.14}$$

The expressions (equation (11.13)) and (equation (11.14)) provide very convenient means of computing the discounted profits. Their validity will be shown in Section X to extend to cases in which q is discontinuous.

The expression

$$q - y/y'$$

which appears in (equation (11.13)) is, in terms of Figure 11.1, the difference between the abscissa and the subtangent of a point on the curve. It therefore equals the distance to the left of the origin of the point where a tangent to the curve meets the q-axis.

The value of the mine when $t = 0$ is, in this notation, J_0^T. It is γ/λ times the distance from the origin to the point of intersection with the negative x-axis of the initial tangent to the curve of monopoly profit.

VII   Retardation of production under monopoly

Although the rate of production may suffer discontinuities in spite of the demand function having a continuous derivative, these breaks will always occur during actual production, never at the end. Eventually q will trail off in a continuous fashion to zero. This means that the highest point of the curve of Figure 11.2 corresponds to $q = 0$. To prove this, we use the monotonic decreasing character of p as a function of q, which shows that

$$y'(q) = p(q) + qp'(q)$$

is, for positive values of q, less than $p(q)$, and that this in turn is less than $p(0)$. Hence the curve rises higher at the y'-axis than for any level maximum at the right.

The duration of monopolistic exploitation is finite or infinite according as y' takes on a finite or an infinite value when q approaches zero. This condition is a little different from that under competition, where a finite value of p as q approaches zero was found to be necessary and sufficient for a finite time. The two conditions agree unless p remains finite while $qp'(q)$ becomes infinite, in which case the demand curve reaches the p-axis and is tangent to it with contact of order higher than the first. In such a case the period of operation is finite under competition but infinite under monopoly. That this apparently exceptional case is quite likely to exist in fact is indicated by a study of the general properties of supply and demand functions applying the theory of frequency curves, a fascinating subject for which space will not be taken in this paper.

Such a study indicates that very high order contact of the demand curve with the p-axis is to be expected, and therefore that monopolistic exploitation of an exhaustible asset is likely to be protracted immensely longer than competition would bring about or a maximizing of social value would require. This is simply a part of the general tendency for production to be retarded under monopoly.

VIII   Cumulated production affecting price

The net price p per unit of product received by the owner of a mine depends not only on the current rate of production but also on past production. The accumulated production affects both cost and demand. The cost of extraction increases as the mine goes deeper; and durable substances, such as gold and diamonds, by their accumulation influence the market. In considering this effect, the calculus of variations cannot be avoided; the following formulation in terms of this science will include as special cases the situations previously treated.

Let x be the amount which has been extracted from a mine, $q = dx/dt$ the current rate of production, and a the amount originally in the mine. Then p is a function of x as well as of q and t. The discounted profit at time $t = 0$, which equals the value of the mine at that time, is

$$\int_0^\infty p(x, q, t) q e^{-\gamma t} dt. \tag{11.15}$$

If exhaustion is to come at a finite time T, we may suppose that $q = 0$ for $t > T$, so that T becomes the upper limit. We put

$$f(x, q, t) = pq e^{-\gamma t}.$$

Then the owner of the mine (who is now assumed to have a monopoly) cannot do better than to adjust his production so that

$$\frac{\partial f}{\partial x} - \frac{d}{dt}\frac{\partial f}{\partial q} = 0.$$

In case f does not involve x, the first term is zero and the former case of monopoly is obtained.

In general the differential equation is of the second order in x, since $q = dx/dt$, and so requires two terminal conditions. One of these is $x = 0$ for $t = 0$. The other end of the curve giving x as a function of t may be anywhere on the line $x = \alpha$, or the curve may have this line as an asymptote. This indefiniteness will be settled by invoking again the condition that the discounted profit is a maximum. The "transversality condition" thus obtained,

$$f - q\frac{\partial f}{\partial q} = 0,$$

that is,

$$q^2 \frac{\partial p}{\partial q} = 0,$$

is equivalent to the proposition that, if p always diminishes when q increases, the curve is tangent or asymptotic to the line $x = a$. Thus ultimately q descends continuously to zero.

Suppose, for example, that q, x, and t all affect the net price *linearly*. Thus

$$p = \alpha - \beta q - cx + gt.$$

Ordinarily α, β, and c will be positive, but g may have either sign. The growth of population and the rising prices to consumers of competing exhaustible goods would lead to a positive value of g. On the other hand, the progress of science might lead to the gradual introduction of new substitutes for the commodity in question, tending to make g negative. The exhaustion of complementary commodities would also tend toward a negative value of g.

The differential equation reduces, for this linear demand function, to the linear form

$$2\beta \frac{d^2x}{dt^2} - 2\beta\gamma \frac{dx}{dt} - c\gamma x = -g\gamma t + g - \alpha\gamma.$$

Since β, c, and γ are positive, the roots of the auxiliary equation are real and of opposite signs. Let m denote the positive and $-n$ the negative root. Since

$$m - n = \gamma,$$

m is numerically greater than n. The solution is

$$x = Ae^{mt} + Be^{-nt} + gt/c - 2\beta\gamma/c^2 - g/c\gamma + \alpha/c,$$

whence

$$q = Ame^{mt} - Bn^{-nt} + g/c.$$

Since $x = 0$ when $t = 0$,

$$A + B - 2\beta g/c^2 - g/c\gamma + \alpha/c = 0.$$

Since $x = \alpha$ and $q = 0$ at the time T of ultimate exhaustion,

$$Ae^{mT} + Be^{-nT} + gT/c - 2\beta g/c^2 - g/c\gamma + \alpha/c - a = 0,$$
$$Ame^{mT} - Bne^{-nT} + g/c = 0.$$

From these equations A and B are eliminated by equating to zero the determinant of their coefficients and of the terms not containing A or B. After multiplying the first column by e^{-mT} and the second by e^{nT}, this gives:

$$\Delta = \begin{vmatrix} e^{-mT} & e^{nT} & -2\beta g/c^2 - g/c\gamma + \alpha/c \\ 1 & 1 & gT/c - 2\beta g/c^2 - g/c\gamma + \alpha/c - \alpha \\ m & -n & g/c \end{vmatrix} = 0.$$

Expanding and using the relations $m - n = \gamma$, and $mn = c\gamma/2\beta$, we have for Δ and its derivative with respect to T,

$$\Delta = (e^{-mT} - e^{nT})g/c + (ne^{-mT} + me^{nT})(gT/c - 2\beta g/c^2 - g/c\gamma + \alpha/c - \alpha)$$
$$+ (m+n)(2\beta g/c^2 + g/c\gamma - \alpha/c),$$
$$\Delta' = (e^{nT} - e^{-mT})[T - 1/\gamma + (\alpha - \alpha c)/g]g\gamma/2\beta,$$

the last expression being useful in applying Newton's method to find T. Obviously, the derivative changes sign for only one value of T; for this value Δ has a minimum if g is positive, a maximum if g is negative.

We may measure time in such units that γ, the force of interest, is unity. If money is worth 4 per cent, compounded quarterly, the unit of time will then be about 25 years and 1 month. With this convention let us consider an example in which there is an upward secular trend in the price consumers are willing to pay: take $\alpha = 100$, $\beta = 1$, $c = 4$, $g = 16$, and $\alpha = 10$. The net amount received per unit is in this case

$$p = 100 - q - 4x + 16t.$$

Substituting the values of the constants, and noting that $m = 2$ and $n = 1$, we have

$$\Delta = \begin{vmatrix} e^{-2T} & e^T & 19 \\ 1 & 1 & 4T+9 \\ 2 & -1 & 4 \end{vmatrix} = (8T+14)e^T + (4T+13)e^{-2T} - 57,$$

$$\Delta' = (e^T - e^{-2T})(8T + 22).$$

Evidently $\Delta < 0$ for $T = 0$, $\Delta = +\infty$ for $T = \infty$, and $\Delta' > 0$ for all positive values of T. Hence $\Delta = 0$ has one and only one positive root. For the trial value $T = 1$ we have

$$\Delta = 5.10, \quad \Delta' = 77.5.$$

Applying to T the correction $-\Delta/\Delta' = -.07$ roughly, we take $T = .93$ as a second approximation. For this value of T,

$$\Delta = -.06, \quad \Delta' = 70.0,$$

whence $-\Delta/\Delta' = .001$.

The most profitable schedule of extraction will therefore exhaust the mine in about 0.931 unit of time, or about 23 years and 4 months, perhaps a surprisingly short time in view of the prospect of obtaining an indefinitely higher price in the future, at the rate of increase of 16 per unit of time.

In order that the time of working a mine be infinite, it is necessary not only that the price shall increase indefinitely but that it shall ultimately increase at least as fast as compound interest.

The last two equations for determining A and B now become, since $e^{2T} = 6.4366$ and $e^{-T} = .3942$,

$$6.4366A + .3942B + 12.724 = 0$$
$$12.8732A - .3942B + 4 = 0.$$

Hence $A = -.866$, $B = -18.13$; so that

$$x = -.866e^{2t} - 18.13e^{-t} + 4t + 19.$$

As a check we observe that this expression for x vanishes when $t = 0$. Differentiating, we have

$$q = -1.732e^{2t} + 18.13e^{-t} + 4,$$

showing how the rate of production begins at 20.40 and gradually declines to zero. Substitution in the assumed expression for the net price gives

$$p = 100 - q - 4x + 16t = 20 + 5.196e^{2t} + 54.39e^{-t},$$

showing a decline from 79.60 at the beginning to 74.90 at exhaustion, owing to the greater cost of extracting the deeper parts of the deposit. The buyer of course pays an increasing, not a decreasing price, namely,

$$p + 4x = 100 - q + 16t = 96 + 1.732e^{2t} - 18.13e^{-t} + 16t.$$

This increases from 79.60 to 114.90.

IX   The optimum course

To examine the course of exploitation of a mine which would be best socially, in contrast with the schedule which a well-informed but entirely selfish owner would adopt, we generalize the considerations of Section III. Instead of the rate of profit pq, we must now deal with the social return per unit of time,

$$u = \int_0^q p(x, q, t)dq,$$

x and t being held constant in the integration. Taking again the market rate of interest as the appropriate discount factor for future enjoyments, we set

$$F = ue^{-\gamma t},$$

and inquire what curve of exploitation will make the total discounted social value,

$$V = \int F dt$$

a maximum.

The characteristic equation

$$\frac{\partial F}{\partial x} - \frac{d}{dt}\frac{\partial F}{\partial q} = 0$$

reduces to

$$\frac{\partial p}{\partial q}\frac{d^2x}{dt^2} + \frac{\partial p}{\partial x}\frac{dx}{dt} - \gamma p = \frac{\partial u}{\partial x} - \frac{\partial p}{\partial t}.$$

The initial condition is $x = 0$ for $t = 0$. The other end-point of the curve is movable on the line $x - \alpha = 0$, α being the amount originally in the mine. The transversality condition,

$$F - q\frac{\partial F}{\partial q} = 0,$$

reduces to

$$u - pq = 0.$$

This is satisfied only for $q = 0$, for otherwise we should have the equation

$$p = \frac{1}{q}\int_0^q p\,dq,$$

stating that the ultimate price is the mean of the potential prices corresponding to lower values of q. Since p is assumed to decrease when q increases, this is impossible. Even if $\partial p/\partial p$ is zero in isolated points, the equation will be impossible if, as is always held, this derivative is elsewhere negative. Hence $q = 0$ at the time of exhaustion.

If, as in Section VIII, we suppose the demand function linear,

$$p = \alpha - \beta q - cx + gt,$$

the characteristic equation becomes

$$\beta\frac{d^2x}{dt^2} - \beta\gamma\frac{dx}{dt} - c\gamma x = -g\gamma t + g - \alpha\gamma.$$

This differs from the corresponding equation for monopoly only in that β is here replaced by $\beta/2$. In a sense, this means that the decline of price, or marginal utility, with increase of supply counts just twice as much in affecting the rate of production, when this is in the control of a monopolist, as the public welfare would warrant.

The analysis of Section VIII may be applied to this case without any qualitative change. The values of *m* and *n* depend on β, and are therefore changed. The time *T* until ultimate exhaustion will be reduced, if social value rather than monopoly profit is to be maximized. For the numerical example given, *T* was found to be 0.931 unit of time under monopoly. Repeating the calculation for the case in which maximum social value is the goal, we find as the best value only 0.6741 unit of time.

For different values of the constants, even with a linear demand function, the mathematics may be less simple. For example, the equation $\Delta = 0$ may have two positive roots instead of one. This will be the case if the numerical illustration chosen be varied by supposing that the sign of *g* is reversed, owing to the progressive discovery of substitutes, the direct effect of passage of time being then to decrease instead of increase the price. In such cases a further examination is necessary of the two possible curves of development, to determine which will yield a greater monopoly profit or total discounted social value, according to our object.

X Discontinuous solutions

Even if the rate of production *q* has a discontinuity, as in the example of Section V, the condition that $\int f\,dt$ shall be a maximum requires that each of the quantities

$$\frac{\partial f}{\partial q}, \quad f - q\frac{\partial f}{\partial q},$$

must nevertheless be continuous.[4] This will be true whether *f* stands for discounted monopoly profit or discounted total utility.

The equation (11.8) may be written

$$\frac{\partial f}{\partial q} = \lambda,$$

which shows, since the left-hand member is continuous, that λ must have the same value before and after the discontinuity.

When *p* is a function of *q* alone, the two continuous quantities may be written in the notation of Section IV, $y'e^{-\gamma t}$ and $(y - qy')\,e^{-\gamma t}$, which shows that y' and $y - qy'$ are continuous. Thus the expression $\lambda\,(q - y/y')$ appearing in (equation (11.13)), is continuous. Consequently the expressions (equation (11.13)) or (equation (11.14)) pertaining to the different time-intervals may simply be added to obtain an expression of the same form. Hence the present value of the discounted future profits of the mine – and therefore of the mine – is in such cases the difference between the values of

$$\lambda(q - y/y')/\gamma$$

at present and at the time of exhaustion.

We are now ready to answer such questions as that raised at the end of Section V as to the location of the discontinuity there shown to exist in the most profitable schedule of production when the demand function is

$$p = b - (q - 1)^3.$$

Since in this case

$$f = pqe^{-\gamma t} = \left[bq - q(q - 1)^3\right]e^{-\gamma t},$$

the two quantities

$$b - (4q - 1)(q - 1)^2,$$
$$3q^2(q - 1)^2,$$

are continuous. Consequently

$$(4q - 1)(q - 1)^2$$

and

$$q^2(q - 1)^2$$

are continuous. If q_1 denote the rate of production just before the sudden jump and q_2 the initial rate after it, this means that

$$(4q_1 - 1)(q_1 - 1)^2 = (4q_2 - 1)(q_2 - 1)^2$$
$$q_1^2(q_1 - 1)^2 = q_2^2(q_2 - 1)^2.$$

The only admissible solution is:

$$q_1 = (3 + \sqrt{3})/4 = 1.1830, \quad q_2 = (3 - \sqrt{3})/4 = 0.31699.$$

XI Tests for a true maximum

The equations which have been given for finding the production schedule of maximum profit or social value are necessary, not sufficient, conditions for maxima, like the vanishing of the first derivative in the differential calculus. We must also consider more definitive tests.

The integrals which have arisen in the problems of exhaustible assets are to be maxima, not necessarily for the most general type of variation conceivable for a curve, but only for the so-called "special weak" variations. The nature of the economic situation seems to preclude all variations which involve turning time backward, increasing the rate of production, maintaining two different rates of production at the same time, or varying production with infinite rapidity. Extremely sudden increases in production usually involve special costs which will be borne only under unexpected conditions, and are to be avoided in long-term planning. Likewise sudden decreases involve social losses of great magnitude such as unemployment, which even a selfish monopolist will often try to prevent. This will be considered further in the next section. It is indeed possible that in some special cases these "strong" variations might take on some economic significance, but such a situation would involve forces of a different sort from those with which economic theory is ordinarily concerned.

The critical tests which must be applied are by the foregoing considerations reduced to two – those of Legendre and Jacobi.[5] The Legendre test requires, in order that the total discounted utility or social value (Section IX) shall be a maximum, that

$$\frac{\partial^2 u}{\partial q^2} = \frac{\partial p}{\partial q} < 0,$$

a condition which is always held to obtain save in exceptional cases. In order that the chosen curve shall yield a genuine maximum for a monopolist's profit, the Legendre test requires that

$$\frac{\partial^2 (pq)}{\partial q^2} = 2\frac{\partial p}{\partial q} + q\frac{\partial^2 p}{\partial q^2} < 0.$$

This means that the curve of Figure 11.1 is convex upward at all points touched by the turning tangent. The re-entrant portions, if any, are passed over, producing discontinuities in the rate of production.

When the solution of the characteristic equation has been found in the form

$$x = \varphi(t, A, B),$$

A and B being arbitrary constants, the Jacobi test requires that

$$\frac{\partial\varphi/\partial A}{\partial\varphi/\partial B}$$

shall not take the same value for two different values of t. For the example of Section VIII this critical quantity is simply $e^{(m+n)t}$, which obviously satisfies the test. The solution represents a real, not an illusory maximum for the monopolist's profit. The like is true for the schedule of production maximizing the total discounted utility with the same demand function. Each case must, however, be examined separately, as the test might show in some instances that a seeming maximum could be improved.

XII   The need for steadiness in production

The demand function giving p may involve not only the rate of production q, but also the rate of change q' of q. Such a condition would display a duality with that considered by C. F. Roos[6] and G. C. Evans,[7] who hold that the quantity of a commodity which can be sold per unit of time depends ordinarily upon the rate of change of the price, as well as upon the price itself. If p is a function of x, q, q', and t, the maximum of monopoly profit or of social value can only be obtained if the course of exploitation satisfies a fourth-order differential equation.

More generally we might suppose that p and its rate of change p' are connected with x, q, q', and t by a relation

$$\varphi(p, p', x, q, q', t) = 0.$$

This presents a Lagrange problem, which can be dealt with by known methods.[8] A further generalization is to suppose that the price, the quantity, and their derivatives are subject to a relation in the nature of a demand function which also involves an integral or integrals giving the effect of past prices and rates of consumption.[9]

Capital investment in developing the mine and industries essential to it is a source of a need for steady production; the desirability of regular employment for labor is another. Under the term "capital" might possibly be included the costs, both to employers and to laborers, in drawing laborers to the mine from other places and occupations. The returning of these laborers to other occupations as production declines would have to be reckoned as part of the social cost. Whether this would enter into the mine-owner's costs would probably depend upon whether the laborers have at the beginning sufficient information and bargaining power to insist upon compensation for the cost to them of the return shift.

Problems in which the fixity of capital investment plays a part in determining production schedules may be dealt with by introducing new variables $x_1, x_2, \ldots$, to represent the various types of capital investment involved. In so far as these variables are continuous, the problem is that of maximizing an integral involving $x, x_1, x_2, \ldots$, and their derivatives, using well-known methods. The simultaneous equations

$$\frac{\partial f}{\partial x_i} - \frac{d}{dt}\frac{\partial f}{\partial x_i} = 0 \quad (i = 0, 1, 2, \ldots; x_0 = x; x_i' = dx_i/dt)$$

are necessary for a maximum. The depreciation of mining equipment raises considerations of this kind.

The cases considered in the earlier part of this paper all led to solutions in which the rate of production of a mine always decreases. By considering the influence of fixed investments and the cost of accelerating production at the beginning, we may be led to production curves which rise continuously from zero to a maximum, and then fall more slowly as exhaustion approaches. Certain production curves of this type have been found statistically to exist for whole industries of the extractive type, such as petroleum production.[10]

XIII Capital value taxes and severance taxes

An unanticipated tax upon the value of a mine will have no effect other than to transfer to the government treasury a part of the mine-owner's income. An anticipated tax at the rate α per year and payable continuously will have the same effects upon the value of the mine and the schedule of production as an increase of the force of interest by α. This we shall now prove.

From the income pq from the mine at time t must now be deducted the tax, $\alpha J\,(t)$. Consequently the value at time τ is

$$J(\tau) = \int_\tau^T [pq - \alpha J(t)] e^{-\gamma(t-\tau)} dt.$$

This integral equation in J reduces by differentiation to a differential equation:

$$J'(\tau) = -pq + \alpha J(\tau) + \gamma J(\tau).$$

The solution is found by well-known methods. The constant of integration is evaluated by means of the condition that $J(T) = 0$. We have:

$$J(\tau) = \int_\tau^T pq e^{-(\alpha+\gamma)(t-\tau)} dt,$$

so that α is merely added to γ.

Quite a different kind of levy is represented by the "severance tax."[11] Such a tax, of so much per unit of material extracted from the mine, tends to conservation. The ordinary theory of monopoly of an inexhaustible commodity suggests that the incidence of such a tax is divided between monopolist and consumer, equally in the case of a linear demand function. However, for an exhaustible supply the division is in a different proportion, varying with time and the supply remaining. Indeed, the imposition of the tax will lead eventually to an actually lower price than as if there had been no tax.

Consider the linear demand function

$$p = \alpha - \beta q$$

and, for simplicity, no cost of production. The rate of net profit, after paying a tax v per unit extracted, will be

$$(p - v)q = (\alpha - v)q - \beta q^2.$$

As in Section IV, the derivative increases as compound interest:

$$\alpha - v - 2\beta q = \lambda e^{\gamma t}.$$

Since ultimately $q = 0$ and $t = T$, we obtain

$$\alpha - v = \lambda e^{\gamma T},$$

whence eliminating λ and solving for q,

$$q = [1 - e^{\gamma(t-T)}](a - v)/2\beta.$$

The time of exhaustion T is related to the amount originally in the mine through the equation

$$\alpha = \int_0^T q \, dt = (\gamma T + e^{-\gamma T} - 1)(\alpha - v)/2\beta\gamma;$$

whence

$$dT = \frac{2\beta\alpha \, dv}{(\alpha - v)^2(1 - e^{-\gamma T})},$$

showing how much of an increase in time of exploitation is likely to result from the imposition of a small severance tax. The effect upon the rate of production at time t is

$$dq = \frac{\partial q}{\partial v} dv + \frac{\partial q}{\partial T} dT = dv\{-1 + e^{\gamma(t-T)}[1 + 2\beta\gamma\alpha/(\alpha - v)(1 - e^{-\gamma T})]\}/2\beta.$$

From the form of the demand function it follows that the increase in price at time t is

$$dp = -\beta dq = dv\left\{\frac{1}{2} - e^{\gamma(t-T)}\left[\frac{1}{2} + \beta\gamma\alpha/(\alpha - v)(1 - e^{-\gamma T})\right]\right\}.$$

If α is very large, then so is T; the expression in curly brackets will, for moderate values of t, differ infinitesimally from $\frac{1}{2}$, reducing to the case of monopoly with unlimited supplies. However, dp will always be less than $\frac{1}{2}dv$ and, as exhaustion approaches, will decline and become negative. Finally, when $t = T$, the price of the tax-paid articles to buyers is lower by

$$\beta\gamma\alpha v/(\alpha - v)(1 - e^{-\gamma T})$$

than the ultimate price if there had been no tax. The price will, nevertheless, be so high that very little of the commodity will be bought.

A tax on a monopolist which will lead the monopolist to reduce his/her prices is reminiscent of Edgeworth's paradox of a tax on first-class railway tickets which makes the monopolistic (and unregulated) owner's most profitable course the reduction of the prices both of first- and of third-class tickets, besides paying the tax him/herself.[12] The case of a mine is, however, of a distinct species from Edgeworth's, and cannot be assimilated to it by treating ore extracted at different times as different commodities. Indeed, in the simple case of mine economics which we are now considering, the demands at different times are not correlated; supplies put upon the market now and in the future neither complement nor compete with each other. Correlated demand of a particular type was, on the other hand, an essential feature of Edgeworth's phenomenon.

The ultimate lowering of price and the extension of the life of a mine as a result of a severance tax are not peculiar to the linear demand function, but hold similarly for any declining demand function $p(q)$ whose slope is always finite. This general proposition does not depend upon the tax being small.

The conclusion reached in the linear case that the division of the incidence of the tax is more favorable to the consumer than for an inexhaustible supply is probably true in general; at least this is indicated by an examination of a number of demand curves. However, the general proposition seems very difficult to prove.

Since the severance tax postpones exhaustion, falls in considerable part on the monopolist, and leads ultimately to an actual lowering of price, it would seem to be a good tax. It is particularly to be commended if the monopolist is regarded as *unfairly* possessed of his property, and there is no other feasible means of taking away from him so great a portion of it as the severance tax will yield. However, the total wealth of the community may be diminished rather than increased by such a tax. Considering as in Section III the integral u of the prices p which buyers are willing to pay for quantities below that actually put on the market, and the time-integral U of values of u discounted for interest, we have in the case of linear demand just discussed,

$$u = \int_0^q (\alpha - \beta q)dq = \alpha q - \frac{1}{2}\beta q^2.$$

If we were considering the portion of this social benefit which inures to consumers, we should have to subtract the portion pq which they pay to the monopolist, an amount from which he would have to subtract the tax, which benefits the state. But the sum of all these benefits is u, which is affected by the tax only as this affects the rate of production q.

If, for simplicity, we measure time in such units that $\gamma = 1$, the rate of production determined earlier in this section becomes

$$q = (1 - e^{t-T})(\alpha - v)/2\beta.$$

Substituting this in the expression for u and the result in U, we obtain

$$U = \int_0^T ue^{-t}dt = (\alpha - v)[4\alpha(1 - e^{-T} - Te^{-T}) - (\alpha - v)(1 - 2Te^{-T} - e^{-2T})]/8\beta.$$

We differentiate U and then, to examine the effect of a small tax, put $v = 0$. The results simplify to:

$$\frac{\partial U}{\partial v} = -(1 - e^{-T})^2 \alpha/4\beta$$

$$\frac{\partial U}{\partial T} = [(T + 1)e^{-T} - e^{-2T}]\alpha^2/4\beta.$$

From the amount initially in the mine,

$$\alpha = (T + e^{-T} - 1)/2\beta,$$

we obtain,

$$\frac{dT}{dv} = \frac{2\beta\alpha}{\alpha^2(1 - e^{-T})},$$

When $v = 0$. Substituting here the preceding value for α we find, after simplification,

$$\frac{dU}{dv} = \frac{\partial U}{\partial v} + \frac{\partial U}{\partial T}\frac{dT}{dv} = -\frac{\alpha}{4\beta}\frac{e^T + e^{-T} - 2 - T^2}{e^T - 1}.$$

The numerator of the last fraction may be expanded in a convergent series of powers of T in which all the terms are positive. Hence dU/dv is negative.

Thus a small tax on a monopolized resource will diminish its total social value, at least if the demand function is linear. Whether this is true for demand functions in general is an unsolved problem.

We have here supposed the tax *v* to be constant, permanent, and fully foreseen. Since an unforeseen tax will have unforeseen results, we can scarcely build up a general theory of such taxes. However, any tax of amount varying with time in a manner definitely fixed upon in advance will have predictable results. In this connection, an interesting problem is to fix upon a schedule of taxation *v*, which may involve the rate of production *q* and the cumulated production *x*, as well as the time, such that, when the monopolist then chooses his schedule of production to maximize his profit, the social value *U* will be greater than as if any other tax schedule had been adopted. This leads to a problem of Lagrange type in the calculus of variations, one end-point being variable. Putting *q = dx/dt* and

$$J = \int_0^T f(x,q,v,t)dt, \quad U = \int_0^T F(x,q,t)dt,$$

the problem is to choose *v*, subject to the differential relation

$$\frac{\partial f}{\partial x} + \frac{\partial f}{\partial v}\frac{\partial v}{\partial x} - \frac{d}{dt}\left(\frac{\partial f}{\partial q} + \frac{\partial f}{\partial v}\frac{\partial v}{\partial q}\right) = 0,$$

so that *U* will be a maximum. In general, of course, a still greater value of *U* would be obtainable, at least in theory, by public ownership and operation.

XIV   Mine income and depletion

With income taxes we are not concerned except for the determination of the amount of the income from a mine. The problem of allowance for depletion has been a perplexing one. It has been said that if the value of ore removed from the ground could be claimed as a deduction from income, then a mining company having no income except from the sale of ore could escape payment of income tax entirely. The fallacy of this contention may be examined by considering the value of the mine at time *t*,

$$J(t) = \int_t^T pqe^{-\gamma(\tau-t)}d\tau.$$

In this integral *p* and *q* have the values corresponding to the time *τ*, later than *t*, assigned by whatever production schedule has been adopted, whether this results from competition, from a desire to maximize monopoly profit, or from any other set of conditions. The net income consists of the return from sales of material removed (cost of production and selling having as usual been deducted), minus the decrease in the value of the mine. It therefore equals, per unit of time,

$$pq + dJ/dt;$$

and from the expression for J, this is exactly γJ. In other words, any particular production schedule fixes the value of the mine at such a figure that the income at any time, after allowing for depletion, is exactly equal to the interest on the value of the investment at that time.

But, although the rate of decline in value of a mine seems a logical quantity to define as depletion and to deduct from income, such is not the practice of income-tax administrations, at least in the United States. The value of the property upon acquisition, or on March 1, 1913, a date shortly before the inauguration of the tax, if acquired before that time, is taken as a basis and divided by the number of units of material estimated to have been in the ground at that time. The resulting "unit of depletion," an amount of money, is multiplied by the number of tons, pounds, or ounces of material removed in a year to give the depletion for that year. The total of depletion allowances must not exceed the original value of the property.

The differences between the two methods of calculating depletion arise from the uncertainties of valuation and of forecasting price, demand, production, costs, interest rates, and amount of material remaining. If the theoretical method were applied, a year in which the mine failed to operate would still be set down as yielding an income equal to the interest on the investment value. This seems anomalous only because of another defect, from the theoretical standpoint, in income-tax laws: the non-taxation of increase in value of a property until the sale of the property. During a year of idleness, if foreseen, the value of the property is actually increasing, for the idle year has been considered in fixing the value at the beginning of the year.

An amendment made to the United States federal income-tax law in 1918 provides that the valuation upon which depletion is calculated may under certain circumstances be taken, not as the value of the property when acquired or in 1913, but the higher value which it later took when its mineral content was discovered. This provision has the effect of materially increasing depletion allowances, and so of reducing tax payments. The sudden increase in value when the mineral is discovered might well be regarded as taxable income, but is not so regarded by the law unless the property is immediately sold. The framers of the statute seem indeed, according to its language, to have considered this increase in value a reward for the efforts and risks of prospecting, which would suggest that it is of the nature of income, a reasonable position. However, the object of the amendment is to treat this increment as pre-existing capital value, to be returned to the owner by sale of the mineral. The amendment appears to be inconsistent and quite too generous to the owners particularly affected.

XV   Duopoly

Intermediate between monopoly and perfect competition, and more closely related than either to the real economic world, is the condition in which there are a few competing sellers. In a former paper[13] this situation was discussed for the static case, with special reference to a factor usually ignored, the existence with reference to each seller of groups of buyers who have a special advantage in dealing with him in spite of possible lower prices elsewhere. More than one price in the same market is then possible, and with a sort of quasi-stability which sets a lower limit to prices, as well as the known upper limit of monopoly price.

For exhaustible resources the corresponding problems of competition among a small number of entrepreneurs may be studied in the first instance by means of the jointly stationary values of the several integrals representing discounted profits. We need not confine ourselves, as we have done for convenience in dealing with monopoly, to a single mine for each competitor. Let there be m competitors, and let the one numbered i control n_i mines, whose production rates and initial contents we shall denote by $q\alpha, \ldots, q_{in}$, and $\alpha_{il}, \ldots, \alpha_{in}$, respectively. The demand functions will be intercorrelated, both among the mines owned by each competitor and between the mines of different concerns. Consequently the m integrals J_i representing the discounted profits will involve in their integrands f_i all the q_{ij}, as well as some at least of the cumulated productions $x_{ij} = \int q_{ij} \, dt$. If the ith owner wishes to make his profit a maximum, assuming the production rates of the others to have been fixed upon, he will adjust his n_i production rates so that

$$\frac{\partial f_i}{\partial x_{ij}} - \frac{d}{dt}\frac{\partial f_i}{\partial q_{ij}} = 0. \quad (j = 1, 2, \ldots, n_i)$$

Continuing the analogy with the static case, we are to imagine that the other competitors, hearing of his plans, do likewise, altering their schedules to conform to equations resembling those above. When the ith

owner learns of their changed plans, he will in turn readjust. The only possible final equilibrium with a settled schedule of production for each mine will be determined by the solution of the set of differential equations of this type, which are exactly as numerous as the mines, and therefore as the variables to be determined. All this is a direct generalization of the case of inexhaustible supplies. But we shall show that the solution tends to overstate the production rates and understate the prices of competing mines.

Doubts in plenty have been cast upon the result in the simpler case, and the reasons which can there be adduced in favor of the solution are even more painfully inadequate when the supplies are of limited amount. The chief difficulty with the problem of a small number of sellers consists in the fact that each, in modifying their conduct in accordance with what they think the others are going to do, may or may not take account of the effect upon their prices and policies of their own prospective acts. There is an "equilibrium point," such that neither of two sellers can, by changing his price, increase his/her rate of profit while the other's price remains unchanged. However, if one seller increases his/her price moderately, thus making some immediate sacrifice, the other will find his/her most profitable course to lie in increasing his/her own price; and then, if the original increase is not too great, both will obtain higher profits than at "equilibrium." But that the tendency to cut prices below the equilibrium is less important than has been supposed is shown in the article just referred to.

With an exhaustible supply, and therefore with less to lose by a temporary reduction in sales, a seller will be particularly inclined to experiment by raising his price above the theoretical level in the hope that his competitors will also increase their prices. For the loss of business incurred while waiting for them to do so he can in this case take comfort, not merely in the prospect of approximating his old sales at the higher price in the near future but also in the fact that he is conserving his supplies for a time when general exhaustion will be nearer and even the theoretical price will be higher. Thus a general condition may be expected of higher prices and lower rates of production than are given by the solution of the simultaneous characteristic equations.

For complementary products, such as iron and coal, the situation is in some ways reversed. Edgeworth in his *Papers Relating to Political Economy* points out that when two complementary goods are separately monopolized the consumer is worse off than if both were under the control of the same monopolist. This assumes the equilibrium solution to hold. The tentative deviations from equilibrium made in order to influence the other party may now be in either direction, according as the nature of the demand function and other conditions make it more profitable to move toward the lower prices and larger sales characterizing the maximum joint profit, or to raise one's price in an effort to force one's rival to lower his in order to maintain sales. When the supplies of the complementary goods are exhaustible, the same indeterminateness exists.

A very different problem of duopoly involving the calculus of variations has been studied by C. F. Roos,[14] who finds[15] that the respective profits take true maximum values. However, as in the static case, no definitively stable equilibrium is insured by the fact that each profit is a maximum when the other is considered fixed, since the acts of one competitor affect those of the other. The calculus of variations is used by Roos and G. C. Evans[16] to deal with cost and demand functions involving the rate of change of price as well as the price. Such functions we have for concreteness and simplicity avoided, but if they should prove to be of importance in mine economics the foregoing treatment can readily be extended to them. (Cf. Section XII.) Evans and Roos are not concerned with exhaustible assets, and assume that at any time all competitors sell at the same price.

The problems of exhaustible resources involve the time in another way besides bringing on exhaustion and higher prices, namely, as bringing increased information, both as to the physical extent and condition of the resource and as to the economic phenomena attending its extraction and sale. In the most elementary discussions of exchange, as in bartering nuts for apples, as well as in discussions of duopoly, a time element is always introduced to show a gradual approach to equilibrium or a breaking away from it. Such time effects are equally or in even greater measure involved in exploiting irreplaceable assets, entangling with the secular tendencies peculiar to this class of goods. With duopoly in the sale of exhaustible resources the possibilities of bargaining, bluff, and bluster become remarkably intricate.

The periodic price wars which break the monotony of gasoline prices on the American Pacific Coast are an interesting phenomenon. Along most of the fifteen-hundred-mile strip west of the summits of the Sierras a few large companies dominate the oil business. In the southern California oil fields, however, numerous small concerns sell gasoline at cut prices. Cheap gasoline is for the most part not distilled from oil but is filtered from natural gas, and may be of slightly inferior quality; nevertheless, it is an acceptable motor fuel. The extreme mobility of purchasers of gasoline reduces to a minimum the element of gradualness in the shift of demand from seller to seller with change of price. Ordinarily, the price outside of southern California is held steady by agreement among the five or six major companies, being fixed in each of several large areas according to distance from the oil fields. But every year or two a price war occurs, in which prices go down day by day to extremely low levels, sometimes almost to the point of giving away gasoline, and certainly below the cost of distribution. From a normal price of 20 to 23 cents a gallon the price sometimes drops to 6 or 7 cents, including the tax of 3 cents. Peace is made and the old high price restored after a few weeks of universal joy-riding and storage in every available container, even in bath tubs. The interesting thing is the slowness of the spread of these contests, which usually begin in southern California. The companies fight each other violently there, and a few weeks later in northern California, while in some cases maintaining full prices in Oregon and Washington. These affrays give an example of the instability of competition when variations of price with location as well as time complicate commerce in an exhaustible asset.

Notes

1 As in "A General Mathematical Theory of Depreciation," by Harold Hotelling, *Journal of the American Statistical Association*, September, 1925.
2 Cf. George W. Stocking, *The Oil Industry and the Competitive System*, Hart Schaffner and Marx prize essay (Houghton Mifflin, 1928).
3 "A Mathematical Theory of Saving," *Economic Journal*, XXXVII (1928), 543.
4 C. Caratheodory, "Über die diskontinuirlichen Lösungen in der Variationsrechnung," thesis, Göttingen, 1904, p. 11. The condition that the first of these quantities must be continuous is given in the textbooks, but for some reason the second is generally omitted.
5 A. R. Forsyth, *Calculus of Variations* (Cambridge, 1927), pp. 17–28.
6 "A Dynamical Theory of Economics," *Journal of Political Economy*, XXXV (1927), 632, and references there given; also "A Mathematical Theory of Depreciation and Replacement," *American Journal of Mathematics*, L (1928), 147.
7 "The Dynamics of Monopoly," *American Mathematical Monthly*, Vol. XXXI (1924); also *Mathematical Introduction to Economics* (McGraw-Hill Book Co., 1930).
8 Cf. G. A. Bliss, "The Problem of Lagrange in the Calculus of Variations" (mimeographed by O. E. Brown), (University of Chicago Bookstore).
9 See "Generalized Lagrange Problems in the Calculus of Variations," by C. F. Roos, *Transactions of the American Mathematical Society*, XXX (1927), 360.
10 C. E. Van Orstrand, "On the Empirical Representation of Certain Production Curves," *Journal of the Washington Academy of Sciences*, XV (1925), 19.
11 A variant is an ad valorem tax. A great deal of information and discussion concerning these taxes is contained in the biennial *Report of the Minnesota*

State Tax Commission, 1928, (St. Paul). From p. 111 of this report it appears that Alabama since 1927 has had a severance tax of $2\frac{1}{2}$ cents a ton on coal, $4\frac{1}{2}$ cents a ton on iron ore, and 3 per cent on quarry products; Montana taxes coal extracted at 5 cents per ton; Arkansas imposes a tax of $2\frac{1}{2}$ per cent on the gross value of all natural resources except coal and timber, 1 per cent on coal, and 7 cents per 1,000 board feet on timber. Minnesota taxes iron ore extracted at 6 per cent on value minus cost of labor and materials used in mining, and also assesses ore lands at a higher rate than other property for the general property tax. These taxes are not based entirely on the conservation idea, but aim also at taxing persons outside the state, or "retaining for the state its natural heritage." Since Minnesota produces about two-thirds of the iron ore of the United States, the outside incidence is doubtless accomplished. Mexican petroleum taxes have the same object. The Minnesota Commission believes that prospecting for ore has virtually ceased on account of the high taxes.

12 *Economic Journal*, VII (1897), 231, and various passages in Edgeworth's *Papers Relating to Political Economy*.

13 Harold Hotelling, "Stability in Competition," *Economic Journal*, XLI (March, 1929), 41.

14 "A Mathematical Theory of Competition," *American Journal of Mathematics*, XLVII (1925), 163.

15 "Generalized Lagrange Problems in the Calculus of Variations," *Transactions of the American Mathematical Society*, XXX (1927), 360.

16 *A Mathematical Introduction to Economics* (McGraw-Hill, 1930).

12
The Economics of Resources or the Resources of Economics

Robert M. Solow

It is easy to choose a subject for a distinguished lecture like this, before a large and critical audience with a wide range of interests. You need a topic that is absolutely contemporary, but somehow perennial. It should survey a broad field, without being superficial or vague. It should probably bear some relation to economic policy, but of course it must have some serious analytical foundations. It is nice if the topic has an important literature in the past of our subject – a literature which you can summarize brilliantly in about eleven minutes – but it better be something in which economists are interested today, and it should appropriately be a subject you have worked on yourself. The lecture should have some technical interest, because you can't waffle for a whole hour to a room full of professionals, but it is hardly the occasion to use a blackboard.

I said that it is easy to choose a subject for the Ely Lecture. It has to be, because twelve people, counting me, have done it.

I am going to begin with a quotation that could have come from yesterday's newspaper, or the most recent issue of the *American Economic Review*.

> Contemplation of the world's disappearing supplies of minerals, forests, and other exhaustible assets has led to demands for regulation of their exploitation. The feeling that these products are now too cheap for the good of future generations, that they are being selfishly exploited at too rapid a rate, and that in consequence of their excessive cheapness they are being produced and consumed wastefully has given rise to the conservation movement.

The author of those sentences is not Dennis Meadows and associates, not Ralph Nader and associates, not the President of the Sierra Club;

it is a very eminent economic theorist, a Distinguished Fellow of this Association, Harold Hotelling, who died at the age of seventy-eight, just a few days ago. Like all economic theorists, I am much in his debt, and I would be happy to have this lecture stand as a tribute to him. These sentences appeared at the beginning of his article "The Economics of Exhaustible Resources," not in the most recent *Review*, but in the *Journal of Political Economy* for April 1931. So I think I have found something that is both contemporary and perennial. The world has been exhausting its exhaustible resources since the first cave-man chipped a flint, and I imagine the process will go on for a long, long time.

Mr Dooley noticed that "th' Supreme Coort follows the iliction returns." He would be glad to know that economic theorists read the newspapers. About a year ago, having seen several of those respectable committee reports on the advancing scarcity of materials in the United States and the world, and having, like everyone else, been suckered into reading the *Limits to Growth*, I decided I ought to find out what economic theory has to say about the problems connected with exhaustible resources. I read some of the literature, including Hotelling's classic article – the theoretical literature on exhaustible resources is, fortunately, not very large – and began doing some work of my own on the problem of optimal social management of a stock of a nonrenewable but essential resource. I will be mentioning some of the results later. About the time I finished a first draft of my own paper and was patting myself on the back for having been clever enough to realize that there was in fact something still to be said on this important, contemporary but somehow perennial topic – just about then it seemed that every time the mail came it contained another paper by another economic theorist on the economics of exhaustible resources.[1] It was a little like trotting down to the sea, minding your own business like any nice independent rat, and then looking around and suddenly discovering that you're a lemming. Anyhow, I now have a nice collection of papers on the theory of exhaustible resources.

A pool of oil or vein of iron or deposit of copper in the ground is a capital asset to society and to its owner (in the kind of society in which such things have private owners) much like a printing press or a building or any other reproducible capital asset. The only difference is that the natural resource is not reproducible, so the size of the existing stock can never increase through time. It can only decrease (or, if none is mined for a while, stay the same). This is true even of recyclable materials; the laws of thermodynamics and life guarantee that we will never recover a whole pound of secondary copper from a pound of primary copper in use, or a whole pound of tertiary copper from a pound of secondary copper in use. There is leakage at every round; and a formula just like the ordinary multiplier formula tells us how much copper use can be built on the world's initial endowment of copper, in terms of the recycling or recovery ratio. There is always less ultimate copper use left than there was last year, less by the amount dissipated beyond recovery during the year. So copper remains an exhaustible resource, despite the possibility of partial recycling.

A resource deposit draws its market value, ultimately, from the prospect of extraction and sale. In the meanwhile, its owner, like the owner of every capital asset, is asking: what have you done for me lately? The only way that a resource deposit in the ground and left in the ground can produce a current return for its owner is by appreciating in value. Asset markets can be in equilibrium only when all assets in a given risk class earn the same rate of return, partly as current dividend and partly as capital gain. The common rate of return is the interest rate for that risk class. Since resource deposits have the peculiar property that they yield no dividend so long as they stay in the ground, in equilibrium the value of a resource deposit must be growing at a rate equal to the rate of interest. Since the value of a deposit is also the present value of future sales from it, after deduction of extraction costs, resource owners must expect the net price of the ore to be increasing exponentially at a rate equal to the rate of interest. If the mining industry is competitive, net price stands for market price minus marginal extraction cost for a ton of ore. If the industry operates under constant costs, that is just market price net of unit extraction costs, or the profit margin. If the industry is more or less monopolistic, as is frequently the case in extractive industry, it is the marginal profit – marginal revenue less marginal cost – that has to be growing, and expected to grow, proportionally like the rate of interest.

This is the fundamental principle of the economics of exhaustible resources. It was the basis of Hotelling's classic article. I have deduced it as a condition of stock equilibrium in the asset market. Hotelling thought of it mainly as a condition of flow equilibrium in the market for ore: if net price is increasing like compound interest, owners of operating mines will be indifferent at the margin between extracting and holding at every instant of time. So one can imagine production just equal to demand at the current price, and the ore market clears. No other time profile for prices can elicit positive production in every period of time.

It is hard to overemphasize the importance of this tilt in the time profile for net price. If the net price were to rise too slowly, production would be pushed nearer in time and the resource would be exhausted quickly, precisely because no one would wish to hold resources in the ground and earn less than the going rate of return. If the net price were to rise too fast, resource deposits would be an excellent way to hold wealth, and owners would delay production while they enjoyed supernormal capital gains.

According to the fundamental principle, if we observe the market for an exhaustible resource near equilibrium, we should see the net price – or marginal profit – rising exponentially. That is not quite the same thing as seeing the market price to users of the resource rising exponentially. The price to consumers is the net price plus extraction costs, or the obvious analogy for monopoly. The market price can fall or stay constant while the net price is rising if extraction costs are falling through time, and if the net price or scarcity rent is not too large a proportion of the market price. That is presumably what has been happening in the market for most exhaustible resources in the past. (It is odd that there are not some econometric studies designed to find out just this. Maybe econometricians don't follow the iliction returns.) Eventually, as the extraction cost falls and the net price rises, the scarcity rent must come to dominate the movement of market price, so the market price will eventually rise, although that may take a very long time to happen. Whatever the pattern, the market price and the rate of extraction are connected by the demand curve for the resource. So, ultimately, when the market price rises, the current rate of production must fall along the demand curve. Sooner or later, the market price will get high enough to choke off the demand entirely. At that moment production falls to zero. If flows and stocks have been beautifully coordinated through the operations of futures markets or a planning board, the last ton produced will also be the last ton in the ground. The resource will be exhausted at the instant that it has priced itself out of the market. The Age of Oil or Zinc or Whatever It is will have come to an end. (There is a limiting case, of course, in which demand goes asymptotically to zero as the price rises to infinity, and the resource is exhausted only asymptotically. But it is neither believable nor important.)

Now let us do an exercise with this apparatus. Suppose there are two sources of the same ore, one high-cost and the other low-cost. The cost difference may reflect geographical accessibility and transportation costs, or some geological or chemical difference that makes extraction cheap at one site and dear at the other. The important thing is that there are cost differences, though the final mineral product is identical from both sources.

It is easy to see that production from both sources cannot coexist in the market for any interval of time. For both sources to produce, net price for each of them must be growing like compound interest at the market rate. But they must market their ore at the same price, because the product is identical. That is arithmetically impossible, if their extraction costs differ.

So the story has to go like this. First open source operates and supplies the whole market. Its net price rises exponentially, and the market price moves correspondingly. At a certain moment, the first source is exhausted. At just that moment and not before, it must become economical for the second source to come into production. From then on, the world is in the singlesource situation: the net price calculated with current extraction costs must rise exponentially until all production is choked off and the second source is exhausted. (If there are many sources, you can see how it will work.)

Which source will be used first? Your instinct tells you that the low-cost deposit will be the first one worked, and your instinct is right. You can see why, in terms of the fundamental principle. At the beginning, if the high-cost producer is serving the market, the market price must cover high extraction costs plus a scarcity rent that is growing exponentially. The low-cost producer would refrain from undercutting the price and entering the market only if his capital gains justify holding off and entering the market later. But just the reverse will be true. Any price high enough to keep the high-cost producer in business will tempt the low-cost producer to sell ore while the selling is good and invest the proceeds in any asset paying the market rate of interest. So it must be that the low-cost producer is the first to enter. Price rises and output falls. Eventually, at precisely the moment when the low-cost supply is exhausted, the price has reached a level at which it pays the high-cost producer to enter. From then on, *his* net price rises exponentially and production continues to fall. When cumulative production has exhausted the high-cost deposit, the market price must be such as to choke the demand off to zero – or else just high enough to tempt a still higher-cost source into production. And so it goes. Apart from market processes, it is actually socially rational to use the lower-cost deposits before the higher-cost ones.

You can take this story even further, as William Nordhaus has done in connection with the energy industry. Suppose that, somewhere in the background, there is a technology capable of producing or substituting for a mineral resource at relatively high cost, but on an effectively inexhaustible resource base. Nordhaus calls this a "backstop technology." (The nearest we now have to such a thing is the breeder reactor using U^{238} as fuel. World reserves of U^{238} are thought to be enough to provide energy for over a million years at current rates of consumption. If that is not a backstop technology, it is at least a catcher who will not allow a lot of passed balls. For a better approximation, we must wait for controlled nuclear fusion or direct use of solar energy. The sun will not last forever, but it will last at least as long as we do, more or less by definition.) Since there is no scarcity rent to grow exponentially, the backstop technology can operate as soon as the market price rises enough to cover its extraction costs (including, of course, profit on the capital equipment involved in production). And as soon as that happens, the market price of the ore or its substitute stops rising. The "backstop technology" provides a ceiling for the market price of the natural resource.

The story in the early stages is as I have told it. In the beginning, the successive grades of the resource are mined. The last and highest-cost source gives out just when the market price has risen to the point where the backstop technology becomes competitive. During the earlier phases, one imagines that resource companies keep a careful eye on the prospective costs associated with the backstop technology. Any laboratory success or failure that changes those prospective costs has instantaneous effects on the capital value of existing resource deposits, and on the most profitable rate of current production. In actual fact, those future costs have to be regarded as uncertain. A correct theory of market behavior and a correct theory of optimal social policy will have to take account of technological uncertainty (and perhaps also uncertainty about the true size of mineral reserves).

Here is a mildly concrete illustration of these principles. There is now a workable technology for liquefying coal – that is, for producing synthetic crude oil from coal.[2] Nordhaus puts the extraction-and-preparation cost at the equivalent of seven or eight 1970 dollars per barrel of crude oil, including amortization and interest at 10 per cent on the plant; I have heard higher and lower figures quoted. If coal were available in unlimited amounts, that would be all. But, of course, coal is a scarce resource, though more abundant than drillable petroleum, so a scarcity rent has to be added to that figure, and the rent has to be increasing like the rate of interest during the period when coal is being used for this purpose.

In the meanwhile, the extraction and production cost for this technology is large compared with the scarcity rent on the coal input, so the market price at which the liquefied-coal-synthetic-crude activity would now be economic is rising more slowly than the rate of interest. It may even fall if there are cost-reducing technological improvements; and that is not unlikely, given that research on coal has not been splashed as liberally with funds as research on nuclear energy. In any case, political shenanigans and monopoly profits aside, scarcity rents on oil form a larger fraction of the market price of oil, precisely because it is a lower cost fuel. The price of a barrel of oil should therefore be rising faster than the implicit price at which synthetic crude from coal could compete. One day those curves will intersect, and that day the synthetic-crude technology will replace the drilled-petroleum technology.

Even before that day, the possibility of coal liquefaction provides a kind of ceiling for the price of oil. I say "kind of" to remind you that coal-mining and moving capacity and synthetic-crude plant cannot be created overnight. One might hope that the ceiling might also limit the consuming world's vulnerability to political shenanigans and monopoly profits. I suppose it does in some ultimate sense, but one must not slide over the difficulties: for example, who would want to make a large investment in coal liquefaction or coal gasification in the knowledge that the current price of oil contains a large monopoly element that could be cut, at least temporarily, if something like a price war should develop?

The fundamental principle of the economics of exhaustible resources is, as I have said, simultaneously a condition of flow equilibrium in the market for the ore and of asset equilibrium in the market for deposits. When it holds, it says quite a lot about the probable pattern of exploitation of a resource. But there are more than the usual reasons for wondering whether the equilibrium conditions have any explanatory value. For instance, the flow market that has to be cleared is not just one market; it is the sequence of markets for resource products from now until the date of exhaustion. It is, in other words, a sequence of futures markets, perhaps a long sequence. If the futures markets actually existed, we could perhaps accept the notion that their equilibrium configuration is stable; that might not be true, but it is at least the sort of working hypothesis we frequently accept as a way of getting on with business. But there clearly is not a full set of futures markets; natural-resource markets work with a combination of myopic flow transactions and rather more farsighted asset transactions. It is legitimate to ask whether observed resource prices are to be interpreted as approximations to equilibrium prices, or whether the equilibrium is so unstable that momentary prices are not only a bad indicator of equilibrium relationships, but also a bad guide to resource allocation.

That turns out not to be an easy question to answer. Flow considerations and stock considerations work in opposite directions. The flow markets by themselves could easily be unstable; but the asset markets provide a corrective force. Let me try to explain why.

The flow equilibrium condition is that the net price grow like compound interest at the prevailing rate. Suppose net prices are expected by producers to be rising too slowly. Then resource deposits are a bad way to hold wealth. Mine owners will try to pull out; and if they think only in flow terms, the way to get out of the resource business is to increase current production and convert ore into money. If current production increases, for this or any other reason, the current price must move down along the demand curve. So initially pessimistic price expectations on the part of producers have led to more pressure on the current price. If expectations about future price changes are responsive to current events, the consequence can only be that pessimism is reinforced and deepened. The initial disequilibrium is worsened, not eliminated, by this chain of events. In other words, the market mechanism I have just described is unstable. Symmetrical reasoning leads to the conclusion that if prices are initially expected to be rising too fast, the withholding of supplies will lead to a speculative run-up of prices which is self-reinforcing. Depending on which way we start, initial disequilibrium is magnified, and production is tilted either toward excessive current dumping or toward speculative withholding of supply. (Still other assumptions are possible and may lead to qualitatively different results. For instance, one could imagine that expectations focus on the price level rather than its rate of change. There is much more work to be done on this question.)

Such things have happened in resource markets; but they do not seem always to be happening. I think that this story of instability in spot markets needs amendment; it is implausible because it leaves the asset market entirely out of account. The longer run prospect is not allowed to have any influence on current happenings. Suppose that producers do have some notion that the resource they own has a value anchored somewhere in the future, a value determined by technological and demand considerations, not by pure and simple speculation. Then if prices are now rising toward that rendezvous at too slow a rate, that is indeed evidence that owning resource deposits is bad business. But that will lead not to wholesale dumping of current production, but to capital losses on existing stocks. When existing stocks have been written down in value, the net price can rise toward its future rendezvous at more or less the right rate. As well as being destabilized by flow reactions, the market can be stabilized by capitalization reactions. In fact the two stories can be made to merge: the reduction in flow price coming from increased current production can be read as a signal and capitalized into losses on asset values, after which near-equilibrium is reestablished.

I think the correct conclusion to be drawn from this discussion is not that either of the stories is more likely to be true. It is more complex: that in tranquil conditions, resource markets are likely to track their equilibrium paths moderately well, or at least not likely to rush away from them. But resource markets may be rather vulnerable to surprises. They may respond to shocks about the volume of reserves, or about competition from new materials, or about the costs of competing technologies, or even about near-term political events, by drastic movements of current price and production. It may be quite a while before the transvaluation of values – I never thought I could quote Nietzsche in an economics paper – settles down under the control of sober future prospects. In between, it may be a cold winter.

So far, I have discussed the economic theory of exhaustible resources as a partial-equilibrium market theory. The interest rate that more or less controls the whole process was taken as given to the mining industry by the rest of the economy. So was the demand curve for the resource itself. And when the market price of the resource has ridden up the demand curve to the point where the quantity demanded falls to zero, the theory says that the resource in question will have been exhausted.

There is clearly a more cosmic aspect to the question than this; and I do not mean to suggest that it is unimportant, just because it is cosmic. In particular, there remains an important question about the social interest in the pace of exploitation of the world's endowment of exhaustible natural resources. This aspect has been brought to a head recently, as everyone knows, by the various Doomsday forecasts that combine a positive finding that the world is already close to irreversible collapse from shortage of natural resources and other causes with the normative judgment that civilization is much too young to die. I do not intend to discuss those forecasts and judgments now, but I do want to talk about the economic issues of principle involved.

First, there is a proposition that will be second nature to everyone in this room. What I have called the fundamental principle of the economics of exhaustible resources is, among other things, a condition of competitive equilibrium in the sequence of futures markets for deliveries of the natural resource. This sequence extends out to infinity, even if the competitive equilibrium calls for the resource to be exhausted in finite time. Beyond the time of exhaustion there is also equilibrium: supply equals demand equals zero at a price simultaneously so high that demand is choked off and so low that it is worth no one's while to lose interest by holding some of the resource that long. Like any other competitive equilibrium with the right background assumptions, this one has some optimality properties. In particular, as Hotelling pointed out, the competitive equilibrium maximizes the sum of the discounted consumer-plus-producer surpluses from the natural resource, *provided* that society wishes to discount future consumer surpluses at the same rate that mine owners choose to discount their won future profits.

Hotelling was not so naive as to leap from this conclusion to the belief that *laissez-faire* would be an adequate policy for the resource industries. He pointed to several ways in which the background assumptions might be expected to fail: the presence of externalities when several owners can exploit the same underground pool of gas or oil; the considerable uncertainty surrounding the process of exploration with the consequent likelihood of wasteful rushes to stake claims and exploit, and the creation of socially useless windfall profits; and, finally, the existence of large monopolistic or oligopolistic firms in the extractive industries.

There is an amusing sidelight here. It is not hard to show that, generally speaking, a monopolist will exhaust a mine more slowly than a competitive industry facing the same demand curve would do. (Hotelling did not explore this point in detail, though he clearly knew it. He did mention the possibility of an extreme case in which competition will exhaust a resource in finite time and a monopolist only asymptotically.) The amusing thing is that if a conservationist is someone who would like to see resources conserved *beyond* the pace that competition would adopt, then the monopolist is the conservationist's friend. No doubt they would both be surprised to know it.

Hotelling mentions, but rather pooh-poohs, the notion that market rates of interest might exceed the rate at which society would wish to discount future utilities or consumer surpluses. I think a modern economist would take that possibility more seriously. It is certainly a potentially important question, because the discount rate determines the whole tilt of the equilibrium production schedule. If it is true that the market rate of interest exceeds the social rate of time preference, then scarcity rents and market prices will rise faster than they "ought to" and production will have to fall correspondingly faster along the demand curve. Thus the resource will be exploited too fast and exhausted too soon.

The literature has several reasons for expecting that private discount rates might be systematically higher than the correct social rate of discount. They fall into two classes. The first class takes it more or less for granted that society ought to discount utility and consumption at the same rates as reflective individuals would discount their own future utility and consumption. This line of thought then goes on to suggest that there are reasons why this might not happen. One standard example is the fact that individuals can be expected to discount for the riskiness of the future, and some of the risks for which they will discount are not risks to society but merely the danger of transfers within the society. Since there is not a complete enough set of insurance markets to permit all these risks to be spread properly, market interest rates will be too high. Insecurity of tenure, as William Vickrey has pointed out, is a special form of uncertainty with particular relevance to natural resources.

A second standard example is the existence of various taxes on income from capital; since individuals care about the after-tax return on investment and society about the before-tax return, if investment is carried to the point where the after-tax yield is properly related to the rate of time preference, the before-tax profitability of investment will be too high. I have nothing to add to this discussion.

The other class of reasons for expecting that private discount rates are too high and will thus distort intertemporal decisions away from social optimality denies that private time preference is the right basis for intertemporal decisions. Frank Ramsey, for instance, argued that it was ethically indefensible for society to discount future utilities. Individuals might do so, either because they lack imagination (Böhm-Bawerk's "defective telescopic faculty") or because they are all too conscious that life is short. In social decision-making, however, there is no excuse for treating generations unequally, and the time-horizon is, or should be, very long. In solemn conclave assembled, so to speak, we ought to act as if the social rate of time preference were zero (though we would simultaneously discount future *consumption* if we expect the future to be richer than the present). I confess I find that reasoning persuasive, and it provides another reason for expecting that the market will exhaust resources too fast.

This point need not be divorced so completely from individual time preference. If the whole infinite sequence of futures markets for resource products could actually take place and find equilibrium, I might be inclined to accept the result (though I would like to know who decides the initial endowments within and between generations). But of course they cannot take place. There is no way to collect bids and offers from everyone who will ever live. In the markets that actually do take place, future generations are represented only by us, their eventual ancestors. Now generations overlap, so that I worry about my children, and they about theirs, and so on. But it does seem fundamentally implausible that there should be anything *ex post* right about the weight that is actually given to the welfare of those who will not live for another thousand years. We have actually done quite well at the hands of *our* ancestors. Given how poor they were and how rich we are, they might properly have saved less and consumed more. No doubt they never expected the rise in income per head that has made us so much richer than they ever dreamed was possible. But that only reinforces the point that the future may be too important to be left to the accident of mistaken expectations and the ups and downs of the Protestant ethic.

Several writers have studied directly the problem of defining and characterizing a socially-optimal path of the exploitation of a given pool of exhaustible resources. The idea is familiar enough: instead of worrying about market responses, one imagines an idealized planned economy, constrained only by its initial endowment, the size of the labor force, the available technology, and the laws of arithmetic. The planning board then has to find the best feasible development for the economy. To do so, it needs a precise criterion for comparing different paths, and that is where the social rate of time preference plays a role.

It turns out that the choice of a rate of time preference is even more critical in this situation than it is in the older literature on optimal capital accumulation without any exhaustible resources. In that theory, the criterion usually adopted is the maximizations of a discounted sum of one-period social welfare indicators, depending on consumption per head, and summed over all time from now to the infinite future. The typical result, depending somewhat on the particular assumptions made, is that consumption per head rises through time to a constant plateau defined by the "modified Golden Rule." In that ultimate steady state, consumption per head is lower the higher is the social rate of discount; and, correspondingly, the path to the steady state is characterized by less saving and more interim consumption, the higher the social rate of discount. That is as it should be: the main beneficiaries of a high level of ultimate steady-state consumption are the inhabitants of the distant future, and so, if the planning board discounts the future very strongly, it will choose a path that favors the near future over the distant future.

When one adds exhaustible resources to the picture, the social rate of time preference can play a similar, but even more critical, role. As a paper by Geoffrey Heal and Partha Dasgupta and one of my own show, it is possible that the optimal path with a positive discount rate should lead to consumption per head going asymptotically to zero, whereas a zero discount rate leads to perpetually rising consumption per head. In other words, even when the technology and the resource base could permit a plateau level of consumption per head, or even a rising standard of living, positive social time preference might in effect lead society to prefer eventual extinction, given the drag exercised by extinction, given the drag exercised by exhaustible resources. Of course, it is part of the point that it is the planning board in the present that plans for future extinction: nobody has asked the about-to-become-defunct last generation whether *it* approved of weighting its satisfactions less than those of its ancestors.

Good theory is usually trying to tell you something, even if it is not the literal truth. In this context, it is not hard to interpret the general tenor of the theoretical indications. We know in general that even well-functioning competitive markets may fail to allocate resources properly over time. The reason, I have suggested, is because, in the nature of the case, the future brings no endowment of its own to whatever markets actually exist. The intergenerational distribution of income or welfare depends on the provision that each generation makes for its successors. The choice of a social discount rate is, in effect, a policy decision about that intergenerational distribution. What happens in the planning parable depends very much – perhaps dramatically – on that choice; and one's evaluation of what happens in the market parable depends very much on whether private choices are made with a discount rate much larger than the one a deliberate policy decision would select. The pure theory of exhaustible resources is trying to tell us that, if exhaustible resources really matter, then the balance between present and future is more delicate than we are accustomed to think; and then the choice of a discount rate can be pretty important and one ought not to be too casual about it.

In my own work on this question, I have sometimes used a rather special criterion that embodies sharp assumptions about intergenerational equity: I have imposed the requirement that consumption per head be constant through time, so that no generation is favored over any other, and asked for the largest steady consumption per head that can be maintained forever, given all the constraints including the finiteness of resources. This criterion, like any other, has its pluses and its minuses and I am not committed to it by any means. Like the standard criterion – the discounted sum of one-period utilities – this one will always pick out an *efficient* path, so one at least gets the efficiency conditions out of the analysis. The highest-constant-consumption criterion also has the advantage of highlighting the crucial importance of certain technological assumptions.

It is clear without any technical apparatus that the seriousness of the resource-exhaustion problem must depend in an important way on two aspects of the technology: first, the likelihood of technical progress, especially natural-resource-saving technical progress, and, second, the ease with which other factors of production, especially labor and reproducible capital, can be substituted for exhaustible resources in production.

My own practice, in working on this problem, has been to treat as the central case (though not the only case) the assumption of zero technological progress. This is not because I think resource-saving inventions are unlikely or that their capacity to save resources is fundamentally limited. Quite the contrary – if the future is anything like the past, there will be prolonged and substantial reductions in natural-resource requirements per unit of real output. It is true, as pessimists say, that it is just an assumption and one cannot be sure; but to assume the contrary is also an assumption, and a much less plausible one. I think there is virtue in analyzing the zero-technical-progress case because it is easy to see how technical progress can relieve and perhaps eliminate the drag on economic welfare exercised by natural-resource scarcity. The more important task for theory is to try to understand what happens or can happen in the opposite case.

As you would expect, the degree of substitutability is also a key factor. If it is very easy to substitute other factors for natural resources, then there is in principle no "problem." The world can, in effect, get along without natural resources, so exhaustion is just an event, not a catastrophe. Nordhaus's notion of a "backstop technology" is just a dramatic way of putting this case; at some finite cost, production can be freed of dependence on exhaustible resources altogether.

If, on the other hand, real output per unit of resources is effectively bounded – cannot exceed some upper limit of productivity which is in turn not too far from where we are now – then catastrophe is unavoidable. In-between there is a wide range of cases in which the problem is real, interesting, and not foreclosed. Fortunately, what little evidence there is suggests that there is quite a lot of substitutability between exhaustible resources and renewable or reproducible resources, though this is an empirical question that could absorb a lot more work than it has had so far.

Perhaps the most dramatic way to illustrate the importance of substitutability, and its connection with Doomsday, is in terms of the permanent sustainability of a constant level of consumption. In the simplest, most aggregative, model of a resource-using economy one can prove something like the following: if the elasticity of substitution between exhaustible resources and other inputs is unity or bigger, and if the elasticity of output with respect to reproducible capital exceeds the elasticity of output with respect to natural resources, then a constant population can maintain a positive constant level of consumption per head forever. This permanently maintainable standard of living is an increasing, concave, and unbounded function of the initial stock of capital. So the drag of a given resource pool can be overcome *to any extent* if only the initial stock of capital is large enough. On the other hand, if the elasticity of substitution between natural resources and other inputs is less than one, or if the elasticity of output with respect to resources exceeds the elasticity of output with respect to reproducible capital, then the largest constant level of consumption sustainable forever with constant population is – zero. We know much too little about which side of that boundary the world is on – technological progress aside – but at least the few entrails that have been read seem favorable.[3]

Perhaps I should mention that when I say "forever" in this connection, I mean "for a very long time." The mathematical reasoning does deal with infinite histories, but actually life in the solar system will only last for a finite time, though a very long finite time, much longer than this lecture, for instance. That is why I think it takes economics as well as the entropy law to answer our question.

I began this lecture by talking of the conditions for competitive equilibrium in the market for natural resources. Now I have been talking of centralized planning optima. As you would expect, it turns out that under the standard assumptions, the Hotelling rule, the fundamental principle of natural-resource economics, is a necessary condition for efficiency and therefore for social optimality. So there is at least a prayer that a market-guided system might manage fairly well. But more than the Hotelling condition is needed.

I have already mentioned one of the extra requirements for the intertemporal optimality of market allocations: it is that the market discount future profits at the same rate as the society would wish to discount the welfare of future inhabitants of the planet. This condition is often given as an argument for public intervention in resource allocation because – as I have also mentioned – there are reasons to expect market interest rates to exceed the social rate of time preference, or at least what philosophers like us think it ought to be. If the analysis is right, then the market will tend to consume exhaustible resources too fast, and corrective public intervention should be aimed at slowing down and stretching out the exploitation of the resource pool. There are several ways that could be done, in principle, through conservation subsidies or a system of graduated severance taxes, falling through time.

Realistically speaking, however, when we say "public intervention" we mean rough and ready political action. An only moderately cynical observer will see a problem here: it is far from clear that the political process can be relied on to be more future-oriented than your average corporation. The conventional pay-out period for business is of the same order of magnitude as the time to the next election, and transferring a given individual from the industrial to the government bureaucracy does not transform him into a guardian of the far future's interests. I have no ready solution to this problem. At a minimum, it suggests that one ought to be as suspicious of uncritical centralization as of uncritical free-marketeering. Maybe the safest course is to favor specific policies – like graduated severance taxes – rather than blanket institutional solutions.

There is another, more subtle, extra requirement for the optimality of the competitive market solution to the natural-resource problem. Many patterns of exploitation of the exhaustible-resource pool obey. Hotelling's fundamental principle myopically, from moment to moment, but are wrong from a very long-run point of view. Such mistaken paths may even stay very near the right path for a long time, but eventually they veer off and become bizarre in one way or another. If a market-guided system is to perform well over the long haul, it must be more than myopic. Someone – it could be the Department of the Interior, or the mining companies, or their major customers, or speculators – must always be taking the long view. They must somehow notice in advance that the resource economy is moving along a path that is bound to end in disequilibrium of some extreme kind. If they do notice it, and take defensive actions, they will help steer the economy from the wrong path toward the right one.[4] Usually the "wrong" path is one that leads to exhaustion at a date either too late or too soon; anyone who perceives this will be motivated to arbitrage between present and future in ways that will push the current price toward the "right" path.[5]

It is interesting that this need for someone to take the long view emerged also when the question at hand was the potential instability of the market for natural resources if it concentrates too heavily on spot or flow decisions, and not enough on future or stock decisions. In the context too, a reasonably accurate view of the long-term prospects turns out to be a useful, maybe indispensable, thing for the resource market to have.

This lecture has been – as Kenneth Burke once said about the novel – words, all words. Nevertheless, it has been a discourse on economic theory, not on current policy. If some of you have been day-dreaming about oil and the coming winter, I assure you that I have been thinking about shadow prices and transversality conditions at infinity. If I turn briefly to policy at the end, it is not with concrete current problems in mind. After all, nothing I have been able to say takes account of the international oil cartel, the political and economic ambitions of the Middle Eastern potentates, the speeds of adjustment to surprises in the supply of oil, or the doings of our own friendly local oligopolists. The only remarks I feel entitled to make are about the long-run pursuit of a general policy toward exhaustible resources.

Many discussions of economic policy – macroeconomics aside – boil down to a tension between market allocation and public intervention. Marketeers keep thinking about the doughnut of allocative efficiency and informational economy and *dirigistes* are impressed with the size of the hole containing externalities, imperfections, and distributional issues. So it is with exhaustible resources. One is impressed with what a system of ideal markets, including futures markets, can accomplish in this complicated situation; and one can hardly miss seeing that our actual oligopolistic, politically involved, pollution-producing industry is not exactly what the textbook ordered. I have nothing new to add to all that. The unusual factor that the theory of exhaustible resources brings to the fore is the importance of the long view, and the value of reasonable information about reserves, technology, and demand in the fairly far future.

This being so, one is led to wonder whether public policy can contribute to stability and efficiency along those lines. One possibility is the encouragement of organized futures trading in natural resource products. To be useful, futures contracts would have to be much longer-term than in usual is the futures markets that now exist, mostly for agricultural products. I simply do not know enough to have an opinion about the feasibility of large scale futures trading, or about the ultimate contribution that such a reform would make to the stability and efficiency of the market for resource products. But in principle it would seem to be a good idea.

The same considerations suggest that the market for exhaustible resources might be one of the places in the economy where some sort of organized indicative planning could play a constructive role. This is not an endorsement of centralized decision-making, which is likely to have imperfections and externalities of its own. Indeed it might be enough to have the government engaged in a continuous program of information-gathering and dissemination covering trends in technology, reserves and demand. One could at least hope to have professional standards govern such an exercise. I take it that the underlying logic of indicative planning is that some comparison and coordination of the main participants in the market, including the government, could eliminate major errors and resolve much uncertainty. In the case of exhaustible resources, it could have the additional purpose of generating a set of consistent expectations about the distant future. In this effort, the pooling of information and intentions from both sides of the market could be useful, with the effect of inducing behavior that will steer the economy away from ultimately inferior paths. It is also likely, as Adam Smith would have warned, that a certain amount of conspiracy against the public interest might occur in such sessions, so perhaps they ought to be recorded and the tapes turned over to Judge Sirica, who will know what to do with them.

Notes

1   *The Review of Economic Studies* published a group of them in the summer of 1974, including my own paper and others by Partha Dasgupta and Geoffrey Heal, Michael Weinstein and Richard Zeckhauser, and Joseph Stiglitz, from all of which I have learned a lot about this subject.
2   As best one can tell at the moment, shale oil is a more likely successor to oil and natural gas than either gasified or liquefied coal. The relevant costs are bound to be uncertain until more research and development has been done. I tell the story in terms of liquefied coal only because it is more picturesque that way.
3   See pp. 60–70 in William D. Nordhaus and James Tobin.
4   This sort of process has been studied in a different context by Frank Hahn and by Karl Shell and Joseph Stiglitz.
5   For example, suppose the current price is too low, in the sense that, if it rises according to the current principle, the demand path will be enough to exhaust the resource before the price has risen high enough to choke demand

to zero. A clever speculator would see that there will be money to be made just after the date of exhaustion, because anyone with a bit of the resource to sell could make a discrete jump in the price and still find buyers. Such a speculator would wish to buy now and hold for sale then. But that action would tend to raise the current price (and, by the fundamental principle, the whole price path) and reduce demand, so that the life of the resource would be prolonged. The speculation is thus corrective.

References

P. Dasgupta and G. Heal, "The Optimal Depletion of Exhaustible Resources," *Rev. Econ. Stud.*, 1974, 3–28.

F. H. Hahn, "Equilibrium Dynamics with Heterogeneous Capital Goods," *Quart. J. Econ.*, Nov. 1966, *80*, 633–646.

H. Hotelling, "The Economics of Exhaustible Resources," *J. Polit. Econ.*, April 1931, *39*, 137–175.

W. D. Nordhaus, "The Allocation of Energy Resources," *Brookings Papers on Econ. Activ.*, 1974, *3*, 529–570.

——and J. Tobin, "Is Economic Growth Obsolete?" in National Bureau of Economic Research, *Economic Growth*, 50th Anniversary Colloq. V, New York 1972.

K. Shell and J. E. Stiglitz, "The Allocation of Investment in a Dynamic Economy," *Quart. J. Econ.*, Nov. 1967, *81*.

R. M. Solow, "Intergenerational Equity and Exhaustible Resources," *Rev. Econ. Stud.*, 1974, 29–45.

J. E. Stiglitz, "Growth with Exhaustible Natural Resources," *Rev. Econ. Stud.*, 1974, 139–152.

M. Weinstein and R. Zeckhauser, "Use Patterns for Depletable and Recyclable Resources," *Rev. Econ. Stud.*, 1974, 67–88.

Part V

The Economics of Renewable Resources

13
Economics of Production from Natural Resources

Vernon L. Smith

I Introduction

This paper attempts to provide a unified theory of production from natural resources. A single model of an industry is used to describe a dynamic process of recovery from such technologically diverse resources as fish, timber, petroleum, and minerals. Recovery from each of these resources is seen as a special case of a general model, depending upon whether the resource is replenishable, and on whether production exhibits significant externalities. A model of centralized management, with particular reference to "common property" resources, such as fisheries, under stationary conditions, is also discussed and compared with competitive recovery in the stationary state.

The paper builds directly upon, and has been much influenced by, the basic contributions of Gordon [6] and Scott [11] [12].

II Environmental technology

The economy of man consumes two fundamental kinds of naturally occurring resources: (1) Replenishable resources, such as fish, timber, bison, and the whooping crane, and (2) nonreplenishable resources, such as petroleum, natural gas, and the products of mines. The second category is often called "exhaustible resources," which is something of a misnomer since both types of resources are capable of exhaustion. The American bison, once of value to the American economy, is such a case, as also were the native trout of Lake Michigan.[1] This particular dichotomy is important analytically in that the first category of resources is capable of regeneration, as man consumes a flow of the resource, while the second represents a fixed stock whose inventory can only be diminished over time.

For purposes of production analysis, one of the most important technological features of a replenishable commercial resource like a fish or timber species is its law of growth. The growth characteristics of a species may be studied in terms of the growth in the number of members, and in the size of individual members [1], or in the aggregate mass of the species [8]. This paper will take a crude macrobiological approach, and deal only with variables which measure the aggregate masses of species. Such an approach is analogous to the aggregate production function hypothesis employed by economists in macroeconomics and growth theory.

The mass growth of a species will depend upon certain internal biological characteristics of the species, and on its environment, i.e., the abundance of food nutrients, and the existence and efficiency of other species which have predator or symbiotic relationships to the given species. We can think of any species to be harvested by man as subject to a "technological" law of growth governed by the ecological characteristics of the biosystem in which it resides [8].

In the simplest model of the technology of a replenishable resource, we consider a single species population with mass X in pounds, board feet, or other appropriate measure of quantity. The ecological balance between this species and its natural environment is postulated to give rise to a law of mass growth of the form

$$X \equiv \frac{dX}{dt} = f(X). \tag{13.1}$$

From the general ecological descriptions usually given for any species [8] as well as for fish [2, pp. 7–8] [4, p. 209] and timber [7] [9] resources, it is reasonable to assume that $f(X)$ has the inverted "U" properties shown in Figure 13.1, i.e., $f(\underline{X}) = f(\overline{X}) = 0$, $f'(X°) = 0$, $f''(X) < 0$, $0 \le X \le \overline{X}$, where $\underline{X}$ and $\overline{X}$ are the minimum and maximum self-sustaining populations, and $X°$ is the population producing the largest sustainable yield or net rate of growth. The yield function $f(X)$ measures the net effect of the birth rate, the growth rate of individual members, and the death rate from natural causes, including predation from nonhuman sources. Populations smaller than $\underline{X} \le 0$, are assumed not to be viable.

The most frequently postulated form for the yield function is the quadratic, giving

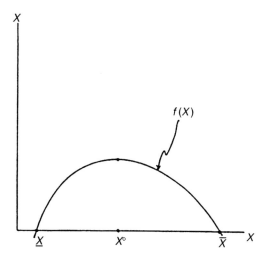

Figure 13.1

$$X = \alpha_0 + X(\alpha_1 - \alpha_{11}X), \qquad (13.1')$$

whose solution, $X(t)$, is the familiar and ubiquitous logistic law of growth [8, pp. 64–76].

In the natural state a replenishable resource, whose law of growth is governed by (13.1), will normally be expected to grow until the stable equilibrium $X = \overline{X}$, $\dot{X} = 0$ is reached. In such circumstances commercial production from the resource by man will begin with these as initial conditions. (Note that $\underline{X}$ is unstable.)

With the entry of man as a predator in the form of an extractive industry – commercial fishing, forest products, and so on – equation (13.1) must be modified to serve as a technological restriction on the activities of the industry. Throughout this paper, in order to sharpen the essential features of the theory and simplify the arithmetic we will assume that recovery from a given resource is effected by K homogeneous firms or units of capital, each producing an output rate, x. Total industry output is then Kx, where both K and x are, in general, variables. Hence, the required technological restriction might be written:[2]

$$\dot{X} = f(X) - Kx. \qquad (13.2)$$

It is understood that x, K, X are each a function of time. Under our assumptions, K is both the number of firms (e.g., fishing boats) in the industry, and a measure of the real capital stock invested by the industry.

Turning now to nonreplenishable resources like petroleum, coal, iron ore, and other products of mines, we note that these form a simple special case of (13.2) in which $f(X) \equiv 0$, i.e., regeneration is assumed to be impossible so that the fixed stock declines at a time rate equal to aggregate industry output.

III   Cost behavior – the technology of recovery

The cost structure of the recovery process varies widely among the major commercial natural resources. Recovery cost in fishing, petroleum and natural gas is uniquely influenced by the "common property" character of these resources [6] [11]. No one has exclusively private rights in ocean fishing nor are such rights feasible to grant when commercial species are migrants. Similarly with crude oil extraction the reservoir's physical boundaries are often unknown, and even unknowable except at prohibitive cost. Such resources may therefore be shared by many private firms. An important consequence of this is that there may be direct and very significant external diseconomies in production, with an attending divergence of private and social optima.

On the other hand, forest and mineral resources are relatively divisible into independent productive units and to this extent are relatvelyi free of significant production externalities.[3] Thus, of the two replenishable resources, fisheries and forests, it is assumed that the former shows significant external diseconomies of production while the latter does not. With the two nonreplenishable resources, petroleum and mining, again, the former is assumed to exhibit significant diseconomies, the latter is not.

In industries such as mining and lumbering, the extractive total cost function for the individual firm is assumed to be of the form,

$$C = \phi(x) + \hat{\pi}, \quad C'(x) > 0, \quad C''(x) < 0, \tag{13.3}$$

where $\phi(x)$ is total (fixed and variable) operating cost,[4] and $\hat{\pi}$ is the normal profit or return on a unit of capital required to hold the unit (or firm) in the industry.

The most natural general hypothesis about total operating cost for the individual fisherman requires it to be an increasing function of the vessel's catch rate, x, but a decreasing function of fish population, i.e., $\phi = \phi(x,X)$, with $\phi_1 \equiv \partial\phi/\partial x > 0$, and $\phi_2 \equiv \partial\phi/\partial X < 0$. The latter specification is implied if it is the case that when there are more fish of a given species they are easier to catch. On the other hand if increases in X cause no change in the density of stocks, as may be the case in some species, then it may be that $\phi_2 \equiv 0$. Externalities enter in an interesting and simple manner: *no individual competitive fisherman has control over population size as a private decision variable yet it enters as a parameter in each fisherman's cost function.* Externalities may also enter via crowding phenomena: if the fish population is highly concentrated, the efficiency of each boat may be lowered by congestion over the fishing grounds.[5] In general then the cost function may include K, and our most general cost hypothesis for the fishing firm is:

$$C = \phi(x, X, K) + \hat{\pi}, \quad C_1 \equiv \partial C/\partial x > 0,$$
$$C_2 \equiv \partial C/\partial X \leq 0, \quad C_1 \equiv \partial C/\partial K \geq 0. \tag{13.4}$$

When $C_2 < 0$, recovery cost exhibits resource *stock externalities*. When $C_3 > 0$, recovery cost exhibits *crowding externalities*. Each case represents an external diseconomy to the industry. Equation (13.4) will serve as the most general cost function with which we shall be concerned. It includes (13.3) as a special case. Another special case is crude oil production, since oil well drilling, development and operating costs are essentially independent of crude production in primary recovery fields (fields subject to natural drive forces).

IV A model of the competitive recovery of natural resources

We propose to characterize the competitive recovery process in any extractive industry by a system of three behavior equations describing the interactions of the resource, individual firms, and the industry. The term "industry" in the case of fishing and petroleum extraction will not necessarily refer to the entire industry, but to the collection of firms exploiting a given fishery or oil reservoir, since in these cases external interdependence is postulated.

The behavior equation for the resource has already been stated in (13.2), and describes the growth or decline of the stock as a function of stock size and industry output.

If we let $\rho(Kx)$ be the total revenue rate from the sale of Kx units of the resource, then revenue per firm is $\rho(Kx)/K$, and, using (13.4) the most general form of the firm's pure or excess profit function is

$$\pi = \frac{\rho(Kx)}{K} - C(x, X, K). \tag{13.5}$$

It is assumed that each firm perceives this profit to vary only with its own output and this only because its private cost is variable with output. Thus price, $\rho(Kx)/Kx$, is perceived as a given constant, and $C(x, X, K)$ is treated as a function only of the private control variable x. The behavior equation for firms is a perceived profit maximizing condition (price equals marginal cost), which serves to determine x as a function of capital and resource stocks depending on revenue, cost and externality conditions, *viz*

$$\frac{\rho(Kx)}{Kx} = \phi_1(x, X, K). \tag{13.6}$$

Some modification of the hypothesis (13.6) must be specified in the case of crude oil production where cost is substantially independent of output, and output depends primarily upon the characteristics of the field and its exploitation. In primary producing fields all crude oil is produced at the surface of a well by the action of one or more naturally occurring underground drives or pressures from edge water encroachment, a gas cap, or gas dissolved in the crude [10, pp. 391–93]. Both the rate of recovery and the cumulative recovery reduces the pressure level. So the output, x, of a given well can be regarded as a decreasing function of aggregate current output, Kx, and a decreasing function of cumulative output, $\overline{X} - X$, or[6]

$$x = g(Kx, X), \quad \frac{\partial g}{\partial(Kx)} \equiv g_1 < 0, \quad \frac{\partial g}{\partial X} = g_2 > 0. \tag{13.6a}$$

Finally, new firms (capital) are assumed to be attracted into the industry when $\pi > 0$, while producing firms are driven out of the industry when $\pi < 0$. Specifically, it is supposed that this flow of capital is proportional to pure profit, or

$$\dot{K} = \delta\left[\frac{\rho(Kx)}{K} - C(x, X, K)\right], \tag{13.7}$$

where $\delta > 0$ is a behavioral constant for the industry.[7]

In summary, our behavioral equation system is

$$\dot{X} = f(X) - Kx, \qquad (I.1)$$

$$\frac{\rho(Kx)}{Kx} = C_1(x, X, K), \quad \text{or} \quad x = g(Kx, X), \quad \text{for crude oil,} \qquad (I.2)$$

$$\dot{K} = \delta\left[\frac{\rho(Kx)}{K} - C(x, X, K)\right], \qquad (I.3)$$

with $f(X) \equiv 0$ for oil, gas and mineral stocks, and $C_2 \equiv C_3 \equiv 0$, for mineral and timber resources.[8] It is further assumed that equation (I.2), whatever its particular form, always provides a unique x for every (X, K) pair (i.e., a mapping $X, K \to x$). Then the system I provides two first-order differential equations in X and K of the form,

$$X = F(X, K) \qquad (II.1)$$

$$K = I(X, K), \qquad (II.2)$$

with initial conditions $X(0)$ and $K(0)$. Where recovery requires specialized capital, exploitation begins with $X(0) = \bar{X}$ and $K(0) = 0$, i.e., the resource is in static mass equilibrium with its environment, and an exploiting industry does not exist. If exploitation begins with a direct transfer of capital from other industries (e.g., haddock and cod fishing vessels shift to lobster), then $K(0) > 0$.

V   The dynamics of competitive recovery

A   General

Equation system II together with the initial conditions describe the velocity of a point in the "phase space" (X, K) i.e., the rates of increase or decrease in (i) the resource stock, (ii) the level of capital investment of the industry.

A static equilibrium or singular point (X^*, K^*) is defined by the property that $F(X^*, K^*) = 0$, $I(X^*, K^*) = 0$. There may be many such points. Two such singular points (P^* and P^{**}) are illustrated in the phase diagram of Figure 13.2 for a replenishable resource. Points in the set defined by $F(X, K) = 0$ correspond to *equilibria between the resource mass and its environment*, while points in the set defined by $I(X, K) = 0$ correspond to *equilibria between the exploiting industry and alternative uses of capital in the economy* as a whole. Both equilibrium relations presuppose instantaneous output adjustment in accordance with firm profit maximization (I.2). In Figure 13.2 it is assumed that $\partial F/\partial K < 0$; for any given

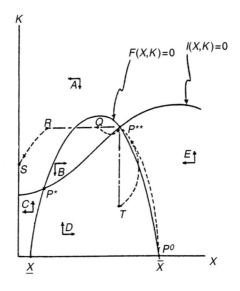

Figure 13.2

resource stock, an increase (decrease) in the size of the industry will decrease (increase) the rate of growth of the resource, i.e., production exceeds the rate of replenishment. Also it is assumed that $\partial I/\partial K < 0$; for any given resource stock, an increase (decrease) in the size of the industry lowers (raises) profit and reduces (increases) the flow of capital into the industry. Conditions for the validity of these two assumptions are stated in the appendix. The assumptions apply only to the illustration in Figure 13.2, and not to the model in general.

Under these assumptions the nonnegative quadrant is partitioned into five regions by the F and I curves. In region A, above both curves, both the industry and the resource stock will decline. In region D, below both curves, both the industry and the resource stock will grow. In regions B, C and E the remaining combinations of growth in K and X occur as shown. The perpendicular arrows in each region indicate in the usual way, the directions of motion along a development path in phase space. If initially the resource population is at $\overline{X}$, and $K = 0$, then (by hypothesis) $\dot{K} > 0$ and capital flows into the new extractive industry reducing the resource mass along the path from P^0 to P^{**} as shown. P^{**} is an equilibrium point for the conditions postulated in the illustration. At P^{**} the industry is in equilibrium with the economy, and the species mass is in ecological equilibrium (total recruitment of new mass equals the harvest rate). The illustration shows P^{**} to be locally, but not globally stable. Thus, suppose having reached P^{**}, there is a sudden reduction in X from natural causes – such as a disease which wipes out the susceptible portion of the species and then disappears. The system is then shifted to the point Q or R. At Q firms suffer losses, and capital starts to leave the industry, while the natural productivity of the resource is increased to a level above harvesting by the industry. The resource mass rises, and the industry declines until the state of the system crosses into region D where the industry is once more profitable. Capital now flows back into the industry, and the resource mass continues to grow until balanced by the industry harvest at P^{**}. If the catastrophe is large, and the system shifts to a point such as R in region A, the resource mass declines, and the yield of the species is lowered. As a result the harvest exceeds the yield, the resource stock falls, and the industry declines until both may be put out of business at S.

The qualitative properties of virtually any conceivable pattern of resource exploitation can be depicted by a phase diagram similar to the illustration of Figure 13.2. Invasion of the resource domain by a new parasite or predator, which becomes a permanent aspect of the environment, can be represented by a downward shift of the F function. F may fall below I so that the invading parasite or predator together with the industrial harvest wipes out the resource and thence the industry. Such was the course of events when the lamprey invaded Lake Michigan destroying both the lake trout and the lake's fishing industry.

From the above illustration it is clear that commercial production from a replenishable resource need not in time destroy the resource. Exploitation by man *may* disrupt a delicate balance which destroys a resource. But the existence of external diseconomies (though it lead to non-Pareto efficient production states) does provide a built-in mechanism tending to resist annihilation of the resource: harvesting depletes the stock, costs rise and, *ceteris paribus*, discourages harvesting, with the possibility if not a guarantee of an equilibrium such as P^{**} in Figure 13.2.

We turn next to an analysis of various special applications and examples of the general model.

B Selling price constant: the fishery

Much of the more systematic literature on resource economics has been concerned with the implications of competitive recovery under conditions of constant price, not only to the individual firm, but also to the individual resource deposit, fishing ground, and so on [2] [6]. It is therefore of some interest to explore the implications of the model for this case.

With selling price, $p \equiv \rho(Kx)/Kx \equiv$ constant, system I becomes,

$$\dot{X} = f(X) - Kx \qquad (IA.1)$$

$$p = C_1(x, X, K) \qquad (IA.2)$$

$$\dot{K} = \delta[px - C(x, X, K)]. \qquad (IA.3)$$

Writing total differentials of equations (IA.2) and (IA.3), and solving for dK/dX, we get

$$\left.\frac{dK}{dX}\right|_{\dot{K}=0} = \frac{-C_2}{C_3}, \qquad (13.8)$$

which is the slope of the $I(X, K) = 0$ function in system II. Hence, if $C_2 < 0$, $C_3 > 0$, i.e., we have external diseconomies from both fish shortage and crowding by vessels, then $I(X, K) = 0$ defines K as an increasing function of X. Every reduction in the fish mass will increase costs, and force some fishermen out of the industry until a new normal-return equilibrium is established.

In like manner, differentiating (IA.1) and (IA.2), with $\dot{X} = 0$, we get

$$\left.\frac{dK}{dX}\right|_{\dot{X}=0} = \frac{KC_{12} + C_{11}f'}{xC_{11} - KC_{13}} \qquad (13.9)$$

for the slope of $F(X, K) = 0$, Since $f' \lesseqgtr 0$, if $C_{12} < 0$, $C_{11} > 0$, $C_{13} > 0$, the sign of this derivative is not determined on the basis of qualitative considerations alone, and may change in the phase space.

Figures 13.3–13.5 illustrate some possible effects of different externality assumptions on industry equilibrium, $I(X, K) = 0$, and several possible solution paths in phase space. In each case it is assumed that

$$\left.\frac{dK}{dX}\right|_{\dot{X}=0}$$

is positive below some value of X, and negative above that value.

In Figures 13.3a and 13.3b, with no resource stock externalities, but with crowding externalities, industry equilibrium occurs at K^* independent of X. A possible path to the equilibrium at P^* is shown. In

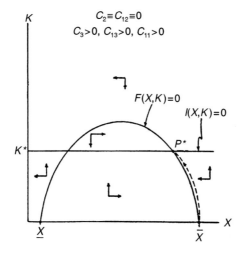

Figure 13.3a

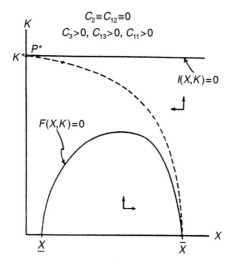

Figure 13.3b

Figure 13.3b the resource is so profitable that it is wiped out before crowding externalities limit the industry's growth.

In Figures 13.4a–c, we assume stock externalities to be significant but no crowding externalities. In contrast to the previous case, industry

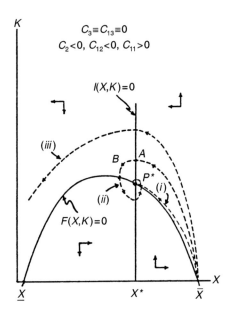

Figure 13.4a

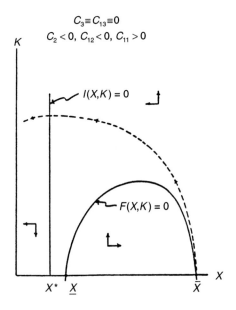

Figure 13.4b

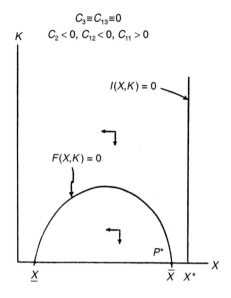

Figure 13.4c

equilibrium is determined at X^* independent of K. Figure 13.4a shows three possible paths to equilibrium: (i) a direct path to P^* with mono-tone growth in the industry and monotone decline in the resource stock to the self-sustaining level X^*; (ii) a cyclical path in which firms respond so quickly to pure profits that when industry equilibrium is reached at A the harvest exceeds the yield of the stock causing the stock to con-tinue falling. But with the stock continuing to fall costs rise, losses are incurred, and firms are forced out of the industry. The declining harvest eventually provides equilibrium of the resource stock, at B but the industry is declining. And so on in a convergent cyclical path with capital flowing in and out in response to cost changes induced by the decline and rise of the stock level; (iii) a path in which the entry speed of new firms is so rapid, and resource stock externalities such, that the stock is depleted before capital outflow due to losses can bring the harvest rate below the yield. Figure 13.4b illustrates the polar case in which the harvest is so profitable that the resource is sure to be depleted, while 13.4c shows the opposite pole where it does not pay to harvest any of the resource. Figures 13.5a and 13.5b illustrate the more general case in which both kinds of externalities are present.

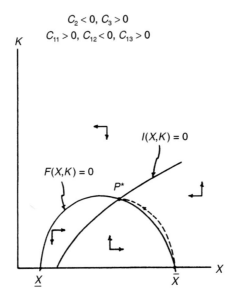

Figure 13.5a

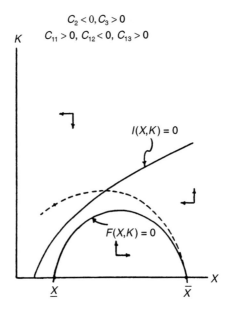

Figure 13.5b

C Mining

We have assumed mining to be the prototype of a nonreplenishable resource with insignificant externalities due to resource scarcity and crowding. Under these assumptions $f(X) \equiv 0$, and $C_2 \equiv C_3 \equiv 0$ in system (IA). Hence, if recovery is profitable, $x = x^0$ is determined by equation (IA.2), and $\dot{K} = \delta[px^0 - C(x^0)] > 0$. Capital flows into the resource at a constant rate, and the depletion rate of the resource is $\dot{X} = -Kx^0$. Figure 13.6 illustrates the equilibrium path to depletion.

D Petroleum

The dynamics of competitive petroleum recovery is slightly more complicated due to externalities. The fixed price equation system is:

$$\dot{X} = -Kx \tag{IB.1}$$
$$x = g(Kx, X), \quad g_1 < 0, \quad g_2 > 0. \tag{IB.2}$$
$$\dot{K} = \delta[px - C_0], \quad \delta = 0, \quad \text{if } px < C_0, \quad \delta > 0 \text{ otherwise.} \tag{IB.3}$$

In equation (IB.3) we impose the condition that $\dot{K} \geq 0$; wells once drilled cannot "flow out" of the resource. With all costs fixed, production continues as long as the natural drive forces persist.

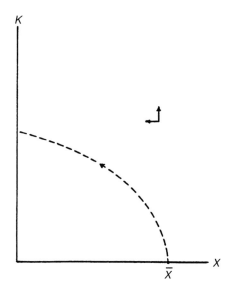

Figure 13.6

Observe first that if it pays to drill any wells at all, then at some point $K > 0$, and, by (IB.3), K can never fall. Hence, $\dot{X} = 0$ in (IB.1) if and only if $x = 0$, i.e., the resource is not in equilibrium until well output is zero. The resource equilibrium set, defined by $F(X, K) = 0$ in system II is here defined by the condition $g(0, \underline{X}) = 0$, where $X = \underline{X}$ is the depleted level of the oil reservoir (Figure 13.7). That is, the primary or free-flow stage of recovery ends at $X = \underline{X}$, when $x = 0$. Similarly, equilibrium in the industry, defined by the function $I(X, K) = 0$ in system II, is here defined by (IB.2) and (IB.3) with $\dot{k} = 0$, or $C_0/p = g(KC_0/p, X)$. Writing the total differential of this last equation and solving for dK/dX, gives the slope of $I(X, K) = 0$:

$$\left.\frac{dK}{dX}\right|_{\dot{K}=0} = -\frac{pg_1}{C_0g_2} > 0. \tag{13.10}$$

Hence, the equilibrium size of the industry is a strictly increasing function of the size of the untapped oil reservoir, X.

The phase diagram for the competitive exploitation of an oil reservoir will therefore appear as in Figure 13.7. Initially, the system is at $P_0(K = 0, X = \overline{X})$, where $\overline{X}$ is the initial level of the oil reservoir stock. Since $I(X, K) = 0$ is shown above P_0, it pays for drilling firms to exploit the resource. Hence $\dot{K} > 0$, $\dot{X} = -Kx < 0$, and the state of the system moves along some path to a point P on $I(X, K) = 0$ as shown. Thereafter, $\dot{K} = 0$, but the stock

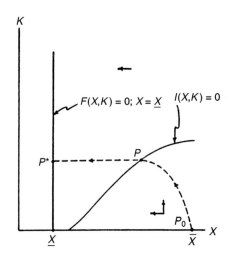

Figure 13.7

decline, $\dot{X} = -Kx < 0$, proceeds apace until $x = 0$ at P^*. The reservoir is depleted, the wells capped and abandoned (unless pumping is profitable).

E Timber

Timber resources are replenishable, but we assume no significant production externalities either from population scarcity or crowding by producers. These assumptions may also apply to exhausted historical species like the whooping crane and the American bison (if both species were so easily harvested that cost was not influenced by population mass). System (IA) becomes:

$$\dot{X} = f(X) - Kx \tag{IC.1}$$

$$p = C_1(x) \tag{IC.2}$$

$$\dot{K} = \delta[px - C(x)] \tag{IC.3}$$

(IC.2) determines x^0. If $px^0 - C(x^0) > 0$ harvesting is profitable, and firms enter the resource. Eventually the entire stand, and all new growth during the exploitation period is exhausted, as illustrated in Figure 13.8.

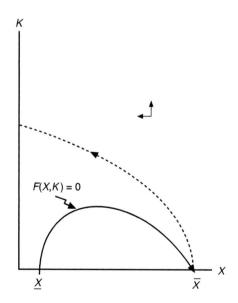

Figure 13.8

Such is the demise of an unappropriated replenishable resource which does not exhibit external diseconomies to the industry.

VI   Centralized fishery management: sole ownership and regulated competition

In the literature of fishery economics the important papers by H. Gordon [6] and A. Scott [11] have emphasized the advantages of unified management or "sole ownership" of the fishing ground as distinct from the unregulated decentralized exploitation of the resource. Sole ownership permits the social costs of production to be borne privately with the result that the private producer has the incentive to manage the resource in the interests of society as well as his own. To see how these results follow using the competitive model of this paper, we must develop the contrasting model of centralized management.

We assume with Gordon and Scott that there are many fishing grounds so that centralizing the ownership (or right of access) of any one does not introduce monopoly elements.[9] We continue to assume steady-state equilibrium, $\dot{X} = 0$. Under centralized management x, X and K will all be decision variables subject to control, in the interest of profit, by the sole owner. His profit function will be $\pi = pKx - KC(x, X, K)$ which is to be maximized with respect to (x, X, K), subject to $\dot{X} = f(X) - Kx = 0$. The Lagrangean is thus

$$\Psi = pKx - KC(x, X, K) + \lambda[f(X) - Kx],$$

and the first order conditions for an interior maximum can be written:

$$\frac{\partial \Psi}{\partial x} = pK - KC_1 - \lambda K = 0$$

$$\frac{\partial \Psi}{\partial X} = -KC_2 + \lambda f'(X) = 0$$

$$\frac{\partial \Psi}{\partial K} = px - KC_3 - C - \lambda x = 0$$

An interior maximum must therefore satisfy the system

$$f(X) = Kx \tag{13.11}$$

$$p - C_1 = \lambda \tag{13.12}$$

$$p - \frac{C}{x} - \frac{KC_3}{x} = \lambda \tag{13.13}$$

$$\lambda = \frac{KC_2}{f'} \tag{13.14}$$

By way of interpreting these conditions, note that total fleet catch, Kx, can be increased either by increasing catch per vessel, x, or by expanding the fleet, K. The Lagrange multiplier λ, in this instance, is the marginal profitability of the total fleet catch (or yield of the fish mass). Condition (13.12) requires the marginal profitability of increasing catch by intensive use of the fleet (i.e., by increasing x) to be equal to the marginal profitability of total fleet catch, λ. Condition (13.13) requires the marginal profitability of the catch from fleet expansion to equal λ. Thus (13.12) and (13.13) state that profitability at the intensive and extensive capital margins must be equal. Finally, KC_2/f' is the marginal external or social cost of the fleet catch. An increase in catch tending to lower the fish mass contributes fishing costs external to the individual boats. Since C_2 is negative while f' may be negative or positive, the question arises as to whether a maximum can occur with negative marginal social cost. It is easy to prove that a global maximum cannot occur at an X^* such that $f'(X^*) > 0$. Suppose we have equations (13.11)–(13.14) satisfied by a point (x^*, X^*, K^*), with $f'(X^*) > 0$. Then we know from the properties of $f(X)$, that there is an $X^{**} > X^*$ such that $f'(X^{**}) < 0$, and $K^*x^* = f(X^*) = f(X^{**})$. But since $C_2 < 0$, $C(x^*, X^*, K^*) > C(x^*, X^{**}, K^*)$ It follows that the point (x^*, X^{**}, K^*) satisfies the constraint, and yields a greater profit. Hence, $f' < 0$ and $KC_2/f' > 0$ in (13.14).[10]

Under competitive harvesting KC_2/f' is a social cost which does not affect firm behavior; but this cost is "privatized" when property rights are vested in a central manager-owner who adjusts his operations according to (13.12) and (13.14) to account for these social costs. Similarly will the central manager adjust for the effects of boat crowding over the fishing ground. Thus in (13.13), multiplying through by x, px is the gross marginal revenue from an additional vessel, C is the long-run direct internal cost, while $KC_3 + \lambda x$ is the long-run marginal external social cost of operating an additional vessel. An addition to the fleet produces external crowding cost at the rate KC_3, and external fish scarcity cost at the rate λx.

For the sole owner when $C_2 \equiv C_3 \equiv 0$, we have the conditions which could be postulated to apply to *appropriated* timber resources. With the appropriation of forest property rights comes an incentive to "conserve,"

and the forest will not be wiped out as in our previous model. The first
order conditions become:

$$f(X) = Kx$$
$$p - C_1 = \lambda$$
$$C_1 = \frac{C}{x}$$
$$f'(X) = 0$$

We see that only in the absence of resource stock externalities is it
optimal to maintain the resource stock at the level which maximizes
recruitment or sustainable yield, where $f'(X^0) = 0$.[11]

   By comparing (13.11)–(13.14) with the system (IA.1)–(IA.3), where
$\dot{K} = \dot{X} = 0$ in the latter, we contrast sole ownership with decentralized
competitive recovery in the stationary state. The two systems differ only
in that the sole owner perceives a *unit catch* cost, $\lambda = KC_2/f'$, and an
annual boat cost $KC_3 + \lambda x$, which is not incurred by the decentralized
competitive fisherman. Theoretically, then, the problem of regulating
competitive recovery can be stated as one of imposing these unper-
ceived social costs on the industry. The partial equilibrium solution to
the regulation problem is to levy an extraction fee $U = KC_2/f'$ per unit
of catch unloaded at the wharf, plus an annual license fee $L = KC_3$
on each fishing vessel.[12] As a consequence profit after taxes to each
competitive fishing vessel is

$$\pi^* = px - C(x, X, K) - L - Ux.$$

   If each fisherman chooses x to maximize π^*, and fishermen, with their
boats, enter the industry as long as $\pi^* > 0$, the equilibrium conditions
become

$$f(X) = Kx \tag{13.15}$$
$$p - C_1 = U \tag{13.16}$$
$$p - \frac{C}{x} - \frac{L}{x} = U \tag{13.17}$$

   This system is identical with (13.11)–(13.14) for centralized management provided only that the regulating authorities are omniscient
enough to fix $U = \lambda = KC_2/f'$, and $L = KC_3$ at optimizing valves satisfying (13.11)–(13.14).[13]

Appendix

In this appendix we consider some qualitative properties of the system (I.1)–(I.3) or (II.1)–(II.2), particularly as the system is illustrated in Figure 13.2.

The following qualitative restrictions on the cost function will be assumed: $C_1 > 0$, $C_2 < 0$, $C_3 \geq 0$, $C_{11} > 0$, $C_{12} < 0$, $C_{13} \geq 0$. Also it is assumed that the demand (or average revenue) function, $p(Kx)/Kx$, is monotone decreasing in Kx. Hence $p' < p/Kx$, and therefore from (I.2) $p' < C_1$.

We first examine the slopes in phase space along the equilibrium sets $\dot{K} = F(X, K) = 0$ and $\dot{K} = I(X, K) = 0$. Setting $\dot{K} = 0$, differentiating the equations (I.1) and (I.2), and eliminating dx/dX by substitution, we solve for

$$\left.\frac{dK}{dX}\right|_{\dot{X}=0} = \frac{(C_1 + xC_{11} - p')f' + KxC_{12}}{x(xC_{11} - KC_{13})} \tag{A.1}$$

If $C_{13} = 0$, or if $KC_3 < xC_{11}$, the denominator of this expression is positive. Since $C_{12} < 0$, $p' < C_1$, with $f' \gtreqless 0$ according as $X \lesseqgtr X^0$ it follows that

$$\left.\frac{dK}{dX}\right|_{\dot{X}=0}$$

is either (i) always negative or (ii) nonnegative for all $X \leq \hat{X} < X^0$, and negative for $X > \hat{X}$. The curve for $F(X, K) = 0$ in Figure 13.2 illustrates this second case.

Setting $\dot{K} = 0$, differentiating (I.2) and (I.3), and eliminating dx/dX by substitution, we solve for

$$\left.\frac{dK}{dX}\right|_{\dot{K}=0} = \frac{KxC_2C_{11} + K(p' - C_1)(xC_{12} - C_2)}{(p' - C_1)KC_3 + (p' - C_1)x(xC_{11} - KC_{13}) - KxC_{11}C_3} \tag{A.2}$$

If $C_{13} = 0$, or $KC_{13} < xC_{11}$ the denominator in (A.2) is negative. If $xC_{12} - C_2 > 0$, the numerator is negative, and

$$\left.\frac{dK}{dX}\right|_{\dot{K}=0}$$

is positive, but if $xC_{12} - C_2 < 0$,

$$\frac{dK}{dK}\bigg|_{\dot{K}=0}$$

may change sign. The curve for $I(X, K) = 0$ in Figure 13.2 illustrates a case in which

$$\frac{dK}{dX}\bigg|_{\dot{K}=0}$$

changes signs once, from positive to negative as X increases from zero. From (A.2) it is clear that many other configurations are compatible with the stated qualitative restrictions.

Now consider the directions of motion in phase space of points in the partitions A–E of Figure 13.2. Differentiating (II.1), or (I.1) and (I.2), with X fixed, gives

$$\frac{\partial \dot{X}}{\partial K} = F_K = \frac{x(KC_{13} - xC_{11})}{C_1 + xC_{11} - \rho'}. \tag{A.3}$$

The denominator is strictly positive. If $C_{13} = 0$, or $KC_{13} < xC_{11}$ then $F_k < 0$. It follows that $\dot{X} < 0$ for all points above the $F(X, K) = 0$ curve in Figure 13.2, and $\dot{X} > 0$ for all points below this curve.

Differentiating (II.2), or (I.2) and (I.3), with X fixed, gives

$$\frac{\partial \dot{K}}{\partial K} = I_K = -\frac{\delta x}{K}\left\{\frac{(\rho' - C_1)(KC_{13} - xC_{11})}{C_1 + xC_{11} - \rho'} + \frac{KC_3}{x}\right\} \tag{A.4}$$

Repeating the previous restrictions on C_{13} and C_{11}, we see that $I_K < 0$. It follows that $\dot{K} < 0$ for all points above $I(X, K) = 0$ in Figure 13.2 and $\dot{K} > 0$ for all points below this curve.

In the special case in which price is constant to the exploited resource $p \equiv \rho/Kx$, $\rho' = p = C_1$, and (A.1) reduces to (13.9) in the text, while (A.2) becomes (13.8).

Notes

1   The two cases are different, however. Neither was exhausted in the physical sense, but in the economic sense. The biotic potential of fish is so large that complete extinction may be very difficult. With the Lake Michigan trout it was invasion by another predator – the sea lamprey – that destroyed the

trout harvest. The lamprey have since been brought under control, and with restocking, the lake may again become an important fishery resource if pollution does not win the battle.

2　More generally, we should write $\underline{X} = f(X, Kx)$. In (13.2) we assume no interaction between the total harvest and the growth properties of the population mass, as likely will be the case if only restricted portions of the age distribution are harvested. Concerning my formulation of the constraint (13.2), and its use in the models to follow, the reader is urged to refer to [3], especially the mathematical appendix and the references cited there. Unfortunately, I suffered the impoverishment of not having acquired a copy of the important Crutchfield-Zellner book until after the present paper had been written. They work with the quadratic form (13.2) in the context of a supply and demand industry model (and again in the treatment of the optimization problem of central management, both static and dynamic). Although my treatment was independent, and differs from theirs, the reader should view the present paper as essentially a generalization and explication of this earlier literature.

3　The specialist will want to take this statement with a grain of salt. In forestry there are obvious externalities with regard to fire control (except remember that we are working with certainty models) and the spread of insects and disease. Also, in mining, one man's shaft may cause cave-ins or water encroachment on another mining property. A general disclaimer is in order: in a paper trying to emphasize the unity of production theory in the natural resource setting, one inevitably does a certain violence to the detailed facts, for there are indeed diverse elements to consider in the various cases of extraction. But the truth of unity, even if partial, is easily obscured by concentrating on more-or-less minor differentiating details.

4　In (13.3) we somewhat oversimplify the view of mining and forestry production. In mining, cumulative output (or the unrecovered stock remaining) may affect cost; for this and other important considerations in mining see [13]. See note 11 for some relevant qualifications applying to appropriated forest resources.

5　A good example is sport fishing for striped bass in San Francisco Bay. The stripers form schools to feed on schools of smaller food fish. The latter are driven to the surface, attempting to escape, and this attracts the gulls to feed. The fishing boats simply motor into the Bay looking for the mass of fighting gulls. The boats congregate around the gulls and then alternate with trolling passes through the concentrated school of stripers. On a busy holiday a considerable waiting line may develop.

6　Alternatively we could write $x = h(K, X)$, $h_1 < 0$, $h_2 > 0$. With secondary (water or gas injection) and stripper (mechanical pumping) recovery fields, the cost function will be as in (13.4). We assume in the text that the ultimate cumulative recovery, $\overline{X} - \underline{X}$ is known and is independent of the production path. In fact, the total free-flow recovery may depend upon the extraction rate. See, for example, [5, pp. 91–92], and the references cited there.

7　In (13.7) we assume capital to be equally mobile out as well as into an industry, i.e., there is no problem of irreversibility. More generally we could write

$$\dot{K} = \begin{cases} \delta_1\pi, & \text{if } \pi \geq 0 \\ \delta_2\pi, & \text{if } \pi < 0. \end{cases}$$

We later assume $\delta_2 = 0$ in the case of oil wells, which clearly cannot be reduced in quantity once drilled.

8   Many variations on the particular forms of these behavior equations could be made. In place of (I.3) some variant of the accelerator hypothesis or an adaptive expectations hypothesis about investment could be introduced. In (I.2) any output adjustment hypothesis might be used in place of the classical – price equals marginal cost. If fishing is concentrated in a single season of the year (such as spawning time), then a difference equation expression of growth-harvest behavior could substitute for (I.1).

9   This assumption is not essential, but keeps the arithmetic simpler. If sole ownership leads also to monopoly, we might still study the efficiency implication of the former uncontaminated by monopoly effects by imposing as an *additional constraint* upon the sole owner the price control condition $p(Kx) \leq Kx\bar{p}$, where $\bar{p}$ is the maximum selling price permitted.

10   Imposing a global maximum criterion is essential here since a "solution" with $X = X^*$ may not only satisfy (13.11)–(13.14) but also the corresponding second-order conditions for a relative interior maximum.

11   This result could be misleading in that it conflicts with some of the forestry economics literature [7], which contains valid arguments against the objective of maximizing sustainable yield. I do not argue that forest managers "should" maximize sustainable yield. This is simply a result of the assumptions made above, and I do not have any commitment to the assumptions. In a model of maximization over time and/or in a model in which forest husbanding costs are introduced and assumed to depend upon forest stock, sustainable yield will no longer be maximized in an optimal program.

With maximization over time, the discounting process will associate interest cost with X because forest growth depends upon X. Even in a static model, if husbanding costs depend upon X, we must then write cost as $C(x, X)$, not because of externalities measured by X, as in fishing, but because appropriation brings the incentive to incur costs of cultivating the stock. In such a case, the first order conditions for the sole forest owner are:

$$f(X) = Kx$$
$$p - C_1 = \lambda$$
$$C_1 = \frac{C}{x}$$
$$\lambda = \frac{KC_2}{f'}$$

However, in contrast with the fishing model, $C_2 > 0$ (husbanding costs increase with the stock). Consequently, for a global maximum, $f' > 0$, and the optimally managed stock is lower than the stock corresponding to maximum sustainable yield.

12 Regulatory devices other than taxes or fees could, of course, be used, such as direct controls on entry [4, p. 214]. But the resulting large rents may induce investment in gear improvement, more intense fishing, and other operating changes which invite more detailed controls. In practice, such direct controls have almost invariably taken the form of devices that reduce efficiency [4, p. 207].

13 There are, of course, other important aspects of the problem of optimal fishery regulation. Of particular importance is the problem of regulating mesh size as a means of selective harvesting [1, 14]. The idea behind mesh control is to limit the harvest to the older, and larger, members of the species whose growth rates are considerably slower than those of the younger members. The present paper has also omitted any explicit analysis of the problem of interspecies equilibrium where more than a single species have commercial value. There is also the interesting problem of optimization over time for centrally managed recovery – a problem in Pontryagin control theory. Such extensions will be treated in separate papers.

References

1 R. J. H. Beverton and S. V. Holt, *On the Dynamics of Exploited Fish Populations*, Ministry of Agriculture, Fisheries and Food, Fishery Investigations, Ser. II, Vol. XIX, London 1957.

2 F. T. Christy and A. Scott, *The Common Wealth in Ocean Fisheries*. Baltimore 1965.

3 J. A. Crutchfield and A. Zellner, *Economic Aspects of the Pacific Halibut Fishery*, Fishery Industrial Research I, US Department of the Interior, Washington 1962.

4 J. A. Crutchfield, "The Marine Fisheries: A Problem in International Cooperation," *Am. Econ. Rev., Proc.*, May 1964, *54*, 207–18.

5 P. Davidson, "Public Policy Problems of the Domestic Crude Oil Industry," *Am. Econ. Rev.*, March 1963, *53*, 85–108.

6 H. S. Gordon, "The Economic Theory of a Common Property Resource: The Fishery," *Jour. Pol. Econ.*, April 1954, *62*, 124–42.

7 G. K. Goundry, "Forest Management and the Theory of Capital," *Can. Jour. Econ. and Pol. Sci.*, Aug. 1960, 439–51.

8 A. J. Lotka, *Elements of Mathematical Biology*, New York 1956.

9 A. L. MacKinney, F. Schumacher and L. Chaiken, "Construction of Yield Tables for Nonnormal Loblolly Pine Stands," *Jour. Agric. Res.*, April 1937, *54*, 531–45.

10 S. V. Pirson, *Elements of Reservoir Engineering*. New York 1950.

11 A. Scott, "The Fishery: The Objectives of Sole Ownership," *Jour. Pol. Econ.*, April 1955, *63*, 116–24.

12 ——, *Natural Resources: The Economics of Conservation*. Toronto 1955.

13 ——, "The Theory of the Mine Under Conditions of Certainty." Ch. 2 in Mason Gaffney, ed., *Extractive Resource and Taxation*, Madison 1967.

14 R. Turvey, "Optimization in Fishery Regulation," *Am. Econ. Rev.*, March 1964, *54*, 64–76.

14
Economics of Forestry in an Evolving Society
Paul A. Samuelson

A debate that has raged for centuries is unlikely to be resolved by me in one lecture. However, I shall do my best to set forth the issues and indicate what ought to be the crucial factors that a jury should consider in rendering its verdict on the matter. The issue is one between forestry experts and the general public on the one side and professional economists and profit-conscious businessmen on the other. At first blush this would seem to suggest that economists are on the side of the interests and are not themselves members of the human race. But, as I hope to show, sound economic analysis is needed to do justice to the cases put forward by either of the adversary parties.

Sustain or not sustain?

To vulgarize and oversimplify, *there has been a tradition in forestry management which claims that the goal of good policy is to have sustained forest yield, or even "maximum sustained yield" somehow defined.* And, typically, economists have questioned this dogma.

If laissez-faire enterprisers tended to be led by that invisible hand Adam Smith talked about to achieve in fact sustained forest yields, and even maximum sustained forest yields, then no doubt there would be a school of economists called into existence to give their blessings to the doctrine of maximum sustained yield. In that case there would be no great debate. The economists in the liberal arts division of the university, on those rare occasions when they deign to think about the practical problems of forest management, would come out with the same conclusions and dicta as would the professional foresters in the school of forestry. Moreover, the professors in the biological departments, and the lay public generally, would heartily approve of the actual solution in this best of all possible worlds.

Life is not like that and it hasn't been for a long time. The medieval forests of Britain, and of Europe, tended to be chopped down as society moved into the Industrial Revolution. The virgin forests that graced the New World when Columbus arrived here have increasingly been cut down once the calculus of dollar advantage began to apply. When I informed a graduate student that I was preparing this lecture, he mentioned to me the rumor that a nearby consulting firm had applied dynamical programming analysis to the problem of how old – or rather how young – a tree should be when it is to be optimally cut in the steady state. Allegedly, its computer spun out of control and generated a negative, or for all I know, imaginary, root for the equation: apparently at realistic profit rates, it doesn't pay to keep a forest in existence at all. This is probably only a tall story, but it does well illustrate the fact that standard managerial economics, and actual commercial practice, both tend to lead to an optimal cutting age of a forest that is much shorter than the 80 or even 100 years one often encounters in the forestry literature.

Externalities and intervention

This apparent clash between economists and foresters is not an isolated one. Biological experts in the field of fisheries are sometimes stunned when they meet economists who question their tacit axiom that the stock of fish in each bank of the ocean ought to be kept as a goal at some maximum sustained level. Similarly, hard-boiled economists are greeted with incredulity if and when they opine that it may be optimal to grow crops in the arid plain states only until the time when the top soil there has blown away to its final resting place in the ears and teeth of Chicago pedestrians.

Everybody loves a tree and hates a businessman. Perhaps this is as it should be, and perhaps after the profession of economics is 1,000 rather than 200 years old, the human race will be as conditioned to abhor economists as it has become to abhor snakes. But really, these matters need arguing in court so the informed jury, and I do mean the informed jury of human beings, can make up its mind.

Let me say in advance of the argument, there is no ironclad presumption that profit seeking laissez-faire will lead to the social optimum. Thus, suppose that a living redwood tree helps purify the air of smoggy Los Angeles. Suppose sowing the land to short-lived pine trees prevents floods 500 miles downstream. Then we may well have here a case of what modern economists recognize as "externalities." We economists these days spend much of our time analyzing the *defects* of competitive free entry and push-shove equilibrium when important externalities are involved. If therefore in the great historic debate on sustained yields, foresters and conservationists had brought into court an elaboration of the respects in which forestry is an activity beset with important externalities, carefully and objectively described, Ph.Ds in economics would be found on both sides of the case under trial. Indeed, if the externalities involved could be shown to be sufficiently important, I am naive enough to believe that all economists would be found on the side of the angels, sitting thigh next to thigh with the foresters. (*All* economists agree? Well, almost all.)

"Private" versus "common" property

Earlier I mentioned fisheries. Even those economists who ostrich-like tend always to play down externalities if they can, have long recognized that there is a "common property" element in hunting and fishing: even though I were to have to pay rent to someone who owns a particular acre of the ocean in order to put down my net there, my act of fishing there can hope to draw on fish with might migrate from nearby acres. So we have in the case of fisheries a special kind of externality that makes in nonoptimal to have *decentralized rent-charging owners* of subdivisions of a common fishing bank. Government regulation and centralized decision making for the whole fishing pool, if it can be arranged in this age of nationalism, is obviously preferable to free competition as Gordon (1954), Scott (1955a), and Crutchfield (1962) have analyzed.

From a cursory glance at the literature of forestry, both technical and economic, I do not perceive foresters to be making as a case for timber what is true for fisheries, or for oil drilling. It is true that forest fires are a hazard that adjacent timber lands may face in common. And if the units of land owned by each forester-owner were very, very small, the externalities between adjacent plots would render decentralized competitive decision-making nonoptimal. However, for the most part, timber ownership will not under laissez-faire tend to stay so pulverized, since it is quite feasible to have the span of ownership widened to the optimal degree without creating monopoly or vitiating the assumptions of workable competition.

At the beginning, therefore, even before entering into the serious argument, let us make a deposition that the following would be a false issue in the debate:

Abolishing private ownership in land or abandoning public regulation of forest land owned by the government is not an alternative to maximum sustained yield that is advocated by anybody. This would certainly result in unnecessary decimation of the forest. Indeed, as Vernon Smith (1968) has shown in one of his models, it could result in extinction of *all* forests; but even if a realistic model of complete push-shove free-free entry led to a maintainable sustained-yield steady state, the average age of the forest stands in such a Hobbesian jungle might well involve rotation periods so short as to be absurd, which is why in medieval Germany severe limits were properly placed on the use by the public of crown and public forest lands.

Competitive land rents

The economists who oppose maximum sustained-yield do not advocate any such absurd push-shove procedure. They assume that the cultivator who plants a tree on one acre of land owns or rents the right to exclusive garnering of the fruits of that which he has planted. Similarly, if I own yonder acre or have leased it from a public or private owner, and if I desist in chopping down a tree that is not yet ripe, I expect to find it still there when I do come to chop it down. In return for this exclusive use of my own area of cultivation, I expect to pay a land rent. If I own the land outright, I pay it *to myself* at an opportunity cost rate that is perfectly well determined in a freely competitive market. Or I pay the rent to a private owner, who knows he can rent that land to somebody else like me if not to me. Or I pay a rent to a government that owns the land.

This rate of land rental can be high or low. If the total amount of land available for growing the timber that society needs, and which is close enough to the market to be able to avoid heavy transportation charges, is severely limited in amount, then the appropriate competitive land rent will be high. If on the other hand land is extremely plentiful, its scarcity rent will be very low. It will not even matter for the purpose of our analysis if well-located land is so plentiful as to be redundant. In that case, its competitive land rent will be zero, but even though land rent is zero I shall still need to have *exclusive* rights to the fruits of my earlier labor and other investment inputs, independently of whether in other acres of the redundant territory push-shove free-free entry is permitted.

Assumptions for the analysis

Let me first review the correct economic principles that would be applicable if forestry can be regarded simply as sources of wood saleable in competitive markets. This initially assumes away externalities such as flood control, pollution abatement, species preservation, vacationers' enjoyments, etc.

Although I am not a specialist in the field of forest economics, I have been reading a couple of dozen different analyses ranging over the last two centuries that grapple with optimal steady-state rotation periods. The economic analysis in most of them is wrong. In some it is very wrong. In others it is not quite right. In at least one case, the remarkable 1849 German article by Martin Faustmann, the analysis does come close to an essentially correct solution.

These remarks are not intended to give a harsh indictment of foresters or of economists who have worked in the field of forestry. The mistakes made in the forestry literature can be duplicated aplenty in the intermediate textbooks of pure economics.

Thus, Irving Fisher was the greatest single economic writer on interest and capital, and his 1930 *Theory of Interest* summarized his life work in that field. Yet at MIT we ask graduate students on quizzes to identify and correct Fisher's false solution as to when a tree should be cut (a false solution that he seems to share with the great von Thunen (1826) and the brilliant Hotelling (1925) as well as with some excellent economists who have written on forestry in recent decades). Again, Kenneth Boulding is one of our leading economists; but his rule of maximizing the so-called "internal rate of return" has led many a forestry economist down the garden path (Boulding 1935). A 1960 review of the literature by G. K. Goundrey comes out with the wrong Boulding solution, and yet his analysis purports to lean on such excellent authorities as Wicksell, Scitovsky, Kaldor, Metzler, and Scott; alas, it did not lean more heavily on Faustmann (1849), Preinrich (1938), Alchian (1952), Bellman (1957), Gaffney (1957), Hirshleifer (1958), and perhaps Samuelson (1937).

If an unambiguous solution to the problem is to be definable, of course certain definite assumptions much be made. If the solution is to be simple, the assumptions must be heroic. These include: (1) knowledge of future lumber prices at which all outputs can be freely sold, and future wages of all inputs; (2) knowledge of future interest rate at which the enterprise can both borrow and lend in indefinite amounts; and (3) knowledge of technical lumber yields that emerge at future dates once certain expenditure inputs are made (plantings, sprayings, thinnings, fellings, etc.). Finally, it is assumed (4) that each kind of land suitable for forests can be bought and sold and rented in arm's length trans-actions between numerous competitiors; or, if the government owns public lands, it rents them out at auction to the highest of numerous alternative bidders and conducts any of its own forestry operations so as to *earn the same maximum rent* obtainable at the postulated market rate of interest. For the special steady-state model, the future prices and interest rates must be assumed to be known constants. Moreover, our problem is not one merely of managerial economics; rather we must deduce the competitive prices that clear the industry's market.

Assumptions would not be heroic if they could be easily taken for granted as being exactly applicable. Stochastic factors of climate, lightning, forest fires, and disease must in real life qualify the techni-cal assumptions made in (3) above. At the least, therefore, as a second approximation, one must introduce probabilities and expected values into the decision calculus.

Similarly, tomorrow's lumber price is not knowable exactly, much less the price of lumber a score of years from now when today's seedling will mature. So, in other than a first approximation, the assumptions under (1) need to be complicated.

Finally, future interest rates are not knowable today. Moreover, the inherent uncertainties involved in interest and profit yields also serve to falsify the assumption in (2) that the enterprise is able at each date both to borrow and to lend in indefinite amounts at one interest rate (even one knowable at *that* date if not now). Once we recognize that the enterprise is in an imperfect capital market, we will not be able to deduce its optimal forestry decisions independently of knowl-edge about its owners' personal preferences concerning consumption outlays of different dates (and concerning their "liquidities" at different dates).

Correct capital analysis

Our problem is now well posed. What principles provide its solution? What is the exact nature of the solution?

(i) Does it yield a steady-state rotation period as long as that which achieves the foresters' traditional "maximum sustained yield"?

(ii) Is the optimal rotation that *shorter* period which maximizes the present discounted value over the first planting cycle of the cash receipts that come from the sale of cut lumber minus the cash expenses of planting and cutting inputs (excluding from the net cash receipts stream any adjustments for implicit and explicit land rent)?

(iii) Is the optimal rotation period that still shorter period which maximizes Boulding's "Internal Rate of Return," computed as that largest rate of interest which when applied to the net dollar cash receipts over one complete cycle reduces the resulting present discounted value to zero (and, be it noted, ignores land rent in setting up the net algebraic cash receipts!)?

(iv) Alternatively, is the optimum the rotation period that results from maximizing (1) the present discounted value of all net cash receipts excluding explicit or implicit land rents, but calculated over the *infinite chain* of cycles of planting on the given acre of land from now until Kingdom Come; or (2) what may sound like a different criterion, the rotation period that results from maximizing the present discounted value of net algebraic receipts over the first cycle, but with the market land rental included in those receipts, it being understood that the land rental that each small enterprise will be confronted with will be the *maximum* rental that ruthless Darwinian competition can contrive?

If you have been testing yourself by trying to answer the objective-type quiz that I have just propounded, you will receive a perfect A+ if you gave the following answers:

(i) No, the rotation period that maximizes sustained yield is so long that, at the postulated positive interest rate and inevitable market rent for land, it will bankrupt any enterprise that endeavors to realize it.

(ii) No, maximizing the present discounted value, over *one* planting cycle, of cash receipts from cut timber sold minus cash receipts for inputs that do planting, thinning, and cutting will give you a somewhat too long rotation period and will not enable you to cover the land rent that will be set by your more perspicacious competitors. However, your error will not be so very great in the case the length of each cycle is very great and/or the rate of interest per annum is very large, so that the discounted value today of a dollar payable at the end of the cycle is negligible. Still, employing this method that is so frequently advocated by sophisticated economists will lead you to the following absurdity: an increase in initial planting cost will have *no effect at all* on your optimal rotation period, up to the point that it makes it unprofitable to put the land you own into lumber, even when you are philanthropic enough to forego obtainable positive land rent. It is a solution that pretends that the Archimedean forest lever never needs the land fulcrum to work with.

(iii) No, ignoring land rent and maximizing the internal rate of return will give you so short a rotation period that, at the postulated interest rate, you will not be able to pay yourself the positive land rental set by competition. Moreover, maximizing the interal rate of return will give you the nonsensical result that you should select the same rotation period when the interest rate, the price of time, is high or low; and, when initial planting costs are zero, it will give a meaningless infinite return.

(iv) Finally, yes, (1) and (2), which really are exactly the same method, constitute the only correct method. The first formulation, in terms of an infinite chain of repeated cycles, was already proposed in the brilliant 1849 German article by Martin Faustmann. A glance at its recent English translation convinces me of his remarkable merit, even though at first glance one does not find in it the exact explicit conditions for optimal cutting age of the forest stand. I do not know that the economics literature caught up with this degree of sophistication prior to the 1938 *Econometrica* survey article on depreciation by Gabriel Preinrich, which was itself a notable anticipation of the dynamic programming that Richard Bellman made routine in the postwar period. The second approach, which I cannot recall seeing explicitly in print, will perhaps be more intuitively understandable at a first approach to the subject; and, in any case, land rent has tended not to be given the proper analysis it needs.

In a moment I shall illustrate all this by means of a specific model, which though not very realistic will be familiar to economists since the time of Stanley Jevons. From it, you will infer the presumption that commercial exploitation of forestry will lead to a departure from the goal of maximum sustained yield even greater than may have been realized by adherents and critics of forestry dogmas. The higher the effective rate of interest, the greater will be the shortfall of the optimal rotation age compared to the age that maximizes steady-state yield. As

312 The Economics of Renewable Resources

the interest rate goes to zero, the economists' correct optimum will reach the limit of the foresters' target of maximum sustained yield. Only if an explicit land rent charge is introduced into the cash stream will Boulding's maximized internal rate of return avoid incorrect results; but in that case, Ockham's razor can cut it down as redundant (worse than that, as involving incomplete, implicit theorizing.) Actually, as we have seen in (2) above, including in competitive land-rent can save from error the popular method of maximizing present discounted value calculated over only the first cycle; however, to know *how much* rent so to include, one must impose the condition that it be just large enough to reduce to zero that maximized discounted value over one cycle, and this rent so calculated will turn out to be after capitalization exactly what the Faustmann-Preinrich-Bellman-Hirshleifer solution deduced. It should be noted that, in the special case where the land for timber growth is redundant and therefore free, maximizing over a single cycle will singularly give the correct answer, and maximizing the internal rate of return will with equal singularity also give the same answer. Since at least one writer, Goundrey (1960), has alleged that timber land in Canada is so plentiful as to be free, it is worth emphasizing that even in this case the three methods nominated by economists will deduce a rotation period significantly shorter than the foresters' maximum because of the positive interest rate. The foresters, without realizing it, are correct only when the true interest rate is literally zero.

The bogey of compound interest

I cannot conclude this general survey of wrong and right ways of analyzing the actual equilibrium that will emerge in the competitive steady-state without expressing my amazement at the low interest rates which abound in the forestry literature. Faustmann, writing in the middle of the nineteenth century, uses a four per cent rate. Thunen, writing at the same time, uses a five per cent interest rate. The 1960 Goundrey survey also uses a five per cent rate. These will seem to an ordinary economist and businessman as remarkably low. The notion that for such gilt-edge rates I would tie up my own capital in a 50-year (much less a 100-year) timber investment, with all the uncertainties and risks that the lumber industry is subject to, at first strikes one as slightly daft. I can only guess that such low numbers have been used either as a form of wishful thinking so foresters or forest economists can avoid rotation ages so short they show up the forester's "maximum sustained yield;" or because the writers have not had the heart to face up to the discounting almost out of existence of receipts payable half a century from now.

Let us make no mistake about it. The positive interest rate is the enemy of long-lived investment projects. At six per cent interest, money doubles in 12 years, quadruples in 24, grows 16-fold in 48 years, and 256-fold in 96 years. Hence, the present discounted value today of $1 of timber harvest 96 years from now is, at six per cent, only 0.4 of one cent!

Foresters know this and fight against compound interest. Thus, an economist cannot help but be amused at the 1925 gem by the Assistant Chief, Board of Research, US Forest Service, Ward Shepard. Entitled "The Bogey of Compound Interest," this argues that if you have forest stand in the steady state, no interest need be involved: your cutting receipts exceed your planting expenses! This is so absurd as to be almost believable to the layman – up to the moment when the economist breaks the news to the farmer, lumber-company president, or government official that he can mine the forest by cutting it down without replanting and sell the land, thereafter putting the proceeds into the bank or into retiring the public debt and subsequently earn interest forever.

"Bogey" has two meanings. The first, which is Shepard's naive meaning, is that compound interest is a fictitious entity which, like the Bogey Man, is wrongfully used to frighten little children. The second and here more legitimate meaning of bogey is that defined in Webster's Dictionary as "a numerical standard of performance set up as a mark to be aimed at in competition." Compound interest is indeed the legitimate bogey that competitors must earn in forestry if they are not to employ their land, labor, and disposable funds in other more lucrative uses.

Competitive theory can be reassuring as well as frustrating to the forester. There is a popular notion that interest calculations may be applied to decisions for next year as against the immediately following years. "But," it is not infrequently argued, "when what is at issue is a tree or dam whose full fruits may not accrue until a century from now, the brute fact that our years are numbered as three score and ten prevents people from planting the trees that will not bear shade until after they are dead – altruism, of course, aside."

To argue in this way is to fail to understand the logic of competitive pricing. Even if my doctor assures me that I will die the year after next, I can confidently plant a long-lived olive tree, knowing that I can sell at a competitive profit the one-year-old sapling. Each person's longevity and degree of impatience to spend becomes immaterial in a competitive market place with a borrowing, lending, and capitalizing interest rate that encapsulates all which is relevant about society's effective time preferences.

Inflation and income taxes

What interest rate is appropriate for forestry? I hesitate to pronounce on such a complex matter. A dozen years ago I might incautiously have said 12 per cent or more. And, just recently you could have got 12 per cent per annum on $100,000 left with safety in the bank for three months. But this of course represented in part the 1974 10+ per cent annual inflation rate, a rate which the price rise in lumber could also presumably share. Indeed timber lands are often recommended as an inflation hedge: if the interest rate is 12 per cent and the price of lumber rises at 12 per cent per annum, it is a standoff and in effect there is a zero real interest rate.

Fortunately, I was able to show back in 1937, correcting a misleading interpretation in Keynes' 1936 *General Theory*, that so long as price changes are anticipatable, it does not matter in what "own-rates-of-interest" you calculate to make decisions (such as at what optimal age to cut a tree), the optimal physical decision will always be invariant. This means that essentially all we need in order to discuss forest economics correctly is to concentrate on (1) the *real* rate of interest (i.e., the actual interest rate on money minus the presumed known rate of overall price inflation), and (2) the real price of lumber outputs and inputs (i.e., the percentage real rate of rise for $P_{lumber}/P_{general}$).

There is another complication. If marginal tax rates are (say) 50 per cent, a 12 per cent yield before tax is a 6 per cent yield after tax. It would seem to make quite a difference for optimal rotation decisions whether we must use a 12 or a 6 per cent discount rate. Actually, and this may seem discouraging to the foresters' dream of maximum sustained yield, one can correctly use the higher pre-tax rate in making optimal decisions provided the income tax authorities really do properly tax true money income at uniform prices. More specifically, I showed in Samuelson (1964) that, if foreseeable depreciation and appreciation are taxed when they occur, a person always in the 50 per cent (or 99 per cent) bracket will make the same optimal decisions as a person always in the zero per cent bracket.

But are actual US or Canadian tax systems "fair" in their income taxation? Of course not. As a forest grows in size and value, instead of taxing this certain accretion of true income in the Henry Simons fashion, the tax is deferrable until the wood is cut. So forestry may provide a "tax loophole," which can distort decisions toward the longer rotation period of the foresters' maximum sustained yield, particularly if capital-gains tax-treatment is available at lower rates.

To sum up, I might mention that William Nordhaus (1974) recently showed at Brookings that *real* profit yields have been falling in recent years. Thus, his Table 5 suggests that real before-tax yields on corporate capital have tended to average only about 10 per cent in the early 1970s as against over 15 per cent 20 years earlier. This seems better for forest economics than in earlier decades, but still bad enough. Tax loopholes may further improve the viability of longer rotation periods. Also, I remember Frank Knight's being quoted as saying that, in effect, *real* lumber prices have risen historically about enough to motivate holding on to forest inventories – a dubious generalization, but one that reminds us that lumber price cannot be taken as a hard constant in realistic analysis. Before a nation, or regions it trades with, completely depletes a needed item, the price of that item can be expected to rise.

Defining maximum sustained yield in a classic case

You might think that the practical man's notion of sustained yield, or of maximum sustained yield, would be clear-cut. But if you do, you haven't had much experience with analyzing so-called common sense notions. Certainly maximum sustained yield in forestry does not suggest all land wasted on soybeans and other goodies should be plowed and planted with trees. Nor does it mean that land devoted to forests should be manicured and fertilized by all the labor in society, labor not needed for subsistence calories and vitamins, in order to produce the most lumber that land is capable of in the steady state.

The amount of lumber a virgin forest is capable of producing in a wild state approaches closer to the notion's content. But biologists have long realized that Darwinian evolution leads to an ecological equilibrium in which many trees grow to be too old in terms of their wood-product efficiency; and, in any case, a virgin forest left unmolested by man is like a librarian's perverted dream of a library where no books are ever permitted to be taken out so that the inventory on the shelves can be as complete as possible.

One presumes that "maximum sustained yield" is shorthand for a reasonable notion like the following:

Cut trees down to make way for new trees when they are past their best growth rates. Follow a planting, thinning, and cutting cycle so the resulting (net?) lumber output, averaged over repeated cycles or, what is the same thing, averaged over a forest in a synchronized age class distribution, will be as large as possible.

Jevons, Wicksell, and other economists have for a century analyzed a simple "point-input point-output, time-phased" model that can serve as the paradigm of an idealized forest. Labor input of L, does planting on an acre of forest land at time t. Then at time $t + T$, I can cut lumber of Q_{t+T}, freeing the land for another input of L_{t+T} and output $Q_{t+2T}, \ldots$, and so forth in an infinite number of cycles. Biology and technology give me the production function relating inputs and output, namely

$$Q_{t+T} = f(T) \tag{14.1}$$

$$f'(T) > 0, \; a < T < b; \; f'(b) = 0$$

Actually, as we'll see, $f(T)$ is short for $f(s, L; T)$, where L is labor input at the beginning of one planting cycle and s is the land used throughout that complete cycle (which can be set at $s = 1$).

In the steady state, a new part of each forest is being planted at every instant of time, an old part is being cut down at age T, and forest stands of all ages below T are represented in equal degree. If we wish to calculate the average product per unit of land of the synchronized forest, we can follow one cycle on one part of the forest, and divide the Q it produces in T periods by T to get average product per year. So one measure of gross sustained yield would be $f(T)/T$. However, this neglects the fact that workers must be paid wages. These are payable in dollars at rate W; and the lumber is sold in dollars at the competitive price P. But we could think of the workers who do the initial planting as being paid off in kind, in lumber they can sell at price P. So their wage in lumber, $(W/P)L$, must be subtracted from gross output $f(T)$ in order to form "average sustainable net lumber yield" of $[f(T) - (W/P)L]/T$.

Figure 14.1 shows the story. The point of maximum $f(T)$ is shown at B, where $f'(b) = 0 > f''(b)$. The point of maximum sustained gross yield T_q, is shown where a ray through the origin, OG, is tangent to the $f(T)$ curve. The point of maximum sustained net yield, is given by tangency at T_n of a similar ray, EN, from the expense point, E, to the net curve $f(T) - (W/P)L$.

Maximum sustained gross yield, as here defined, is at a maximum, not when $T = b$. To wait until each tree slowly achieves its top lumber content is to fail to realize that cutting the tree to make the land available

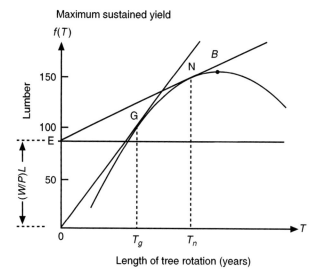

Figure 14.1 T_g is rotation period for maximum *gross* sustained yield irrespective of initial planting costs. T_n is rotation period for maximum *net* sustained yield.

for a faster-growing young tree is truly optimal. Ignoring all wage subtractions, sustained yield of gross lumber is maximized at the lower rotation age, T_g, defined by

$$\max_T[f(T)/T] = f(T_g)/T_g, \tag{14.2}$$

where

$$f'(T_g) = f(T_g)/T_g, \quad T_g < b.$$

Since a short rotation period makes us pay the same wages more often, once we introduce wage subtractions, we arrive at a forester's true "maximum sustained (net) yield" at a rotation age somewhat greater than T_g namely at T_n defined as

$$\max_T[f(T) - (W/P)L]/T = [f(T_n) - (W/P)L]/T_n, \tag{14.3}$$

where[1]

$$f'(T_n) - f(T_n)/T_n = -(W/P)L/T_n, \quad T_g < T_n < b.$$

This provides us with an unambiguous and useful definition of "maximum sustained net yield." And it is this definition of sustained yield that I shall compare with what will actually emerge as steady-state competitive equilibrium, and with the various optima that one or another economist has proposed when poaching on the territory of forest economics.

The true competitive solution

The above Jevons model will illustrate the false economic solutions and the correct solution.

First, consider the most popular method which maximizes present discounted value or PDV, calculated over one planting cycle only and involving cash receipts other than land rent. This gives T_1, defined by the equations below as

$$f(T_1)e^{-rT_1} - (W/P)L \geq 0 = \underset{T}{Max}[f(T)e^{-rT} - (W/P)L],\qquad(14.4)$$

where

$$f'(T_1)/f(T_1) = r$$

and

$$T_1 < b \quad \text{when} \quad r > 0,$$

where r is the market-given competitive interest rate at which everyone can borrow and lend in unlimited amounts. This is the famous Jevons relation, which had already been glimpsed by Thunen and which Fisher was later mistakenly to apply to a forest growing on limited land. (Only if land is so abundant as to be redundant and rent-free, so that P/W falls to equal $f(T_1)L^{-1}$, will T_1 give the correct competitive rotation period of the forest. As we'll see, the correct rotation period, call it T_∞, will be shorter than T_1; but unlike T_1 it must always fall short of T_n.)

A defect in many good economic discussions is to present alternative maximum criteria, as if it were a matter of choice which to adopt. One such is to maximize the so-called internal rate of return, defined by

$$\underset{T}{Max}\,\rho = \underset{T}{Max}\{T^{-1}\log[f(T)(P/WL)]\} = r_i = f'(T_i)/f(T_i),$$
$$= T_i^{-1}\log[f(T_i)(P/WL)] = r_i \qquad(14.5)$$

where

$$f'(T_i)/f(T_i) = T_i^{-1}\log[f(T_i)(P/WL)]$$
$$T_i < T_1 \quad \text{when} \quad r_i > r.$$

Anyone who misguidedly adopts this foolish T_i rotation period will find that he either goes broke or is permanently sacrificing return on original capital that could be his. (To prove that $T_i < T_1$, note that increasing r can be shown to lower T_1; also note that for $r = r_i$, T_1 and T_i would coincide. Hence, the T_1 for smaller r would be greater than T_i. QED)

Finally, as Faustmann showed in 1849, the correct description of what will emerge in competitive forest-land-labor-investment equilibrium is an optimal rotation period shorter than the forester's T_n and Thunen-Fisher's T_1, but longer than Boulding's T_i, namely T_∞ as defined by either of the following equivalent formulations.

$$R_\infty \underset{T}{Max} Rs = \underset{T}{Max} R \quad \text{for} \quad s = 1, \text{subject to}$$
$$0 = \underset{T}{Max}\left\{Pf(T)e^{-rT} - WL - R\int_0^T e^{-rT}dt\right\}$$
$$= Pf(T_\infty)e^{-rT_\infty} - WL - R_\infty[1 - e^{-rT_\infty}]r^{-1} \tag{14.6a}$$

or,

$$\underset{T}{Max}[Pf(T)e^{-rT} - WL]\left[1 + e^{-rT} + (e^{-rT})^2 + \ldots\right]$$
$$= \underset{T}{Max}[Pf(T)e^{-rT} - WL]/[1 - e^{-rT}]$$
$$= \underset{T}{Max}(R/r) = [Pf(T_\infty)e^{-rT_\infty} - WL]/[1 - e^{-rT_\infty}] = R_\infty/r, \tag{14.6b}$$

land's value, where

$$f'(T_\infty) - rf(T_\infty) = +r[Pf(T_\infty)e^{-rT_\infty} - WL]/[1 - e^{-rT_\infty}]$$
$$= r(R_\infty/r) = r \ land \ value = R_\infty$$
$$T_i < T_\infty < T_1 \quad \text{and} \quad T_\infty < T_n \quad \text{for} \quad R_\infty > 0. \tag{14.6c}$$

The first line of (14.6b) is the correct Faustmann-Gaffney-Hirshleifer formulation. Its equivalence with the maximum-land-rent formulation of (14.6a) is seen from solving the last relation of (14.6a) for R and noting its equivalence with the second relation of (14.6b) except for the extraneous constant r.

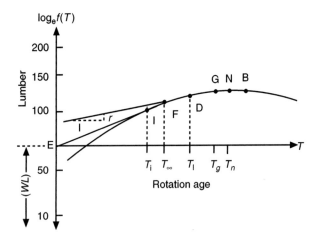

Figure 14.2

Figure 14.2 shows the familiar relation among the different rotation periods. Note that a reduction in P/W would lower the curve in the figure until at the zero-land-rent state the line through E with slope r would just touch the new curve at the new *coinciding* points T_i and T_1 and T_∞. It can be shown that, as $r \to 0$.[2]

Digression: labor and land variable

The general problem recognizes that Q_{t+T} output can, for each T, be affected by how much labor, L_t, one uses initially and how much land, $s_{t,t+T}$, one uses throughout the time interval t to $t + T$. Hence, we replace $f(T)$ in the steady state by

$$Q = f(s, L; T) \equiv \lambda^{-1} f(\lambda s, \lambda L; T) \tag{14.1'}$$

and $f(\ )$ concave in (s, L) jointly; $f(\ )$ can be smoothly differentiable in the neoclassical fashion, or it can take the fixed-coefficients form $f(Min[s/\alpha, L/\beta]; T)$ where (α, β) are positive constants that can be set equal to unity by proper choice of input units. For brevity, I analyze the neoclassical case.

Using the rate of interest (r) as a discount factor, economists like von Thünen and Irving Fisher favored cutting trees when percentage growth of gross lumber just equals the interest rate, giving T_1 as optimal age where D's slope just equals r on ratio chart. Boulding and those who say, maximize internal rate of return, select lower T_i where slope of ray through E is at its steepest because of tangency at I. Correct competitive solution is that of Martin Faustmann (1849), which maximizes *present discounted* value over infinity of cycles (not just one cycle as with Fisher): correct T_∞ is between T_i and T_1 and maximizes land rent of steady-state forest. If $r \to 0$, $T_\infty \to T_n$, the point at which the net sustained yield is maximized.

Competitive equilibrium requires, for given $(r, W/P)$,

$$0 = \underset{T,s,L}{Max}\left\{f(s,L;T)e^{-rT} - (W/P)L - (R/P)s\int_0^T e^{-rt}dt\right\}$$
$$= f(s_\infty, L_\infty; T_\infty)e^{-rT_\infty} - (W/P)L_\infty - (R/P)_\infty s[1 - e^{-rT_\infty}]r^{-1} \qquad (14.7)$$

where $[L_\infty/s_\infty,\ T_\infty,\ (R/P)_\infty]$ are roots of

$$e^{-rT}\partial f(1, L/s; T)/\partial L = W/P \qquad (14.8a)$$

$$e^{-rT}\partial f(1, L/s; T)/\partial s = (R/P)[1 - e^{-rT}]r^{-1} \qquad (14.8b)$$

$$\partial f(1, L/s; T)/\partial T - rf(1, L/s; T) = (R/P) \qquad (14.8c)$$

These equations are not all independent; and, of course, even if total land available for forestry, $\bar{s}$, is knowable in advance because such land has no other viable use, we need to know the consumer's demand for labor, and the workers' supply of labor to forestry as against alternative uses, before the extensive scale of (Q_∞, L_∞) are determined. It is worth noting that, in the steady state, there is a fundamental three-variable factor-price frontier of the form

$$r = \psi(W/P, R/P) \qquad (14.9)$$

where χ is a monotone-decreasing function that has contours that are convex. Figure 14.3 shows such contours for equi-spaced values of r: the fact they are alternately bunched and spread out indicates that, in the Sraffa fashion, the relation between r and any one variable can be wavy, with variable curvature.

Simple general equilibrium: static and dynamic

An oversimplified case can illustrate the general equilibrium of lumber and other prices, and can show that some efficiency properties are

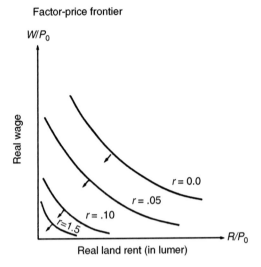

Factor-price frontier

Figure 14.3   The higher the rate of interest, the lower will be the land rent that
can be earned in forestry for each real wage given in terms of lumber price. The
tradeoff between such real wage rates and land rents will be the convex contours
of frontiers shown here; however, equal increments of profit rate may have quite
unequal shift effects upon contours.

produced by that equilibrium. Suppose the total supply of land is fixed
at $s = \bar{s}$, and that it is suitable only for forestry. Suppose the total steady-
state supply of labor is fixed at $\bar{L}$, to be divided between L for forestry
and $\bar{L} - L$ for the other (composite) good. Let Q be the steady-state
output of wood, as produced by the production function in (1'); and let
C be the output of the other good, which is producible instantaneously
from $\bar{L} - L$ alone, by $C = (\bar{L} - L)/c$. Finally, suppose everyone spends his
income on lumber and the other good in the same way whether rich
or poor, and in the same way as does any other person. Therefore,
demand curves can be regarded as generated by the "homothetic" col-
lective utility function, $U[C, Q] \equiv \lambda^{-1} U[\lambda C, \lambda Q]$, where U is a concave
first-degree-homogeneous function with standard regularity properties.
With the interest rate at which society neither saves nor dissaves given
by time preference rate ρ, so that $r = \rho > 0$, the full equilibrium is defined
by

$$C = (\bar{L} - L)/c \tag{14.10a}$$

$$Q = f(\bar{s}, L; T)$$

$$W/P_c = c^{-1} \quad (14.10\text{b})$$

$$W/P_Q = e^{-pT} \partial f(\bar{s}, L; T)/\partial L$$

$$P_Q/P_c = c^{-1} e^{pT} [\partial f(\bar{s}, L; T)/\partial L]^{-1}$$

$$\partial f(1, L/\bar{s}; T)/\partial T - pf(1, L/\bar{s}; T) = (R/P_Q) \quad (14.10\text{c})$$

$$P_Q/P_c = \frac{\partial U(C, Q)/\partial Q}{\partial U(C, Q)/\partial C} \quad (14.10\text{d})$$

Here (14.10a) gives the steady-state production functions. (14.10b) gives the labor and land marginal productivity relations, discounted when necessary, and with the implied steady-state price ratios (14.10c) gives the Faustmann optimal-rotation relation to determine T_∞. (14.10d) gives the needed demand relations. Note that, with T determined, we can use (14.10a) to express the right-hand side of (14.10d) in terms of L as the only unknown; substituting the right-hand side of (14.10b) last relation into the left-hand side of (14.10d), (14.10d) become one implicit equation for the one unknown, namely L. So an equilibrium does exist (and, under strong sufficiency conditions, it may well be unique). However, is there anything at all socially optimal about this positivistic competitive solution? Is there ever any "intertemporal efficiency" to this market equilibrium? The answer can be shown to be yes in a certain definable sense.

Specifically, imagine a Ramsey planner who maximizes an integral of discounted social utility, with discounting at an exponential rate of time preference, $r = \rho$, in exp $(-\rho t)$. His steady-state optimality relations will be of the exact same form as the steady-state competitive relations.

The following simple example can help to illustrate the general principles involved.

Optimal programming and forestry rotation

Thus, restrict T to only integral values – say to either $T = 1$ or $T = 2$; and replace the quality in (14.10c) that determines T_∞ by a corresponding inequality condition. And suppose a planner for this society acts to solve a Ramsey (1928) optimal-control problem, namely for t restricted to integral values,

$$Max\sum_{t=0}^{\infty}U[C(t),Q(t)]e^{-\rho t} \text{ subject to} \qquad (14.11)$$

$$C(t) \le c^{-1}[L - L_1(t) - L_2(t)]$$

$$\bar{S} \ge S_1(t) + S_2(t) + S_3(t)$$

$$L_i(t) \ge 0, S_i(t) \ge 0$$

$$Q(t) = f[S_1(t-1), L_1(t-1); 1] + f[Min[S_2(t-2), S_3(t-1)], L_2(t-2)],$$

with specified initial conditions

$$L_1(-1), S_1(-1), S_2(-2), S_2(-1), S_3(-1).$$

Such a problem is known to have a determinate solution, with implied optimal T_∞ rotation periods that can prevail at each time. And normally it will have the property that as $t \to \infty$, the optimal solution approaches the "turnpike" defined by the steady-state equations (14.10) above, once they are modified for discrete time periods. Of course, for still lower ρ, a different solution will be optimal, and presumably the optimal T_∞, call it $T_\rho = 1$, becomes optimal in the steady state. See Samuelson (1973b) for indicative analysis concerning the dynamic aspect of profit-including prices.

Non-steady-state considerations

The forester's notion of sustained yield is a steady-state notion. The economist's shorter rotation period for the forest, due essentially to a positive interest rate, is also a steady-state notion. But life is not now in a steady-state. It never was. It never will be. Incessant change is the law of life. You might correctly infer from this that economists' simple notion of stationary equilibrium needs to be generalized and replaced by the notion of a perpetual Brownian motion, as dramatized by the perpetual dance of the colloidal particles one sees in the microscope as they are buffeted to and fro around an average position of equilibrium by ever-present molecules, numerous and random, but unseen. A beginning has been made at the frontier of modern economics toward replacing equilibrium by an *ergodic probability distribution*. Since my time here is limited, I shall only refer to the works of Mirrlees (1965), Brock and Mirman (1972), R. C. Merton (1975), Samuelson (1971). But it is not the purely probabilistic perturbation of equilibrium that is important for the great debate on sustained yield. What is important is the realistic presence of *systematic trends* or *transients*, which move away from one steady-state equilibrium and which need not settle down to a newer one. It is no paradox that steady-state analysis is useful in the understanding of realistic trend analysis.

Foresters are concerned with sustained yield precisely because they have lived in a world where virgin stands have been decimated. It is only too easy to understand why, with new technologies and consumer tastes and with the cheapening of transport of exports to affluent North America and Western Europe, much land that was once devoted here to trees is transferred to other uses.

We have seen that the rotation age in the virgin forest is greater than what competitive enterprise will countenance. Indeed, were it not that, so to speak by accident, historical governments own much timber land, there would be even fewer trees in North America today. Our analysis warns that applying what is sound commercial practice to government's own utilization of public forests, or what is the same thing, renting out public land to private lumbering interests at the maximum auction rent competition will establish – this is a sure prescription for future chopping down of trees.

No trees left?

Is this prospect a good or bad thing? That cannot be decided in advance of lengthy discussion. Surely, from the vantage point of the final third of the twentieth century, few will agree with the beginning-of-the-century claim of Fernow (1913) that wood is our most important necessity, second only to food in societal importance. Wood is only wood, just as coal is only coal, plastics are only plastics, and, some would say, as bubblegum is only bubblegum. Proper transient analysis does not justify the implied fear that, once forests cease to be cultivated at maximum sustained yield, the descent is inevitable to the hell of zero timber anywhere in the world where we engage in trade. As wood becomes scarce, it will become more expensive. As it becomes expensive, people will economize on its use. But so long as there remain important needs for wood that people will want to satisfy, the price of wood will rise to the level necessary to keep a viable supply of it forthcoming. This in a sense is a "doctrine of sustained yield," but of course not the traditional forester's doctrine of maximum sustained yield. Indeed, by contrast with deposits of oil, coal peat, and high-concentration ores, all of which are constantly being irreversibly mined, trees bottle up sunshine into cellulose in a reversible cycle.

Nothing said so far should rule out that, in a world where preparation for war is only prudent, governments may have some interest in subsidizing activities that will lower the probability that in emergency times the nation will find itself bereft of steel, uranium, food, energy, and certain kinds of wood. This is not ruled out by sound economics; but it is only fair to mention that economists have a good deal to say by way of criticism of the efficiency with which governments program their subsidies for national defense purposes.

Conservation and flood control

When people in a poor society are given a choice between staying alive in lessened misery or increasing the probability that certain species of flora and fauna will not go extinct, it is understandable that they may reveal a preference for the former choice. Once a society achieves certain average levels of well-being and affluence, it is reasonable to suppose that citizens will democratically decide to forego some calories and marginal private consumption enjoyments in favor of helping to preserve certain forms of life threatened by extinction. It is well-known that clearcutting forests is one way of altering the Darwinian environment. Therefore, pursuit of simple commercial advantage in forest management may have as a joint product reversible or irreversible effects upon the environment. When information of these tradeoffs is made available to the electorate, by that same pluralistic process which determines how much shall be spent on defense and other social goods, and how much shall be taxed for interpersonal redistributions of income, the electorate will decide to interfere with laissez-faire in forest management. This might show itself, for example, in forest sanctuaries of some size located in some density around the nation: the optimal cutting age there and indeed the whole mode of timber culture will have little to do with Faustmann copybook algorithm. Or, putting the matter more accurately, I would have to say the future vector of real costs and real benefits of each alternative will have to be scrutinized in terms of a generalization of the spirit and letter of the Faustmann-Fisher calculus.

Everything said about species conservation can, with appropriate and obvious modifications, be said about the programming of a nation's geographical resources to provide benefits for vacationers, campers, sportsmen, and tourists. Even the unspeakable fox hunter is an endangered species, and it is part of the political decision-making process to decide at what sustained level he is to be permitted to flourish.

Beyond pointing out these simple truisms, I need only mention in the present connection that, when a sophisticated cost-benefit calculus is applied to each of these areas, it is unlikely the optimal solution will include many virgin forests located in inaccessible places. Land use is shot through with externalities. Zoning, public regulations, and various use taxes will presumably be the rational way recommended by economists who study these matters. The organization of land use activities is likely, in the good society, to fall heavily inside the walls of government and regulatory authorities; but there seems reason to believe part of the problem can be effectively franchised out to enterprisers motivated by the hope of financial return. So far, in awarding television licenses or gasoline and restaurant franchises on public highways, governments have been disappointing in the efficiency with which they have worked out such arrangements. But this does not necessarily mean that turning over our landscape to the untender mercies of push-shove laissez-faire is better, or more feasible, than improving the efficiency with which the public sector organizes these activities.

Earlier I accepted the denial that externality problems which crop up in fisheries are equally applicable to forest economics. But that was in connection with the forest merely as a producer of cellulose. Ecologists know that soil erosion and atmospheric quality at one spot on the globe may be importantly affected by whether or not trees are being grown at places some distance away. To the degree this is so, the simple Faustmann calculus and the bouncings of the futures contracts for plywood on the organized exchanges need to be altered in the interests of the public (i.e., the interests of both Pareto-optimality and interpersonal-equity). Again, when the implied optimal sustained yield pattern comes to be estimated, it might well involve numerous clusters of trees planted hexagonally over much of the nation's terrain, rather than huge isolated forest reserves.

The claims of posterity

My time is almost up. Yet I've only been able to scratch the surface of what needs to be explored in depth by catholic men of good will. At the least I must conclude by touching on an issue that goes to the heart of the controversy. Suppose that the competitive interest rates which will guide commercial forestry practices turn out to be very far from zero – say, 10 percent or even more. Must one necessarily accept this penalty on the use of time as the untouchable correct rate of discount a good society will want to recognize in its capital and intergenerational decision-making? This is not an easy question to answer. My earlier equation systems (14.7) and (14.8) show there are indeed theoretical models from which market solutions emerge which *also agree* with a technocrat's computation of a society's welfare optimum. So perhaps there is some presumption in favor of the market solution, at least in the sense that a vague burden of proof can be put against those who argue for interferences. At least many of today's mainstream economists would so argue.

I personally think the issue is more open. But I do not wish to pronounce on a matter that time does not permit us to do full justice to. Let me simply conclude therefore with some overly brief comments.

(i) Economists like Cambridge's Pigou and Ramsey, or such Rawlsian writers as Phelps and Riley (1974), have asserted that we ordinary citizens in our day-to-day and lifetime decision-making about spending, consuming, and saving actually act in *too myopic* a way. If we display time-preference rate of 6 or 10 percent per annum, those rates are not the law of Moses and the Prophets. When we gather together periodically to form social compacts, set down constitutions, and elect representative legislators, a democracy may well decide that government coercion (involving taxing, fiscal changes in the public debt, and control by the central bank of the money supply) ought to alter the trends of capital formation and the amounts of capital bequeathed by each generation to subsequent generations. This is an argument for having lower interest rates at some future date when the policies described have become effective. It is not necessarily an argument for programming the use of publicly-owned forests now with a hypothetical interest rate much lower than interest rates that prevail elsewhere. The latter rates may very well be needed to ration optimally the supply of capital in its actual limited state.

(ii) There is still some debate among economists as to whether the interest rates appropriate for a government to use should be at all lower than those of private enterprise, and in particular, of the smaller private enterprises and corporations. Marglin (1963) has argued in this fashion, and so in a sense Arrow and Lind (1970) seem to have argued. Hirshleifer (1966) has given arguments against such a dichotomy; Diamond and Mirrlees (1971) have applied the powerful techniques of Ramseyian second-best analysis to analyze the problem. Pending the ultimate verdict of the informed jury in this matter, it seems safe to guess that no simple historical notion of "maximum sustained yield" will be likely to be recommended as optimal.

Whatever else my analysis today may have accomplished, I daresay it will provide corroboration to the old theorem that, when economists and forecasters meet to reason together, economists are likely stubbornly to act like economists. This is an indictment to which I would have to plead guilty, and throw myself on the mercy of your indulgent sentence. Let the penalty fit the crime!

Bibliographical notes

Rather than burden my text with footnotes, I include here some sketchy comments on previous writings. The notion is ancient that wood is so important and the time periods of forestry are so long that the state cannot leave the matter to commercial laissez-faire. See, for example, the Roman and German background as discussed in Fernow (1902, 1913); Fernow takes for granted that the ideas of Adam Smith are pernicious when applied to long-lived forests.

The foresters' notion of "sustained yield," with allowable cut to be regulated by how much the average tree age is above or below the optimal age that maximizes steady-state lumber yield per acre is already present in the 1788 "Austrian Cameral Valuation Method." With a little charity, we might interpret this as an attempt to reduce cut of trees below the age T_g at which $f'(T_g) = f(T_g)/T_g$ (as in my Equation (14.2)), and to encourage cut at older ages.

In the early nineteenth century discounting future receipts at compound interest had reared its head. A momentary 1820 flash of insight by Pfeil, which he later regretted, called for "a rotation based on maximum soil rent" (Fernow 1913, p. 139), as in my Equation (14.6). Von Thunen (1826, 1966, Hall English edition, p. 121) seems to anticipate the (incorrect!) Jevons-Fisher relation $f'(T_1)/f(T_1) = r$ (of my Equation (14.4)) in his statement: "When the right methods are adopted, only trees of the same age will stand together; and they will be felled (just?) before the relative increment in their value sinks to ($r =$) 5 percent – the rate of interest I have assumed to prevail throughout the Isolated State."

The highwater mark comes in 1849 when Martin Faustmann corrects an attempt by E. F. von Gehren to use present discounted values to put a fair price on (1) forest land taken by eminent domain for alternative agricultural uses, and (2) existing forest stands on that land. Because von Gehren uses too long a rotation age for his postulated interest rate, applies bad approximations to true compound interest, and mistakenly values unripe trees at their then-current wood value rather than at their best future value properly discounted, he arrives at wrong and inconsistent results. He concluded, for example, that land value is negative when he subtracted too high a stand value from total land-cum-stand value.

Faustmann corrects all this, applying the infinite cycle formula – maximum $[Pf(T)e^{-rT} - WL]$ $[1 + e^{-rT} + ...]$ for our idealized case – as in my Equation (14.6b). He shows that evaluating each tree or age-cohort, or evaluating a synchronized forest, must always lead to the *same* result, a truth denied as late as 1951 by Lutz and Lutz (1951, p. 33). I rely on the excellent translation of Faustmann and von Gehren given in Gane (1968). In my quick reading, I judge Faustmann to know how to calculate the correct optimal rotation age; but I cannot recall exactly where he has done so, if he has indeed done so.

By this century, Irving Fisher (1906, 1907, 1930) has made present discounted value calculations standard in the economics literature. However, Fisher (1930, p. 161–165) still incorrectly calculates over one cycle rather than over an infinity of repeated cycles, deducing in effect as mentioned the relation for T_1 of my Equation (14.2), rather than the right Faustmann-Ohlin-Preinrich-Bellman-Samuelson relation for T_∞ of Equation 14.6c. Hotelling (1925) also concentrates on one cycle of a machine; and Goundrey (1960) claims the economist writers on forestry like Scott (1955a and b) are still concentrating on one cycle. Lutz and Lutz (1951) give numerous alternatives including the correct infinite-cycle, but they fail to deduce just *when* this correct method is mandatory (and, as noted, they become confused on the synchronized-forest case). Preinrich (1938), Alchian (1952), Bellman (1957) provide more accurate discussion of the infinite-cycle case: but until this present paper, I have not seen an adequate elaboration of the maximum-land-rent aspect of the forestry problem. Hirshleifer (1970, p. 88–90) has the correct Faustmann solution and refers in his work to Gaffney (1957). I have to agree with Gaffney that Fisher is wrong, even though Hirshleifer is right in thinking that his principle of maximizing a *proper* PDV is not wrong. Ohlin (1921), I belatedly discover, gives an exactly correct analysis.

The "internal rate of return," r_i, today quite properly associated with Boulding (1935, 1941 and 3 later editions), was already explicitly or implicitly in Bohm-Bawerk (1889), Fisher (1907), Keynes (1936).

Samuelson (1937) and Hirshleifer (1958) have debunked "maximizing" this r_i as a proper goal for decision-making by either a perfect or an imperfect competitor, but the corpse will not stay buried. Under free-entry and perfect competition, maximizing proper PDV *happens when PDV is zero also* to make r_i by tautology at a maximum. The only other possible defense for maximum-r_i is farfetched in any application, but has to my knowledge independently been glimpsed or proved by Boulding, Samuelson, Solow, Gale, and Chipman. If there is available to you a time-phased vector of net algebraic cash receipts, which you can initiate at *any* intensity *with no diminishing returns* (as you force down lumber prices, force up wage rates, run out of free forest lands, and bid up the land rent you must pay!), then any dollars that you initially have can ultimately be made, by investment and reinvestment into the postulated golden goose, to grow proportionally to $e^{r_i t}$; hence, having a higher r_i will ultimately come to dominate any lower r_j. However, under these unrealistic assumptions, r_i will come to form r, the market interest rate, itself; for if one could borrow at $r < r_i$, infinite scale would be optimal for this activity, a "meaningless" situation in a finite world; or, in the present application, the fact that trees grow on finite land will require positive rent payments that undermine any excess of r_i over r.

I found Goundrey (1960) a valuable survey, even if in the end he mistakenly comes out in favor of maximum internal rate of return. For the forestry literature on sustained yield, see items like Shepard (1925) and Waggener (1969).

On the proper discount rate to be used for governmental welfare decisions, see Ramsey (1928), Marglin (1963), Arrow and Lind (1970), Hirshleifer (1966), and Diamond and Mirrlees (1971).

Notes

1 Note that, as $(W/P) \to f(T)/L$, so that land rent is zero even at $r = 0$, $T_n \to b$.
2 This is better brought out by my maximum rent formulation of (14.6a) than by Faustmann's infinite number of cycles as in (14.6b) here. Thus for $r = 0$ (14.6a) becomes equivalent to

$$\text{subject to } 0 = \underset{T}{Max}\left\{f(T) - (W/P)L - R\int_0^T dt\right\}$$

Maximize R, namely

$$\underset{T}{Max}\{[f(T) - (W/P)L]/T\} = [f(T_n) - (W/P)L]/T_n$$

where T_n is defined by my earlier equation (14.3). B. Ohlin, I now learn, worked out much of this as a graduate student: cf. Ohlin (1921).

References

Alchian, A. A., 1952, *Economic Replacement Policy*. The Rand Corporation, Santa Monica, Calif.

Arrow, K. J. and Lind, R. C., 1970, "Uncertainty and the evaluation of public investments," *American Economic Review, 60*, 354–378.

Bellman, R., 1957, *Dynamic Programming*. Princeton University Press, Princeton.

Boulding, K. E., 1935, "The theory of a single investment," *Quarterly Journal of Economics, 49*, 475–494.

——, 1941, 1948, 1955, 1966. *Economic Analysis*. Harper & Bros., New York.

Brock, W. and Mirman, L., 1972. "The stochastic modified golden rule in a one sector model of economic growth with uncertain technology," *Journal of Economic Theory* (June).

Crutchfield, J. A. and Zellner, A., 1962, "Economic aspects of the Pacific halibut fishery," *Fishery Industrial Research I.*, US Dept. of the Interior, Washington, DC.

Diamond, P. A. and Mirrlees, J., 1971, "Optimal taxation and public production I–II," *American Economic Review, 61*, 8–27, 261–278.

Faustmann, M., 1849, "On the Determination of the Value Which Forest Land and Immature Stands Possess for Forestry," English edition edited by M. Gane, *Oxford Institute Paper 42*, 1968, entitled "Martin Faustmann and the Evolution of Discounted Cash Flow," which also contains the prior 1849 paper by E. F. von Gehren.

Fernow, B. E., 1902, *Economics of Forestry*, Thomas Y. Crowell & Co., New York.

——, 1913, *A Brief History of Forestry*, 3rd Edition, University Press Toronto, Toronto.

Fisher, I., 1906, *The Nature of Capital and Income*, Macmillan, New York.

——, 1907, *The Rate of Interest*, Macmillan, New York.

——, 1930, *The Theory of Interest*, Macmillan, New York, particularly pp. 161–165.

Gaffney, M., 1957, "Concepts of financial maturity of timber and other assets," *Agricultural Economics Information Series 62*, North Carolina State College, Raleigh, NC, September.

Gordon, H. S., 1954, "The economic theory of a common-property resource: The fishery," *Journal of Political Economy, 62*, 124–142.

Goundrey, G. K., 1960, "Forest management and the theory of capital," *Canadian Journal of Economics, 26*, 439–451.

Hirshleifer, J., 1958, "On the theory of optimal investment decision," *Journal of Political Economy, 66*, 198–209.

——, 1966, "Investment decision under uncertainty: Applications of the state-preference approach," *Quarterly Journal of Economics, 80*.

——, 1970, *Investment, Interest and Capital*, Prentice-Hall, Inc., Englewood Cliffs.

Hotelling, H., 1925, "A general mathematical theory of depreciation," *Journal of the American Statistical Association," 20*, 340–353.

Lutz, F. and Lutz, V., 1951, *The Theory of Investment of the Firm* (particularly Chs. 2 and 8), Princeton University Press, Princeton.

Marglin, S. A., 1963, "The social rate of discount and the optimal rate of investment," *Quarterly Journal of Economics, 77*, 95–111.

Merton, R. C., 1975, "An asymptotic theory of growth under uncertainty," *Review of Economic Studies, 42*, 375–394.

Mirrlees, J. A., "Optimum accumulation under uncertainty," Unpublished MS, December 1965.

Nordhaus, W. D., 1974, "The falling share of profits," *Brookings Papers on Economic Activity*, Okun, A. M. and Perry, G. L., eds., pp. 167–217. The Brookings Institution, Washington, DC.

Ohlin, B., 1921, "Till fragen om skogarnas omloppstid," *Ekonomisk Tidskrift*, "Festschrift to Knut Wicksell."

Phelps, E. S., and Riley, J. G., "Rawlsian growth: Dynamic programming of capital and wealth for intergenerational maxi-min justice," Columbia University and UCLA. (Paper for private circulation, early 1974.)

Preinrich, G. A. D., 1938, "Annual survey of economic theory: The theory of depreciation," *Econometrica*, 6, 219–241.

Ramsey, F. P., 1928, "A mathematical theory of saving," *Economic Journal*, 38, 543–559.

Samuelson, P. A., 1937, "Some aspects of the pure theory of capital," *Quarterly Journal of Economics*, 51, 469–496. Also reproduced in Stiglitz, J. E., ed., *Collected Scientific Papers of Paul A. Samuelson*, 1, pp. 161–188, MIT Press, Cambridge, Mass. 1966.

——, 1964, "Tax deductibility of economic depreciation to insure invariant valuations," *Journal of Political Economy* (December), 604–606. Also pp. 571–573 in Merton, R. C., ed., *Collected Scientific Papers of Paul A. Samuelson*, 3, MIT Press, Cambridge, Mass. 1972.

——, 1971, "Stochastic speculative price," *Proceedings of the National Academy of Sciences, USA*, 68, 335–337. Also pp. 894–896 in Merton, R. C., ed., *Collected Scientific Papers of Paul A. Samuelson*, 3, MIT Press, Cambridge, Mass. 1972.

——, 1973 (a), "Reply on Marxian matters," *Journal of Economic Theory*, 11, 64–67.

——, 1973 (b), "Optimality of Profit-Including Prices Under Ideal Planning," *Proc. Nat. Acad. Sci., USA*, 70, 2109–2111.

Scott, A., 1955 (a), "The fishery: The objectives of sole ownership," *Journal of Political Economy*, 63, 116–124.

——, 1955 (b), *Natural Resources: The Economics of Conservation*, University of Toronto Press, Toronto.

Shepard, W., 1925, "The bogey of compound interest," *Journal of Forestry*, 23.

Smith, V. L., 1968, "Economics of production from natural resources," *American Economic Review*, 58, 409–431.

Thunen, J. H. von, 1826, *Isolated State*, English edition edited by Peter Hall, 1966. Pergamon Press, London.

Waggener, T. R., 1969, "Some economic implications of sustained yield as a forest regulation model," Contemporary Forestry Paper 6, University of Washington.

Further Readings

The following suggestions are designed to help the reader further explore the topics covered in this volume. The list is selective rather than comprehensive and draws more heavily from journal articles than from books or other sources.

I The intertemporal problem

Arrow, Kenneth J. and Kruz, M., "Optimal Growth with Irreversible Investment in a Ramsey Model," *Econometrica*, 38, 331–44, 1970.

Dasgupta, S. and Mitra, Y., "Intergenerational Equity and Efficient Allocation of Exhaustible Resources," *International Economic Review*, 24, 133–53, 1983.

Eckstein, Otto, "Investment Criteria for Economic Development and the Theory of Intertemporal Welfare Economics," *Quarterly Journal of Economics*, 71, 56–85, 1957.

Giancarlo, Marini and Posquale, Scaramozzo, "Overlapping Generations and Environmental Control," *Journal of Environmental Economics and Management*, 26(2), 200–9, 1994.

Gray, L. C., "The Economic Possibilities of Conservation," *Quarterly Journal of Economics*, 27, 497–519, 1913.

Grossman, Gene, M. and Krueger, Alan B., "Economic Growth and the Environment," *Quarterly Journal of Economics*, 110(2), 353–77, 1995.

Hirshleifer, J., "Investment Decision Under Uncertainty: Choice-Theoretic Approaches," *Quarterly Journal of Economics*, 79, 509–36, 1965.

Howarth, Richard B. and Norgaard, Richard B., "Environmental Valuation Under Sustainable Development," *American Economic Review*, 82, 473–7, 1982.

Marglin, Stephen A., "The Social Rate of Discount and the Optimal Rate of Investment," *Quarterly Journal of Economics*, 77, 95–111, 1963.

Mishan, Ezra J., "The New Welfare Economics: An Alternative View," *Journal of Economic Literature*, 21, 691–705, 1980.

Rawls, John, *A Theory of Justice*, Cambridge, Mass.: Harvard University Press, 1971.

Rowse, John, "Discount Rate Choice and Efficiency in Exhaustible Resource Allocation," *The Canadian Journal of Economics*, 23(4), 772–90, 1990.

Samuelson, Paul A., "The Pure Theory of Public Expenditure," *Review of Economics and Statistics*, 37, 387–9, 1954.

Solow, Robert M., "Intergenerational Equity and Exhaustible Resources," *Review of Economic Studies (Symposium) 1974*, 29–46, 1974.

Weitzman, Martin L., "On the Environmental Discount Rate," *Journal of Environmental Economics and Management*, 26(2), 200–9, 1994.

II Externalities and market failure

Ayres, R. U. and Kneese, A. V., "Production, Consumption and Externalities," *American Economic Review*, 59, 282–97, 1969.

Atkinson, S. E., "Pollution Permits and Acid Rain Externalities," *Canadian Journal of Economics*, 16, 704–22, 1968.
Baumol, William J., "On the Taxation and the Control of Externalities," *American Economic Review*, 62, 307–22, 1972.
Boyd, Roy, Krutilla, Kerry and Viscusi, Kip, W. "Energy Taxation as a Poicy Instrument to Reduce CO2 Emissions: A Net Benefit Analysis," *Journal of Environmental Economics and Management*, 29(1), 1–24, 1996.
Crocker, T. D., "Externalities, Property Rights and Transaction Costs: An Empirical Study," *Journal of Law and Economics*, 14, 451–64, 1971.
Fisher, Anthony and Peterson, F. M., "The Environment in Economics: A Survey," *Journal of Economic Literature*, 5, 361–71, 1976.
Forester, B. A., "Pollution Control in a Two-Sector Dynamic General Equilibrium Model." *Journal of Environmental Economics and Management*, 4, 305–12, 1977.
Hanemann, Michael, W., "Valuing the Environment through Contingent Valuation," *The Journal of Economic Perspectives*, 8(8), 19–43, 1994.
Mishan, Ezra J., "The Postwar Literature on Externalities: An Interpretative Essay," *Journal of Law and Economics*, 14, 451–64, 1971.
Polinsky, A. M., "On the Choice Between Property Rules and Liability Rules," *Economic Inquiry*, 18, 233–46, 1980.
Randall, Allan, "Market Solution to Externality Problems: Theory and Practice," *American Journal of Agricultural Economics*, 54, 175–83, 1971.
Sedjo, Roger A., Wisniewski, Joe, Alaric V. and Kinsman, John D., "The Economics of Managing Carbon via Forestry: Assessment of Existing Studies," *Environmental and Resource Economics*, 6, 139–165, 1995.
Smith, Kerry V., "Detrimental Externalities, Nonconvexities, and Technical Change," *Journal of Public Economics*, 4, 289–95, 1975.
Stewart, Frances and Ghanif, Ejaz, "How Significant are Externalities for Development?," *World Development*, 19, 569–94, 1991.
Tietenberg, Tom, "Tradable Permits for Pollution Control When Emission Location matters: What Have We Learned", *Environmental and Resource Economics*, 5, 95–113, 1995.

III   Property rights, institutions and public choice

Alchian, Armen A. and Demsetz, Harold J., "Property Rights Paradigm," *Journal of Economic History*, 33, 16–27, 1973.
Bishop, Richard C., "Endangered Species and Uncertainty: The Economics of a Safe Minimum Standard," *American Journal of Agricultural Economics*, 60, 10–18, 1978.
Bromley, Daniel W., "The Ideology of Efficiency: Searching for a Theory of Policy Analysis," *Journal of Environmental Economics and Management*, 19, 86–107, 1980.
Castle, Emery N., "Property Rights and the Political Economy of Resource Scarcity," *American Journal of Agricultural Economics*, 60, 1–9, 1978.
Chen, Shenshen, "On the Question of Ownership and Property Rights," *Chinese Economic Studies*, 23, 3–99, 1989.
Gopalakrishnan, Chennat, "The Doctrine of Prior Appropriation and Its Impact on Water Resource Development," *American Journal of Economics and Sociology*, 32, 61–72, 1973.

Commons, John R., *The Legal Foundations of Capitalism*, Madison: University of Wisconsin Press, 1968.

Meade, J. E., *Efficiency, Equality and the Ownership of Property*, Cambridge, Mass.: Harvard University Press, 1965.

Meza, David de and Gould, J. R., "The Social Efficiency of Private Decision to Enforce Property Rights," *Journal of Political Economy*, 100, 561–80, 1992.

Mishan, Ezra J., "Pareto Optimality and the Law," Oxford Economic Papers, 19, 255–87, 1967.

Mishan, Ezra J., "Property Rights and Amenity Rights," in *Technology and Growth: The Price We Pay*, New York: Praeger Publishers, 1970.

Pearce, Peter H., "Property Rights and the Development of Natural Resource Policies in Canada," *Canadian Public Policy*, 14, 307–20, 1988.

Posner, Richard A., *Economic Analysis of Law* (2nd edition), Boston and Toronto: Little, Brown and Company, 1977.

Schmid, Allan A., *Property, Power and Public Choice: An Inquiry into Law and Economics*, New York: Praeger Publishers, 1987.

Terrebonne, Peter R., "Property Rights and Entrepreneurial Income in Commercial Fisheries," *Journal of Environmental Economics and Management*, 28(1), 68–82, 1995.

IV The economics of exhaustible resources

Kolstad, Charles D., "Hotelling Rents in Hotelling Space: Product Differentiation in Exhaustible Resources Markets," *Journal of Environmental Economics and Management*, 26(2), 163–80, 1994.

Chakravorty, Ujjayant and Krulce, Darrell, "Heterogeneous Demand and Order of Resource Extraction," *Econometrica*, 62, 1445–52, 1994.

Chermak, Janie M., "A Well-Based Cost Function and the Economics of Exhaustible Resources: The Case of Natural Gas," *Journal of Environmental Economics and Management*, 28(2), 174–89, 1995.

Cole, H. S. D., et al., *Thinking About the Future: A Critique of the Limits to Growth*, Chat and Windus for Sussex University Press, 1973.

Cummings, Ronald G., "Some Extensions of the Economic Theory of Exhaustible Resources," *Western Economic Journal*, 7, 201–10, 1969.

Dasgupta, Partha and Heal, Geoffrey, *Economic Theory and Exhaustible Resources*, Cambridge, Cambridge University Press, 1979.

Farzin, Y. H., "The Time Path of Scarcity Rent in the Theory of Exhaustible Resources," *The Economic Journal*, 102: 813–30, 1992.

Gopalakrishnan, Chennat, Khaleghi, Gholam H. and Shrestha, Rajendra B., "Energy-Non-Energy Input Substitution in U.S. Agriculture: Some Findings," *Applied Economics*, 21, 673–9, 1989.

Halvorsen, Robert and Smith, Jim R., "A Test of the Theory of Exhaustible Resources," *Quarterly Journal of Economics*, 106, 123–40, 1991.

Heal, Geoffrey M., "Depletion and Discounting: A Classical Issue in the Economics of Exhaustible Resources," in *Natural Resource Mathematics*, ed. R. McKelvey, Providence, RI: American Mathematical Society.

Levhari, David and Livian, Nissan, "Notes on Hotelling's *Economics of Exhaustible Resources*," *Canadian Journal of Economics*, 10, 177–92, 1977.

Malueg, David A. and Solow, John L., "Monopoly Production of Durable Exhaustible Resources," *Economica*, 57, 29–47, 1990.

Meadows, D. H., et al., *The Limits to Growth*, New York: Universe Books, 1972.

Pindyck, Robert S., "Uncertainty and Exhaustible Resource Markets," *Journal of Political Economy*, 99, 681–721, 1980.

Quven, N. V., "Exhaustible Resources: A Theory of Exploration," *Review of Economic Studies*, 58, 777–89, 1991.

Slade, Margaret, "Trends in Natural-Resource Commodity Prices," *Journal of Environmental Economics and Management*, 9, 122–37, 1982.

Stiglitz, Joseph E., "Monopoly and the Rate of extraction of Exhaustible Resources," *American Economic Review*, 66, 665–61, 1976.

Vousden, N., "Basic Theoretical Issues in Resource Depletion," *Journal of Economic Theory*, 6, 126–143, 1973.

Weitzman, Martin L., "The Optimal Development of Resource Pools," *Journal of Economic Theory*, 12, 351–64, 1976.

Yacov, Tsur and Zemel, Amos, "Uncertainty and Irreversibility in Ground Water Resource Management," *Journal of Economics and Management*, 29(2), 149–51, 1995.

Zilberman, David, "Technological Change, Government Policies, and Exhaustible Resources in Agriculture," *American Journal of Agricultural Economics* 66(5), 634–40, 1984.

V The economics of renewable resources

Adelai, L. A. and Rodin, E. Y., "Optimal Management of Renewable Economic Resources in a Model with Bertalanffy Growth Law," *Mathematical and Computer Modeling*, 12(7), 821–9, 1989.

Anderson, Lee G., *The Economics of Fisheries Management*, Baltimore: Johns Hopkins, 1977.

Berck, Peter, "Economics of Timber: A Renewable Resource," *Bell Journal of Economics*, 10, 447–62, 1979.

Bowes, Michael D. and Krutilla, John V., "Multiple Use Management of Public Forestlands," in *Handbook of Natural Resource and Energy Economics*, Vol. 2, ed. by A. V. Kneese and J. L. Sweeney, Elsevier Science Publishers, 1985.

Clark, Colin W., *Mathematical Bioeconomics: The Optimal Management of Renewable Resources*, New York: Wiley, 1976.

Clark, Colin W., Clarke, Frank H. and Munro, Gordon R., "The Optimal Exploitation of Renewable Resource Stocks: Problems of Irreversible Investment," *Econometrica*, 47, 25–47, 1979.

Dasgupta, Partha, *The Control of Resources*, Cambridge: Harvard University Press, 1979.

Donald E. Campbell and Jerry S. Kelly, "Trade-Offs in the Spatial Model of Resource Allocation," *Journal of Public Economics*, 60(1), 1–20, 1996.

Gopalakrishnan, Chennat, "Natural Gas from Seaweed: Is Near Term R&D Funding by the US Gas Industry Warranted?," *The Energy Journal*, 6(4), 129–37, 1985.

Goundrey, G. K., "Forest Management and the Theory of Capital," *Canadian Journal of Economic and Political Science*, 26, 439–51, 1960.

Kolberg, William C., "Models of Renewable Resource Management," *Land Economics*, 68(1), 11–27, 1992.

Levhari, D., Michiner, R. and Mirman, L. J., "Dynamic Programming Models of Fisheries," *American Economic Review*, 712, 649–61, 1981.

Lyon, K. S., "Mining of the Forest and the Time Path of the Price of Timber," *Journal of Environmental Economics and Management*, 5, 345–56, 1971.

Merrifield, John and Firoozi, Fathali, "Renewable Resource Use: Transition from Capture to Allocation and Optimal Stock Recovery," *Journal of Environmental Management*, 44(3), 195–211, 1995.

Plourde, G. C., "Exploitation of Common Property Replenishable Resources," *Western Economic Journal*, 9, 256–66, 1971.

Schworm, William E., "Monopolistic Control of a Common Property Renewable Resource," *Canadian Journal of Economics*, 16, 275–87, 1983.

Smith, Vernon L., "Control Theory Applied to Natural and Environmental Resources: An Exposition," *Journal of Environmental Economics and Management*, 4, 1–24, 1977.

Tahvonan, Olli, "On the Dynamics of Renewable Resource Harvesting and Pollution Control," *Environmental and Resource Economics*, 1(1), 97–117, 1991.

Turvey, Ralph, "Optimization in Fishery Regulation," *American Economic Review*, 54, 64–76, 1964.

Walter, G. R. "Economics of Multiple-Use Forestry," *Journal of Environmental Economics and Management*, 5, 345–56, 1971.

Warford, Jeremy and Parto, Zeinab, "Natural Resource Management in the Third World: A Policy and Research Agenda," *American Journal of Agricultural Economics*, December 1990, 1269–73.

Author Index

Subject Index

accelerator hypothesis, 302
adaptive expectations hypothesis, 302
agricultural uses, 329
air pollution, 50
Alabama, 256
Alaska, 189
American bison, 279, 295
American Indians, 167, 169
American Pacific Coast, 254
applied economist, 159
Arkansas, 256
asset equilibrium, 263–64
Australia, 182
"Austrian Cameral Valuation
    Method," 329

backstop technology, 8, 262, 270
bargaining solution, 4, 5
benefits and costs, 3, 5, 62, 69, 70,
    72, 73, 74, 75, 164, 171, 172,
    210, 326
benefit-cost analysis
    see cost-benefit analysis
biological research, 188
biology, 178, 179
bionomic ecosystem, 178, 192, 193,
    198
biosystem, 280
Britain, 305
business cycle, 68

California, 222, 254, 255
California oil companies, 222
Canadian Atlantic Coast, 181, 189
Canada, 188, 312
capital, 15, 29, 38, 40, 44, 174, 175,
    182, 222, 245, 260, 281, 282,
    284, 285, 286, 287, 291, 293,
    297, 301, 308, 309, 319, 327, 328
    marginal efficiency of, 15, 16, 20
    market, 14, 15, 29, 54, 55, 309
    social productivity of, 16, 20, 27
    theory, 13–14

capital-gains tax, 315
centralized decision-making, 306
Chicago, 305
coal, 223, 253, 256, 262, 263, 274,
    282, 325
Coase theorem, 4
collective action, 212, 216
collective choice, 207, 208
collective good, 152, 158, 212, 213,
    214, 383
common-property resource, 5, 6, 109,
    178, 190, 191, 192, 282, 306
    economic theory of, 178–203
    see also natural resources, fisheries
competition, 223, 224, 226, 227, 228,
    234, 250, 252, 255, 306
conservation movement, 221, 222,
    226, 306
corporations, 5, 39, 40, 42, 44, 46,
    48, 71, 174, 175, 328
corporate taxes, 38, 42, 56
cost-benefit analysis, 13, 20, 37, 327
crude oil, 262, 282, 283, 284

democracy, 207, 209
Department of the Interior (US), 272
development, 3, 77, 82
differential equation, 244, 253, 285
discount factor, 239
discount rate, 13, 18, 37, 39, 41, 44,
    45, 47, 49, 50, 52, 53, 55, 56, 57,
    60, 73–74, 228, 267, 269, 314,
    327
    calculation of, 13
    definition, 2
    risk and, 42, 55
    types of, 14
duopoly, 223, 252, 254
dynamic programming, 305, 311

ecological equilibrium, 182, 183, 286,
    315
ecological system, 191

economic efficiency, 5, 159, 205
economics of forestry
competitive land rents, 307–08
competitive solution, 318–20
compound interest rate analysis,
312–14
externalities and intervention,
305–06
labor and land variable, 320–21
optimal programming
rotation, 323–34
optimal rotation period, 309–12
maximum sustained yield, 304,
315–18
simple general equilibrium, 321–23
sustainability, 304–5
Economics of Welfare, The, 87, 117
Edgeworth-like box diagram, 146
eminent domain, 329
endangered species, 326
England, 181
energy, 262, 326
entropy, 271
environment, 8, 280, 285, 326
amenities, 2
ambient, 83
climatic changes and, 83
costs, 2, 4, 76, 82
deterioration in, 3, 76
irreversible effects on, 49, 78, 81,
82, 83, 301, 325, 326
pollution control and, 83
pollution damages to, 76, 83
preservation of, 78, 79, 82
uncertainty, 76, 77, 80, 81
see also externalities, natural
resources
ethics, 23
Europe, 305
exhaustible resources, 1, 7, 8, 9, 221,
222, 223, 227, 228, 236, 252,
254, 258, 259, 260, 263, 265,
268, 269, 270, 272, 273, 274, 279
application of calculus of
variations, 223, 229, 235, 250,
254, 255, 256
cumulated production and, 235–39
discontinuous production and,
241–43

duopoly in, 252–55
economics of, 221–56
free competition and, 224–26
impact of taxes on, 245–50
maximum social value and, 226–28
monopoly and, 228–34
optimum mine exploitation under,
239–41
peculiar problems of, 221–23
tests for a "true maximum" under,
243–44
externalities, 1, 3, 4, 5, 6, 38, 44, 48,
52, 53, 138–154, 155, 164, 165,
166, 167, 169, 170, 171, 172,
173, 174, 175, 204, 206, 208,
210, 211, 213, 214, 216, 266,
273, 274, 279, 283, 284, 288,
291, 301, 302, 305, 306, 308,
327
and political organization, 6–7
classification of, 3–4
"crowding," 283, 289, 297
definition (concept) of, 3, 138
diagrammatic depictions, 146–47,
157
internalization of, 6, 9, 156, 164,
165, 166, 171, 172, 173, 174
investment as a public good and,
47–50
marginal, 138, 139, 140, 141
non-pecuniary, 164
Pareto equilibrium, 149, 150, 152
pecuniary, 139, 140, 164
"pigovian solution" to, 151
"political," 7, 216
production, 139, 282, 295
stock, 283, 291, 298
technological, 4, 139, 140

Faustmann calculus, 327
Faustmann optimal-rotation, 323
fish, 221, 223, 279, 280, 283, 288,
300, 306
fisheries, 6, 9, 178, 186, 187, 287,
301, 305, 306, 327
bionomic equilibrium in, 192–94
centralized management of,
296–300
common-property nature of, 189